The
New
Brick
Reader

The
Brick

New Reader

Edited by Tara Quinn

ANANSI

This edition published in 2013 by
House of Anansi Press Inc.
110 Spadina Avenue, Suite 801
Toronto, ON, M5V 2K4
Tel. 416-363-4343
Fax 416-363-1017
www.houseofanansi.com

Distributed
in Canada by
HarperCollins Canada Ltd.
1995 Markham Road
Scarborough, ON, M1B 5M8
Toll free tel. 1-800-387-0117

Distributed
in the United States by
Publishers Group West
1700 Fourth Street
Berkeley, CA 94710
Toll free tel. 1-800-788-3123

Library and Archives Canada Cataloguing in Publication

The new Brick reader / edited by Tara Quinn.

A collection of literary essays, interviews, memoirs, travelogues,
belles lettres, and unusual musings previously published in Brick.
Issued in print and electronic formats.
ISBN 978-1-77089-408-2 (pbk.). — ISBN 978-1-77089-409-9 (html)

1. Canadian literature (English) — 20th century.
2. Canadian literature (English) — 21st century.
3. Authors, Canadian (English) — 20th century — Anecdotes.
4. Authors, Canadian (English) — 21st century--Anecdotes.
5. Authors, Canadian (English) — Interviews.
I. Quinn, Tara, 1980–, editor of compilation

PS8251.N49 2013
C810.8'0054   C2013-903779-9   C2013-903780-2

Library of Congress Control Number:
2013941770

Cover design: Brian Morgan
Text design and typesetting: Brian Morgan

We acknowledge for their
financial support of our publishing program
the Canada Council for the Arts, the Ontario Arts Council,
and the Government of Canada
through the Canada
Book Fund.

Printed and bound in Canada

CONTENTS

Reading Time: four minutes

Brick has always been a magazine cobbled together by writers who seem to have a slanted perspective of the literary world around them. We have published articles where writers celebrate other writers—Robert Hass on Tomas Tranströmer, John Berger on Pier Paolo Pasolini, Roberto Bolaño on Nicanor Parra, Don DeLillo on Thelonious Monk and Glenn Gould. But we have also published somewhat strange pieces: one on fishing by Graham Swift, one on writers who wrestle, and a piece by a well-known Toronto lawyer whose shoes were stolen by Jean Genet when he stayed at the lawyer's house (what did he expect?). Over the years we have run interviews with Kazuo Ishiguro, W. G. Sebald, Anne Carson, Zadie Smith, and Mavis Gallant, as well as many others. William Gaddis has mused on Herman Melville's impressions of Cologne Cathedral, Patricia Rozema has written about what it was like to direct Harold Pinter in a film, Jeffrey Eugenides remembered John Hawkes as a teacher, a prisoner in San Quentin interviewed the mystery writer Donald Westlake, and the son of a scientist wrote a personal memory about "How Scientists Party." It is as if anything around us can be somehow gathered and carried in the canoe or the split-pea shell that is *Brick, A Literary Journal*.

To some of us it feels that *Brick* began in the Middle Ages. It was started by Jean McKay and Stan Dragland in 1977, and the magazine has gone on from there in various shapes and sizes in the hands of three other publishers: Linda Spalding, Michael Redhill, and Nadia Szilvassy. But throughout all these years—more than thirty-five now—its editors have always been writers. Right now there is an editorial board of six. Some prefer to act as "scouts" for what might be out there—a conversation with a writer, or some idea that can perhaps be encouraged into an essay. Some prefer the more triage-like role of judging what is really good. But most of all we are enthusiasts for what is interesting—to us first of all, and then hopefully to our readers.

One of our consistent desires is that writers from elsewhere rub up against writers from Canada, and we want established writers to meet with newer writers in our pages. So we invite artists and writers from all over the world as well as welcome the strange and random pieces that come over the transom—one man whose job it was to destroy books in a library found a book of poetry there, read it, admired it, and promptly reviewed it for us (*Brick* 90). We have had recipes based on road kill (*Brick* 77), a piece on a strange underground cult in Paris (*Brick* 85), and one on the souls of dogs (*Brick* 80). In another era we would have asked the author of *Moby Dick* for a chowder recipe, or Henry James for a monthly list of his dinner invitations, or Dorothy Wordsworth for her recommended map of rural walks.

Sometimes we ask a range of writers to deal with one of those essential questions, such as "What would you have been if you were not a writer?" ("A dog," said Robert Creeley; "A rock guitarist," said Ian McEwan; "An actor," said Edmund White; "Dead," said Russell Banks.) And in a recent issue we asked writers and artists about their favourite endings in novels. Of course there are internal battles within the editorial board. I have pushed for years for the magazine to be printed on pink paper like the *Financial Times,* and for all of our articles to have a line at the start that gives the approximate reading time of the piece, as magazines did in 1950s England, just so that we could reprint Yeats's "Sailing to Byzantium" and list the reading time as somewhere between seventeen seconds and twenty-five minutes. I never was able to convince the others. The final selection can also lead to fights. Even for this anthology, many of the editors wanted Helen Garner's wilder article on experiencing a high colonic cleanse as opposed to her more reasonable piece on an Antarctic journey.

There were other problems in earlier times. The number of typos in *Brick,* for instance. Accusations from writers have been constant and furious over the years. A reference to a "puppy" as opposed to a "poppy" in David Malouf's book, *An Imaginary Life.* A reference to "the police at 4 a.m." as opposed to Alberto Giacometti's *The Palace at 4 a.m.* (that article written by Alice Munro). So we were proud when we published a piece by Harry Mathews that was proofread so many times it seemed faultless to us. But Mr. Mathews wrote a terse letter from France complaining we had left out a whole page of his well-argued essay. Similarly, we did once leave out a stunning first paragraph of a piece by Rohinton Mistry, though we managed to reprint it in full in our first *Brick Reader.* All of this was not helped by a fictional Cecily Moos (she with the roving umlaut), who pretended to be the new copy editor for the magazine and then proceeded to publish brief editorials in *Brick* chiding the other editors for their bad grammar and lazy work on the magazine. Cecily Moos in fact found a large fan base among our readers, although she was the invention of one of our male editors who often writes under a female pseudonym.

We have from time to time wanted to change the subtitle of the magazine from *A Literary Journal* to something more inviting. Why, I don't know. The poet bpNichol suggested *Brick,*

A Magazine for the Idle Rich. But of course there are too many of those already. They fill the racks, and we rather hope *Brick* is an antidote. We all know that there are only a few real magazines remaining, somewhat like icebergs. And newspapers tend to notice a magazine only when it dies, which is cold comfort.

So why do we carry on, "pledging our troth" to our dear readers? One reason might be that as writers we bring out a book, with luck, every four or five years, and *Brick* allows us to feel we have a new literary work twice a year. And there is great pleasure in making this collage-like object—this *bricolage*—as we are all ardently and even furiously involved in editing, layout, and paste-up. Producing a magazine is also a sure-fire way of merging with a larger community of artists, finding echoes of interests among them, and allowing them a place to walk, to talk, to think, to muse. While we do publish some fiction and poetry, we at the magazine are mostly interested in what lies behind those works. A culture does not reside just in books, Cynthia Ozick says, but in the tensions and the ideas behind them. We are interested in the seedbed, where the enthusiasms and cross-fertilizations occur, and we see the magazine as a stage for ideas and the personal voice.

Finally, and perhaps this is the real reason for doing *Brick,* there is the pleasure of making something while being part of a community. Writing is mostly a secretive and solitary act where conversation is a curse, and an open telephone or a lunch meeting is a path to destruction. But anyone who has worked in theatre or film recognizes the abundant pleasures of working in a group. *Brick* allows us that. The opinions and participation of all of us involved with the magazine—writers, designers, publishers, contributing editors, distributors—leads to eye-rolling and argument, but we grudgingly know that the magazine will probably become better as a result. So that, in a way, *Brick* is not just the representation of the community of artists around us, but also the portrait of the group that makes it.

—*Michael Ondaatje*

THE LOVER OF THE HUMMINGBIRD

Remembering John Hawkes

JEFFREY EUGENIDES

TWENTY YEARS AGO I arrived on this campus intent on fulfilling my father's greatest fear—while making him pay for it—of having his son ruined by the Liberal Eastern Establishment. At the time I didn't know what the Liberal Eastern Establishment was. Its major recommendation lay in my father's opposition to it. If I'd been asked to describe this group, I would have offered only superficial details: the wrinkled broadcloth shirts, the flood pants, the Latinate vocabulary, the lock-jaw speech.

I had chosen Brown chiefly because of the presence on its faculty of one John Hawkes. Hawkes's books, which I only dimly understood, had enchanted me ever since I'd pulled my first copy off a high school teacher's bookshelf when I was fifteen. I don't want to be hyperbolic about the moment but it retains in memory all the annunciatory trumpets of an epiphany. I can remember reading the words "New Directions" on the spine. I can remember studying the picture on the cover of a muscular, nearly anatomized Caribbean woman posed before a blazing sun. Most of all, I remember the intoxicating effect the prose had on me, like a dangerous throat-burning Scandinavian liqueur. The narrative voice seized me in a way all the noisy art forms of the time (which have only grown noisier since then) somehow didn't. I felt right away, reading the first paragraph of *Second Skin*, that I was in the presence of the qualities Nabokov considered the hallmarks of art: curiosity, tenderness, kindness, ecstasy.

I set out on my pilgrimage my first day here on College Hill. Consulting my campus map, I located Horace Mann. I studied the directory inside the door. With mounting excitement I climbed the steps. Everything was old in the way I wanted it to be. The stairs creaked; the radiators gave off a smell of rust, the smell of the Ivy League, which I inhaled deeply as I searched for the right room. At the end of the hall, in a forlorn office clearly used for perhaps three hours each semester, sat a man with owl-shaped eyeglasses the colour of congealed honey. He looked up at me.

"Are you the lover of the hummingbird?" I asked.

And in that unmistakable voice, putting aside his insistence that you should never confuse a novel's author with its protagonist (because he could see that such a distinction would have been lost on the kid in his doorway), Professor Hawkes answered in the affirmative.

And so it was that Jack Hawkes became for me the living embodiment of the Liberal Eastern Elite. It turned out they didn't wear broadcloth shirts. They wore navy-blue or white turtlenecks, chinos, and tweed jackets. They didn't speak in lock-jaws but in a voice, well, like Jack's, something between the cry of an eagle and the whine of a very intelligent bookish asthmatic child…. you all know the voice, you can hear it now, saying the things Jack used to say. "But what about the character's eyes? Look how the author describes his eyes. These aren't eyes. They're gonads! In Freudian terms the eye is always a gonad!"

Or when he forgot somebody's name: "It's the synapses!"

Or regarding literary poseurs: "To glorify not the writing but the writer, to be concerned with the role of the writer in society rather than the work itself, that is something which, I must say, I strongly resist."

This last remark was delivered to me. Because pretty soon in our dealings with each other Jack realized that my interest in him extended beyond my admiration for his books. One day during my freshman year I came into class and sat next to Jack. I bent over to lay my books on the floor. While I was down there, though, I took the opportunity to stare under Jack's seat.

In an instant Jack was shouting. "You even want to know what kind of shoes I wear?"

I was horrified at being caught, at having my idolatry exposed. I blushed and sat back in my seat and tried from then on not even to look at Jack's shoes.

Among my pitiful efforts that first semester in Beginning Fiction, I remember one moment when Jack gave me encouragement, a memory still more dear to me than any subsequent praise or favourable review. We were given an assignment to describe a single mundane moment with utmost dramatic effect. I had described—taxidermied, really—a little girl in the act of turning on a light switch. But generous Jack found some promise.

"I love this little girl," he shouted. "I want to eat this girl!"

That was a lesson I've never forgotten: try to make every page of prose edible.

AMONG THE MOST edible pages in our literature surely are those written by John Hawkes. Open any book, anywhere, and the feast is laid out before you. I've always agreed with Proust's insistence that you can measure a writer's talent from any paragraph in any book. Just for fun, in preparing these remarks, I opened a few of Jack's books at random. From *The Cannibal*: "And old Herman, fully awake, touched the soft fur with his mouth, and felt the wings through the cotton dress, while in the far end of town, a brigade of men passed shallow buckets of water to quench a small fire." From *The Blood Oranges*: "I swayed, I listened, I shaded my eyes, knowing that Catherine was indeed asleep and that Fiona's haste was justified but futile and that the light itself had turned to wind or that the wind had somehow assumed the properties of the dawn light." From *Sweet William*: "There I was, standing on racing turf at last. Through the shredding curtains of that brisk dawn mirage, a fusion of fog and filmy light and dark shadows, I was able to make out the quarters of the track, as well as the darkened shape of the grandstand, which was like an abandoned ship on its side."

Not only was Jack a wonderful writer; he was a truly first-rate hypochondriac. "Nobody has a cold, do they?" was his usual greeting to our class. If a sufferer were identified, Jack quarantined the poor student in a remote armchair before administering himself the booster vaccine of a glass of Soave Folonari. Of course Jack had had asthma since childhood and needed to guard against flus and colds. And, having done some teaching now myself, I understand the temptation to view students less as presidential material than viral. Nevertheless, one of the strangest things I ever learned about Jack, and something that impressed upon me the mysteriousness of human character (another literary lesson, I suppose), was the following. One of the last times I saw Jack, at a lunch with Rick Moody, Jack, a man who had fled the slightest cough or sniffle, calmly mentioned over a rich dessert that doctors had just determined that his main cardiac arteries were occluded by eighty or ninety percent. He seemed—and again I have only that one afternoon to go on—almost fascinated with the diagnosis, as though the heart condition in question was something he was thinking about giving to one of his characters. And so, to all the other qualities I admired about Jack Hawkes, I had to add another: courage.

That final lunch was not without its sadder aspects. Jack was concerned about his book, *The Frog*, which had come out that year. He was afraid it wasn't doing well enough to suit his publisher and he asked Rick and me if we thought there was anything we could do, down in New York, to give the book some added attention. It was an uncomfortable moment, which I can only compare, in my own experience, to the time my own father, late in life, asked to borrow money. It went against the natural order of things. And we were standing in the middle of a gravel parking lot, in Providence, which is always a sad thing, and Jack looked frail in the harsh light. But no sooner had this unease descended on us than Jack, synapses still intact, summed up the entire situation and, waving his hand, dismissed the whole idea.

In retrospect, I think he was stripping from himself the last shreds of the mantle I had forced on his shoulders so many years ago when I barged into his office quoting *Second Skin*. He was telling me that he was a writer and, like any writer, he worried about the fate of his books in the world. He was telling me, now that I was old enough to understand, exactly what kind of shoes he wore. And what kind of shoes, in emulating him, I had squeezed myself into.

It was my good fortune to study with the great cantankerous Hawkes and to know him as a teacher and as a friend, to enjoy his kindness and humour, his histrionic self-dramatizing, his pagan vitality, and to hear from his own lips the natural flow of his eloquence and the utterly original workings of his fine and incomparable mind.

When I graduated, I wrote a note of thanks to Jack, most of which I've forgotten. The last line, however, comes back to me. "I will always begin with what you taught me." That is as true today, as we gather here to celebrate the man and his work, as it was in 1983. I want to say, God Bless John Hawkes, but it doesn't feel right. Jack was an existentialist. He told me once that he liked the idea that we create our work out of the void. So rather than address Jack in heaven, I'll end by saluting the god he spoke of most often, the imagination, specifically the imagination of John Hawkes, which bodied forth from the void of his many brilliant books.

THE WRITER'S LIFE

ELIZABETH HAY

T HE UNIVERSITY WOMAN who picked me up at the train station was in her fifties, a solid woman with an unruly mass of grey curls and very small hands. Her name was Debbie. Straight away she told me that her book club had discussed my new book the week before, "and to tell you the truth, I like *It's Snowing in Havana* better." She was driving me to this selfsame book club for a potluck supper after which I would speak to the University Women's Club as a whole, but first we would pick up her son from his windswept bungalow on the highway. "This is Elizabeth Gray," she said to him as he slid into the back seat. "Hello, Miss Gray," he said.

I liked Debbie of the small hands. She was blunt when she talked to me and funny when she talked to herself. "This is Pharmaceutical Row," she said of the road we were on. "All these companies get rich making drugs to fight cancer, and you wonder why they never find a cure. Shame on you, Debbie. Did you say that?" and she slapped her left hand.

I was tired, having been on trains since nine in the morning and it was now a quarter to four. I was also hungry. So I was thinking gratefully and peaceably about the potluck supper that would precede my evening chore when she snapped my head around by saying the potluck-supper people would expect me to say something too. I would have to sing for my supper.

"I guess I should have told you," she said. "But don't worry. Just talk about anything. Talk about the writer's life."

I turned my head away from her and flailed my eyes at the skimpy fields lying between the swirl of highways that is southwestern Ontario — where to look outside is to feel you'll never escape the inside of a car — and thought, these university women think I am light on my feet, or is it quick with my tongue? Won't they be surprised.

We dropped off the son and drove on to the big suburban house where I would finally get fed. There the door was opened by a pretty woman who said to me, "Beth?"

"Liz," I said, with some firmness. "Liz."

About a dozen women came to the potluck supper. They arrived one after the other. Each one shook my hand gingerly, then stepped back two feet. No one said a word about that book of mine they had discussed the week before, whose main character was a real sad sack by the name of Beth.

They approached me, and I can't resist calling them my readers, my readers approached me as though I were a salt lick in a field and they had had quite enough salt for now. I sat on the one uncomfortable chair in a room where there were two sofas and several inviting armchairs. The chair was black, straight-backed, and directly in line with a shaft of sunlight

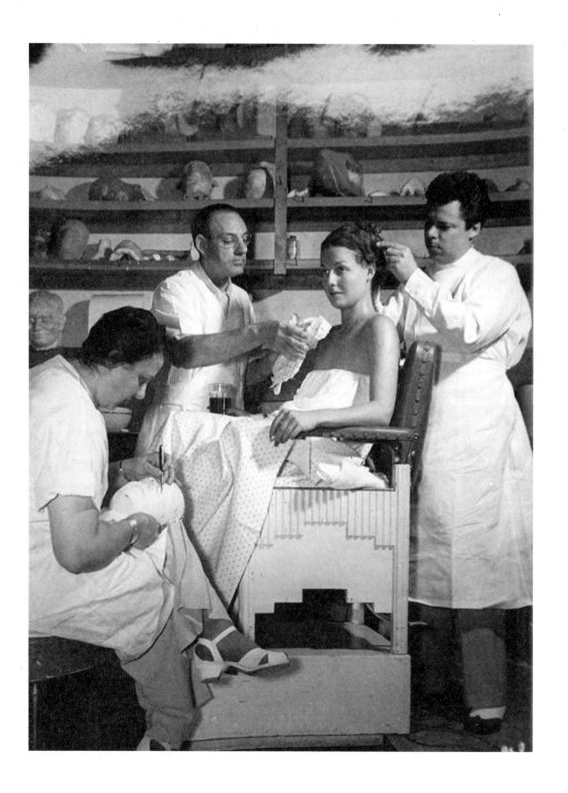

that got me right in the eye. After only a few minutes Debbie said, "Well. We're ready," and all fell silent so that I, blinking in the straight-backed chair, could talk.

Now in my panic, staring out at those pathetic fields, I had decided I would talk about the night and day of the last six months. I would just let rip for about ten minutes, and then, surely, they would give me something to eat. So I began. I said I would tell them about the so-called glories of the writer's life. *Small Change*, I said, had been published at the end of April and by June I had lost so much weight from having offended so many people that I went to the doctor who said, Let's do some blood work, and while we're at it, let's do a hormone test. A week later when I called her to get the results, she said, Well, your blood is fine. But that hormone test? It shows that you're post-menopausal. That period you had in May? That's the last period you'll ever have. And if you start to bleed again? Call me right away.

That was a bracing phone call. To be so ancient yet so liberated and in one fell swoop. The worst is over, I thought to myself, and I didn't even know it had begun.

In my exuberance I made the mistake of phoning my mother. "It's all sunshine and roses from here on," I said.

"Well," she said, "I'm glad you're so exhilarated. I certainly hope," she said, "that it shows in your writing." There was a pause for emphasis. "It is — so — bleak," she said.

She gave the word *bleak* the drawn-out, downward force of a camel's foot on a desert rat.

The university women laughed. "Only a mother," they said, shaking their heads.

As it turned out, the doctor was wrong and all the tests I went through that summer were unnecessary, and my mother was wrong too, in a way, because one fine day at the end of September I got a phone call saying I had been shortlisted for the Governor General's Award. I said to the university women, "It was like being lifted out of the gutter. It was like getting diplomatic immunity. My parents were proud. My friends were impressed." SIX WEEKS LATER there was another nomination, this time for the brand new Impossible-to-Remember-the-Name-of-This-Award Award. And for this award there was a luncheon, and because they were paying I booked myself a first-class train ticket, something I had always wanted to do so that I could enjoy the free wine, the hors d'oeuvres, the chocolates, and the liqueurs to say nothing of the meal, only to discover when I got to the train station at a quarter to six on the morning of the big day that the train had been cancelled though no one had seen fit to inform me. So I got myself a plane ticket — and if you want to know how much it costs to fly from Ottawa to Toronto on the same day you buy your ticket, it's $519.00 — I got myself to Toronto, I got myself to the lunch at the Sheraton Hotel, and there I sat down beside Austin Clarke.

Here I paused to tell the university women that one of the great difficulties of being a writer is meeting other writers whose work you have never read. I had never read one of Austin Clarke's books, but that morning in the airport bookstore I had taken his book off the shelf and read the first few pages, which, I was glad to discover, I liked very much.

Hello, I said, leaning to my right, I'm Liz Hay. And I'm Austin Clarke, he said, leaning to his left. Love your writing, I said, leaning to my right. Thank you very much, he said, leaning to his left. No booze, I said, leaning to my right. Six dollars for a glass of wine, he said — which made me sit straight up. We should never ever travel without a flask! I said. You're quite right, he agreed. Then, leaning to his left, he asked, "And are you in this same line of work?"

"Austin," leaning to my right, "I'm on the same shortlist you're on."

And he was beautifully embarrassed.

That was my little spiel. I was ready to eat but the university women were not. They had questions, all of which I answered with alarming indiscretion. Do you write every day? they wanted to know. And I told them about Trollope and the turnips. Yes, I said, I write every day so it's hard to understand why I produce so little. Once, I said, I went to the library and got out a book about writing novels and I was thunderstruck to read about the way Trollope wrote his. He used to pull his watch out of his pocket, place it on the table and say to himself, Three pages every half hour, and he wrote for three hours a day. It's true that for half that time he reread and revised previous pages, but still, that's nine pages a day, day after day. Having read this I said to myself: That is so ruthless it should really suit you.

It also put me in mind of dinnertime with my father. You won't know this, I said, but I'm the daughter of a high school principal who brooked no resistance at school or at home. Several nights a week my mother would serve turnip for supper. She never softened the blow. Always she served them mashed up with all their stringy fibres intact so that you had to sieve them through your teeth. I would sit at my place, to the left of my father, putting off my wretched fate until finally he would remove his wristwatch, put it on the table directly in front of him, and say, Elizabeth. You have TWO MINUTES to finish your turnips. "So," I said to the university women, "now I put my watch on my desk and say to myself, Elizabeth, you have TWENTY MINUTES to write your way out of this mess."

They asked about my children and I talked about the horrors of family life, dwelling on the slough of surly despond that every single Sunday turns out to be. They asked if I knew many other writers and I said, "Oh, I hate writers."

Then we ate our tasty turnip-free supper after which Debbie took me to her house, where I would sleep, so that I could drop off my bag, and from there we went to the school auditorium where I was scheduled to speak. I said to Debbie on the way, "I like being my own warm-up act. I think I'll do this all the time."

THE MAIN EVENT went quickly. The woman who introduced me to the University Women's Club as a whole was not one of the potluck women, but she was, of course, a university woman. She was very young. She was nervous. She introduced me as the author of *Small Changes*, nominated for the Governor General's Literacy Award.

It's taken a long time but I can finally sign my name, and you can too, so long as you don't give up.

I told them my two jokes, the one about the working title of my book being *Fights I've had with Various Schmucks, Especially Myself*. Actually, it was *Fights I've Had with Various Shitheads*, but I never say that because I'm a university woman too. And the one about the person who told me she thought *Small Change* was so bleak it was exhilarating. After reading it she went to work and for the first time in her professional life she actually yelled at people. So taken aback was her boss that he insisted she go on a two-week vacation. I said, "That's what the blurb on the back of the book should say. Read this book, and get two weeks off."

I also read one of the stories and talked in what must have been a heart-rending way about the book in general because afterwards a woman in her early thirties with long, light brown hair came up to me and said, "You remind me so much of my sister. Tell me. Did writing your book help you with all of your difficulties? Do you think it would help my sister if she became a writer? Because she is so troubled."

Another woman, and this woman I had noticed right away and liked in the same moment because she looked like an elderly Simone Signoret's plain sister — an experienced woman of the world, surely European — this woman said to me, "Are you still as super-sensitive as you were in the book, or have you gotten over that by now?"

At least I had an answer for that one.

"I'm hard as nails," I said.

AN INTERVIEW WITH W. G. SEBALD

JAMES WOOD

THIS CONVERSATION was part of a series called *The Writer, The Work*, hosted by the PEN American Center. It took place in New York City on July 10, 1997, when the only book of W. G. Sebald's in English was *The Emigrants*. *Brick* published the interview the following spring (in issue number 59), and with the exception of the final three paragraphs of the following introduction, it was then reprinted without alteration in 2001.

WALTER BENJAMIN *said that all great works found a new genre or dissolve an old one. The Emigrants is such a book.*

It tells the story of four men, all swept by history and internally menaced. The first, Dr. Henry Selwyn, is discovered by Sebald in 1970 in a country house near Norwich, in England. He seems to be an aristocratic hermit. He has abandoned his large house and lives primarily in a stone folly, a turret he has built in his garden. His relations with plants and animals is stronger than his relations with humans. Slowly his story emerges. He left Lithuania in 1899 and his family disembarked in London, thinking it was New York. Selwyn changed his name, married, went to Cambridge, travelled, and became a rural doctor. Dr. Selwyn, sometime after he met and told Sebald his history, shot himself dead.

*The second story concerns Paul Bereyter, who taught Sebald when the author was a child. In 1984 Sebald hears that Bereyter committed suicide by lying on the local railroad tracks, and he be-*gins to ask around about the source of his misery. He discovers that Paul Bereyter was one-quarter Jewish, that he was consequently banned from teaching—in the mid-thirties, at a time when he was just beginning—that he served in the German army during the Second World War, and that he resumed teaching. But like all of Sebald's subjects except his last, Paul Bereyter's soul began to fall victim to a wasting disease, an inner dwindling. He retired from teaching. His eyesight failed and he killed himself.*

The third story is about Sebald's great-uncle, Ambros Adelwarth, who came to America in the 1920s, worked as a servant for a family, the Solomons, on Long Island, but ended up in a mental asylum in Ithaca, where he died.

The fourth story is about a painter named Max Ferber, whom Sebald met in Manchester.

Much has been said, rightly, about the extraordinary originality of the book. We may find frail precursors, possibly in Stendhal's autobiography, The Life of Henry Brulard, *an unstable book which is adorned—as* The Emigrants *is adorned with photographs—with Stendhal's own unreliable drawings. We may find precursors in the nineteenth-century German tradition of "tales," of narrators meeting people who then recount their life histories. One thinks particularly of the Austrian writer Adalbert Stifter, whom Sebald has written about. In a more contemporary vein, Nabokov has clearly influenced Sebald.* Speak, Memory, *Nabokov's autobiography, has photographs in it, though they are captioned and reliable. But his first novel written in English,* The Real Life of Sebastian Knight, *is a fictionalized account, made to look real, of the life of a writer. This dilemma, the dilemma of fictionality at its most acute, is one of Sebald's great themes.*

The fastidiousness of this book is remarkable, and yet it is not a dead fastidiousness. All those who read it note the patterning of certain motifs, such as gardens and gardening, or the appearance of Nabokov, direct or indirect, in each tale. The book is a great one because it forces the largest abstract questions on us, while never neglecting our hunger for the ordinary. It is full of this extraordinary, careful detail, which is part of what makes it also funny. Few people have mentioned its comedy, but surely the book does have a lugubrious comedy, and that slight tincture of vulgarity, of the sensational, which great books need if they are not to be ethereal.

One thinks, for instance, of Dr. Selwyn inviting people to dinner and giving them only seasonal vegetables from his own garden, or of Elaine, his servant, bringing food in on a portable hot-plate, which Sebald describes as "some kind of patented design dating from the thirties." Note the word "patented." A less careful writer would have omitted that word, but that word, with its ridiculous presumptions, is what makes the sentence funny. Or Mrs. Irlam, in the last story, with her English contraption, The Teas-maid, *which makes tea for you in the mornings, and a photograph of which Sebald diligently reproduces as if it were an ethnographical specimen.*

The photographs—some of which may not refer to the subjects of Sebald's tales—tease us as Goethe meant to tease us when he said this to Eckermann, in 1827: "What else is a novel but an unheard-of event which has actually happened?" The book's constant sense of bringing into permanent visibility something which has happened and which has disappeared, its profound meditation on the fictionality of memory and its deep comedy, all unite in a passage near the beginning of the story about Ambros Adelwarth. Sebald goes to visit his uncle Kasimir, on the Jersey beach, to find out about his great-uncle. His uncle looks at the ocean: "I often come out here," said Uncle Kasimir, "it makes me feel that I am a

long way away, though I never quite know from where." Then he took a camera out of his large-check jacket, and took this picture, a print of which he sent me two years later, probably when he had finally shot the whole film, together with his gold pocket watch."

The gentle irony is so subtle. The photo of Sebald by Uncle Kasimir is reproduced, but is too dark to decipher. You look at it and you try to see Sebald in it and you cannot. It may or may not be the author. It hardly matters. The suggestion is ripe enough: the paragraph has the determination of a Renaissance still life. The sense of time slowed and mastered and then lost is given in the mention of the pocket watch. That detail of the film returned two years later, "probably when he had shot the whole film," tells us about a life, without a strong sense of self-visibility: Uncle Kasimir's is not a life with much need of photographs. Neither does Sebald have much sense of self-visibility. Yet the mastery of his book is that he palpates so much into visibility, so delicately and so beautifully.

THE EMIGRANTS *was Sebald's first book to be published in English; it was swiftly followed by three further works,* The Rings of Saturn, Vertigo, *and* Austerlitz. *Tutored by* The Emigrants, *we began to learn how to read this strange writer, to find amidst the sublimity, melancholy, and abysmal autumn of his writing, more vulgar arts, such as comedy, slyness, even a measure of gothic suspense. Thomas Bernhard was revealed as an influence, along with Beckett. In particular,* The Rings of Saturn, *which folded a great deal of arcane information and storytelling into a long hike through Norfolk and Suffolk, revealed the "English" side of Sebald (who lived in Norwich for thirty years): a writer alive to the grey frustrations and daily eccentricities of English life. One had a sense of a writer settling—insofar as Sebald could settle anywhere—into his borrowed landscape. It was enormously exciting to ponder his next experiments; no contemporary writer was less predictable.*

But like Italo Svevo, who had a few years of international fame before dying after a car accident, Sebald was shortly silenced.

He died in a car accident at the end of last year, at the age of fifty-eight. Along with all the more personal and selfish responses to his death, I recall saying to myself, as I looked at the bald headline of The New York Times *("German novelist dies"): "But he had only just got started!" As readers, we were just getting used to his magical presence. And as English readers, we were just getting used to the idea of new books by Sebald, of books as yet unwritten. And I recalled, of course, my only meeting with him: the evening on which I conducted this interview, followed by dinner, in New York. Like his writing, Sebald was calm, surreptitiously funny, erudite, and oddly pure. He was easy to warm to: handsome, fair, high-coloured (his cheeks brushed with a down of tiny blood vessels), and grief-eyed. Above all, one was struck by the eyes, which slanted downwards, and quickly became melancholy. His grey moustache acted, visually, as a kind of bourgeois correction to aesthetic preciousness; it gave him the aspect of a burgher, a solid, dependable witness. Only his heavy smoking suggested the immense nervous energy that shapes his works.*

I think he enjoyed playing the melancholic German, and then surprising expectations by being funny and easy. He said that one of the elements of English life he most liked was English humor. "What's German humor like?" I asked him. "Oh, it is absolutely dreadful," he said. "Have you seen any German comedy shows on television?" I had not. "They are simply indescribable," he said, stretching the word in his long, lugubrious accent. "Simply indescribable." And then our host asked him if, given his new success, he might be lured from his old vicarage in Norwich to come to America. Perhaps he could teach at Columbia for a year, or take one of the generous fellowships at the New York Public Library. America lay at his feet. America, our host seemed to suggest, is success's real address. England…well, England is what everyone knows it to be—what Larkin called fulfillment's desolate attic. Sebald looked at our host, seemed to consider the idea for a minute, and then said quietly and firmly: "Oh no, I don't think so."

—*James Wood*

JW Can I start by asking you about this question of precursors? The book's originality makes the business of searching for tracks unusually pointless and difficult. But I did want to ask you how the form, particularly with the photographs and this question of the fictional and the factual, came about.

WGS The inclusion of pictures in the text had to do with the process of writing, which began to develop quite late in my career. As you may know, I was just an ordinary academic until not all that long ago. I gradually drifted into creative writing—as one generally calls it—in my mid-forties, out of a sense of frustration with my academic profession, I imagine, and simply because I wanted to find an escape route out of it, something I could do in the potting shed, that no one would know about.

The first prose work that I did is a text, also composed of four discrete pieces, called *Vertigo*, but could also mean legerdemain. It has in it a chapter—I think it's the first, if I remember correctly—precisely about Stendhal, and includes some of those drawings from *La Vie d'Henri Brulard* that you have mentioned. The process of writing, as I drifted into it, was in many instances occasioned by pictures that happened to come my way, that I stared at for long periods of time and that seemed to contain some enigmatic elements that I wanted to tease out. So they did form the instigation for trying to write this kind of thing. Because of that, they have kept their place. It eventually became some sort of habit, of including these pictures. I think they do tell their own story within the prose narrative and do establish a second level of discourse that is mute. It would be an ambition of mine to produce the kind of prose which has a degree of mutedness about it. The photographs do, in a sense, help you along this route.

JW A banal but unavoidable question is—to get it out of the way—to ask you roughly what proportion of those photographs refer to their subjects.

WGS This question is one that I am asked quite frequently. A very large percentage of those photographs are what you would describe as authentic, i.e., they really did come out of the photo albums of the people described in those texts and are a direct testimony of the fact that these people did exist in that particular shape and form. A small number—I imagine it must be in the region of ten percent—are pictures, photographs, postcards, travel documents, that kind of thing, which I had used from other sources. They are, I think, to a very large extent documentary.

JW By way of concentrating on one story and giving a sense of how you discovered, manipulated, and crafted the material, perhaps I could ask you very loosely about the first story, Dr. Henry Selwyn—how that came to you, how you elicited information, and then the process of shaping it.

WGS The Henry Selwyn story is the first one in the book and it's the shortest one. That is an indication of the fact that it was very difficult for me, afterwards, after this man had taken his life, to go back to the family and ask probing questions. It was also difficult because Henry Selwyn and his wife lived very largely separate lives. Hence it would have been extremely difficult to go back to her and sound her out about the motives that might have led her estranged husband to do what he did.

The information which is offered in the story is actually very sparse, in this particular case, and is no more than I actually obtained from him during the time when he was still alive. I would probably have been unable to decipher the truth behind his decision to take his life, if he had not, at a very late stage in that life, volunteered, as it were, in a very short conversation that we had after we moved out of his house, to tell me about his childhood in Lithuania and his emigration to England. It was only because

I had this fragmentary piece of information that I could reconstruct very large gaps in between what presumably this particular trajectory was all about. But as the story is described, with all its gaps and elisions, it is very much like I experienced it.

JW In some senses the fragmentariness of the information is useful to you fictionally. One of the uncanninesses of the book is that, while at one level there are obvious reasons for this kind of despair and inner dwindling that I spoke about, at another there's something mysterious about what exactly prompts this.

WGS The four people whose lives are described in those texts are people who escaped the direct impact of persecution, whom one would count amongst those whom Primo Levi called "*I SALVATI*" as opposed to "*I SOMMERSI.*" What particularly interested me, as I began to think about these lives, was the time delay between a vicariously experienced catastrophe and the point at which it overtook these people, very late in life, i.e., the phenomenon of old age, suicide, and the way in which these kinds of drastic decisions are triggered by things that lie way back in time. The mentality of people who are approaching old age—and I think this is something that most people do experience—the fact that the older you get the more the passage of time between your present age and your childhood or youth begins to shrink somehow. You see things that are very distant with extreme clarity, very highly exposed, whereas things that happened two or three months ago somehow vanish. It's this re-creation of the past, in the minds of those people, that was something that interested me, beyond the immediate cause that led them to take their lives.

JW This re-creation, as your book constantly suggests, is the activity of memory but is also like the business of making fiction. It's imaginative, it's open to strange appropriations and errors and so on. This particular fictional form, even without the photographs, is likely to raise the question of what is imagined and what is recalled. For instance, when Paul Bereyter's friend is describing the loss of Paul's eyesight, you write, "he contemplated the mouse-grey world (his word) before him." As you're reading that you think, it seems fifty/fifty whether it *is* in fact his word or your word. I'm not interested in whose word it is, but something about this fictional form, the form of quasi-documentary, automatically raises the question, I think.

WGS I think any form of fiction does that to a certain extent. It leaves you always unclear as to how much was invented, how much refers in the text to real people, real incidents in time. The classic case of this I think are in the novels of Thomas Mann, which outraged all those who thought they had been portrayed in them, unkindly. To a certain extent I think this is always there.

But what I'm trying, fairly consciously beyond that, is to precisely point up that sense of uncertainty between fact and fiction, because I do think that we largely delude ourselves with the knowledge that we think we possess, that we make it up as we go along, that we make it fit our desires and anxieties and that we invent a straight line of a trail in order to calm ourselves down. So this whole process of narrating something which has a kind of reassuring quality to it is called into question. That uncertainty which the narrator has about his own trade is then, as I hope, imparted to the reader who will, or ought to, feel a similar sense of irritation about these matters. I think that fiction writing, which does not acknowledge the uncertainty of the narrator himself, is a form of imposture and which I find very, very difficult to take. Any form of authorial writing, where the narrator sets himself up as stagehand and director and judge and executor in a text, I find somehow unacceptable. I cannot bear to read books of this kind.

JW Does this aversion have anything to do with contemporary notions that this sort of omniscience, a Jane Austenesque omniscience, is not possible, for whatever reason, in our secularized world? This is not, I suspect, a theoretical abstraction — it's a real unpleasantness you feel about this kind of narration?

WGS It is an unpleasantness, and I suppose it's a question of manners. If you refer to Jane Austen, you refer to a world where there were set standards of propriety which were accepted by everyone. Given that you have a world where the rules are clear and where one knows when trespassing begins, then I think it is legitimate, within that kind of context, to be a narrator who knows what the rules are and who knows the answers to certain questions. But I think these certainties have been taken from us by the course of history, and that we do have to acknowledge our own sense of ignorance and of insufficiency in these matters and therefore to try and write accordingly.

What you say is quite correct, that it gives me an unpleasant feeling to read this kind of book and I'd much rather read autobiographical texts of a Chateaubriand or a Stendhal, that sort of thing. I much prefer *La Vie d'Henri Brulard* to *La Chartreuse de Parme*, for instance. I find there is a degree of realness in it with which I can calculate. Whereas with the novels, I find we are subjected to the rules and laws of fiction to a degree which I find tedious.

JW This is a question which your photographs force and exaggerate, because they ask us to reflect on what's imagined and recalled. But I think also an extra pathos is that they refer not only to something that has happened and that is past, but that all photographs refer to what is just about to happen, after the frame ends. Therefore, they all gesture ahead in some way. Is there some connection between that and something inherent in nostalgia, which also looks both ways, backwards and forwards? For nostalgia is utopian, an escape as well as a sentence.

WGS Photographs are the epitome of memory or some form of reified memory. What has always struck me—not so much about the kinds of photographs that people take now in large quantities—about the older photographs, taken at the time when people had their picture taken perhaps two or three times in a lifetime, and they have something spectral about them. It seems as if the people who appear in these pictures are kind of fuzzy on the edges, very much like ghosts which you may encounter in any of those streets out there. It is that enigmatic quality which attracts me to these pictures. It's less the sense of nostalgia but that there is something utterly mysterious in old photographs, that they are almost designed to be lost, they're in an album which vanishes in an attic or in a box, and if they come to light they do accidentally, you stumble upon them. The way in which these stray pictures cross your paths, it has something at once totally coincidental and fateful about it. Then of course you begin to puzzle over them, and it's from that that much of the desire to write about them comes.

JW I think also the peculiar poignancy of the photographs, as they are arranged in this book, is that documentation is such a fraught subject, as it relates to the Holocaust. There's an extra pathos if these photographs are telling us that the German desire to silence and end witness has been beaten. On the one hand the book tells us that, and on the other, more complicatedly, it also tells us *not* to look in these photographs for the life, because it isn't fully there; it's opaque and mysterious.

WGS Yes, and there are one or two instances in the text which point to the unreliability precisely of these sources. There is in the final tale a photograph which depicts the burning of books on the *residenzeplatz*. One of the characters in the story says that this picture was a falsification, that the great pall of smoke that rises from the burning books was copied into the picture, subsequently, because they were unable to take a proper photograph in the evening, when this burning of books did occur. The Fascist newspaper journalists at that time chose a photograph which showed any old assembly on the *residenzeplatz* and copied that pall of smoke into it. So it seems like a document but in fact it's a falsification. The character then says, this is how it began, with this kind of thing, and like this particular falsification, so everything was a falsification, from the very start. And that pulls the rug from under the narrator's business altogether, so that as a reader you might well ask, What is he on about? Why is he trying to make us believe that these pictures are real? It is this kind of strategy, of making things seem uncertain in the mind of the reader, which the narrator pursues fairly deliberately.

JW Can I just ask you, as a step down from the more abstract questions, about the third story—great-uncle Adelwarth, and a bit along the lines of my question about Dr. Selwyn—to ask you how much of that story you already knew, how much you had to find out, and how much you had to invent?

WGS In one sense, this was the story that concerned me most immediately because it concerned my own family. As the opening of this particular story says, I came across this great-uncle of mine, when I was a small boy, only once, and he seemed to me even then—at any rate, in retrospect—as quite an extraordinary character who didn't fit the family mode. Then, as one does as a child or as someone who grows up, one forgets about it altogether for years on end. It was about fifteen years ago, when I came to this city, first of all to give a paper at the Goethe Institute, I took the occasion to go out to New Jersey and visit my relatives, who lived there. I looked through—as is my habit!—through the old photograph albums that my aunt had. And there was this picture of this great-uncle of mine, in Arab costume—a photograph taken in Jerusalem in 1913. It was a photograph that

I had never seen before and that somehow illuminated instantly, for me, who that man was and how he came to be like he was.

I did not know at that point about the way in which he had ended, but I knew that his psychological dispositions, from looking at that picture and from the predilections that he had, were such that his own family could not acknowledge them. I took it from there. This was the starting point for exploring this particular life further. I asked my aunt to tell me as much as she knew about this particular life, and I asked my uncle, and all that is recorded in this story. Then I also travelled to some of the places which figured in their accounts. So I did go to Deauville, for about a fortnight, and rummaged around there to see what I could find. I did not go to Jerusalem. The great-uncle and Cosmo Solomon, the young man who he looks after, travelled together in 1913 to Jerusalem, via Constantinople. If you go to present-day Jerusalem, I imagine you will find precious few traces of what Jerusalem looked like in 1913. If I had gone there in order to try and find location material, for that part of the story, I would have been led up the garden path. What I worked from in this particular case were old travelogues, going to Chateaubriand's *Itinéraire à Jerusalem*, of which there are many quotes in this particular passage, to travelogues written by a German geologist, in the late nineteenth century, to material of that kind.

So the text is constituted from material which comes from diverse, discrepant sources which exist at various levels, i.e., historical material, material collected personally by the narrator, and stories told to the narrator by other people.

JW One of the things that must strike readers of this book in English is the exquisite care of the prose and of the translation. There is a tension, almost contradiction, between the elusiveness, mysteriousness, opacity of the ma-terial, and the forceful, almost fanatical extremism of the qualifying words, which reminded me of Thomas Bernhard—a kind of extremism of language going alongside this unlocatability. For instance, Paul's whole manner at that time was "extraordinarily composed," Uncle Adelwarth had the "greatest difficulty with everyday tasks," Max Ferber remembers seeing ships in Manchester and remembers it as an "utterly incomprehensible spectacle." The language is constantly enforcing a kind of extremism, and this goes alongside something unextreme. I wanted to ask you about that. And then a larger question, about how you worked with the translator.

WGS These qualifying words, that are introduced in almost every sentence, are certainly a tribute to Thomas Bernhard, who used what I would perhaps try to describe as periscopic writing. Everything that the narrator relates is mediated through sometimes one or two other stages, which makes for quite complicated syntactical labyrinthine structures and in one sense exonerates the narrator, because he never pretends that he knows more than is actually possible.

That extremism that you refer to is, I think, also present in Thomas Bernhard, to a much greater extent. He really indulges in hyperbole, all along. I have tried to preserve some of this, because Thomas Bernhard did mean a great deal to me, in more than one way. What that extremism to me seems to indicate is the things that do stick out in your mind, they're always superlatives, they're always exaggerations. This is what you don't forget. The telling of a tale is an exaggeration in itself. We all know that. When we tell our stories at dinner parties, and your wife can't bear to listen to that story any more, because every time you tell it it becomes more extreme! It becomes more grotesque and more bizarre and funnier, or more boring as the case may be. But it is inherent, I think, in the business of storytelling—that drive towards the extreme.

AN INTERVIEW WITH W. G. SEBALD

JAMES WOOD

THIS CONVERSATION was part of a series called *The Writer, The Work*, hosted by the PEN American Center. It took place in New York City on July 10, 1997, when the only book of W. G. Sebald's in English was *The Emigrants*. *Brick* published the interview the following spring (in issue number 59), and with the exception of the final three paragraphs of the following introduction, it was then reprinted without alteration in 2001.

WALTER BENJAMIN *said that all great works found a new genre or dissolve an old one. The* Emigrants *is such a book.*

It tells the story of four men, all swept by history and internally menaced. The first, Dr. Henry Selwyn, is discovered by Sebald in 1970 in a country house near Norwich, in England. He seems to be an aristocratic hermit. He has abandoned his large house and lives primarily in a stone folly, a turret he has built in his garden. His relations with plants and animals is stronger than his relations with humans. Slowly his story emerges. He left Lithuania in 1899 and his family disembarked in London, thinking it was New York. Selwyn changed his name, married, went to Cambridge, travelled, and became a rural doctor. Dr. Selwyn, sometime after he met and told Sebald his history, shot himself dead.

*The second story concerns Paul Bereyter, who taught Sebald when the author was a child. In 1984 Sebald hears that Bereyter committed suicide by lying on the local railroad tracks, and he be-*gins to ask around about the source of his misery. He discovers that Paul Bereyter was one-quarter Jewish, that he was consequently banned from teaching—in the mid-thirties, at a time when he was just beginning—that he served in the German army during the Second World War, and that he resumed teaching. But like all of Sebald's subjects except his last, Paul Bereyter's soul began to fall victim to a wasting disease, an inner dwindling. He retired from teaching. His eyesight failed and he killed himself.*

The third story is about Sebald's great-uncle, Ambros Adelwarth, who came to America in the 1920s, worked as a servant for a family, the Solomons, on Long Island, but ended up in a mental asylum in Ithaca, where he died.

The fourth story is about a painter named Max Ferber, whom Sebald met in Manchester.

Much has been said, rightly, about the extraordinary originality of the book. We may find frail precursors, possibly in Stendhal's autobiography, The Life of Henry Brulard, *an unstable book which is adorned—as* The Emigrants *is adorned with photographs—with Stendhal's own unreliable drawings. We may find precursors in the nineteenth-century German tradition of "tales," of narrators meeting people who then recount their life histories. One thinks particularly of the Austrian writer Adalbert Stifter, whom Sebald has written about. In a more contemporary vein, Nabokov has clearly influenced Sebald.* Speak, Memory, *Nabokov's autobiography, has photographs in it, though they are* about writing novels and I was thunderstruck to read about the way Trollope wrote his. He used to pull his watch out of his pocket, place it on the table and say to himself, Three pages every half hour, and he wrote for three hours a day. It's true that for half that time he reread and revised previous pages, but still, that's nine pages a day, day after day. Having read this I said to myself: That is so ruthless it should really suit you.

It also put me in mind of dinnertime with my father. You won't know this, I said, but I'm the daughter of a high school principal who brooked no resistance at school or at home. Several nights a week my mother would serve turnip for supper. She never softened the blow. Always she served them mashed up with all their stringy fibres intact so that you had to sieve them through your teeth. I would sit at my place, to the left of my father, putting off my wretched fate until finally he would remove his wristwatch, put it on the table directly in front of him, and say, Elizabeth. You have TWO MINUTES to finish your turnips. "So," I said to the university women, "now I put my watch on my desk and say to myself, Elizabeth, you have TWENTY MINUTES to write your way out of this mess."

They asked about my children and I talked about the horrors of family life, dwelling on the slough of surly despond that every single Sunday turns out to be. They asked if I knew many other writers and I said, "Oh, I hate writers."

Then we ate our tasty turnip-free supper after which Debbie took me to her house, where I would sleep, so that I could drop off my bag, and from there we went to the school auditorium where I was scheduled to speak. I said to Debbie on the way, "I like being my own warm-up act. I think I'll do this all the time."

THE MAIN EVENT went quickly. The woman who introduced me to the University Women's Club as a whole was not one of the potluck women, but she was, of course, a university woman. She was very young. She was nervous. She introduced me as the author of *Small Changes*, nominated for the Governor General's Literacy Award.

It's taken a long time but I can finally sign my name, and you can too, so long as you don't give up.

I told them my two jokes, the one about the working title of my book being *Fights I've had with Various Schmucks, Especially Myself*. Actually, it was *Fights I've Had with Various Shitheads*, but I never say that because I'm a university woman too. And the one about the person who told me she thought *Small Change* was so bleak it was exhilarating. After reading it she went to work and for the first time in her professional life she actually yelled at people. So taken aback was her boss that he insisted she go on a two-week vacation. I said, "That's what the blurb on the back of the book should say. Read this book, and get two weeks off."

I also read one of the stories and talked in what must have been a heart-rending way about the book in general because afterwards a woman in her early thirties with long, light brown hair came up to me and said, "You remind me so much of my sister. Tell me. Did writing your book help you with all of your difficulties? Do you think it would help my sister if she became a writer? Because she is so troubled."

Another woman, and this woman I had noticed right away and liked in the same moment because she looked like an elderly Simone Signoret's plain sister — an experienced woman of the world, surely European — this woman said to me, "Are you still as super-sensitive as you were in the book, or have you gotten over that by now?"

At least I had an answer for that one.

"I'm hard as nails," I said.

That invariably begs the question of what actually is the truth, because last time you told the story it wasn't like that, it was much less extreme, much less funny. If you then get a good audience reception, with a story that is untrue, and there happens to be a witness present who knows it's untrue, that puts you into a position of extreme discomfort. All of a sudden you are no longer a storyteller but you're an impostor.

It's all that sort of thing which is at the heart of fiction writing, quite generally. That is certainly there. You try to atone for that frivolity in other ways, i.e., by trying to be as faithful as you possibly can in all areas where meticulousness is possible. That tends to be very largely about objects rather than people. You never really know what these people felt but you can just possibly imagine what the mulberry tree might have meant to them, or a certain arrangement of another kind or a certain *intérieur*. It's at that level that you try to make up for your lapses, as it were, of reliability, that might otherwise be present.

Do you want me to say something about this translation business? Well, there are many reasons why German texts don't really get noticed in the Anglo-Saxon world. There is a natural gradient out of English, which is such a dominant language, into all other minor languages. German certainly is rapidly beginning to acquire the status of a minor language, together with Italian and French. We know that the French are acutely worried about the dwindling of the presence of French on the world stage. There's a natural gradient out of those languages. Whilst the English had a very highly developed translation culture, in the nineteenth century when people like Coleridge and so on were very closely liaised with the German culture, that has largely fallen by the wayside, for historical reasons not least. It was the preposterousness of the second empire, it was German Fascism that reinforced the insularity of the British. In the post-war years, if it hadn't been for the émigrés, I think nothing would have got translated. All the books that did get translated into English—Heinrich Böll, Günter Grass, the early Handke—were almost all translated by one man, by Ralph Mannheim.

JW   On a different tack, I wanted to ask you—and again, unobtrusively—a little bit about your own relation to emigration and your home country.

WGS   That is quite a difficult chapter, of course. I came to live in England by some kind of historical accident. I left Germany when I was twenty-one, for the simple reason that I found it was impossible, at Freiburg University, as it then was, in the early sixties, to pursue what I was interested in.

It is something that one doesn't really understand very well now, but in the early 1960s the German departments in German universities were staffed, at the senior level at any rate, by people who had received their training in the 1930s, who had done their doctorates in the 1930s, who had very frequently not just toed the line but actively contributed, through their writing, to that culture of xenophobia which had developed from the early years of this century in that country. Of course, they had been reconstructed in the post-war years, but this past which was theirs was nevertheless present. To this day there come to light cases which are so bizarre that you can scarcely credit them. It was about a year or two ago—I don't know whether it appeared in the press here—it became public that one of the more important professors at one of the universities had invented for himself a totally new biography in the immediate post-war years, had gone to the lengths of writing a second doctorate, so that he could prove that he was another person.

That I ended up in Manchester was again rather a fluke. I knew hardly any English at the time, and I had no idea what England was like. I didn't know it was divided into a green and a black part, and I had absolutely no intimation what sort of a city Manchester might be.

I think my arrival in Manchester cast me into turmoil. It took me not a whole year but about three or four months until I had roughly found my bearings. As a very young man, Wittgenstein came to Manchester as an engineering student. This was something that I didn't know when I came to Manchester, and that I only gradually found out about.

You know how it is, when you consider your own life, and you realize fortuitously somehow that your passage through this world crossed somebody else's path. It seems to give your own life added value or significance, for some curious reason. When I first read Elias Canetti's autobiography, the first volume, which begins with this wonderful description of his transplantation from Bulgaria to Manchester, and I learned that he lived in the Palatine Road, where I had lived as well for some time, it meant something to me. I knew even then that it couldn't possibly mean something in the real sense, but it still does somehow. And this is the case also with this Wittgenstein pattern, which is a very faint one in the book, with scarcely noticeable resonances. It was initially, I think, the fact that he had been in Manchester, where I was at roughly the same age. That also, when I thought back to that other life, of my primary school teacher, Paul Bereyter, it seemed to me uncannily similar to the time which Wittgenstein, in his misguided idealism, spent as a primary school teacher in this beastly village in upper Austria. There's a quite extraordinary tale, where he attempted to live the life of a

saint, but at the same time constantly lost his temper with these stupid peasant children, and clipped them about the ears and so on. It was coincidences of this kind, so woven into the schoolteacher's story … there is a faint, second Wittgenstein foil. I think many of us find it difficult to deal with this philosophical thought, because we're all out of our depth, when we get into it, most of us are. But his private life or his person has something endlessly fascinating about it. It has so many things in it that one wants to know about that one cannot get away from it. I had the intention of doing a film script on Wittgenstein at one point, and did a rough draft for it, so it's something that may yet happen. Still, in England, I'm not at home. I consider myself as a guest in that country. But what I appreciate very much is the almost total absence in that country of any authoritarian structures.

In England, people respect privacy, scrupulously, i.e., you can leave your house in the morning in your underwear and nobody will bat an eyelid! A friend of mine once broke an ankle on the beach. There was nobody else there except an elderly English couple sitting in a car, having a cup of tea. He was desperately trying to catch their attention so that they could call an ambulance. In order to do so, he tried to make his way towards them, very much like a soldier in the battlefield. They just looked at him quizzically and didn't say anything. They just thought this is how he goes for his walk and that's fine, it's his business! Sometimes it can become a bit extreme, but generally it's a very pleasant country to live in and I'm quite glad that I'm being tolerated there.

LE BATEAU IVRE

(The Drunken Boat)

Stanzas 4-6

Westmark
HOTELS
ALASKA/YUKON

Whitehorse
March 4
2002

Rimbaud around 1869-70
LSH 02

(Stanza 4)

La tempête a béni mes éveils maritimes.
Plus léger qu'un bouchon j'ai dansé sur les flots
Qu'on appelle rouleurs éternels de victimes,
Dix nuits, sans regretter l'oeil niais des falots!

4

[Out] at sea, storms filled my night watches with joy;
lighter than a cork I danced across (waves) known
as the [timeless] rollers of drowned men, for ten
nights, never missing the vapid eyes of the quay-

Combers?

[ceaseless]?

5

lanterns in port. Sweet as the ~~████~~ tart flesh of green
apples to a child, salt water seeped through my thin
pine [hull] and splotches of vomit and cyan wine
washed over me, swept anchor and rudder clean

enjambment justified?

[shell]

6

away. And ever since that time [I've] I have merged ~~by the~~
in the sea's deep poem, steeped and milky with stars,
suckling the green azures, where at times the rapt,
pale flotsam of a drowned man pensively hovers;

or 'infused'

not quite right for "ravie"

le mot est "coque" — hull but also shell [of egg or nuts]

BARGAINS WITH THE LAND

ROBERT FYFE

THERE'S A PITCHER in the left foreground of Brueghel's *Harvesters*. Made of clay, partially hidden by a veil of standing grain, it divides the painting. In front of it, a field of stubble bears witness to the progress of the harvest; behind it, stretching down the hill to the harbour and village in the distance, a golden field of ripened grain, a wash of yellow so vital that it seems belly gold—rich, filling, satisfying.

On the stubble opposite the pitcher, a disparate group sits under a pear tree. A woman, head covered with a kerchief, is pouring something into the bowls of the men and women sitting in a circle sharing their mid-day meal. One of them twists around to cut into a loaf of bread. The bread is evidence, proof of the unity of the growing grain and the people who harvest it. The action says simply: labour equals life; by the sweat of your brow shall you live. For these people, surrounded by this curiously solid-looking field of grass, labour equals *abundant* life.

This is Demeter's feast. The Barley Goddess is everywhere in this scene, smiling on the fruits of humankind's most shocking revolution: a sceptred stalk of wild grass artificially selected, nurtured, generation after generation, until its head grows heavy with excess life. The painting is a celebration of agrarian tools and patient technology, of a world made gentle through cultivation.

Further to the right there is a line of trees. Under one of them a boy is stooped, picking apples. Around him, single apples are scattered against the stubble. But they look odd, these apples—all the same size. Perspective would dictate various sizes to represent them scattered under the circumference of the tree. Here, they seem to be suspended in the air over the bent back of the boy.

Floating apples? The eye climbs up to the branches of the tree. Isn't there an odd bulkiness to those branches? And then you see, high in the thinnest branches—where his weight and strength would be enough to shake the fruit tree—a second childish figure.

This is no accidental gathering of windfalls. The children's labour contributes to the variety of the harvest. There is no indication that the adults are directing this activity; this is what children can do to help and so they do it.

The eye is pulled back across the painting toward the pitcher in the grain. We go past the central figure: a man sprawled drunk with the sun (and maybe with John Barleycorn too), limbs unjointed, falling where they may in his deep oblivious sleep. He seems to float, emphasizing by contrast the purposeful activity around him.

Then we see a man with a scythe on his shoulder and a jug like the one standing in the grain under his arm. Angling through the waist-high grain, he is walking toward the pear tree and his lunch.

Finally, the eye meets a man swinging a cradle scythe, stepping forward with that effortless coordination which means: a) this is not only a habit, this is a life-work, and b) the blade is so finely whetted that at each sweeping automatic stroke, the standing grain falls sighing.

Ask why this figure is still working when everyone else has stopped and the significance of the clay jug becomes clear. It has been set down as a mark. "I will work to here," he might have said. "When I reach the jug, it will be time to stop." And so he would have proceeded, the goal always ahead of him, with no backward turning to break that rhythm of goal-setting and deferred gratification that is the essence of civilization.

There is nothing heroic about this last working figure, no indication that the others are admiring his personal dedication, just as no notice is taken of the boys harvesting the apples, of the man asleep, of the man walking toward the tree, or of the woman filling the bowls. All is graceful, nothing wilful. We have stumbled upon, have been shown the essence of, a community of curious bipedal creatures who, in spite of individual differences, have somehow joined forces to transform the landscape they inhabit.

The painter here has made a judgement, a valuing of certain human qualities: social organization (those preparing the meal, those working in the field, the activities in the tiny village in the distance, the trading ship in the bay); and there is discrimination (yes, they have cleared the land to plant the grain to make the bread, but they have left the pear tree and they will work around the apple tree). Brueghel has selected details to show us a particular community's bargain with its landscape.

Perhaps this is the true subject of all important landscape paintings—what makes them more than just a recording of a picturesque view—this bargain struck over and over again in different places by different people and made visible for the community to see and reflect on.

THIS MUST be true even when there are no human images included inside the frame. The Group of Seven reflect not only the Canadian northland, but also the Canadian people. The bargain we see in their paintings is an uncompromising one on both sides. On the one hand there are stone-faced mountains and endless miles of carelessly elegant spruce, pine, and birch. On the other, just outside the frame, are the miners, loggers, trappers who work beneath these cool peaks and wind-tortured branches only so long as it takes to dig or kill or cut something out.

We need to know this about ourselves; our history is built on these bargains. We need to admit that what we see in these images is ourselves.

Yet, while it is perhaps our basic bargain, it is not our only one. From the very first, from the time of Champlain's habitation, fields were cleared for planting grain around stockades full of beaver pelts. And long before that, squash and corn were the secret weapons of the invading Iroquois who challenged the hunters and trappers (Algonquin, Montagnais) and drove them further north. The "other" bargain we have historically made with nature is in the tradition that Brueghel shows us.

It is one of the marks of genius in the paintings of Carl Schaefer that they continue the record of this other negotiation. Schaefer's insistent choice of agricultural subjects has resulted in his portrayal as a "regionalist," a characterization that he sometimes agrees with. But such praise inevitably turns his work into a side issue in the history of modern art. Looking at the paintings from the vantage point of Brueghel's *Harvesters*, which records the central place of agriculture in our civilization, we see that Schaefer's work is actually part of a Great Tradition. He offers us a reflection of ourselves that we ignore at our peril. On the radio I hear several young painters agree that landscapes are no longer relevant since the population now lives next to each other, not nature. We like to think that we have come far past that first great revolution, but it is this first technology that still provides our most basic buffer against entropy. What is the news, then, that we can read in Schaefer's landscapes? The bargain seems a standoff at best, a truce with more than a hint of an approaching storm in the sky.

BRUEGHEL CELEBRATES a civilization built on agriculture. For Schaefer — although it is through eyes familiar with a working farm that he sees the world — a simple celebration is seldom possible.

Two of his watercolours appeared in the seventy-fifth anniversary show at Central Tech, a Toronto high school with a tradition of hiring practising artists as teachers. Fired by the T. Eaton Company at the first sign of the Depression, with a wife and a young son to support, Schaefer gratefully accepted an offer to teach there part-time in 1930. The paintings themselves come from a later period, 1958, and from a different place, the countryside around Doon in Waterloo County, Ontario.

One is titled *Wheat Stook, Waterloo County*. There were both bravado and a sense of remembered hurt in Schaefer's voice when, seeing it hung again, he called it "the first portrait of a wheat stook." Agriculture could hardly have been a fashionable subject in the days of Frank Sinatra and Elvis Presley, in the heyday of the New York abstract scene. Critics have often objected to Schaefer's exclusion of the human figure.

The stook stands on a stubble field that rises toward the right, and fills the frame. A lean-to construction of golden bundles, it begins with a pyramid base but springs open at the top, the heads of one sheaf — heavy with ripening wheat — spilling out toward us and to the left in a curve as full and natural as gravity.

The pyramid supporting its curve is set down on a knife-edge diagonal formed in a stubble field by a binder as it cut now the length, now the width, of the field. But even in the mathematics of these shapes, Nature appears, irrepressible: green weeds spring up between the cut grain stalks. Plantain, vetch, and scotch thistles stretch toward the light that heats the earth now that the crop is cut. Above and around the stook are the dark clouds that hang so ominously in so many of Schaefer's paintings. "Contrast," he shrugs, "necessary so you can see the yellow and orange." But he adds: "…The dark clouds, they're there to glorify the subject, you see? …Glorify the subject."

There are no harvesters in this painting, but their presence is here, the bargain they have made with Nature implicit in the geometry imposed on the landscape. You imagine yourself following the churning blades of the binder, picking up a bundle, stuffing it under your arm, then a second and a third until you can set them down, knowing how to lean first two together and then the third to form a tripod, knowing the angle that will draw gravity from the ground, to keep these bundles of light grass standing even if it blows up a storm, knowing that the axis of the wedge of straw you are building must lie north and south so that the grain will dry evenly, rather than bake on one side and stay wet in its own shade on the other.

And knowing south from the way the sun beats on your back, knowing that this last sheaf, splaying sideways as you place it, will form the final buttress, knowing that the structure is complete and that it's time to start again as you turn to follow the thrumming binder knives…and stoop to pick up the next bundle…

The instantaneous and instinctual creation of the stook makes it an ideal subject for the watercolour medium, which Schaefer likes to say is more like handwriting than something continually reworked. It's done instantly, on the spot.

> Walking across the field, you'd see something…stop, look again, and there it was, you see…then I'd turn my back on it, find a comfortable place to set up, bit of shade or whatnot, and get it down.

This is how Schaefer describes the process that produced *The Silent Land*, the second watercolour in the Central Tech show. Completed in the same year, 1958, while he taught at the Doon School, it shows the familiar golden field of standing grain forming a wedge on the right-hand side angling toward a narrow sky. But the major part of the painting, filling the whole of the fore and left middle ground, is a rich, dark, freshly ploughed field, furrows stretching to the centre of the horizon. The land is almost flat, showing only the slightest suggestion of the rocky skeleton that is so important for Schaefer.

> The Group of Seven showed us the shape of the great Pre-Cambrian Shield. I went north too and painted that country. And when I came home, I could see, under the grain fields, under the soil, the great eskers shaping the land. Just as powerful as the Canadian Shield but submerged. You have to look beneath the surface and know the anatomy of the land to be able to paint it.

It is often said that Schaefer is not a "colourist," but there is a deep significance in colours for him. The field is dark earth colour, not the muddy brown of the academy painters who, even now, draw his contempt for having pandered to a Canadian middle class hungry for the look of the old masters. There is nothing homogeneous or approximate in the colour of this ploughed land. Approaching the horizon, there seems to be a green wash over the furrows, new growth or the stray edges of the overturned turf blanded by the distance into a haze that teases the eye. Is there green there or isn't there?

"True colour is only found in shade," Schaefer tells his students. Here, in places, along the edges of the furrows, the absence of colour; tiny stretches of white paper, pockets of not-colour, show where there is light, glinting white light, reflected either from "plough down zillion shine"—solid turf cut so cleanly that the face reflects the sky—or glinting from stretched shallow pools of water in the furrow troughs left from a recent rain.

All these lines and especially the line marking the stark division between the newly ploughed hayfield and the swatch of harvest-ready grain, all these draw the eye to the centre of the horizon and to the dark solitary wall of the woodlot. Untouched by the surrounding farms perhaps because the land it sits on is too wet, or perhaps because it would be a sin to slash and burn *all* the forest, each and every branch that year after year laid down dark earth—untouched, it stands for everything that is closed and obscure to humankind. For Schaefer, the woodlots are fortresses, with palisades and battlements. A bargain is struck.

But it is a bargain struck 150 years ago and caught in these paintings—perhaps as a warning, even then. In Waterloo County today the woodlots are still there except where developers are carving them up into exclusive sites. There still are some towns whose population over the last hundred years has hardly changed except where the farmland bordering the town has been peeled back.

TWO OTHER Schaefer watercolours were on view recently in the Canada Packers show at the Art Gallery of Ontario in Toronto. J. S. McLean, president of a meat-packing plant, was an important collector of Canadian art. Although most of Schaefer's paintings were sold to farmers or schoolteachers who would save up or buy on time, McLean seems to have been an example of the kind of "patron of the arts" that is as endangered today as the woodlots.

Sponsoring companies today expect their logo to appear as advertising ("What's in it for us?"). An actress points out the billboards at the O'Keefe Centre (now the Sony Centre), which

shout the Broadway name of the ten-year-old touring show and the name of the sponsor but no performers' names.

McLean seems not to have had that kind of need to mix business with his interest in art. He was influential in building the Bain Avenue co-operative housing project (which continues to provide affordable housing for some Toronto artists), and Schaefer believes McLean was responsible for finding him an apartment there when he lost his job at Eaton's. There were social occasions when McLean would talk to Carl about art and artists, try to make sense of this part of his life: the significance of a Carmichael that held a special place over his mantelpiece, and, on a day when there were fifteen paintings by David Milne spread out over his bed…. "which one do you like best?" "Nothing to choose between them. They're all masterpieces…." "I thought that maybe an artist's eye…." "Not a question of liking, they are all perfect in their own way, you see…."

In 1940, Schaefer became the first Canadian to win a Guggenheim Fellowship for visual arts. It meant that he had to travel to the States, since that was one of the conditions of the grant. It meant storing furniture, leaving a studio he was comfortable in, and it meant delays in getting a visa since, with his German name ("not only Schaefer but 'Karl,' you see") he was potential spy material. In the middle of these delays came news from the Guggenheim Foundation that the money had been split with a Mexican painter. It was Vincent Massey who helped sort out the diplomatic mess and it was J. S. McLean who sent Schaefer a cheque to cover the shortfall. In return, McLean got first choice of the paintings done over the year.

The year spent in Vermont (1940 to 1941) ended with an offer for a well-paid position at a Midwestern University. Schaefer had seen both sides of the American interest in the war. He was arrested for painting a bridge because it might be used as a blueprint for a terrorist attack. Then, after reading a newspaper from home and telling his friendly postmistress that "things were going badly in the war," he was shocked when she replied, "What war?" He decided not to take the teaching job.

BACK IN Toronto, he decided to record the manufacture of huge crankshafts for corvettes being cast in the John Inglis factory. Inglis gave permission to do the drawings, though at first they showed no interest in paying for them. But when McLean heard about Schaefer's interest, he commissioned a series of watercolours to record his own contribution to the war.

Visking Hams, Rolling Room was done in the Canada Packers plant on St. Clair Avenue in 1942. In it, a large dark room is lit by a single overhead light, its shade throwing a cone of light sharply over the heavy ceiling beam that frames the top of the picture, more diffusely over a pair of vertical pipes on the two-toned blue wall that forms the right side of the frame. The light finally bounces off the tan floor, highlighting the back of a worker's baggy trousers. This man stands between the viewer and a large bench around which ten or so workers bend inward over their work. There are rows of golden-tan humps. Unlike the others, he is not bent forward but leaning to the right, his whole body braced by a hand against the rim of the table. Just behind him there's another figure, billed cap, arm pointing to the figures opposite, mouth open facing toward the stretching man. But the eyes, just the slightest indication of white, are not looking at his fellow workers, they are turned on us, the outsiders, interlopers almost embarrassed in this room of ritual labour.

Singer, Wiltshire Process for Export is part of the same series. Here, "singer" means something that singes, not someone who sings. We are outside on the roof of the plant in a world of sheet-metal vents and chimneys. Eyes are drawn first to a dense, detailed light-brown smoke filling the top right-hand third of the frame. What it represents is obscure at first. The darker brown girders with diagonal cross-struts that surround this haze draw attention down to the muddy tar-black roof. Round vent pipes with conical rain-hats thrust through the roof on the right to close the frame. Just to the left, a length of this same pipe lies on its side — why? And why are there loose pipes up here? — and points across to the two large vents that dominate the left-hand side of the frame. They too are made of sectioned sheet-metal tubes, each surrounded at its base by flashing that, through an intricate series of creases, bends, cuts, and folds, changes from a circular opening where it wraps around the vent-pipe to a rectangular one where it meets the roof. Tar laps up over the flashing, light reflecting on the creases where it bends flat; rainwater will pool here but there will be no leak to rot the roof deck.

The tops of these large vents are hooded like cowelled monks. Rooster-comb vanes on top keep them pointed away from the wind, thereby allowing them to draw the stale air and stench from the building. But the weather must be uncertain today, the wind calm, or else one of the joints designed to let the hood turn freely is bound, for one of the dark, rectangular faces is turned outwards toward the viewer and the other points back across the roof to the bright central haze.

There, represented by the sparest of lines, are the outlines of a front trotter and two hogs' snouts pointing to the sky, hung from a pair of two-by-eights on edge, thrown across the scaffolding. Under them, two open vents, intense heat escaping from their gaping mouths and making the space white, obscuring the carcasses within and creating currents in the still air that carry the singeing smoke away, darkening the sky. Hams for England, enduring the Blitz. Wiltshire hams, requiring a singeing process not usual here across the Atlantic. Thus the temporary scaffolding, the open vents, vent pipes lying on their sides waiting for a return to normal.

The following year Schaefer went to England as a War Records Artist for the Royal Canadian Air Force. For the next four years he painted Spitfires, Lancasters, a still life of a twisted belt of bullets. Then, twelve years later, he was back in Waterloo County, looking at wheatfields and woodlots.

So, finally, does the work of Carl Schaefer show us clearly the position we have inherited? Does it show us how we are connected to the great tradition of negotiating our place in nature? Is it enough that it reminds us that we no longer know what to bid in the upcoming round of negotiations with our landscape?

What the paintings are not:

They are not nostalgia. Looking at an architectural conservation magazine, Schaefer says: "Don't misunderstand. I'm not against change. Things have to change. But these barns and houses and schoolhouses…what is special about them, why I spent so much time painting them, is the way they fit into the landscape." The paintings value the connection between things, between the wheatfield and the woodlot, between geometry and nature.

And where are these connections today? How long before the museum audience standing before Brueghel's jug finds its iconography obscure because these people have never worked in a field of grain, never known the dust and heat, the simple things like water jugs. How long before we forget what a stook is, or a binder?

These paintings are not a plea for naturalism. Schaefer liked to admonish his students that "Nature is a tyrant," warning them against a slavish imitation, against a popular realism that relishes technical accuracy and so sidesteps the hard bargaining with nature that is the true purpose of a landscape. Such a representation is really just another way of ignoring nature, a kind of ecological sycophancy in the face of a tyrant.

These paintings are not a side issue, ignorant of the concerns of "modern" art. "Here," says Schaefer, taking up a paper napkin and smoothing it out on his knee, hands too stiff to sketch the idea on paper. "This was the problem for Mondrian. An empty rectangle like this, it's open, at ease. Now…" He folds the height of the napkin once. "Draw a line here and suddenly, there it is, contrast. Now the shape is narrow, tense. This square here"—an imaginary line follows his finger, crossing the fold—"is balanced by a two-square space here…" Or again, "Cezanne wanted to find a way to paint not only this"—he points at a chair in the middle of the room—"or this"—he points at the wall beside him—"but this!" He waves his arm in the empty space between the two. "And to do it with colour!"

WHAT I SEE in the paintings:

Discrimination. Not all things are equal, homogeneous. A river in which liquid chemicals flow like water becomes polluted. A society that brings everything into the marketplace and has no other way to value things is polluted too.

Judgment. One thing is better than another because it is connected, it takes other things into account. It's not a comfortable attitude to live beside. Schaefer has never been easily popular. People sometimes smile and remember, "Ah, yes, the complainer."

Schaefer knows he makes people uncomfortable. "Even Lillian said, 'The reason you have so much trouble, Carl, is that you preach too much.' But, you see, I was raised a Christian and preaching was a duty. Even in the art world the word had to get out, the truth had to be told."

I WANT TO
SPEAK ILL OF THE DEAD

JANE RULE

I FIRST UNDERSTOOD how competitive grief can be, sitting with my grandmother and her sister-in-law who were discussing the hats they would wear to my grandfather's funeral before he had died. Spinster aunt Gussie was chiefly irritated that her younger brother was dying first, leaving her with no one to see her out, but she comforted herself with the vindictive pleasure of saying to my grandmother, "He wants to be buried by his first wife, you know." "It's all right with me, as long as she's dead," my grandmother replied. It was Gussie who insisted on an open casket, presenting a corpse no one recognized except those few of us who had tended him in his last months. Even to me he didn't look real, simply a central prop for the ritual drama.

My grandfather Rule was on the dock to see me off on my first trip to England and dropped dead of a heart attack before I arrived. The day I heard the news, I had a date to go to Madame Tussaud's Wax Works. I went. Sleeping Beauty's mechanism was broken; she had stopped breathing. There were famous criminals wearing signs that read, "Dressed in his own clothes." Grandfather Rule had been wistful about fame, imagined founding a university which would be named after him. "Oh, beloved man," I thought. "This is all it is, to be a wax doll in this vast mausoleum."

My little grandmother had been cremated before I arrived home. My brother and I went to the funeral parlour to collect the ashes. There was no funeral. People where she lived assumed it would take place in Eureka where her ashes were to be placed in the family mausoleum. The family there assumed it had already taken place. As we were having breakfast at the airport waiting for our flight, Mother said, "Mother never would fly. 'Over my dead body,' she said." Her ashes sat on the fourth chair at the table. If the chief mourner bids you laugh, you laugh.

At four o'clock in the morning of the day Grandmother Rule died, my mother announced, "There will be no grief," as my father talked to his sister on the phone. They did not go back for the funeral.

By now all those old people have outdied my mother's refusal to mourn them, and she remembers them quite conventionally as better than they were, more attractive, brighter, kinder, and nicer to her than they were. She doesn't speak ill of the dead. Perversely I, who mourned each one uncertainly and in secret, remind her of their failings and tyrannies. I don't want the dressed-up wax effigies. I want the real people rampaging around in my imagination as they had in my life. I've never learned to let go of anyone I have loved, living or dead.

When my father was in a coma, dying, my sister offered to be the one to keep watch. "Maybe it's too hard for you, Mother." My mother looked at my sister and said, "He's mine, after all." Months after he died, my brother said to me, "Didn't he shoot you once?" He had, accidentally, while cleaning his shotgun. When it went off, a few pellets ricocheting off the tile floor into my thigh, Mother said in a plaintive voice, "Oh, Art, don't do that." "That proves he loved you best," my brother said. I didn't keep watch while my father died. There was no funeral. I didn't join other members of the family who scattered his ashes on a river where he had taught us all to fish.

I sat with the image of him crawling naked down the hall of my house after a heart attack and then a stroke had felled him, an animal struggling to find a hiding place away from all the helpless witnesses to his last indignity. I was enraged that such a thing had happened to him. It was an anger so fierce it frightened me, for there was no rational place to direct it. I found myself resentful of everyone else I loved because they became for me inevitably vulnerable to similar defeats, at least some of them before my own.

"When I miss him," my mother says, "I remind myself he would have been a vegetable, and I promised him I wouldn't let that happen."

WHEN YOU'RE in your sixties before you lose a parent, something in you has learned to hope it won't have to happen. Oh, I've rarely thought I'd die before my parents did. But I must have thought they might just manage to put dying off indefinitely. Obviously what I did not do was prepare myself, learn how to grieve properly and get beyond grief into acceptance.

So I go back to those earlier family deaths to listen again to the messages I heard. Did I learn that grief is a form of vanity to be avoided at all costs—or, if not avoided, certainly hidden from sight? Do not compete for a place at the bedside, for a handful of ashes. Do not weep or in any way call attention to yourself because grief isn't about the dead. It's about the living feeling sorry for themselves. Then I think grumpily, what's so morally reprehensible about feeling sorry for yourself?

My father's death was different from those other deaths. I had important relationships with all my grandparents, but they were people apart from me. In my relationship with my father there was, well hidden most of the time even from me, a child, dependent and defiant. We were often separated from my father when I was a child. Before the war he was a travelling salesman, on the road much of the time. Each summer Mother took us to her family's summer place in the redwoods where my father joined us for only two weeks of the long summer holiday. When he was with us, he was the playful, loving, teaching parent. Though lessons of most sorts were focused on my brother, I was allowed to learn, too, even the cleaning of a fish and the firing of a gun. He was the parent we wanted to please, even to impress, because he pleased and impressed us, so tall, so handsome, so good at everything, a national swimming champion, a player of any musical instrument he picked up, a builder of anything from a fence to a house. His absences only more sharply defined his presence until the war came, and he went away to sea for three years.

I was twelve when he left, fifteen when he came home bewildered by teenaged children who had learned to live without him and were restive under his resumed authority and his repossession of our mother. We had taken up bowling, a sport he had never tried. The first time he went with us, he beat us soundly, expecting us to be reassured by his superiority. He said of my brother's poor grades in school, "With half the effort you could do twice as well as your sister." He took me alone on a short business trip with him and said, "You know, your mother talks to me and keeps me entertained." "I guess I'm more like you," I said, and he knew it was not a compliment. We did better out fishing the river together or picking fruit, anything where our attention didn't have to be directly on each other.

I don't suppose I knew it then, but I didn't want to be under his spell again. I may have wanted to punish him for having been away those three long, hard years. I may have wanted to protect myself from needing him again.

When I left home to go away to college and to travel in Europe, my grandmother said, "You're breaking your father's heart." "He was gone for three years," I said, "and I coped. It's his turn now."

He tried to take an interest in things that interested me. When I was home from college talking about being a writer, he decided he should show me how to write a story that would sell. He wrote one and asked which was the highest-paying magazine. "*The Ladies' Home Journal*," I told him. The story came back with a rejection slip, the best confirmation I could have that my choice of career was the right one for me. He said wistfully, "You're now climbing in trees too high for me to get you down." "You've taught me to do it for myself." But what had really taught me was his absence. Did I never forgive him for it? Was some part of me left in a tree I couldn't get down from without him?

Because I didn't marry, he didn't give me away as he did his younger daughter. It was agreeable to him if I wanted to live at home and write, but, if I wanted to be independent, I must earn my own way. It seemed a more reasonable expectation to me than it did to him who was never really comfortable about my providing for myself. For the first several years he sent me a small allowance which he could ill afford. He came to visit with expensive gifts, hi-fi sets, typewriters. He built cupboards, bookshelves, wine racks, finally several rooms in the house I live in now. He was in his seventies by then, still swimming in the Masters program, assuring that his team stayed first in the nation.

He wouldn't swim in the pool I had put in. Was it too small in comparison to the public pools he was used to? "He was funny about some things," my mother says. I think it felt unseemly to him that I should have provided such extravagance for myself. He played my hi-fi which wasn't as fine as his, but he'd given it to me.

Before they made their last visit, my father had set the destination as something to get well enough to do. "I'll sit on the deck and swim in the pool." He did both. And then he died. "He did what he set out to do," people said. "He won his last race."

My father was a kind and generous man to many people. He was a kind and generous father to all his children, forgiving us our failures, accepting what he couldn't easily understand. Perhaps for him taking that final swim, old champion in his daughter's small pool, was an act of humility he thought he owed me or I wanted.

I've been perching in this tree of raging grief ever since. "Face it, sweetie," my father said to me once when I complained about unequal salaries for women at the university, "it's a man's world." "I will not!" I retorted. "I'll change it." His laugh rang out surprised and at the same time recognizing the will in me he'd had to contend with since I was a small child.

I sulk and mutter, surrounded by his gifts, not just the bookcases and the very walls of my study but such silly things as a wind-up Victrola to have music even in a power failure. He gave me that when I stubbornly refused to put in a generator he would have provided.

If I never quite managed to forgive him for going away to war, how on earth am I going to learn to forgive him for dying? Thinking I have to is, I suppose, another way of refusing his death. But what a horrible example he has set for everyone else I love!

It's the tree of life I'm in, Father, Sir, Dad, and you don't get me down, and I don't get myself down either. I fall, after you.

THE WRITINGS OF HUGH MACLENNAN

ALISTAIR MACLEOD

I N NOVEMBER of 1990, I was in Scandinavia giving a series of lectures on Canadian literature. I began in Denmark at the University of Aarhus and moved then to Copenhagen and then to the Lund University in Sweden and eventually to Helsinki. The audiences were receptive and warm and exceedingly well informed. The name of Hugh MacLennan occurred and reoccurred in the questions and in the discussions that followed my more formal presentations. It was obvious that he was well thought of and well known and was regarded by many scholars, students, and interested members of the general public as perhaps the major Canadian writer.

I returned home suffering the effects of jet lag and went almost immediately to bed. The next day while going through the correspondence and the newspapers which had accumulated during my absence I encountered for the first time the news of Hugh MacLennan's death. To my colleagues and to my wife, I said, "Hugh MacLennan is dead." "Yes," they said, seeming surprised, "we thought you knew. He died the day you left." His passing was already almost "old news" to them and we looked at each other with different kinds of wonder. I could not, at first, fathom that while I was talking about him in the present tense in Scandinavia, his life had already slipped into the realm of the past, back in the Canada which he so loved. I felt in a small,

selfish way that I had been betrayed by a force that I could not understand, but there was, of course, no one to blame. I knew, though, that my life in the future would be different because of the passing of this man. His journey and, I suppose, that portion of my own — the years in which I knew him — had come to an end. The motto of the clan MacLennan is "The Ridge of Tears."

Hugh MacLennan's journey began in the west Highlands of Scotland, in that region which still today seems supervised by that range of majestic mountains which they call "the sisters of Kintail." Kintail lies at the head of salt water on the west coast and faces, in its own way, what is referred to in Gaelic as *an cuan siar*, the western ocean. Kintail is (was) the home of his father's people and, perhaps, of all MacLennans. It twas the birthplace of my own great, great, grandmother, Christine MacLennan, who crossed *an cuan siar* when still a young girl and married, at age seventeen, a man nearly twice her age. When I was a boy my grandfather and his sisters had tintype photographs of the young woman they still referred to as "Grandma MacLennan." She looked like someone who might be entering grade eleven and it is hard to imagine that hundreds upon hundreds of us today had our genesis within her slender body.

Coming to Cape Breton's Victoria County, Hugh MacLennan's ancestors seemed to set about establishing themselves as rapidly and as firmly as possible. Focusing their eyes determinedly upon the future, they decided with equal determination "not to cast a backward glance." The subsequent journey is quite well documented. As members of the family left the rocky soil of the marginalized West Highlands, so did they eventually leave the less than receptive soil of Victoria County, seeking advancement through the mastering of English and through the opportunities offered by higher education. All of it worked according to plan. After MacLennan's father completed his medical studies, he practiced for a time in Glace Bay, MacLennan's birthplace. Glace Bay at the time was a "big place" by Victoria County standards. The coal mines boomed and the workers flooded in from the surrounding rural areas. Most of the workers were Gaelic-speaking Highlanders, coming for financial reasons to work for the often-exploitative coal companies and to lives which often led to violent confrontations and ended in the brutal deaths of far too many. However, if Glace Bay was a "big place" for the Gaelic-speaking miners desperately seeking work, it was not necessarily a "big place" for a practitioner of medicine, and subsequently MacLennan's father moved to Halifax, "the biggest place" to be found within the Maritimes. MacLennan at the time was seven years old.

FROM HALIFAX, MacLennan, as we know, went forth as a Rhodes Scholar to Oxford and then to Princeton. He became, in a sense, a "citizen of the world" although eventually returning to Canada. When he did return, he settled in Montreal, which was at that time Canada's largest city. As Glace Bay seemed too small for his father's ambitions so too did Halifax seem small to MacLennan himself. In his various essays he describes the Halifax of his boyhood as a "small town" and in *Barometer Rising* there are various viewpoints regarding the city. To the Cape Breton men who come there (again seeking work) it is a "big place" where they can broaden their horizons, get rid of their, perhaps, cumbersome Gaelic accents and prepare their children for life in the twentieth century — mainly it seems through

studying math and science. To those who have grown up there, however, it is perceived as a kind of colonial backwater which the more ambitious strive to leave, seeking the ever-bigger centres of Montreal and Boston or perhaps even the cities of Europe. Geoffrey Wain, whose family seems to have been in Halifax forever, blusters, "I've wasted a whole lifetime in this hole of a town. Everything in this damn country is second-rate. It always is in a colony." The omnipresent idea is that the major rewards are to be found in the future of the larger centres and not in any rural enclave or second-rate small town. It is a message which seems to have been fostered by MacLennan's father and one which MacLennan heeded well.

PART OF MacLennan's success as "modern man" was no doubt due to following his father's advice on preparing for the future while forgetting about the relatively near and perhaps unpleasant past. Even his classical studies focused on a past which was so distant and remote that it had almost become "new" again to those studying it. The "far" past rather than the "near" past. This is, of course, the almost-standard immigrant wish associated with the new world: things will be better if we but work hard enough and take advantage of our given opportunities. The world is all before us and the past is best forgotten; especially if that past seems to contain little of practical use in the new world — only the baggage of racial memories, archaic languages, outworn religions, and outmoded customs. As well as responses to life which seem to be quaintly irrelevant for the years that lie ahead.

The picture of MacLennan's father hurrying him past the brawling Glace Bay miners on Saturday night is a vividly recurring one. There is the circle of pale men up from the underground squatting on their haunches in their "miner's crouch" with their huge pan-shovel hands hanging heavily between their knees. They have come to watch "the fights" and in the semi-darkness their drunken Gaelic voices rise in ancient war cries directed at the bare-fisted men within the circle. There are the grunts and the curses and the sounds of fists on flesh; the blood and the broken teeth. It is not a particularly edifying sight and one can hardly blame "Dr. Sam" for wishing to remove his child from such an environment. It is obvious that the "doctor's son" is destined for another life than this and that such a circle is not to be his. "If this is the present," one can almost imagine the elder MacLennan thinking, "it will soon become the past."

Today there are those who believe that this headlong race into the future was not without its price. It is true that the sad history of the Highlands was not something to be pored over by Dr. Sam and members of his family. The circumstances of the original family's leaving Kintail were never discussed and it seems, thankfully, soon forgotten. During his years of study at Oxford, MacLennan never visited the Highlands. He had no great desire to do so and his father seemed to discourage it. "My father was also the reason why I never visited the Highlands when I was a student in the Old Country," he wrote in "Scotchman's Return" after a superficial visit in 1958 when he was fifty-one.

His observations in "Scotchman's Return" may indeed seem strangely naive to those immersed in the Celtic world. They also reflect his father's admiration for all things English—including the language and the progressive push toward the urban centres. Commenting on the Highland roads, MacLennan observed, "The roads were built by some English general, I think his name was Wade, who had the eighteenth-century English notion that if he built roads the communications between the clans would improve." To many in the Highlands the name of General Wade is anathema. After fighting against the Highlanders in the first Jacobite Rebellion of 1715, Wade shrewdly realized that one of their advantages was their near-inaccessible landscape—cut up as it was by mountains and water. He devised the roads and "forty stone bridges" as a means of getting his armies to a previously inaccessible people "and with great tact disarmed the clans." However, thirty years later the "clans" marched again and once more Wade was sent to meet

them. This time he was an older man in his seventies and, unable to stop their initial rapid advance, retired in favour of the younger Duke of Cumberland who eventually triumphed at the Battle of Culloden. To some, the praising of Wade for his road building is a little like saying Mussolini made the trains run on time. But of course there is always the danger of political interpretation and there is an old couplet which states:

Had you seen these roads before they were made
You would lift up your hands and bless General Wade.

This appreciation for things English, such as General Wade's roads, runs through much of "Scotchman's Return." In commenting on the Highlanders' immigration to Canada, MacLennan states, "With them they brought—no doubt of this—that nameless haunting guilt they never understood, and the feeling of failure, and the loneliness of all warm-hearted, not very intelligent folk so outmoded by the Anglo-Saxon success that they knew they were helpless unless they lived as the Anglo-Saxons did, failures unless they learned to feel (or not to feel at all) as the Anglo-Saxons ordained...."

Further commenting on the beauty of the landscape, MacLennan states that such beauty is dangerous and uses the analogy of Ulysses and the Sirens. While Ulysses, with good common sense, stopped the ears of his sailors, so that they would not be "wrecked" by the beauty, Highlanders seemed slow to learn the lesson. "Beauty," MacLennan writes, "is nearly the most dangerous thing on earth, and those who love her too much, or look too deeply into her eyes, they pay the price for her, which often is an empty stomach and a life of misunderstanding."

THE "BEAUTY" of the Gaelic language in the rural glen is also given short shrift: "The Gaelic tongue sounds soft and lovely, but compared with English and French it is a primitive means of communication. The ancestors of almost a quarter of modern Canada never did, and in their native glens they never could, develop even the rudiments of an urban culture." This image of the original Highlanders as "warm-hearted, not very intelligent folk" is, admittedly, one which causes some discomfort if not even stronger feelings among those who would champion "the Celtic view." It is closely aligned to the view of MacLennan's father that Highlanders function well when they are being dictated to but should never be put "at the helm" of anything. It is a view which is, perhaps, uncomfortably close to the old argument against black quarterbacks or black managers in baseball, except that in this case the speaker is himself a member of the alleged "not very intelligent" minority.

MacLennan's intellectual acceptance of his father's view is echoed especially in his two most "Highland" novels, *Barometer Rising* and *Each Man's Son*, which were published in 1941 and 1951 respectively. In each of these novels there are strong arguments presented for the "improvement" of Highlanders, those "warm-hearted, not very intelligent folk." The thrust is generally to become "more English" by going into and mastering the English world in accordance with Dr. Sam's worldview. Thus, in *Barometer Rising*, the Frasers go to Montreal and South Africa and Neil Macrae is educated in Montreal and at the Massachusetts Institute of Technology. Members of the previous generation include John Macrae who leaves Cape Breton to develop his gifts as a boat builder and dies disillusioned in Boston, Angus Murray who leaves Cape Breton to further his studies in medicine, and Alec MacKenzie, the "primitive man" who leaves Cape Breton and lives "just long enough to bridge the gap out of the pioneering era and save his children from becoming anachronisms." MacKenzie's son, Norman, is, sure enough, studying math and science and his "voice had lost its native Gaelic accent; Halifax had flattened it out." "Later than usual," we are told, "Alec's family had begun to follow the traditional pattern of Nova Scotia Highlanders. They had consciously given up the land and the fisheries for a life in the town." "Later than usual," is, in this case, 1917.

In *Each Man's Son*, arguably MacLennan's best novel, Daniel Ainslie struggles long and hard with the issue of whether or not he is wasting his gifted surgeon's skills on the people of Cape Breton. Perhaps he should go to Europe? Perhaps to the United States? When he dreams of the life he wishes to give Alan, his surrogate son, it is a life far away from the grimy coal towns of Cape Breton. It is again a life of math and science and he sees Alan "as a young man crossing the grass of an Oxford quadrangle with young Englishmen as his friends." There is also the depiction of the close to "cartoon-like" Highlanders who are constantly saying "efferybody," "whateffer," "chesus," "wass," "hass," "hisself," etc. These people who may or may not be examples and descendants of those "warm-hearted, not very intelligent folk so outmoded by the Anglo-Saxon success" are often seen as inhabiting a mental darkness as black as the coal tunnels of their underground employment. Worshipping physical strength at the expense of mental prowess, they are given lines like those of Angus the Barraman as he feels young Alan's biceps: "You whill haff to grow like a son of a bitch to be as strong as your father.... Maybe you whill haff the big brain, like the doctor." These contrasting views of "what to do with Highlanders" are at the centre of much of MacLennan's serious writing. Should they leave or should they stay? Should they live by their minds or by their bodies? And in any case is there a price to be paid for the made decision? There seems to be no simplistic solution.

Those who go into medicine like Angus Murray and Daniel Ainslie have left their humble Cape Breton origins to be successful in the Anglo-Saxon world. Still they are haunted by the "old sorrow" and/or "the beauty of the world." They find it difficult to be motivated by money and the conventional methods of advancement mean little to them. "I guess I was never interested enough to find out," says Angus Murray in one such conversation with Geoffrey Wain on the subject of "advancement." Wain responds, I guess, with typical Anglo-Saxon exasperation, "You're hysterical Murray, and you're being a fool. If you'd done more thinking and less talking in your life, you'd have a little more money in your pocket today."

BOTH MURRAY and Ainslie are troubled, in spite of themselves, by the loss of their complicated and often harsh religious beliefs and the customs associated with such ways of life. Murray is still affected by Cape Breton funerals and "by the sight of a whole community standing about the grave of someone who had been a part of the lives of them all." Daniel Ainslie at a crisis point in his life goes to visit his patron and surrogate father, Dr. Dougald MacKenzie. In a near-delirious state he remembers MacKenzie saying

> that it was possible for a scientific medical man of experience to believe in the efficacy of prayer. Was that three months ago or three minutes ago? It was hard to know. He could hear his own voice saying over and over, *But how can you?* then MacKenzie asking him what he thought of when he imagined God. There jumped into his mind the image of a tight-skinned dog with green eyes, standing before him with muscles rippling under its tawny hide. Then it disappeared.

AFTER THE bloodbath which follows Archie MacNeil's return, Ainslie in another moment of crisis again encounters this vision: "When he closed his eyes he saw the beast again, the tight-skinned, tawny green-eyed dog with the small ears. It was standing over the blood and its eyes were on his face."

Both Murray and Ainslie make spiritual and physical journeys to the Cape Breton farmsteads of their fathers. There they see the buildings fallen into disrepair and the hayfields yielding to the advances of the relentless and reclaiming spruce. It is obvious that neither man can return to such a life. In each case, we are told of the family's sacrifice so that the "chosen" son might somehow be successful, progressive, and increasingly "modern."

Big Alec MacKenzie's worldview is either more complicated or just more simple. He may indeed, in 1917, be "later than usual" in moving his family from Cape Breton to Halifax and he may indeed be the "primitive man" who realizes his children will be "anachronisms" if they cling to the Gaelic language at the expense of math and science. His "primitivism" may account for his frequent unease within the urban confines of Halifax. Often he misses his original landscape and the slower time of the past:

> shadows travelling the steep hills of the Cape Breton shoreline; pockets of mist, white as fleece in the sunshine along the braes opposite Boulardarie; a feeling that time did not matter much, a sense that when a man planted a field or built a boat he did so to meet a season not a timetable; a habit of rising with the sun instead of an Ingersoll alarm-clock.

MacKenzie in spite of, or because of, his "primitive values" is probably the most noble character to be found in *Barometer Rising*.

In Daniel Ainslie's earlier-mentioned vision of Alan "as a young man crossing the grass of an Oxford quadrangle with young Englishmen as his friends," there is the kind of buoyant hope that one might associate with the advice given by Dr. Sam to his young and enthusiastic son. Alan MacNeil and his potential, perhaps, represent MacLennan's view of a kind of "Highland Darwinism"—given the fact that the fittest will indeed survive and even triumph if but given the opportunity. The childless Daniel Ainslie sees his surrogate son as "giving himself a continuance out of the ancient life of the Celts into the new world."

As mentioned earlier, those who are most appreciative of "the ancient life of the Celts" may find this headlong rush to worship at the shrine of anything English a bit disconcerting. And indeed there may be some yearnings and whisperings of the heart that even an Oxford quadrangle full of young Englishmen may not quite settle.

A number of years ago, I heard a well-respected member of a Celtic studies department state that "Hugh MacLennan did nothing for *our people*" (italics mine). Close to the same time period, I found myself at a gathering of educators at Edinburgh University. By some circumstances I found myself backed into a corner by a man from Nova Scotia who began to extol the merits of his particular area of the province. "I know,"

I said, "I'm from Inverness." "Ah yes," he said and continued his pontification. I realized then that he thought I was from Inverness, Scotland, instead of the more humble one in Nova Scotia. And as I became more conscious of both his manner and content I feared the inevitable later embarrassment for us both. Finally I was able to say, "I'm from Inverness, Nova Scotia, from Cape Breton." He was silent for a moment before the expected embarrassed rage. "Well," he said, "you've lost your lisp." "Pardon?" I said. "You don't," he said, "say 'wass' and 'hiss' and 'efferybody' anymore." Ah well. You cannot please all of the people, etc. I relate these two scenes to illustrate some of the complexities associated with those who may be "right" in some eyes but at the same time "wrong" in others. To be sure there are those who may have quivered at MacLennan's penchant for saying "Scotch" instead of "Scottish" while simultaneously persisting in pronouncing his birthplace *Glace Bay* rather than the common "Glace Bay," the pronunciation used by the local people.

SOME OF us do what our fathers tell us to do and some of us do not. Some people left the Highlands with bitterness and rage, some with a sorrow and a sense of loss that they carried all their lives and passed on to succeeding generations. Some left with indifference. And some were, no doubt, glad to see the last of "the sisters of Kintail" or other "majestic" landscapes which seemed to them more negative than positive. Some individuals wish never to leave their parental roofs nor their familiar neighbourhoods. Others cannot wait to get away and, once having left, wish never to return. We cannot blame those who wish to leave unhappy homes and we cannot reasonably expect them to pass on, to succeeding generations, what to them were bad memories. Dr. Sam, it seemed, believed, as did his own father, that he was doing the "right thing" by delving into the future rather than the past. He obviously did not wish himself nor members of his family to be "anachronisms" in the twentieth century. It is hard to lay blame.

BUT STILL there is the old haunting question which comes to those who may slam one door behind them only to see the doors before them not as totally opened as they might have hoped. In the *New York Times Book Review* for April 21, 1291, Anthony Burgess reminisces about his past in an essay entitled "Joseph Kell, V. S. Naipaul and Me." Among other issues, Burgess discusses one of the problems of the contemporary British novelist, namely "knowing who to write for." He also discusses the contemporary author's relationship to his present time and to his past and to the language, region, and country of his birth. Writing of himself from his own continental exile, Burgess states:

> I am still a child of cold England, but only in the sense that I love its language and its literature. I cannot go back there to live, and on brief visits, I see myself as an outsider. The rift of religion, region and class should have been healed a long time ago, but it is not. Like a colonial, I have a sense of exclusion, a chip on the shoulder.

There seems to be no getting over this personal "condition" as Burgess sees it, himself having passed the prescribed biblical age limit. For him, it seems that in spite of himself he and his dazzling accomplishments will always be by "patrician" standards from the "wrong" religion, the "wrong" region, and the "wrong" class. Perhaps, in the end, he writes, "the children of industrialism and the scions of land, or of Bristol commerce, have little to say to each other." On reading this, I was reminded of Hugh MacLennan's "journey." Earlier than most authors, MacLennan seemed to know "who to write for" and his acceptance of Canada as a setting for his novels seemed never in doubt. Not for him the vague "North American cities" and the embarrassment associated with using Canadian settings. "I realized I could only write out of this country because it is a part of me, and I realized no writer has ever written out of anything except what he knows best," he once said. As he was unembarrassed about the country as a whole, so too was he unembarrassed about its regions. It may be argued that because he saw himself as from "the new world" he so loved, he was free from the residual prejudices that Burgess finds so lingeringly repellent. And yet. But still.

SOME YEARS ago, in Halifax, I stood beside Hugh MacLennan on the occasion of his receiving an award from the Writer's Federation of Nova Scotia. The award was in recognition of his lifetime accomplishments and intended as a tribute to him as an outstanding literary figure from his home province. He was very moved by the ceremony and in his acceptance speech said in a strong, emotional voice, "I never wanted to leave Nova Scotia, I was forced to leave it."

Perhaps, like Burgess, he was but expressing an old sorrow, tinged with a certain sense of residual bitterness. When MacLennan graduated from Oxford, he apparently applied for a position as a classics professor at one of the Nova Scotian universities. According to legend he was passed over for the job which went instead to one of those young Englishmen who might well have been his friend "crossing the grass of an Oxford quadrangle." Some may say that the decision affected MacLennan all of his life and that it resulted in a feeling similar to that expressed by Burgess: that he felt "like a colonial" with the accompanying "sense of exclusion" and the closely related "chip on the shoulder." The concept that British-born professors were (are) somehow better equipped to teach Canadian students than Canadian-born professors is unfortunately a "colonial" idea which dies hard among the less imaginative of our academic institutions. To "try to be English" was, perhaps, in MacLennan's case not quite good enough to get him the position he wanted in the end. And perhaps one can hardly lay blame if he felt, again like Burgess, that being "modern" or "cosmopolitan" did not open all doors in the end. Delving into the future may be of limited value to those who are interested in delving, instead, into the past. And the reverse, of course, is true as well. And "tradition" may well be a two-edged sword which forever threatens the divided self.

Hugh MacLennan was Canada's first major novelist. By focusing on the future he crafted a vision of what he felt Canada might potentially be. This vision, perhaps, was born out of a strong intellectual rigor based in turn on discipline and hard work. One associates this kind of rigour with the pioneering spirit bent on creating a firm place to stand within the new or modern world. He maintained, almost until the very end, this clear-sightedness and firm commitment. Yet sometimes, like Angus Murray, he heard the echo of "the old sorrow" even as he contemplated "the beauty of the world." And sometimes, like Daniel Ainslie, he saw the vision of the tawny green-eyed beast standing too near the pool of blood. Perhaps he did not seek these sensory perceptions, heard them rather than listened for them, saw them even with eyes averted. There was deep within him a strain that whispered that the appreciation of beauty and loyalty was not, after all, wasted in the modern world, although, indeed, they might often appear to be so.

IN ANOTHER century, Matthew Arnold, that man of the most divided self, wrote most movingly of the tension between freedom and responsibility. Abandoning his lyric inclination he chose instead the path of "duty" and took upon himself the burden of saving modern England from the encroaching march of what he viewed as the Philistine forces. Someone once said of Arnold that he thrust his "gift" in prison until it died. The lives of the "Scholar Gypsy" and the "Forsaken Merman" were not for him, in the end, quite dutiful enough although he often heard the whisper of their voices. Not surprisingly, Arnold was intrigued by the lives of the ancient Celts. "They went forth to the wars but they always fell," he said of them in one of his essays. Well, I suppose we all fall sooner or later. When the ancient Celts roamed Britain, interacting with the spirit world and creating their heartbreakingly beautiful jewellery, it seemed, even then, that they could not last in practical terms. When the invaders came, the Celts painted their own bodies blue with a mysterious clay they found within their mystical valleys. Whether they did this to give them courage or for decoration's sake we do not know. Nor do we know if they did it to make themselves more beautiful or more fearsome. It worked about as well as one might expect. As well as it did for most aboriginal peoples who trusted (and who trust) to bodily decoration in the face of iron and steel.

"To be a Celt is never to be far from tears," Angus L. Macdonald, the former premier of Nova Scotia, once said to Hugh MacLennan. It was a statement he was fond of quoting. Macdonald was born some two miles from where I sit as I write this; in yet another Nova Scotian autumn. The house of his birth is gone now and if he himself were alive, he would be 101. Yet on the high hardwood hills above his birthplace the leaves are a riot of yellow and russet and red when touched by the glory of the declining but still-strong autumnal sun. Their beauty highlights the transience of their season. Some days ago, a relative of Macdonald's mentioned to me that she often walks within that landscape. Sometimes, she said, she drives her car to where the landscape either begins or ends at the tidemarks of the sea. There, she said, she feels herself in the presence of "the people" who were the ancestors of so many.

Some twenty-five miles to the northeast of where I sit is a sign that reads "MacLennan's Cross." Although one is tempted to leap into symbolic and ambiguous interpretations, the original designation was but to indicate a road which "crossed" or went across the mountain and the landscape of the MacLennans. Some years ago a man hauling hay from the area said to me that there was a surplus of hay there because there were so few people left to harvest it. Hugh MacLennan lies far from MacLennan's Cross. His journey has taken him inland far from the tidemarks of either the beginning or the end of Canada. Far from "the other side" of his ancestor's "western ocean" which became, in turn for him, the eastern sea. Geography is, after all, a matter of perspective and MacLennan was a great geographer.

Some years ago, I heard Alasdair Fraser, the Scottish violinist who now lives in California, play a lament entitled "The Leaving of Kintail." It was so grindingly melancholy that it caused the hair on one's neck to prickle. But that again, I guess, is a matter of perspective. The music did not cause "everyone's" hair to prickle any more than "everyone" might feel the presence of "the people" within a certain landscape. I do not know if Hugh MacLennan's ancestors ever heard "The Leaving of Kintail" or if my own great, great grandmother heard it when directing her girlish footsteps toward the western ocean. Perhaps, if they heard it, they were glad to let it fall behind. Some carry "the old sorrow" longer than do others.

MY OWN sorrow at the loss of Hugh MacLennan is both literary and personal. I miss him as one misses an intrepid pioneer who was among the first to map the rivers and blaze the trails of a new country while suffering great hardship and neglect within that process. "It is possible to lead a literary life within this country," this early cartographer seems to have said. "Follow me; it will not be easy but worthy in the end. Press on. Don't turn back." In some ways he was like those hardy fur-trading explorers he was so fond of writing about in so many of his essays.

On a personal level he was kind and generous and unflinchingly loyal. I will miss, in my own selfishness, his solicitude and support and the many kind words he sent my way. He made my own journey, thus far, much smoother than it might otherwise have been and I will, within the future, miss the company of such a special kind of fellow-traveller. The ancient Celts believed that they were integrated with the elements of earth, air, fire, and water, and that they were part of the never-ending circle. It is comforting in such linear times to think of journeys which evolve rather than terminate. Perhaps all contradictions will be resolved through the spirit in the wind. *Fois t'anam*. Peace to his soul.

GARRY WINOGRAND'S MOMENT OF EXPOSURE

MICHAEL HELM

THE AMERICAN photographer Garry Winogrand once said that when he looked through his viewfinder and saw something familiar, he'd alter the composition by backing up or changing the lens (or tilting the shot—Winogrand often imposed a grade on his subjects), somehow complicating the frame. When I think of Winogrand, as opposed to a photo by Winogrand, I think of two things. One is the instinct to complicate the frame.

The other is a Lee Friedlander photo of Winogrand and his nine-year-old daughter, taken a few months before his death of cancer. She's on his knee, turned slightly toward her father, her eyes sidelong on him, and he's looking out of the frame and into the distance, perhaps into a continuation of the parkland that extends behind them and into the posited foreground on which we, the viewers, stand. The picture captures the most private of moments in the most public of spaces, a congruence that makes Winogrand the subject in more ways than one. Winogrand's photos often suggest that there is no public world; there are only private worlds that sometimes collect for the sake of appearances. Much of his work focuses on people in groups—on a New York street, at a rodeo, a zoo, an airport—but even in those shots which capture a social moment (two weathered cattlemen, one black, one white, shaking hands; a couple dancing close, looking out at other couples dancing) there is often something intensely personal. It's there in the faces. It's in the clothes, or the bodies' implied movements. These are pictures of people in their concealings. And, too, there's something beyond the human subjects themselves—seeming accidents of light or line—that separates the viewer from the viewed by making him complicit with chance.

The chance, it would seem, is divined. The tradition that runs from Cartier-Bresson and Kertész through to Winogrand (and some of Friedlander) involves impressionistic photographers who find coherences in uncontrived moments. And though the Europeans especially looked for a composition of elements that was somewhat formal, these photos are unstylized. When the elements form a pattern—visual or even thematic—they do so accidentally. The photographer's contribution is to see chance, or conjure it, and of course, in editing, to choose quite consciously the exposures which work best. In a 1975 review of Winogrand's work, Janet Malcolm describes his pictures as being "touched with the element of risk." In the shots he chose to exhibit, the method survives into the frame.

Winogrand once described a Robert Frank photo as "the photographer's understanding of possibilities.... When he took that photograph he couldn't possibly know—he just could not know—that it would work, that it would be a photograph. He knew he probably had a chance."

It's in this moment—the moment of the exposure—that the photographer is closest to possibility. Said another way, here he is most alone. It's easy to forget this originating moment in art, especially in an art that involves technology, under the artist's control, in so many stages of composition. But (and this is perhaps especially true of the silent arts) it's the moment wherein the mind of the maker meets that of the beholder. The two of them are there in this fragment of space-time that is neither the thing photographed nor the perfect representation of that thing, but rather something new, so that what has been fixed is not exactly what is re-animated in the viewer. That is, they are both there, and both utterly alone.

In a Winogrand frame, then, are traces of intention (design) and chance. But chance is a principle, not something brought entirely to hand. I find Friedlander's photo especially compelling for yet another reason—here Winogrand looks very like my father did in the months before his death. The long white hair combed back. The same mouth, same face, really. And my father's eyes. The photo is black and white but his eyes must have been my father's certain shade of grey. Here's a rare likeness, an instance of resemblance as distortion, a thing looking so much like another that you, or rather I, can't see it. I have no idea what anyone else would see here, but the same is true of any shared perception. There is a common area (a public space) where we may come to some consensus about a work of art, but if the art is especially powerful, our responses are likely to be inadequate. Unsettled and alone, we reach for language.

An aesthetic encounter involves two contrary impulses: the need to meet art and the need to dispel it, to uncomplicate. It is only this second impulse which is open to public discussion, largely because such discussion, whether with ourselves or in the public forum of criticism, is precisely what shelters us from art. The private encounter sometimes terrifies us and sends us running to the safety of the reduced, secondary perceptions of the common response. We resituate our experience within one or another tradition—within language, really—and falsely assume a measure of control. Interpretation, then, not as "the revenge of the intellect upon art," as Sontag wrote in 1964, but as shelter. When art disturbs, pronouncement calms.

Critical language is most often linear, its locomotion a dull step. So many critical pieces read like labanotation applied to Nijinsky, whose perfect dance, we remember, was in the mind and at the end wouldn't be reduced even to his expressive talents. To be truly, perfectly alone with art, for the artist or the audience, is to risk finding a place outside the social, a sometimes permanently isolated state.

Whether or not this is an old, romantic observation laid out on a blanket statement, it seems true in the particular case of Winogrand. His mature work takes such a path from the safely public world of magazine photography to the terrifying, private world of his final months. Perhaps his best-known photos are those of animals at the Bronx Zoo and Coney Island in the early 1960s, pictures full of life, captured and recontextualized. Given the compositional subject of these shots, the conceptual subject concerns something like the confining power of ritual perception, a saw of such age as to prove that any quickening art surpasses the very responses it invites, especially the trite reductions that could apply equally to bad art or, for that matter, to workplace warnings, accident reports, or headstones. The true subject of these photos, so many of which seem intricately, implausibly composed, is chance. And "chance," as Antonin Artaud said, "is myself." To understand the statement with any empathy is to understand the world as a place of perpetual becoming. Though it persists without us, we are capable, at least, of recognizing something there.

As interest in his work grew, as Winogrand was made public, he was asked to explain his pictures and himself to interviewers or students, and offered only vague answers. He said he took pictures to see what the things he was interested in looked like as photographs. He said there was no one way a photograph should look. Yet how could he be expected to explain the accidental? By 1967, when he was featured along with Friedlander and Diane Arbus in the Museum of Modern Art's exhibition entitled *New Documents*, the role of chance in his work was still larger. In the preface to *Winogrand: Figments from the Real World*, the Museum of Modern Art's John Szarkowski writes, "As his motifs became more complex, and more unpredictable in their development, the chances of success in a given frame became smaller." In the years that followed, the chances of success, at least as defined by Szarkowski, all but disappeared.

AT THE time of his death in 1984 Winogrand had left thousands of rolls of film undeveloped; in the last two years of his life he'd made a third of a million exposures that he'd never looked at. After some debate about what to do with these rolls — two camps of Winogrand's friends and curators squared off to argue politely whether the film should be developed — the shots were eventually turned into contact sheets and made available for research, though not for sale.

Szarkowski reports that they are full of technical flaws, the "most remarkable" of which "is his failure to hold the camera steady at the moment of exposure." Critics speculate that the "errors" might be attributed to Winogrand's acquisition of a motor-driven film advance for his Leica cameras, or his preference in the final months for shooting from a moving car, or his loss of subject, or the painkillers he'd grown increasingly dependent on since back surgery in 1975. But to search after cause here is certainly to see too narrowly. The errors exist in the photographs, but Winogrand wasn't making photographs. He was occupying the viewfinder and making of the shutter release a kind of acknowledgement or affirmation or question, perhaps — we couldn't possibly know. Whatever Szarkowski's good intentions — besides being an important critic, he has done much to bring attention to the man whom he considers "the central photographer of his generation" — and whether or not Winogrand's final work should have been brought to light, these are private recordings that call for something other than responses based upon the usual concerns of critics who willfully fail to account for a mind reduced to its apprehensions.

After his death, Winogrand the person is represented publically in the remembrances of friends. In anecdotes he is sociable. He tells jokes, sometimes about himself. He leads a class of students into a gallery and shouts out the news of their arrival. Ben Lifson describes him as someone whose particular way of hating silence involved bringing those around him to speech. "If we were alone…or at a restaurant…. when the conversation ended I had the sense that I had been with a crowd." He recalls that Winogrand "never left his apartment or a hotel room he was coming back to without turning on the radio or the TV almost full blast. He said it was to scare off burglars. I think it was also because he couldn't bear even the thought of a silent room." In the light brought to his final years by critics, even these stories, told with humour, in fondness, portray a public man with unguessable private fears.

As part of his cancer therapy Winogrand completed a form asking him to identify ways in which he had contributed to his illness. He mentions having ignored his body's warning signs, and confesses unresolved feelings of regret over the failure of his first marriage. In the last space on the form he wrote, simply, "hopelessness and helplessness about the world."

The words tempt us to choose from among the persistent fallacies through which artists are read into their work. Uncertainty can have the frame but we'd rather it was contained therein. Yet there are intriguing ambiguities about Winogrand's last two years. Why did photographs come not to matter to him even as he sought after the exposures? Was the act of shooting merely a ritual of the kind used to ward off chance, or was it a way of acknowledging possibility and, perhaps, hope? Why, during his last months, did Winogrand photograph his daughter each morning as she boarded her school bus? Did he suppose he could hold in time someone he loved? A question underlying all these: Can the world be made over again? It's one of those unstated questions that draw us to art in the first place.

Our aesthetic encounters are not public, but a thousand times private, and so beyond language in its social function. This is not to say, as is fashionable, that the specialized languages of criticism or theory are meaningless or valueless, a position which dismisses much of intellectual history as dung, and judges each parade by its leavings. Rather, the best public response to a beautiful thing is one which acknowledges the complications in the frame and knows when to leave off speculation. The case of Winogrand proves that the larger the conclusions, the less likely they are to measure up to the subject. In his last years, Winogrand himself resisted the need to find final forms, knowing too well that the final forms find us. The thought is speculative, admittedly, and maybe it's fanciful, but it's one I'm alone with when I think of Winogrand's photos, and of those moments that came to be enough for him.

WHAT I'D BE
IF I WERE NOT A WRITER...

E. ANNIE PROULX

IF I WERE not a writer I would be a glider pilot. No. I would be someone who draws, not a draughtsman, but a traveller with a crowquill pen and india ink, a swamp cartographer in a canoe, paddling through snaggy waters and hauling the boat over beaver dams, cross-hatching my damp paper by firelight. Or I would hire out as a shooter (with cannon) of lawnmowers, a blower-up of stripville architecture. On weekends I would search for blewits and fragrant black trumpets, trade them for sofas and weathervanes. I would be a scholar of eyeglasses, or a vintner. At night I would print money on my cellar handpress. I would be a kettledrum player for Arvo Pärt, or a telephone operator in western ranch country. I might be a woodworker making red cabinets of cherrywood, or a magician with the power to turn red cabinets of cherrywood into trees—all furniture, all over the world, would in one instant revert to tree form at my signal. I would be an accordion repairer and, in inner ear, catch the echoes of the first notes ever played on each instrument. I am attracted to the growing of chile peppers, especially the chile pequin or bird's eye. I would be a bottler of iceberg water, sell the stuff in blue-green mason jars. The needle arts might be my calling, not hem-letting and seam-easing, but embroidered vests for urban novelists, with a variety of pictured bullets flying out from the buttonholes. And when I got too old and too crazy and too blind and too confused to follow any of these trades or occupations, I would become a taxi driver.

DIONNE BRAND

A VERY UNHAPPY woman with three or four children, incompetent at housework, neglectful of the children, chronically depressed or at least chronically depressed and not knowing what it was. Or, a very unhappy woman living alone having failed a commercial course of typing and shorthand but having developed a florid handwriting style and loving fountain pens, sitting in a very small room at the back of a neo-colonial government office filling in forms, a job my mother with a little bribery would have secured for me. Or a very unhappy woman who having decided that these alternatives were unbearable walks barefooted with newspapers on her head the length and breadth of streets in San Fernando, Trinidad, taking swigs from a bottle of rum. Selling fish. I love red snapper. And the way that women who sell fish on the side of the road scale them and gut them while they're still gasping.

A bass player in a steel band or a bass player in a jazz trio all just for the cool not to actually become proficient at any instrument since all I ever did as a child was avoid chores and lessons by hiding under the bed reading. Running track, a career which came to a halt when glasses were prescribed for me at eleven—this one I grieve for still, to burst into speed and power like Evelyn Ashford, to pump thigh muscles like Florence Joyner, and to become only the second woman in history, after the magnificent Wyomia Tyus, to win the hundred-metre dash in two consecutive Olympics.

A very unhappy nurse or teacher or dietary assistant or domestic worker in Sudbury, which is where I lived unhappily at seventeen, or a very unhappy insurance claims clerk in a slate-grey office tower on University Avenue, Toronto. Surely supervisor by now, but not necessarily, hovering over the shoulder of a young, very unhappy woman making sure that she codes the claims right. Probably a union organizer, just to save my life, if I were a nurse or a teacher or a dietary assistant or a domestic worker or an unhappy insurance claims clerk in a slate-grey office tower on University Avenue in Toronto.

An urban guerrilla in a clandestine cell red-eyed and calculating which is the most urgent reason for writing.

SALMAN RUSHDIE

I ALWAYS WANTED to be an actor in spite of early reverses. I started out at the age of seven as a pixie in a school play in Bombay. My costume was made of orange crepe paper and halfway through the little pixie dance I had to do with several other pixies, it fell off.

When I was twelve, I played the part of the "Promoter" (that is, prosecutor) in Shaw's *Saint Joan*. I had to sit at a table in a grubby white cassock and make copious notes with a quill pen. The only quill pen that could be found in Bombay was actually a ballpoint with a large red feather attached. I scribbled away merrily. After the play someone congratulated me on my performance and said that they had been especially impressed by the fact that I had been able to write for so long without ever needing to dip my quill pen into the ink.

At school in England the difficulties continued. In one pro-

duction I played a swarthy Latin hound who got poisoned at the end of Act One. I was permitted a wonderfully melodramatic death scene full of staggers and clutches at the throat, before crashing down behind a sofa. In Act Two, however, I had to lie behind the sofa for an hour with my leg sticking out. Stagehands climbed up above the stage and dropped peanut shells on to my face, trying to make my legs twitch. They succeeded.

Next I was cast as one of the lunatics in Friedrich Dürrenmatt's *The Physicists*, but then illness struck down the boy actor playing the megalomaniac hunchback woman doctor in charge of the lunatic asylum in which the play is set, and I was told to take over. (It was a single-sex school, so we were obliged to follow the boys-only casting philosophy of the Elizabethan theatre.) I wore thick tartan leggings, a tweed skirt, and a Mad Cherman Akzent. The play was not a success.

At Cambridge I built myself a putty nose extension for a part in an Ionesco play, but on the first night, bending over a lady's hand, I squished my fake hooter sideways and looked more like the Elephant Man than I would have liked.

In a badly under-rehearsed production of Ben Jonson's *The*

point that such figures are often men, I also sported a prominent black Zapata moustache. My friend the now-successful writer still threatens from time to time to publish photographs of this performance.

After playing the blonde, I understood that I had a limited future in this line of work and ceased to tread the boards. The itch remains, however. A few years ago another frustrated actor, the writer, editor, and publisher Bill Buford, suggested that we should sign up one summer in the most out-of-the-way American summer-stock company we could find and spend a few happy months playing pixies, swarthy Latins, cassocked prosecutors, mad doctors, etc. It never happened, but I wish it had.

Maybe next year.

ROBERT CREELEY

FINALLY MY own choices in so-called life seem to have had the character of opinions, whether or not I might eventually have approved them. Better to think of them as the moves possible within a characteristic maze. Some were clearly wise, at least in hindsight. Others only boxed me in more.

Whatever, one doesn't just stand there, like they say, and my sister Helen early made a pattern for me in some sense intentional, which I think I still follow, at least in imagination. For her books were powerful instruments and she took hold of them with great appetite and particularity. She still does. Really from the time I think I've had a conscious sense of her, words, written and said in all senses were the power she most valued.

Did I then become a writer because of sibling rivalry? I don't think I had any clear sense of what a writer was or did, and a poet was even more vague to me as an actual person. What else might I have wanted to be, then? Growing up in the small farm town West Acton, Massachusetts, where my mother was the town nurse and our only parent, I think I thought first of being a veterinarian. It seemed useful and I much liked animals. But when I went away to school in my high school years, the glamour of reading and writing really got to me, and when it came

Alchemists, playing to a first-night front row full of English Literature professors, I suddenly understood that the line I was speaking was the answer to the question I was about to be asked. The whole cast immediately panicked and began improvising in something like Jonsonian metre, trying to find our way to a bit—any bit—we knew. It took what seemed like hours, but we managed it. Not one of the assembled luminaries of the Cambridge literature faculty noticed a thing.

After graduating I spent a while involved in London fringe productions. In a production of Megan Terry's *Viet Rock* I was required to insult an audience full of people in wheelchairs, attacking them for their apathy about the war. Why were they not marching in protest, why had they not been at the Grosvenor Square demonstration confronting the mounted police, I demanded righteously. The wheelchair people hung their heads, abashed.

In another production I went back into drag, wearing a long black evening gown and a long blonde wig to play a sort of Miss Lonelyhearts figure in a play written by a friend who has since become a successful writer. To make the Nathanael West-ish time to settle on a college, I chose Harvard which offered me nothing other than admission, just that I had a sort of *Jude the Obscure* sense of its grandeur as the cradle of great authors. So off I went on the insurance money paid for the accident causing the loss of my left eye at five. Again it seems hardly a logically determined provision.

In any case, what else I might have been other than at first a writer manqué, and then a poet in spite of himself, and finally a writer in some sense more truly, I don't know. I don't believe in careers and have never had one. I do things because either I can or I have to, as either writing or teaching, which last occupation has also been one I've had for years now. I've taught every grade except the sixth all the way from first to so-called doctoral dissertation. I am a father, which is certainly a real thing to be, and all the more so in my own case, given my father died when I was still very young.

I know well there are many who practice a life as a potential and therefore calculate as shrewdly as possible just what their resources are and how best they can make use of them. It seems a wise course of action, although I've never really done things that way. Do I think that life will find me? Do I believe that life, however to call it, will make its own way? Yes, said my mother, but surely you can help it along?

One time the poet Basil Bunting told me he was about four, sitting on the hearth rug in front of the fireplace of his parents' home with the fire blazing, etc. The grown-ups were discussing the Sino-Japanese conflict, he recalled, when it was borne in upon him that he was a poet, which was a difficult information in that he didn't know what a "poet" was. But he knew he was one nonetheless. I believed him.

I don't really know what I am in any fixed sense. Think of W. C. Williams's poignant exclamation in "The Desert Music": "I *am* a poet! I / am. I am. I am a poet, I reaffirmed, ashamed…" I felt that exactly.

Is there something else I might otherwise do? Perhaps you can tell me. It's never too late to learn, like they say.

C. D. WRIGHT

Whenever I see poet Bruce Weigl he says he is thinking about "giving it up." And I say, "You always say that," and he says, "Yes, but this time I really mean it." I have noticed, he does not give it up. This year he published translations of *Captured Documents*, poems of Vietnamese soldiers; last year his own "captured documents." This does not mean that he does not on some level mean business. I too think of throwing in the rag. Of warming my hands over a barrel of paper. The waste, the excesses, the obnoxiousness, the rue, the wrong words in the wrong place…. The fuming, the feuding, the perfect insurmountable indifference of everyone who isn't similarly afflicted. Then there is the dream of being useful. And the contrary dream of oblivion. The deep stream of Lethe. And the sybarite's dream of more gratifying options. Of painting and eating the paint. The ascetic's dream of living without so many ways to say it, less the dust and clamour and clutter of words. Paper kept clean. Or trees kept standing.

If I had gone to the right schools, and been properly turned out, I am afraid of what my life might have been—lawyer or lawyer's wife, congresswoman or congresswoman's wife. Had I been in California or New York, given my temperament and my age, I would be doing hard time now — Weatherwoman in the East, Symbionese Liberation Army corps in the West. Being from the Upper South, the rural South, spared me the urban guerrilla prison blues. I am aware of at least some of the inert ingredients which made of me an American artist of the language variety: the generational margin of economic safety which allowed me the loving pursuit of art, the absence of art in my locale coupled with the proliferation of utterance, of paper, of transcripts and books in my parents' house; the nearsightedness which made the books such a comfort. And the encounter with a writer who abetted the remote possibility of writing into a hair-raising reality.

I continue to evaluate the prospect of other futures (not to mention other pasts): I would have a bait shop on the White River, maybe a failed resort on the same property. I would definitely have riverfront. I would undoubtedly sell shiners and nightcrawlers and pork — rinds and light bread. I would not bother a soul. I would welcome well-meaning strangers and my funniest, best-read old friends. I would occasionally harbour unarmed fugitives. I would look for the news from the poets (I would have enough scratch for subscriptions), and I would get the word on the weather from trusted neighbours. I am sure I'd have a small garden, and bring in hornet's nests and gourds to beautify the house. I'd have a bottle tree, an artesian well. I could elaborate even more. It has become easier to cultivate this dream, the dream of oblivion, than the one of being useful. That is very difficult. In our society. In our time. I always thought I should have worked for the Works Project Administration. Given a hefty fellowship, I tried to enact a micro-WPA on my own. But it is very difficult. One needs a society which recognizes itself in need to receive it. The dream of being useful, really useful, that is the mother of dreams. That one is still in its infancy.

MARGARET ATWOOD

I USED TO think that if I weren't a writer I would be a painter. Then I thought that if I weren't a writer I would be a designer. Then I thought that if I weren't a writer I would be a scientist. Then I thought that if I weren't a writer I would be a cabinet maker. Then I thought that if I weren't a writer I would be a dancer. Then I thought that if I weren't a writer I would be an historian. Then I thought that if I weren't a writer I would be an opera singer. Then I thought that if I weren't a writer I would walk around in strange clothing talking to myself.

Now I think that if I weren't a writer I would be an amoeba. That's what keeps me writing.

GRAEME GIBSON

HAD I NOT been a writer I would have resembled, even more, the harebrained character in Kapuscinski's *The Emperor*, of whom it was said: "'Hailu must have started to think. You can see that he's sad.' That's how it was then. Those who surveyed the Empire and pondered their surroundings walked sadly and lost in thought, their eyes full of troubled pensiveness, as if they had a presentiment of something vague and unspeakable."

RUSSELL BANKS

DEAD. Would've been stabbed or beaten to death or shot dead at age nineteen or twenty, drunk and swinging fists in the parking lot of a bar in Lakeland, Florida. It really is that simple.

SITES OF CITATION

PETER HARCOURT

"APRÈS TOUT, JE SUIS CON," declares Michel Poiccard at the beginning of Jean-Luc Godard's first feature film, *À bout de souffle* (*Breathless*) (1959). "If you've got to do it, you've got to do it." In this way, the character played by Jean-Paul Belmondo proclaims himself the inverted heir of the existential philosophy of Jean-Paul Sartre. For Michel, what he is is not determined by what he does: what he does is determined by what he is.

This sense of a predestined universe runs throughout Godard's films. Beginning with philosophy, it passes through politics on to, in the late works, a kind of mysticism. But always, everywhere, Godard contests this predestination: he wrestles with it in the effort to confer upon his characters an illusion of freedom—perhaps to seize that illusion for himself.

If the films of Jean-Luc Godard are formally the most original in the history of cinema, if Godard is, indeed, the Picasso of cinema, his films also bear traces of the work that precedes him, both in literature and in film. Although astonishingly inventive, his films are indebted to the culture that subtends them. What Godard is able to do is determined less by who he is than by what has been done before.

Initially this habit of citation seemed like clever name-dropping. With the passing of time, however, it offers evidence of an intense humility. Especially in the late works, Godard becomes the vehicle through which other voices regroup and speak again within our culture in fresh and illuminating ways.

Tracking down these voices in post-literate North America will provide projects for film scholars for decades to come. Let us glance, however, at how this strategy of citation works in a few of his films, how it ironizes his practice and subverts any sense of a confident interpretation. Let us examine how his cinema differs from conventional narrative by a constant deferral of constructed meaning, how (as theorists might say) the play of the signifiers outruns the assumed stability of the sign.

IF THE opening scene of *À bout de souffle* contains a reference to *The Killer Is Loose* (1956), a little-known film by Budd Boetticher, later on when Michel and Patricia (Jean Seberg) go to see a Western at the Napoléon cinema off the Place de L'Étoile, we notice from the marquee that it is playing a Boetticher film. But what do we hear? Certainly not the dialogue from an American Western.

First we hear a man's voice (which we will learn to recognize as Godard's) saying something like:

Beware, Jessica. Embraces are a chisel eating away at the years. Avoid, oh avoid shattering memories.

A woman's voice then replies:

You're wrong, Sheriff. Our story is as noble and tragic as a tyrant's mask. Who can remain untouched by the pathos of our love?

IN THIS one moment, marginal to the action of the film, Godard has drawn from poems by both Aragon and Apollinaire. While critic Michel Marie has identified these moments for us, it is Jean-Louis Leutrat who, writing in a recent tribute to Godard published by the Museum of Modern Art, leaves us *breathless* with his grasp of the Godardian allusion.

> In *Bande à part* (*Band of Outsiders*), there is a reference to Raymond Queneau's novel *Odile*; in fact, a passage from the novel is read out loud by Franz, book in hand: the story of M. Delouit, told by Anglareès. In reality, the character in the novel whose name is Anglarès never does give this absurd little narrative, which is taken from *Nadja*. But Queneau, through the figure of Anglarès, is settling his accounts with Breton. We could see in this no more than simply a knowing wink, but when the narrator says, "Beneath skies of crystal, Arthur, Odile, and Franz crossed bridges suspended over motionless rivers. Nothing moved yet on the palaces' fronts. The water was stagnant. A taste of ashes flew in the air," the spectator recognizes a montage of four of Rimbaud's texts: *Les Ponts, Le Bateau ivre, Aube*, and *Phrases*.

OF COURSE we do. We needed only to be reminded! Similarly, during the key, romantic moment in *Alphaville* in which Eddie Constantine walks through the rooms of his hotel suite, only to find Anna Karina lurking behind the door of each one of them, uncultured North Americans might assume the poetic dialogue is derived from Paul Éluard's *Capitate de la douleur* (since the text is in evidence). Actually it comprises

> some fifteen fragments borrowed from the following slim volumes: *Le Dur désire de durer, Le Temps déborde, Corps mémorable*, and *Le Phénix*. The title, *Capitate de la douleur*, is just one more fragment.

IT IS this density of allusion that once prompted a colleague, Jacques Rivette, to accuse Godard of practising "intertextual terrorism." Intertextual his work surely is; and this intertextuality registers an inclination to synthesize fragments of the works that have informed his sensibility, which have moved him by their insight. "Photography is truth," Godard once affirmed, "and the cinema is truth twenty-four times a second." It is this kind of assertion that so annoys his detractors but which bears witness to his desire to discover the wisdom of life within the authority of aphorism.

While *Bande à part* (1964) draws much of its commentary from a number of French texts, at one moment in the film Godard also reworks Shakespeare to extraordinary effect.

Our three protagonists — Franz, Arthur, and Odile (Sami Frey, Claude Brasseur, and Anna Karina) — are taking English lessons. In a "gangster" film, this fact in itself is preposterous; but the English lesson we witness is particularly absurd.

As they file into the classroom of a little building off the Champs Élysées, the agitated English teacher (who in any case is French) scribbles on the blackboard *Classique = Moderne* and coaxes Odile into supplying the full sentence from the writings of T. S. Eliot: "All that is new is by that fact traditional." She then declares that today they will not concern themselves with touristic matters but must learn to spell Thomas Hardy, which she scribbles on the board, followed by Shakespeare.

In this little love-and-heist film, does Godard know about Eliot's work on tradition and the individual talent? Does he also know that Thomas Hardy has written some of the finest, most desperate love poems in the English language? While it is hard to imagine, the allusions are there (at least for anglophone viewers), dancing within our perception as we attempt to find a place for ourselves in the film.

The abbreviated history lesson is followed by that core of language learning throughout French culture — a *dictée*.

But the *dictée* also provides material for translation. The text is from Shakespeare's *Romeo and Juliet*, which the frenzied teacher dictates in French, to be translated back into the original English. If that in itself is insufficiently uncanny, Godard unfolds the text backward!

Beginning with Juliet's discovery of the self-poisoned Romeo, the dictation cuts back to Romeo's early declaration of the inescapable powers of love:

> *A thousand times the worse to want thy light*
> *Love goes towards Love as school-boyes from their books*
> *But Love from Love, towards schoole with heavie lookes.*

MEANWHILE, GLANCES are exchanged between Franz and Odile and Odile and Arthur, as each man through his gaze vies for her favour. Arthur also passes her a note, adding to the intertextual extensions of this film.

> *tou bi or*
> *not tou bi*
> *contre votre poitrine,*
> *it is ze question*

The *dictée* continues with four lines cunningly plucked from the sonnet that serves as Prologue to the play.

> *In fair Verona where we lay our Scene ...*
> *A paire of starre-crossed lovers, take their life ...*
> *The fearfull passage of their death-markt love ...*
> *Is now the two houres trafficque of our Stage.*

Next it passes through Mercutio's disquisition on dreams and Romeo's premonition of "untimely death," although the two bits are assigned respectively to Romeo and Juliet. It then concludes with Juliet's prophetic lament: "O Fortune, Fortune, all men call thee fickle." The scene wraps up with the teacher offering the students three seconds to hand in their translations and with a student asking her how to say in English "a big, one-million-dollar film."

ABOUT THE same time as *Bande à part* was made, during a press conference at Cannes, Godard got into an argument with Henri-Georges Clouzot, the distinguished director of conventional thrillers like *La Salaire de la peur* (*Wages of Fear*) (1953) and *Les Diaboliques* (1955). "Surely, Monsieur Godard," Clouzot concluded in exasperation, "even you believe a film must have a beginning, a middle, and an end." "Of course," replied Godard, "but not always in that order." This much-rehearsed anecdote is generally taken as a joke; but as I have perhaps implied, Godard's inversion of linear narrative is not performed merely for comic effect.

In the example from *Bande à part*, while the entire situation is risible in the extreme, the inversion of *Romeo and Juliet* compounds the predestination of the story, invalidating all sense of cause and effect. In parallel ways, Hardy's greatest love poems — "The Voice," "After a Journey," "A Wet August" (among others) — are all about a love not imaginatively grasped until it was too late, until the woman was gone or dead.

Furthermore, for all Eliot's determination to bring modernism to English verse in the 1920s and, along with Ezra Pound, to "make it new," whatever was really new had already been done, leaving the two Americans dependent upon a poetry of allusion, ransacking the past for their strategies and metaphors, adding to tradition but by that very gesture, automatically becoming part of it. Godard has always claimed that he has invented nothing, that he has just picked up things that have been lying around. This confession is again an indication of humility. Godard's distinction resides in the fact that he has picked up from such a wide variety of artifacts and has rearranged them dynamically so as to change their perspective.

Reviewing *Forty Guns* (1957), a little-known Sam Fuller movie, for *Cahiers du cinéma*, Godard singles out a favourite moment. Gene Barry is courting the "ravishing" Eve Brent, making her debut in this film. "Eve sells guns," writes Godard. (Actually, she manufactures them.)

> Jokingly, Gene aims at her. The camera takes his place and we see Eve through the barrel of the gun. Track forward
>
> until she is framed in a close-up by the mouth of the barrel. Next shot: they are in a kiss.

Similarly, during the prolonged bedroom scene in the middle of *À bout de souffle*, Patricia rolls up a poster and we see Michel in a close-up through the improvised cylinder. Next shot: they are in a kiss.

In *Bande à part*, when Arthur, Franz, and Odile dance their Madison number in a Parisian café, the style of its capture in a continuous take arguably derives from the title number of Busby Berkeley's MGM musical *For Me and My Gal* (1942), while the actual choreography suggests the staccato gestures characteristic of Bob Fosse's "Steam Heat" number in *The Pajama Game* (1957).

In this way, Godard's art is an art of collage — indeed, of cubist collage. Disparate fragments are seized from here and there, from high and low culture, from Rimbaud and Hollywood, and forged together into new cinematic gestures, implying several points of view.

As in cubist painting, the tone remains unstable. Are these works comic or tragic? Does the poetry elevate the images or do the images debase the poetry? Are all the intertextual references merely playful, perhaps even mocking; or are they an essential part of the film's meaning, of its yearning toward both signification and significance? Even when we cannot seize the allusions, we know they are there. They reveal their presence in the disparity of tone, through (for example) the elevated commentary that throughout *Bande à part* accompanies the deadpan antics of the characters.

In this apparently simple, virtually throwaway film, Godard inflects every element of his craft. Even the opening titles fuse character and function. In compressed blocks we read:

JEANLUC
CINEMA
GODARD

Finally, if the film draws upon sources as diverse as Rimbaud and the Hollywood musical, in tone at least it has itself become the template for the early films of Wim Wenders and Jim Jarmusch and leads directly to the work of the Finnish cinematic dadaist Aki Kaurismäki, supremely to the direct *hommage* to *Bande à part* detectable in Kaurismäki's *Ariel* (1989). That which is most modern is automatically most classical. That which is most innovative inevitably becomes part of an evolving tradition.

GODARD'S WORK divides easily (although not exclusively) into four periods. First we have the Romantic period, from 1955 to 1968. Next there is the Political period, the time of the Dziga Vertov group in which Godard worked with Jean-Pierre Gorin (1968–1972). Overlapping this and still ongoing (the major source of Godard's income) is his Television period, which was already under way when he made *Numéro Deux* in 1975. This is also the time that he began his long collaboration with Anne-Marie Miéville which, in varying degrees, continues today. Finally (or most recently?) is his Reflective period, characterized by a return to his native Switzerland, to what is visually a more conventional cinematic aesthetic, and to a more settled concern with character and story (1979 to the present day).

Godard's cinema has always displayed an uncertain sense of story, a refusal to wrap his images around a coherently sequential plot. From *Une Femme Mariée*, which Godard described as "Fragments of a Film shot in 1964," to *Passion* (1981) in which the Italian producer keeps running through the film crying out in despair, "*Una storia! Una storia!*", Godard has always had an uneasy relationship with narrative.

Passion is interesting in terms of this uneasiness. It is about a filmmaker trying to make an impossible film, a film that consists of the photographic re-creation of classical paintings—apparently a static project. Yet the allusions in this film form before our eyes—Rembrandt's "The Night Watch," Goya's "The Third of May," Ingres's "The Turkish Baths," and Delacroix's "The Entrance of the Crusaders into Constantinople"—all of which are narrative paintings! Back in the 1950s for Alexandre Astruc, the fundamental problem of cinema was "how to express thought." Godard solves this problem by refusing the simplifications of a confident narrative march from a beginning, through the middle, to an end.

The question most often posed by a Godard film is not the standard one, "Why are the characters behaving in this way?" but rather the more demanding "Why is Godard doing this?" Unlike conventional film narratives (from which by mute agreement the author is absent), Godard's work is informed by a sense of his own presence. Sometimes it is his voice—*À bout de souffle*, *Vivre sa vie* (*My Life to Live*) (1962), *Bande à part*, *Deux ou trois choses que je sais d'elle* (*Two or Three Things I Know About Her*) (1966); sometimes his appearance—*Le Mépris* (*Contempt*) (1963), *Pravda* (1969), *Prénom Carmen* (*First Name Carmen*) (1982), *King Lear* (1987). But always there is the felt presence of his artistry: shaping, selecting, punning, citing, inverting, interrogating—determined to achieve a cinema not just of pleasure but of thought.

Thought is provoked less through subject matter (the traditional way for "serious" films) than by strategies of construction. His puns and citations compound this process. They "square" the signifier. When we hear the voice of Aragon in a Budd Boetticher Western within a gangster film by Godard, we are invited (if we are able) to imagine connections between Aragon, Godard, Boetticher, Westerns, gangster movies, and the characters in the film. Similarly, Godard's references to

Shakespeare are both ironic and transformational.

Détective (1984) is a film that no one admires, apparently not even Godard. I think it is a masterpiece. As I have written about it elsewhere, I shall here only mention that one of the characters is called Uncle William-Prospero, another is Ariel, and the film is indeed about regeneration after punishment against all odds. It also ends with a flurry of magical tricks that, with a hop, skip, and a jump, brings to this remarkable film something like a happy resolution. If at the end of *The Tempest*, Shakespeare is willing to renounce his magical wand, by the end of *Détective*, Godard is still very much in possession of his.

GODARD'S MOST extended reference to Shakespeare occurs in *King Lear* (1987). This too is a film that no one takes seriously—not Godard, not Menahem Golan (the producer for Cannon Films who signed the contract with Godard on a paper serviette on the terrace of the Hôtel d'Angleterre during the Cannes film festival in 1986), not the audiences—who haven't been allowed to see it. But it now exists on video with all the glory of its stereophonic sound. It is, as I shall argue, a wonderful film. It is also eccentric—a film "shot in the back" as an opening title informs us. While we listen to Golan on the phone arguing with Godard about getting the film ready for Cannes in 1987, we hear Godard reluctantly concede, "and anyway, this picture—what the hell!"

Evidently, Godard's *Lear* was to have starred Norman Mailer with his daughter Kate as Cordelia; and originally Mailer was to have written the script, transforming *Lear* into a Mafia tale. The egos, however, were too conflicting. As we watch Mailer and Kate go through their first scene together, we hear Godard explaining in a distorted voice, as if talking like a gangster: "It was not Lear with three daughters. It was Kate with three fathers: Mailer as a star, Mailer as a father, and me as a director. It was too much indeed for this young lady from Provincetown."

When we see the scene again, Godard's voice continues: "After the fifth take of the first shot, the great writer left the set. He took off for America, as he said—he and his daughter first class, his daughter's boyfriend, economy."

Godard enjoys working into his films the difficulty of making films. In *Prénom Carmen*, he presents himself as a "washed up" filmmaker seeking refuge in an asylum. After a discussion of the need for stars and story in *Tout va bien* (1972), for about five minutes—it feels like five minutes!—we watch a whole series of cheques being signed, the money needed to pay for cast and crew. In *Lear*, the producer's voice and Mailer's "star" behaviour play a similar role. But after this prologue—itself somewhat Shakespearean—Godard's *King Lear* begins.

SHAKESPEARE'S *Lear* evokes a time of upheaval and change in which nature herself has become unnatural. It is a time of solar eclipses, when storms rage and blood ties betray, when "Madmen leade the Blinde."

Godard's *Lear* takes place after Chernobyl, after much of life and culture have been destroyed. Emerging from the tall grasses of Nyon in Switzerland comes William Shakespeare Jr. the Fifth, played by the theatrical wizard Peter Sellars. WSJ.5 has been hired by the Cannon Cultural Group to reconstruct the works of his famous ancestor and has come to Nyon to consult Professor Pluggy, a mischievous creature (like the Fool in Shakespeare's *Lear*) played in this film by Godard himself, bedecked with Rasta locks of RCA television cables that don't connect to anything but which exist (as my friend Erin Manning has suggested) as "wires of possibility."

If Shakespeare's *Lear* is about legitimacy and continuity within his kingdom, so is Godard's within the realm of cinema. During the opening moments, photographs of great directors like Bresson, Pasolini, and Lang flash on the screen. We hear WSJ.5 saying: "Robert, yes; Pier Paolo, yes; Fritz, yes." At the same time, as a stand-in for Godard, WSJ.5 is troubled by his assignment: "Why did they pick me? Twenty years later I still wonder. Why not some other gentleman from Moscow or Beverly Hills? Why don't they just order some goblin to shoot this twisted fairy-tale?"

In his task of reconstruction, WSJ.5 decides to concentrate on the story of the old man and his daughter, now played with fine intensity by Burgess Meredith and Molly Ringwald. Godard's use of Shakespeare's text is disjunctively selective. Yet the essence is there—the concern with continuity, something that Don Learo feels Cordelia's silence denies him.

While dealing with (at times quite movingly) the tensions that occur between Learo and Cordelia, Godard transforms her denial into declaration, into an affirmation of her physical self. She is the "virtue" of silence, determined to resist Learo's "power" over language, his addiction to words. Godard's *Lear* thus becomes an exploration of the inadequacy of language, especially in the realm of morality and aesthetics, in its inability adequately to apprehend the beauty of the world.

A central moment in this film has less to do with Shakespeare than with Godard, although the impulse toward synaesthesia derives from the play. In Shakespeare's *King Lear*, after Gloucester has been blinded, he claims that he sees things "feelingly," to which Lear replies:

What, art mad? A man may see how this world goes,
    with no eyes.
Looke with thine eares…

So too, in Godard's *King Lear*, WSJ.5 explains:

for Learo, to hear is to see. A man may see how the world goes with no eyes. Look with thine ears…. This is what he tries to do…. In listening to his daughters, he hopes to see their entire bodies stretched out across their voices.

Meanwhile, we see Cordelia, dressed in white, leading a white horse through wintry woods toward the lake, radiant in the physical presence of her silence. wsj.5 concludes:

> So that he can silence this silence, he listens as if he's watching television. But Cordelia, what she shows in not speaking is not nothing but her very presence, her exactitude.

Springing from these dilemmas, the film becomes an extolment of images over words. More than any other film, it explains the abrupt change in his aesthetic, the radiant visual beauty of the late films.

WHILE GODARD'S early work had it own kind of beauty, it was often a poster beauty, sometimes a pop-art beauty. Primary colours prevailed with very little shading. The more political his films became, the more Godard mistrusted the sensual power of images. During his Dziga Vertov period, he sometimes even crossed them out on the screen. Images were the carrier of bourgeois ideology. The project in the early 1970s was to replace false images with true words, with language that could contest the seductive power of sight.

Perhaps through working in television, perhaps through his contact with Anne-Marie Miéville, perhaps following in the footsteps of Pasolini with his privileged notion of "im-sign," certainly through the failure of the politics of that period, by the time Godard returned to Switzerland and made his comeback film, *Sauve qui peut (La vie)* (*Every Man for Himself*) (1979), he had espoused the image in all the subtlety of its three-dimensional depth and the potential chiaroscuro of its modelling. During an extended moment in *King Lear*, Godard explains why.

Pluggy, wsj.5, and others are in some sort of screening room. There is a battery of control panels on the left and two television monitors on the right, one on top of the other. Now sporting dark glasses and a red toque, Godard is designing his own projection box, first with a light bulb, then with sparklers. "Tell me, Professor," says wsj.5 as he enters the room. "Show, not tell," returns Godard, who then begins an extended disquisition on what we might call the transcendent quality of images, on their ability to manifest the world.

Throughout this long dissertation, accompanied by changing images on those two television screens, Godard is suggesting that while words divide, images unify.

> The image is the pure creation of the soul. It cannot be born of a comparison but of a reconciration of two realities that are more or less apart.... The more the connection between the two realities, the stronger the image will be, the more it will have emotive power.

Meanwhile, on the other stereo track, we hear gulls loudly calling, virtually drowning out the words which Godard is perhaps shy at sharing with us in such an offbeat film—a film shot in the back! In any case, it is the reality of images that Godard is discussing plus the superiority of reality itself. "Nature's above Art, in that respect," says Godard, echoing Lear, as gulls cry out concordance. If Godard once displayed a mistrust of images, he is now concerned with the divisive falsity of words.

This concern also explains his addiction to citation. When words are drawn from other texts, they are already part of culture, which is almost part of nature—certainly of human nature. If their origins are elsewhere, they have stood the test of time. They must embody truth—the truth of human nature, within culture; like the truth of cinema, twenty-four times a second.

The pain shared by Don Learo and Cordelia is snitched from bits of Shakespeare taken from all over the play. Learo fears that, in his distress, "I am not in my perfect mind." He then returns to a refrain that occurs several times in the film: "Go too, they are not men o' their words; they told me I was everything [They are not men o' their words.]" To give Cordelia more presence than, through her silence, she can have in this film, Godard twice grants her a few lines from

Sonnet 47, allowing her voice to confirm the value of sight:

> Betwixt mine eyes and heart a league is tooke,
> And each doth good turnes now unto the other,
> When that mine eye is famisht for a looke,
> Or heart in love with sighes himself doth smother;
> With my loves picture then my eye doth feast.
> And to the painted banquet bids my heart ...

As we hear these words, we see an image of Vermeer's "Girl with Turban," her eyes looking out at us; and then, over a photo of Orson Welles, Learo continues:

> Come not betweene the dragon and its wrath,
> I lov'd her most, and thought to set my rest
> On her kind nursery. Hence and avoid my sight:
> So be the grave my peace ...

To emphasize Cordelia's martyrdom, Godard bestows upon her some lines from St. Joan, citing the text of her trial from the film by Robert Bresson. Indeed, after receiving two telexes from Gloria and Regina with all their obsequious flattery, as in the play, Cordelia must die — in the film, sacrificed by her father.

She is led in her white robe from her white horse and laid out upon a rock looking over the lake, her body indeed stretched out across the silence of her voice.

> ... she's gone forever.
> I know when one's dead, and when one lives.
> She's dead as earth: Lend me a Looking-glasse,
> If that her breath will mist or staine the stone,
> Why then she lives.

KING LEAR is difficult to write about. It is the first of Godard's truly contrapuntal works, utilizing stereo channels to obtain different sonic effects that both complement and contest one another. As Learo and his daughter sit at the dinner table in the Hôtel Beau Rivage in Nyon, Learo reminiscing about his gangster days with Bugsy Siegel and Meyer Lansky, preparing his memoirs, bits of Shakespeare often appear as whispers on the other track, declaring the predetermined fate of the characters, suggesting the grieving life within.

Again and again, however, Godard returns to the opening moments of Shakespeare's play, to Cordelia's refusal — which is at the same time her affirmation. As WSJ.5 explains: "It's not that she hasn't said anything. She has said nothing. No thing." Indeed, the words "No thing" keep appearing as an intertitle throughout this twisted fairy-tale, reminding us (in an intricately French way) of the presence of absence.

For all its silliness — and on the surface, it is a silly film — like other Godard films it addresses the pain of loss and the desire for renewal — possibly for forgiveness. But the loss endures, allowing Godard (uncharacteristically) Edgar's terminating rhymes that end the most despairing of Shakespeare's great plays:

> The waight of this sad time we must obey,
> Speake what we feele, not what we ought to say:
> The oldest hath borne most, we that are yong,
> Shall never see so much, nor live so long.

EXCEPT THIS is not the end of Godard's film. Since *King Lear* begins with a prologue involving Norman Mailer, it ends with an epilogue involving Woody Allen. As Mr. Alien, Allen slouches by his Steenbeck, wearing a black Picasso T-shirt — like all Godard's troubled males, weighed down by the burdensome responsibilities of modernity. Just before he died, Professor Pluggy had suggested that Mr. Alien might be able to help WSJ.5 to finish his film.

Mr. Alien is editing, stitching the film together, first with a safety pin, then with a needle and thread — a playful absurdity that nevertheless emphasizes the tactility of film, a tactility absent from video. Since the film must come to an end, this film about No Thing, Godard plays it off with Mr. Alien's face in profile, reciting Shakespeare's sonnet of imminent termination, Sonnet 60. WSJ.5's voice echoes after him, as if learning the lines. The final couplet is withheld. There are no closing titles, just the sound of gulls, cut off in mid-screech. The film is over.

TRAGICALLY FUNNY, hilariously sad, the films of Jean-Luc Godard gain their power from his unflagging attempts to make sense of the absurdities of the world. In their combination of the throwaway and the considered, they depict both the playfulness of life and its painful seriousness — the ludic and the agonistic. "What I want," he once said back in the 1960s, "is to capture the definitive by chance." I think he has.

In the early days championed as a political radical, Godard has been recently all but abandoned. Yet his late work is astonishing. Ravishing both to eyes and ears, it elevates our senses while confounding our comprehension. As allusive as ever, the citations have become ever more esoteric, at least for North Americans — certainly for me.

In 1990, drawing upon the services of Alain Delon and Elena Torlato-Favrini, Godard produced *La Nouvelle Vague*, the very title of which alludes to the film movement in the 1960s in which he played such a vital part. Suffocatingly beautiful, it contains a philosophical gardener as choric commentator whose discourse derives from sources as familiar as William Faulkner and as arcane as Jacques Chardonne. Containing bits from Baudelaire (in French) and from Dante (in Italian), the film passes through contempt toward forgiveness, through money toward love, and through death to resurrection. Punctuated by intertitles that are often in Latin, it begins with the announcement, "Incipit Lamentatio" and concludes with the finality of "Consumatum Est." It is (so far) the master work of his Reflective period.

With each new film, Godard reinvents himself, drawing upon the scraps of culture that circulate in his head, determining his existence but enabling him as an artist to achieve ever-fresh configurations of aesthetic synthesis. If the world of Jean-Luc Godard enacts a determined universe, it is determined not just by ideological preconceptions (as the political left was wont to claim) but by all the achievements of past poetry and cinema, in both French and English. Whatever the value of this adduction of texts, they are splayed out before us, like Cordelia's body across her voice, vibrant within their transformational contexts for all to see.

"Not to know but to see," as Professor Pluggy/Godard keeps saying in *King Lear*. To see is to experience. To see is to be amazed — to be touched by wonder. To see, finally, is to understand (without preconception) the cinema of Jean-Luc Godard.

DON'T GO OUT OVER YOUR HEAD

JIM HARRISON

OF LATE I've determined that I am largely unfit for human consumption. We can think of ourselves accurately as five billion tiny fish swirling in a big green pond and I've only had passing contact with one in fifty thousand which seems more than enough. This idea came to mind recently when I finished the last stop on the last book tour of my life which came by happenstance in a foreign country, Canada, a somewhat alien and mysterious country to Americans. The pork sausage at the Park Hyatt in Toronto was the best in my long experience and I felt inclined to stay there indefinitely. Doctors recently have come to highly recommend the diet of pork sausage, room-temperature Swedish vodka, and the stray pack of airline peanuts found in one's briefcase. If you crave greens you merely eat the leaves off the fresh flowers in your room. If they make you ill, stop eating them.

Toronto seemed like a good place to end a public literary career, partly because I felt at home in the many wooded ravines and kept a sharp single eye out for places I might pitch a tent and lay out my sleeping bag. In the United States these marvellous ravines would likely have been bulldozed long ago for no particular reason. One reason to live in a ravine is so you don't have to go to the airport to fly home. Airports and office machinery lead the list of our current humiliation. Another reason to stay in Toronto is that the people are antiquely polite. I could see I wouldn't be turned away at men's clothing stores for being poorly dressed as I have been in New York City.

I've spent most of my life out in the water over my head and I want to come to shore if, indeed, there is a shore. Right after World War II, my father, grandfather, and uncles built us a cabin on a remote lake for nine hundred bucks' worth of materials. The lake was about fifteen miles from our home in the county seat where my father worked as the government agriculturist advising farmers. My uncles who had recently returned from the war were in poor shape in mind and body and so was I from a rather violent encounter with a little girl that took the sight from my left eye. My response, wonderfully close at hand, was to spend all of my time swimming and fishing and wandering in the woods. Every morning at breakfast my iron mother (of Swedish derivation) would say, "Don't go out over your head."

Consequently I've spent a lifetime doing so. There is a beauty in threat. A rattlesnake is an undeniably beautiful creature as is a pissed-off mountain lion, or a grizzly bear hauling off an elk carcass. The boy loves the icy thrill of taking a dare and running through a graveyard at night. Why not drop ten hits of lysergic acid and go tarpon fishing? Why not hitchhike to California with twenty bucks in your pocket? We can be perplexed and wanton creatures with all of the design of the Brownian movement. When I begin a novel I always have the image of jumping off the bank into a river at night. There is no published map for the river and I have no idea where it goes.

Of course deciding to avoid the public doesn't mean I'm going to stop writing my poems and novels, which are my calling. I've looked into the matter and it will be easy to Cryovac my work like those vain bodies suspended in liquid nitrogen and encased in aluminum tubes. They could have been stored in Saddam Hussein's underground palace, but it turned out that our intelligence was in error and he didn't have an underground palace.

Meanwhile, as I try to make my way to shore I have a number of significant projects and questions in mind, especially whether or not dogs have souls. Rather than stray off into the filigree of mammalian metaphysics my research into this question, already considerable, is dwelling on diet, with many clues coming from the coordinates in diet between humans, who presumably have souls, and dogs, who don't—or so it was established by the Catholic Church in the ninth century when it declared that animals don't have souls because they couldn't monetarily contribute to the church.

To start at the beginning we have to posit that reality is an aggregate of the perceptions of all creatures. This broadens the playing field. I was never a member of the French Enlightenment and most of my sodden but extensive education didn't stick. All I recall from my Ph.D. in physics at Oxford is that the peas were overcooked, the sherry invariably cheapish, and that in the sixties in England there were thousands of noisy bands with members wearing Prince Valiant hairdos. I survived on chutney and pork fat and the sight of all the miniskirts that rarely descended beneath the hip bones. No, all of my true education has come from the study of six thousand years of imaginative literature. As Andrei Codrescu said, "The only source of reliable information is poetry." In addition I am widely travelled and have lived my life in fairly remote and vaguely wild locations where the natural world teaches its brutally frank lessons and where the collective media has no more power than a meadow mouse fart on a windy night. Prolonged exposure to nature gives one a sort of *grammatica pardo*, a wisdom of the soil.

Just the other day a woman, a rather lumpish friend, said to me over a lunch of squid fritters, "My life is so foreign, I wish it were subtitled like a foreign movie. Just this morning I noted that unlike me songbirds never seem overweight."

"O love muffin," I said, "life properly perceived is alien, foreign, utterly strange. If life seems familiar you're afflicted with lazy brain. Birds don't plump up because they have no sphincter muscle. They let go fecally on impulse. This would work out poorly in human concourse though it would seem appropriate in politics."

A literary scientist must take note of disparate elements. In the very same newspaper the other day I noticed two important items. The world's oldest man, a 113-year-old from Japan, said, "I don't want to die." (He's evidently waiting for an alternative experience.) In the second article a young woman who is an ultra marathoner wasn't feeling well and did thirteen "stop-and-squats" in a hundred-mile race that she won. It seemed a tad narcissistic to count, but more important she appeared to possess a genetic glitch that made her part bird.

Dogs have great powers of discrimination. They are said to have less than a quarter of the number of our taste buds, but this is more than compensated for by their vast scenting powers. Rover can be snoozing way out in the yard, but if you begin to sauté garlic he's suddenly clawing at the door. The intense happiness you see in French dogs is doubtless due to superior leftovers. I noted that in over two decades at my cabin, my bird dogs were francophile. They loved Basque chicken, the heavy beef stews called *daubes, cuisse de canard* which is a wonderful duck preparation from southwest France, and Bocuse's *Bécasse en salmi*, a rather elaborate woodcock recipe. It should be said that during hunting season it is hard to maintain the weight and strength of an English setter or a pointer. If you're walking five miles a setter or pointer might cover thirty-five if it's high-spirited. Compared to Labradors, setters can be finicky eaters. One of mine named Rose learned to refuse Kraft Parmesan in favour of Parmigiano Reggiano.

Labs, however, show their love of nature by eating it. My Scottish lab, Zilpha, loves to eat the gophers caught by her housemate, an English cocker named Mary. I've tried without success to rescue cheeping gophers from Zilpha's capacious mouth. She loves green apples though they make her intestinally restless. This omnivorous capacity can be a problem as a recent x-ray showed that she was failing to digest some deer hooves. She is an obedient bird dog and we had a grand dove season along the Mexican border, though she pretended she couldn't find the last bird of the year and on opening her jaws I found the feather evidence. Zilpha, however, is not in the league of a previous Sandringham Lab who once made it in a hipcast to the top of the counter and ate a bunch of bananas, a pound of butter, and a dozen eggs (in the shell).

We had a bitch Airedale named Jessie whose favourite snack was snakes, which she would catch and shake into manageable pieces, while another Airedale, Kate, never got beyond voles, popcorn, and pizza crusts in her preferences. A squeamish French Brittany who fishes with us likes Spanish Zamora or eight-year-old Wisconsin cheddar but will not touch fine salami because it is an Italian product. His name is suitably Jacques and he refuses chicken and pork but is frantic for beef in a hot Korean marinade.

But do dogs have souls? Of course they do for reasons I have delayed. Many scientists like myself have wondered at the sheer number of androids that have infiltrated our population. The obvious test is the absence of the belly button but a primary diet of fast food is also a good indicator. You can also add as evidence the reading of fast food–type books — ninety-nine percent of all published books here in the United States — and the predominance of television in their lives. The average bitch mutt is an absolute Emily Dickinson of the soul-life compared to the large android portion of our population.

In this slow swim toward shore I have been considerably impeded by my defect of Lab-like eating the world. I don't mean just the food but every aspect of life on Earth. My esteemed mind doctor of thirty-five years has been helping me banish this nasty habit. As a literary scientist I must remember that our work disappears quickly like a child's money at the county fair. A certain austerity is required if I'm ever to touch the bottom. Never again will I eat a fifteenth-century recipe, a stew of fifty baby pig noses a dear friend in Burgundy prepared for me. It did look peculiar with all of those tiny nostril holes pointing toward the heavens beyond the kitchen ceiling. His Alsatian dog, Eliot, had scented these noses when still in the refrigerator and was frantic for his portion.

In order to sense the rather obvious souls of dogs we must first admit that much of life is inconsequential, a matter of frying eggs over and over, moment by moment, or daily playing "The Flight of the Bumblebee" on an accordion at an amateur show. This is because we're seeing life from our own point of view. In order to clearly see a dog's soul you must give up the hopeless baggage that is your personality. Dogs and other creatures are made nervous by our errant personalities that herky-jerkily infest the atmosphere. Forget your ninny self-profile and become accepting as your dog. You must totally absorb the dimension of stillness to fully meet the otherness of this creature, at which point you'll have at first what you think is a metaphysical experience, and later realize is a birthright because you are nature too. Not surprisingly this attitude or state of being is also of great advantage in writing poems, novels, or cooking. Why get in the way of the actual ingredients? I'm not saying this is easy. It took me fifteen years to get a flock of chihuahuan ravens to take a walk with me down on the Mexican border. Until last April I was properly on probation.

Once within the lucidity of extreme grief I was lucky enough to see the soul of a dog. She was in extreme pain and we rushed her to the vet in the middle of the night. I was holding her big body in my arms as if she were Juliet or Isolde and after the fatal injection I saw her soul shimmer out of her body. Frankly, the vision was a little banal like a science fiction movie but life is like that.

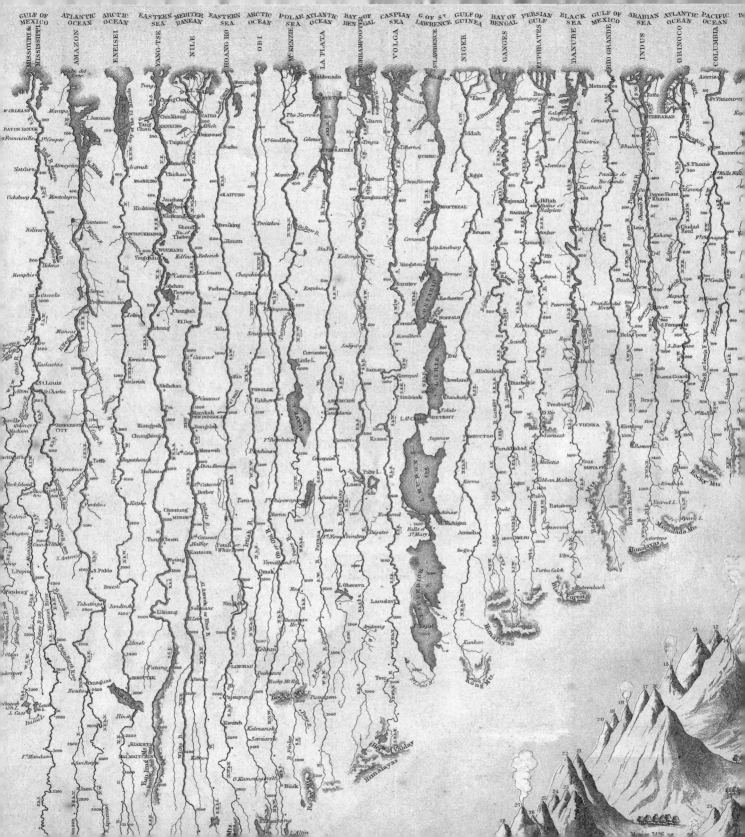

ANTARCTIC VOYAGE

HELEN GARner

THEY SAY that tourist ships to Antarctica, even more than ordinary human conveyances, are loaded down with aching hearts. Deceived wives and widowers, men who've never loved and don't know why, Russian crew forced to leave their children behind for years at a time, grown women who've just buried a beloved parent, people with cancer travelling to the cold before they die. They say people come here looking for "solace." And then there are the married couples: how calm the old ones, how eager the new!—but isn't a couple the greatest mystery of all?

THE HATS. Oh, they're terrible. One woman broaches the deck pulling on a thing shaped like a sponge bag, made of purple polypropylene. A little old lady is wearing a grey wool bonnet straight out of a Breughel painting. A young bloke in spectacles sports a cap of multicoloured segments, topped with a twirl and several small silver bells.

My own headgear, a hideous borrowed job featuring red earmuffs and a peak, is still stuffed into a corner of my suitcase, down in cabin no. 521 which I'm to share with a perfect stranger called Robyn (and I've forgotten my earplugs).

So far, an hour after we've embarked from Ushuaia, an Argentine port in Tierra del Fuego, I am still stubbornly refusing to believe in the cold, though my fingers have shrunk so thin that my wedding ring keeps sliding off, and my eyes and nose are streaming. *If you fall overboard*, states the Lonely Planet Guide grimly, *you will die*. I'm not the Antarctic type. I'm hanging out for a short black. I'm not adventurous, and I'm too sad to be sociable with strangers.

Stop whinging. As the late summer Saturday afternoon draws on, we chug down the Beagle Channel, a body of calm water that splits the bent nib of South America into Chile and Argentina. The channel lies along a row of high, impossibly sparkling-topped mountains, each with its diaphanous scarf of cloud. Our ship is the *Professor Molchanov* out of Murmansk in the former Soviet Union, where, they say, scores of ships lie at anchor, unused, unwanted, rusting—the detritus of empire. Our crew is Russian; our captain, though only thirty-eight, is an ice-master. "I look young," he says, "but I am old inside." He is also, various women agree later in the bar, "a dish."

"Haven't you taken a seasick pill yet, Helen?" asks Terry, a vet from Brisbane. "Take one. Take one *now*." I obey. By 8 P.M. I am nodding off at the dinner table among my fellow adventurers, most of them shy, many of them older than I am. In the early hours of Sunday morning we turn out of the Channel and into the Drake Passage—where, while everyone but the crew is sound asleep, we hit a force-seven gale which will rage unabated for two days and nights.

The pills knock out nausea, but the simplest tasks—going to the lavatory, getting dressed—become Herculean. Robyn and I lurch past each other in the cramped space of our cabin, flung against walls and cannoning off cupboard fronts. Somehow a lifeboat drill is achieved, after which we hibernate. Our porthole is bisected by a madly tilting grey line. I am in love with my bunk, so narrow and perfect, like the single bed of childhood.

Sometimes Ann, the Aurora doctor, materializes: next to my drugged head, holding out a bottle of lemon-flavoured water, a handful of dry biscuits. Morning and evening a quiet voice comes over the tannoy into the cabin. Greg Mortimer, experienced mountaineer and leader of our "voyage" (no one calls it a "tour" or a "trip" and since the storm began I have stopped seeing this as pretentious), has a knack of saying only what's required, without embellishment. To city people disturbed by the screaming wind, his voice is comforting. "Sleep well," he says at night, like a competent, benevolent father.

By Monday evening the huge waves smooth out. People creep from their burrows. Some have, incredibly, been unperturbed, attending learned disquisitions in the bar on the habits of penguins. Other voyagers confess to having spewed in public—a great leveller. Thea, the woman in the Breughel bonnet, shows off a carpet burn the size of a dollar coin on her forehead. Everyone is friendlier since the storm: now we are shipmates. Around 9 P.M. we gather on the bridge to keep vigil for our first iceberg. This far south, in February, it doesn't get dark till after eleven. The bridge is a serious place, of work and watching. The Russian officers are big blokes smelling of cigarettes, with moustaches and silver teeth, and voices that rumble up from deep in their torsos. They murmur to each other, slip out onto the deck for a smoke, stand at the wheel or bend over charts spread on drawing boards. We are shy of them and keep stepping out of their way.

Out on deck the air is gaspingly cold but the evening sky is pretty, the water a steely, inky grey-blue. Suddenly there's a moon riding tranquil between layers of bright cloud. Leaning over the rail I see my first tiny chunk of ice bobbing past, very close to the ship's side. At once I'm seized by an urge to compare it with something, with anything: it's the size of a loosely flexed hand, palm up; like a Disney coronet with knobbed points; as hollow as a rotten tooth. For some reason I am irritated by this urge, and make an effort to control it.

Inside the bridge is warm and dim. Thirty people stand about talking, but intent on the greying line that divides sea from sky. *There it is—there's one. And another.* The first iceberg is only a pale blip on the horizon. The second is greyer, straighter-sided, more "like a building." Night thickens as we approach them. Iceberg number one is unearthly, mother-of-pearl, glowing as if with its own inner light source. People grow quiet, their social chatter stills. The only sounds are the buzz and hum of the radar, the dull rumble of the engine, and out on deck the rushing of the wake.

Then somebody begins to liken the iceberg to a face. "It's got a sad eye. See its nose?" On and on people go: it's like a sphinx, a Peke's face, an Indian head with its mouth open. Again I am secretly enraged by this, and by my own urgent desire to do the same. I stare at the iceberg as it looms two hundred metres away on our port side. It gleams with a pearly purity. It's faceted: creamy on the left, whiter on the right. It looks stable, like an island rather than something floating. Water riffles around its foot. I strain and fail to see it only in abstract terms. I don't *want* to keep going "like, like, like." But I can't stop myself.

ON TUESDAY morning we slip out of the Bransfield Strait into the misty mouth of the Antarctic Sound. While dressing I glance on the porthole and see a tremendous iceberg—big as two houses—shaped like a chunk of frozen cloud sliced off by a downward stroke of a spatula. The tilt of its top is the cleanest, most perfect line I've ever seen. Rush up on deck, rugging up as I run. The water is as flat and as lumpy with ice scraps as the surface of a gin and tonic.

In the fog the monster bergs are everywhere. *Molchanov* cruises among them, gently. Each one is fissured, flawed with a wandering seam of unnatural cellophane blue-green, almost Day-Glo: older ice, someone explains, more densely compressed. A lump of ice needs to be only the size of, say, a small washing machine for this faery green to be present in it, like a flaw in an opal.

"Unrool, idn't it," murmurs big Dave the diver, a Queenslander with huge square teeth.

It's hopeless, trying to control the flood of metaphor. People cry out in wonder. Look—a temple, with pillars. The white-ridged sole of a Reebok. There's one with a carved spine. Hey—an aircraft carrier! A flooded cathedral. Somebody's been at that one with a melon-baller. Suddenly, we glide into an area of small ice chunks, like the aftermath of an explosion—pieces no bigger than a folded sheet, a dish-rack, a car engine.

Exhausted with the ecstasy of it, you turn your eyes away for a moment to rest—and the sun breaks through the cloud cover to reveal a whole further field of icebergs—great flaring blocks of perfect, piercing silver.

The fog lifts further. There it is—the Antarctica Peninsula, continent of dark rocks, of ridged and bony snow. They want us to climb into an inflatable, flat-bottomed Zodiac and set *foot* on it? My stomach rolls with excitement and fear.

I wish I didn't have to write about this. I wish I could find a silent spot and hide in it to gaze and gaze; or crawl back into my bunk and sleep off the wonder. Instead I go to breakfast. There's bacon. You can smell it all over the ship.

OUR FIRST trip ashore, to Brown Bluff, is apparently to be about penguins. Urk. I've got feather-phobia: birds revolt me. We are told that our behaviour on land must leave no trace: no "toiletting"; no food or drink; and we are strictly forbidden to take anything away, not even a shell, a stone, a tiny bone. Tubs of water will be provided on *Molchanov*'s deck for our return; we must scrub every scrap of penguin shit off our boots, or else the air inside the ship will become unbearable.

The Zodiacs rise and fall at the bottom of the gangway, down which we blunder in single file, puffy in our grotesque wet weather gear of Gore-Tex, rubber, Velcro, and large coarse zips.

As we bounce across a kilometre of water toward a line of brown and white cliffs, the penguin stench hits us: shit and feathers, with an overlay of fish.

On the stony beach, people fan out with their camera equipment and become solitary. Each photographer attempts to establish an intense relationship with an individual penguin. One tiptoes past these strivings, feeling like an intruder.

I note with relief that some penguins are not waddling about on their flabby feet, or standing in forward-slanted throngs on points of land, but are lying, singly or in twos, flat on their bellies on the grey rocks, their eyes closed to slits, doing nothing at all. Just loafing about. I long to emulate them. But I'm afraid even to seal myself on a rock. What if I fall asleep and get left behind?

This is of course impossible, due to a rigorously enforced system of tags, labels, life-belt counting, and so on—but it's my first twinge of primal dread, mixed with a swooning sensation. I'm tired. I'm guilty about not liking penguins. I'm cold. I have to keep wiping my nose. I'm incapacitated by all these bulky clothes. I'm lonely because everyone else is hiding behind a camera. Everywhere I turn my view is blinded by some keen bean with a tripod. I fight the sense that a person with a camera has a prior right to any view we both happen to be looking at. I am being driven insane by photography.

Okay, one sub-group of the voyage is actually there to be

coached by Darren, a tall quiet young professional photographer from Brisbane; but your average punter on board has brought at least one camera and several kilometres of film. I have left my Pentax at home. I tell incredulous shipmates that it's too old and heavy to carry, but the real reason is that at the pre-trip briefing a couple of months ago, people spoke so fanatically of bringing a backup camera in case their main one fell overboard or got splashed in the Zodiac that it brought out the party-pooper in me. I determined on the spot that I would go to the icy continent in a state of heroic lenslessness; that I would equip myself with only a notebook and a pen.

But I forgot something. The cold.

Two degrees Celsius doesn't sound that scary, specially if you've been reading about Shackleton's journey in the open boat, or Apsley Cherry-Garrard's "Worst Journey in the World"—tales in which temperatures of seventy below scarcely raise an eyebrow. Still, the Aurora people urge us over and over again to take the cold seriously, to dress in layers against it, to keep dry, to wear several pairs of gloves. I have brought cotton ones, wool ones, and a pair of mittens made of stiff stuff like leather. Have you ever tried to take notes wearing boxing gloves?

With my huge bulging paws I wrestle the notebook and pen out of my pocket and start *describing things*, partly to justify my presence, partly to keep from falling asleep. "Penguins: ridiculous, helpless-looking creatures, always in a flap. A penguin looks like a person trying to walk in an inverted sack; it has to strain its feet apart to keep the neck of the bag open round its ankles. The cliff tops are crenellated: you expect to see the feathered heads of Indian warriors peep over them; it's like Arizona."

Oh, shut up, smart-arse.

I stow the book and sit down gingerly on a little point of rock, out of the wind. In this bay the sound of the ocean is hushed. Further around the rocky beach stands a wall of ice. Its vertical face is nicked with tiny hollows, in each of which there lurks a droplet of the same secret, tawdry green that seamed this morning's icebergs.

A chunk of ice the size and shape of a double bed (with base) detaches itself from near the top of the wall, and floats gracefully down and out of my line of sight—slow, ethereal. But it lands with a shocking roar and a smash and there's a fluster in the water, which dies away. Back inside the ice river there's a constant groaning and creaking, an occasional crack like a pistol shot.

Mild sun shines on my upturned face. None of these gargantuan catastrophes has anything to do with *me*. Nothing is my fault. While the ice behaves as it must, I am permitted to sit here on a rock, strangely at peace.

SOMETHING FUNNY happens to time, down here. The nights are so short and the light's so foreign, we're so buffeted by weather, bombarded by new sights, wrung out with wonder that the memory starts to pack up. We lose our grip on the sequence of events. Cameras are impotent against the slippage. The Aurora people work late into the night to counteract it: each morning we wake to find, under our cabin door-handle, a two-page account of the activities of the previous day, complete with map, and a plan for the day ahead. This is not just the usual Aurora efficiency: it's protection against an attack of severe existential anxiety.

AT THE lunch table Nicola and Sue, Aurora workers, relate how they lassoed a small iceberg and brought it back for cubes in the bar. "We were hauling and hauling! It was like a birth! And suddenly there was this great big THING in the Zodiac! Just as well there were no men there! If there'd been men they would've gone 'Stand back, girls! Let *me* handle this!' We were determined—we were like 'This iceberg is not going to beat us!'" The sole bloke at the table, Michael, a quiet man with a modest, introverted demeanour, who has lost his toes and parts of his feet to frostbite on Everest, sits looking on half smiling.

"The food on this ship is great," says another woman at the table, lifting her forearms off the cloth, which is dampened to prevent the plates from sliding about. "It must be the cold—I've been eating four times my usual rations and I'm *not even putting on weight!*"

That night we sail into our second storm, force ten on the Beaufort scale. It is colossal. I hardly sleep. Never before has it been strenuous just to lie down. I'm stiff from neck to feet all night long. In daylight, speechless people stagger hand over hand along the corridors and up to the bridge, where there are rails to grip, and one grips them hard, gulping and shaking, exhilarated, scared.

The sea is a heaving grey field of waves as big as apartment blocks, which rise with majestic deliberation and smash themselves over the bridge. For a few seconds after each impact, the ice fragments cascading down the glass blot out the world, then camouflage it, abstracting it into wild patterns of white, grey, and streaming loden green.

Hanging on with aching arms, flexing my knees and swaying with the madness, I begin to understand that the *Professor Molchanov* is not just a dead contraption of rivets and chunks of metal, but an entity, a living being. The *it* transforms into a *she*. She bounds, throbs, moans. She has a sense of her own springy wholeness, as she quivers on the lip of a wave gathering herself for the next plunge. The aliveness, the working *beingness* of her goes straight to the heart: I admire her, she moves me. For the first time in my life I understand how one can love a ship.

"My feeling of this part of Antarctica," says Greg, "is usually much more gentle. But this time it showed itself in a really raw way. We got a faceful."

THE NEXT evening we go ashore at Half Moon Island, to inspect a penguin rookery. While we're beaching the first Zodiac, a sudden wind springs up and slashes across the bay, making the water bristle. The stones underfoot, as we scramble out of the boats and up the steep beach, are grey and clanking, big as bread-and-butter plates. Camera mania flourishes at once, obliterating all social contact: I mooch about on my own, crabby and left out.

A lone penguin, separated from its fellows, stumps along beside me on its damp pink feet. We cast an ill-tempered glance at each other. It's a companionship of sorts, I suppose. I am just starting to appreciate the pearly sheen of its dress shirt when it loses interest and staggers away behind a beautiful old clinker-built rowboat which has sagged and half collapsed on the stones. I slog on by myself up to the saddle, where I am rewarded by a splendid vista: white peaks all scumbling down on the other side of a narrow channel in which mad dark water is bumping with frozen lumps. The wind up here ("cleanest air in the world") nearly bowls me over. *Breathe it, Misery Guts, and let that be enough.*

Way down behind me, there's a commotion at the water's edge. A bunch of tiny people are struggling to drag the second Zodiac, then the third, up on the beach. The light is weakening and the wind is growing stronger by the minute. On the crest I'm having to crouch and claw at the ground so as not to be blown off my feet. *Professor Molchanov* looks very small out there in the bay, and awfully far away.

I scramble crab-wise down to the shore. Seven people are battling to hold the third Zodiac steady. Waves are slopping over its stern, crashing and dragging at it; it's filling with water, we can't pull it up. Night's coming, there's a harsh side-on swell, and why *should* the wind drop?

It doesn't help that only a metre away from our struggles, a single penguin is frolicking in the dark water, as carefree as if the sun were beaming down at noon. While the humans shout and haul and groan, it loops and dives and twirls, merry as an otter.

The sky is so pure it hurts to look at it. The wind whips fine grit off the stones and slashes it into our streaming eyes.

My stomach knots in animal dread, a horror of cold. How will we get through this night? Has *Molchanov* got another boat to save us?

At the far end of the beach we can see a clump of small huts on bare, dark scree. No lights, no sign of life—only the blue and white Argentine flag painted on the roof: Camara base. Oh God. I picture the whole gang of us shuddering all night in a pile on the floor of the biggest hut, having *broken in.*

Over the wind Greg shouts at us: "Walk around the shore to the base! We'll bring the boats across! It's calmer there!" I set out to trudge a kilometre on the big shifting stones, my head seething with thoughts of the pathetic will I hastily scrawled the night before I left home, of bequests I made to certain people which I now suddenly and savagely regret.

Someone shouts to me and points to a dark thing squirming among rocks two metres away—a seal, the size of a terrier. I give it one look before the photographers descend on it with their ravening lenses. I keep stumping along in my brand new gumboots, leaning forward and stabbing my toes in among the stones, the only way to make progress against the cold wall of wind. My eyes pour liquid. I keep overtaking older couples struggling along in the same bent posture. They look up as I steam past, but in our scarves and sunglasses and headgear we don't recognize each other. We drive onwards, toes first, leaning into the wind.

Aurora Sue has somehow got to Camara beach before us, and is talking with a big, mustachioed Argentinean scientist in polar gear. She shouts, "There's room for all of us to sleep here if we have to!" Straggling in, people jockey for position out of the wind behind a tiny orange hut right near the water's edge. We huddle there in a clump, giggling feebly. Here come our Zodiacs, bounding across the fierce, darkening bay.

Greg has got soaked to the groin. His gumboots are full of water. He upends and empties them, wrings out his sop-

ping socks and stoically pulls them back on to his blue feet. A woman says to him, "You must be freezing." He shrugs manfully "Oh—not specially…" "I mean your feet must be freezing," she insists. "Well…" he says, looking away as if embarrassed; then, in a rush: "Oh, none of that stuff—*yes!* They *are!*" He gives a sudden laugh and throws both arms round her in a quick hug. This guy has climbed Everest? K2? And he mocks his own tendency to macho posturing? No wonder we all—women and men—adore him.

On the strength of his self-awareness I fight a powerful temptation to break the rules and pocket an orange pebble. I win; but my righteousness will never quite comfort me for the fact that I have not got that small bright stone, which signalled to me from among the big grey ones, and which that night I so badly wanted, and still do.

The captain has brought the ship closer in, to give us a lee. We zip splashily home. On deck, scrubbing off the penguin shit, we are already heroes to ourselves, staring-eyed, laughing a bit too wildly, half hysterical with relief and foolishness.

A woman asks Greg, "Tell me the truth—were you scared?" He shakes his head. "No. I knew the worst that could happen was we'd get a bit wet. It's the wind that makes people panic. It's like standing under a helicopter, when everybody's shouting."

"OF COURSE we're *exploiting* the penguins," says an earnest woman from Canberra. "A bunch of ignorant tourists staring at them as they go about their business."

"I don't think they feel exploited, though," says Greg with a straight face. "Beautiful as they are, it's a pretty small brain."

FORGIVE ME, but I'm not here for the wildlife. Of course I crane to see the seals, dumb and smooth as slugs, trailing blood-coloured shit as they slither off floes at our approach. Of course I gasp at the soaring of the giant petrels. Of course I race up on deck at the shout, "Sperm whale! Port side!" and hang over the rail, excited by the grand dark thing heaving just below the surface and blowing with a hollow rush. And when only the rind of a whale can be seen from a following Zodiac, when with a casual flip of the tail it's gone—of course with the others I groan in disappointment, and sit gripping the Zodiac side in the keen wind, shrunken and shuddering with cold, heart in mouth, nose running, eyes watering, scanning scanning scanning…

But in my heart all I want to do is go out in the boats to "look at ice." Seals, penguins, and whales, to me, are only distractions from the bliss of this.

Where to find a language for these miraculous frozen forms? Couldn't there be poetry in the ship's library alongside the glossy photo books? Doesn't someone in Shakespeare wake from a dream about "regions of thick-ribbed ice"? Would Gerard Manley Hopkins have found words for these teeming variations on *surface*?

On outings to Paradise Bay and to the "city of bergs" off Pleneau Island, we learn calm from Greg, who never calls for silence but simply manifests it, sitting beside the outboard with his handbacks resting on his thighs, his eyes squinting. The minute people stop ripping and adjusting Velcro, or tearing open film packets, we start to hear the sound the brash ice is making. It's whispering all around us: chinking, rustling on the gentle swell. We sit. We stare.

The colour of an iceberg, or of a glacier wall, is impossible to name. You call it white, but when you swing your eyes away and back, you see it's the most delicate, the palest and yet the greyest green. Mint? The Nile? A no-colour. Water colour. Cloud colour. Again and again the eye returns to feast on the crumpled mystery of ice. One plumbs the word-well. The bucket comes up empty.

People whisper helpless clichés. *Magic. Wonderland.* Not good enough. The forms are inhuman, but to name them we need the vocabulary of the body, of carpentry, dressmaking, masonry—all the beautiful crafts of people's hands. Pocked.

Dimpled. Chiselled. Chamfered. Bevelled. Ruched. Frilled. Saw-toothed. Cloven. Striated, stippled, puckered, fringed, trimmed, carved, scrolled—or simply folded and scratched.

On the way back from Paradise Bay, at nightfall, sitting in a silent row along the rim of the Zodiac, we pass a toppled, majestic thing—an iceberg like an immense coroneted head. Wagnerian? Arthurian? *Look on my works, ye mighty, and despair.* A monarch brought low, shamed, blinded, submerged to the temples. Resting his cold cheek among the ripples.

I FIERCELY wish I had no prior inkling of this place, that everything I'm looking at was completely new to me. I hate movies and TV and videos. People with cameras are busybodies, writers are control freaks, spoiling things for everyone else, colonizing, taming, matching their egos against the unshowable, the unsayable. I long to have come down here in a state of infantile ignorance. Is this a rebirth fantasy? Or perhaps it's what Greg means when he says, "the power of this place quietens and humbles even the dickheads."

The morning we go in the boats to the Hydrurga Rocks (penguins, seals, and a particular bird which hovers, head into the ferocious wind, right next to my shoulder as I stand wobbling on the ridge, crazy with the brightness of the world and the faraway satin peaks, wanting to yell with joy), a photographer loses his grip on a white plastic bag. The wind whisks it out of his hand and away it soars, inflated, skimming the surface of the water like a big white bubble of poison. We all stand transfixed, mouths gaping with horror. Later I hear that one of the blokes has chased it in a Zodiac and managed to pick it up; but the distress I felt at the sight of its escape still astonishes me.

NO ONE ever wants to look at my slides!" laments Vern cheerfully. "Can't even get m' children to look at 'em! Never mind—they're for my own pleasure."

On *Molchanov*'s deck after an outing, I see two men, half

in jest, point their cameras at each other. Like two tired cowboys in their penguin-shit-stained wet weather gear and boots, they thrust their lenses right into each other's faces. Stand-off. "Go on—take it!" says one. "*I'm* not taking a shot!" cries the other—"I only want to stop *you* from taking one!"

What *is* this thing about cameras? Around them seem to constellate such deep anxieties. In spite of my bravado about going lensless, I've actually got a throwaway camera in my cabin, having cracked in Ushuaia ten minutes before we boarded the ship. I want to leave it hidden in a drawer—though I confess that I took it to the "city of bergs" and got shots that I scanned at home and now never think to look at—because I am engaged in a battle with the terror of forgetting, which drives people to raise a camera between themselves and everything they encounter—as if direct experience were unbearable and they have to shield themselves from it, filter it through a machine, store up a silent, odourless version of it for later, rather than endure it now.

But doesn't my wretched notebook (which the wind tore out of my pocket on Hydrurga Rocks; which would have followed the airborne plastic bag if I hadn't stamped on it with my heavy boot in the nick of time)—doesn't a notebook perform the same function? Why can't we let experiences lay themselves down in us like compost, or fall into us like seeds which may put forth a shoot one day, spontaneously, as childhood memories do, in answer to the stimulus of ordinary life? "Take it home," says Greg, "and plant it somewhere."

"The morning star was over the mountain," says a man to his wife at dawn on our last day, as *Molchanov* slides back up the flushed glass floor of the Beagle Channel, "*but I didn't photograph it!*" He is apologizing to her for having missed something—but I want to kiss him, I want to shake his hand!

We disembark at Ushuaia in bright morning sun. There's a beech forest high up there behind the town: Greg and another mountaineer jump into a rattly old taxi and make a dash for the trees, to touch and smell foliage briefly before they set out, the same afternoon, back to the peninsula on the last voyage of the season.

So this is the end. But toward 4 P.M., I get the strangest feeling that I have to go back to the wharf. What nonsense! How sentimental! I can't stay away. I drift down there, furtive in my Patagonia jacket with its penguin motif, and to my surprise I find half a dozen shipmates rambling down to the water as well—only casually strolling, mind you, to get their land legs—merely chancing to be wandering in that direction.

We stand looking up at *Molchanov*'s clean side, a bunch of sad dags clustering on the dock. We've said goodbye to everyone in sight but we need to stay right to the end. I can't believe the way my chest muscles are being squeezed by an emotion I don't have a name for. Even hulking Dave the diver owns up to it: we hardly dare look at each other. To see strangers on board our ship, leaning over the rail in a proprietary manner as she edges out and turns to face the glistening channel, is painful—enraging. She was *our* ship, and we've already been replaced.

A CONVERSATION
WITH DAVID MALOUF

MICHAEL ONDAATJE

MO   David, you were born in Australia. At what age did you begin to write? Were you conscious of wanting to be a writer early on?

DM   I started to write stories when I was a kid, what I thought were novels, which I'd bash out on an old Royal typewriter…I might have been about thirteen, fourteen. They were sort of reflections on the kind of things I was reading. They were no good at all, they weren't serious attempts. They were imitations, I think, more of films than any novels. Films are what I really grew up with, as well as writing. Then I started to write poetry when I went to university—I was probably about sixteen or seventeen. I still thought that what I eventually wanted to be was a fiction writer. None of the fiction I tried to write ever worked, it seems to me; but in poetry I got to the point of writing something I thought was publishable long before I got to the same point in fiction. I ended up publishing three books of poetry before I published a novel.

MO   Most of the people I know who are poets and novelists began as poets and then became novelists as their grasp perhaps got larger.

DM   Yes. One of the things I discovered which I found interesting is that the reason I couldn't write the prose is that I could never find the right tone. I was always trying to write something that seemed to be too elaborate and indirect and roundabout. What I discovered when I settled down to write the third version of *Johnno* was that I'd already hit the tone almost ten years before in poems that I'd written. All I had to do was go to a poem like "The Year of the Foxes" and look at that, then simply sit down and write in that tone of voice. It was a little autobiographical poem, actually about my mother, but its tone was perfectly straightforward and easy, and worked utterly in the poem. It's still one of my most successful poems. It seems extraordinary to me that it took me so long to realize that all I had to do, when I sat down and wrote prose, was to pick up on that same voice which was both comfortable for me and properly expressive of me.

MO   Was it comfortable for you in the sense that it was your voice? Or was it another voice?

DM   I think it was my voice. Maybe because the poems were short and because I knew exactly what was the small dramatic incident I wanted to talk about, I didn't feel as self-conscious about that as I did about beginning a prose work. It was when I got rid of that self-conscious, round-about, indirect thing that I thought belonged to the kind of prose I wanted to write, and realized I could do something in a straightforward way and let the complexity come in a different way, it was only then that I could write the book. I tried to write *Johnno* at least twice before I finally began that. I'd always been starting in the wrong place. First of all it began as a third-person narrative, which was wrong, and it was only when I said, okay, I could accept the role of the narrator for this material rather than trying to disguise my role in it, that I could write the book. But going back to your previous thing, I'd always thought of myself as wanting to write fiction.

MO The only other example I know of someone who's worked the other way (other than Thomas Hardy) is Robert Kroetsch, who began as a novelist and then in mid-career began to write wonderful poetry. In some ways I think he's much more radical as a poet than as a novelist. There are lots of writers who wished to be filmmakers—or who were influenced by films. Is this true of you?

DM I think it's our generation. We're people who grew up with a double inheritance in that way: film shaped the whole of our visual imagination. But reading gave us those things which a film can't do, that ability to deal with the interior world. What I'm interested in, in books, is that interior world. But people often look at the books and say, Oh, these will make great films, because they see that minute by minute there's a visual sense working there. And you have to keep saying to them, no, there's nothing there that finally matters that can be presented in a film.

MO I know. I think there's an attempt by most writers to write against the possibility of a film. Even someone like John Fowles has written screenplays and I think as a result of that maybe tried to write works that could not be filmed.

I think most writers today are doing that, as a sort of defence of their work, while using the elements of film.

DM Yes. Generally speaking, if you look at a scene in a book of mine there are two characters sitting there saying nothing. From an observer's point of view, everything is happening! That is what writing can do, which film can't do.

MO Do you think there are films that do represent that interior world? Do you see a possibility of film being able to capture that in some way?

DM I think films always have to suggest it. I think that very often great performances, or great performers on film, can suggest to you that there's an interior world there which is being expressed in their body gestures or their facial expressions, but which are not going to be expressed—but they *are* being expressed, visually. There are a lot of actors who are like that. For example a young actor like Matt Dillon who's really not a very good actor but somehow he can express a sense of baffled emotions, inarticulate anguish or something like that, which is what the film needs, underneath what is being visually presented. I think a lot of that comes through the actors. We have to pick that up and almost create for ourselves from what's being expressed, because it is inarticulate.

MO When you grew up in Australia, what other influences were there for you? Were the books that influenced you Australian books? Or books from England?

DM There were almost no Australian books. I don't think many people read them, although the general reading book we had in primary school did have a lot of Australian material: a lot of poems, and writers like Henry Lawson. But the kind of books I really grew up on, the books I was reading at around twelve, were the usual strange mixture of things like *Captain Marriot*, *Moby Dick*, *Northwest Passage*, *Wuthering Heights*, *Pride and Prejudice*, *The Hunchback of Notre Dame*, and strange books like *Barnaby Rudge* ... that kind of range.

MO That's a more classical series of books than I suspect

someone of twelve in England was reading.

DM   Maybe. I don't know. I know they're the books that I
read the year I was twelve; I can remember the Christmas
holidays, when you'd go to the beach and take all the books
you'd been given for Christmas. I was reading them because
they told me things about the world that I wanted to know.
These days there tends to be a kind of specialized literature
for young teens, all about how they should cope with, oh,
the fact that their mother's a lesbian or their father's gay or
their family's breaking up, or something like that. Yes, kids
are worried about those kinds of things too, but I think what
kids really want to know is how strange and passionate and
cruel and unpredictable the world is. The big revelation to
me was something like *The Hunchback of Notre Dame*.

MO   What did that book show you?

DM   There was a lot of sex in it. Of the nineteenth-century
kind, which is fetishized sex, and which, it seems to me,
presents sex in *just* the way that kids really can grasp it; that
is, it's not straightforward, but somehow it connects with
your real emotional and real fantasy world. The way the
Victorians—Dickens and somebody like Hugo or Dumas,
whom I also read loads of—deal with sex is just the way it
needs to come into the unconscious and conscious fantasy
world of a twelve- or thirteen-year-old. That's what I was
discovering about that.

Suburban life everywhere is fairly unpassionate. Your
parents, and your teachers, are always presenting you with
a world where you are meant to be unpassionate and not
excessive. And what those books are presenting you, whether it's *Wuthering Heights* or *The Hunchback of Notre Dame*, is a
world in which everything goes to the extreme, where big
passions are involved. I think that kids at a certain stage of
their growth need to feel that that's one of the possibilities
in the world.

All experience as it comes to kids is experience that eventually has to be judged against the real world. Part of our
process of growing up is determining what is possible and
what is not possible. To have these examples of the excessive, the grandly destructive—we need to know that stuff.
It's not what our teachers or our parents are going to tell us
about, the possibilities of the world. I find it very difficult to
know—and you may be able to tell me—how much that
is a part of a kind of colonial growing up.

It seems to me that one of the things when you grow
up—in our generation anyway—in the colonies was always to believe that real life was happening somewhere
else, that you were away from the centre of it and England,
as it was then, was where real passions were acted out, real
relationships occurred, real conversations took place, real
history happened. Our only version of that was these books.
So part of our coming to terms with real life was coming
to terms with the fact that our version of what life at the
centre was like was this one that had been entirely created
through literature. Whether, if you lived at the centre, you
would have had the same feeling or not, I can't tell.

MO   Remember when we were talking at that conference
in Wales and you were saying that in some senses we on
the edge—whether it was Australia or Sri Lanka or Canada—because we were watching what was happening in
England and were influenced by it in numerous ways—we
tended to read the best literature. There was a classical sense,
or a sense of not a canon exactly but books that had been
winnowed down to important books one should read, and
I think we read them. Also I think we had a sense of reading books that were about individuals within a context of
history. Books such as *With Wolfe in Canada*, *With X in Bor-
neo*...always an individual at a historical moment.

DM   Yes. There was a very long time in which the people at the
edges—Australians, New Zealanders, Canadians, South Af-
ricans—kind of didn't want to know one another; it was too
embarrassing to see another version of yourself, really. We
felt there was nothing to be gained by a relationship with

people who were also on the periphery. What we wanted was a relationship with people at the centre.

But once you'd done that, made that contact, it is interesting to see what we've shared in the way of growing up, our reading, and the relation of all of that to the centre. It was only when I came to England at the age of twenty-four that I discovered that England was completely different, life in England was a different thing from what I had extrapolated from the reading of English fiction.

One of the things I discovered was that Australia, for example, was not a reflection of southern England at all; it was a reflection of northern England and Scotland. That's true, I'm sure, of Canada as well. All those things that I took for granted as being English were really provincial English. And that, too, was strange.

MO   Are you talking about a value system?

DM   Yeah. The whole way of life as it was lived in Australia was a way of life that was immediately familiar to me when I went to live in Liverpool. Even simple things, like calling the meal in the middle of the day "dinner" and the evening meal "tea" and the kind of food you ate was really northern English food. The entire vocabulary was northern English. When I first went into a schoolroom in London and said to the kids, "Get the reading books out of the press," they'd no idea what I meant; that's called the cupboard, in southern England, but in Liverpool the kids said, "Will I get the books out of the press, sir?" If you said to a kid in London, "Will you do a message for me?" nobody knew what you were talking about. But in northern England and in Scotland that's what people would say.

MO   What does that mean?

DM   It means, "Will you run an errand for me?" What you said in Australia was, "Would you do a message for me?" or "Would you go a message for me?" So, immediately you were aware you were in a place where Australian speech comes from. People often assume that Australian language is a derivative of Cockney. It really isn't. It's a derivative of northern English speech mixed with Scottish and Irish. So, already that literature—which was largely literature of southern England—was at one remove from the reality that I discovered when I arrived. But that, nevertheless, was the reality out of which I'd made my own vision of the language world I was going to write in.

MO   There are a couple of writers we've talked about in the past who are important to you not as touchstones but as something else—a cloud somewhere—and those are Balzac and Kipling. Would those be two of the major writers for you or not?

DM   Not really. I'm fond of Kipling, but Kipling's not central to me in that kind of way. I would have said amongst European writers it's Balzac and Tolstoy and later Thomas Mann who would be the three I'm most interested in and read most. Amongst the English novelists in some ways it's Conrad, but that turns out to be so for almost everybody.

MO   Yes, Conrad and Yeats. What is it about Conrad that appeals to you?

DM   I'm a writer who is very interested in the conventions of the male world of work and play. That's very much Conrad's field, and it has a very complex language, a very complex set of conventions for dealing with feeling, that I've always been interested in. Language is absolutely central to Conrad. I sometimes feel that it's the people who are on the periphery of English who feel they're not dealing with it in a way that can be taken for granted, either because they're colonial or peripheral speakers of it, or because they've got it late, like Conrad. It was not their language. It wasn't inevitable; the language was an accident. So it seems enormously precious and enormously interesting to them. I strongly suspect that for a lot of people who are not born in England, Conrad is a wonderful example of somebody who is mesmerized by the riches of the language and who sees himself, as a writer, as a creation of that language. Whereas if you were writing in England there could never have been another language and it's just what you deal with daily. It is for us, too, but it seems like a miraculous gift.

MO It's interesting because I think a lot of people who think about Conrad look right through the language. They don't see him as a good writer. They talk about the three hundred adjectives and adverbs found on two pages of *Heart of Darkness*. I think when they look at Conrad they're looking at the skeleton of a theme or a plot in a book like *Heart of Darkness* or *Nostromo*.

DM But it is the language, isn't it?

MO I think it is. He and Ford, they were obviously sculptors of some kind.

DM A Conrad story or passage seems to me to be absolutely inconceivable except in that language which he has such a dense feel for; it's got all the senses in it. Often people talk about it only in visual terms, and it is that, but it's got every other kind of sense in it. The other great thing about Conrad is that it is subjective writing. Brilliantly objective as all the observation seems to be in the visual world — and this is going back to what we were talking about in the beginning — he is one of the people who is essentially writing about interior movements and discoveries, in a most wonderfully masculine kind of way. There's nothing pretentious or precious about it. It seems to belong simply to a kind of bluff world. These are always the people he's dealing with, these sailors are workingmen. Yet he's able to suggest this complex and rich interior world which is a moral world.

MO I keep thinking of a lot of things you're saying in terms of your recent novel, *Remembering Babylon*. In many ways the description of the people in that book seems to be at first judgmental — they seem to be just bluff, external types. But then what we are being gifted with is this internal and moral world that percolates into the characters of that community.

DM I think that's one of the things that fiction can do that nothing else can do. Part of the burden that's put on you as a writer is to take characters or situations that seem, in a stereotyped kind of way, to be merely surface, and then to discover what is going on underneath there, that those situations and those people do have a dense and rich and complex inner life, although it might not necessarily be expressive in their words. It's the writer's business to discover words for what they apprehend but can't necessarily express or articulate. Again it's that business of what writing is meant to do, which is to take the object and subjectify it. That's the subject of writing!

MO Was that one of the reasons you selected that third-person voice in the new book?

DM I wanted a situation where you see something from many different points of view, in each case subjectively, so that you'd get that sense that there are many ways in which any situation is seen. Part of the complexity of what is happening is that different people are seeing the same event in different ways. In *Remembering Babylon* I wanted to be able to have characters see one another in a crude way, and I'd think at first, yes, this is what this character is like. But somewhere later in the book, you get inside that character and he's quite different. He's being seen even by the people within the book. That seems to me to be true to the way life is.

MO I was moved so much in the new novel, at those moments when you go past the surface portrait and we discover the husband and the wife and that remarkable scene where she talks about what she wanted to be. But also what stunned me was the shape and the structure of the book. Was that something you had imagined beforehand? Or was it something that evolved?

DM No, that always has to evolve. The thing I find most exciting about starting on a book is that although you know that there's something in there that's drawing you, often you don't know what it is. You say to yourself, Why this subject rather than another? What is it here that's hooked my conscious or unconscious in some way that means I have to go with it? Finding out what that is through the book, letting the book be the shape of the discovery, is the entire excitement of the writing. You hope, if that is how it happens to you as you go along, that will be the same kind of sense of discovery for the reader. There are things obviously you discard ... possibilities. In that book in particular ... I just notice, from reviews often and people's more conventional expectations, when they sometimes don't like the way in which those conventional expectations get thwarted. There are several possibilities there that Jimmie, for example, will pick up an axe and go for the settlers. There are some people who expect the book to go that way and want it to go that way, or they expect the whole community to turn on him and treat him in some more overtly brutal way than he's been treated. And that's another possibility which I didn't take up. Or they want to see the community go out and massacre all the aborigines, which is not what happens. When you're going along, you make those choices which are shaping the book. But often, as you know, you're avoiding just those things that readers are expecting to happen and which is what you don't want to happen.

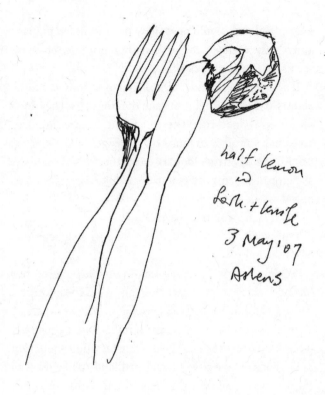

half lemon
in
fork + knife
3 May '07
Athens

MO   Avoiding the expected movie. I thought his entrance into this community and that strange ripple effect, which got larger and larger — it was two months, and then five years or ten years by the end — was beautiful and a wonderful way of placing that incident within a history. The last pages were beautiful. I was in tears at the end. I didn't know why or what was happening. It was again something to do with that language. There was some hope there that was startling.

DM   Yes, the ending of any book just has to be right, and you never know quite what that's going to be. You keep going with it, believing that you're going to find the ending which will be the right ending. I think there are a lot of people, readers of or commentators on this book, who were very surprised by the leap forward at the end, and they wanted to know more clearly what happened to Jimmie; they wanted his story to be more central to the book than I really wanted it to be.

MO   But in a way that story has already been told, in up to twenty novels in Australia.

DM   Yes, sure, sure. I wanted him to walk out of the book as he came into it, in a kind of mysterious way. It seemed important to me that his silence should be given its proper weight. In that book it really is the silence of the aborigines. There's a mystery about that silence that has to be paid proper tribute to. It's also the silence of all of those lives that don't come fully articulated either into history or into fiction. Paying a proper respect to the mystery of that silence is important. So he does go out with his own life mysteriously about him and what his end is is hinted at or guessed at, but we don't necessarily know. What you do get is his effect on those children, so there is a carrying forward of his life, as our lives do carry forward, in the memories and their effects on other people.

MO Do your novels get called poetic novels? And is this a term you object to strongly?

DM Yeah, you do get called "poetic." These days I try to write a really straightforward and transparent language. I try to make the language absolutely transparent and straightforward, but I do want the language to be dealing with things which are just at the edge of expression or just at the edge of apprehension. If that's what poetry brings into the novel then it's a damn good thing.

MO I think it's amazing how when people talk about a poetic novel they assume it's something precious and abstract.

DM It's true that novels like mine (but there are many kinds of novels, we can do with as many kinds of novels as anybody can think up to write) and maybe novels like yours, too, move from epiphanic moment to epiphanic moment with a kind of magnetic pull between those moments, which is meant to hold the novel together. That's okay. I can't see anything wrong with that kind of novel. It's the kind I like to read. I can't see why I shouldn't write it.

MO Yeah. I was thinking about the thing you were saying about having more of a variety of novels. What tends to happen with critics is that if they're looking at a book of yours or of anyone's, they'll say, This book doesn't do this, as if the novel was supposed to do everything, or this writer was supposed to represent all aspects of society.

DM Or that there's only one kind of novel which they know about, a novel with this kind of plot and these kinds of characters. I love Balzac, but I can't write and don't want to write another Balzac novel or a version of a Balzac novel. If anybody were to say to me, what was the model for *Remembering Babylon*, it's very, very far from the model; it's that wonderful, late story of Tolstoy's called *Hadji Muràd*.

It's a fabulous little novel. No one would look at my book and say it was that story, but that was kind of what I had in mind. So there is a kind of classical model, but my work's not going to come out anything like that.

MO Looking back on your earlier novel, *An Imaginary Life*, how do you see it now?

DM It's still the book of mine that in some ways is my favourite. That may only mean it's the one that now I feel absolutely comfortable with. Yet it too began as a book I felt uncomfortable with, as with any new book. It's like a piece of clothing, it takes a while to work your way into it and feel that it fits you comfortably, and I think that's how it should be. But I can't remember that book, except that it began in a very strange way. I wrote a scene from it — which is a key moment in the book — before I knew what book it belonged to. It's the scene where Ovid sees the poppy. I knew it was Ovid, but I didn't know whether it was just a piece of writing or a scene for a novel or a prose poem. I wrote that three weeks before I suddenly thought of sitting down and beginning the book. Then I think the whole book was written and typed up within seven or eight weeks. People are always talking about the ideal conditions for writing. The ideal conditions for writing are whatever that particular work demands. After I'd written that passage, I started that book at the beginning of November, and it was a time when I had a thousand HSC papers to mark, the equivalent of university entrance exams, and seven hundred first-year poetry papers to mark. I used to get up in the morning, write the book from six until eight in the morning, then have breakfast and spend the whole of the rest of the day marking papers.

MO My god!

DM And the whole book got written in that marking period! It was obviously just what I needed. When you see the manuscript, there are a few changes of words here and there, a couple of paragraphs that go and a couple of paragraphs that change their order, but virtually nothing else, there's no shaping, nothing. So I'm fond of it also because I think if you're very lucky you sometimes get one gift book and that was it! It's never going to be as easy again.

MO Do you rewrite a lot?

DM I do, yes.

MO And did you write a lot more than what ended up in *Remembering Babylon*?

DM Not with that one so much, but certainly things are longer in their expression and you cut them back…you look and say, this isn't necessary, or this has already been said, or there's a quicker way of saying that. So there's a lot of cutting in that way. I write by hand.

MO So do I.

DM I love those first horrible, unreadable drafts with all their scratchings out. Often you get to a place where something that's difficult is happening and you know you're going to have to rewrite that paragraph five, six, twenty times if it's necessary, just to get it right. It's always amazing that you have in your head this platonic idea of what right is going to be, you know how far you are from it in the first draft. But often the real germ of that is in the first draft. Often when you're writing—I'm sure you find that too—you write away from that, and you get so far away from it you know you've lost it and you're going to have to go back to that first draft. Sometimes there's just a single word there, or a single little idea which is what you have to go back to. I love that process of writing.

MO I do too. There is a real pleasure also in using the page and the pen.

DM What's always amazing to me is that your mind has to be working in that finicky way, with details and paragraphs, and yet in some other kind of way, which you can't determine and which is utterly mysterious to you, you've got to have this other rhythm which is the big sweep through the book. So that when people are reading it, what they feel is this movement straight through the book and which is sweeping them on. You've got to sustain that over months.

MO Or years, for me!

DM It's really mysterious that, how something has to be working on those two levels, where one thing is sort of hovering and hardly moving, like a—

MO Plumb-bob.

DM Yeah, over the page, over the little sentence and the phrase, and yet some other part of you is whoosh! Straight through the book.

MO There's something about that scope that's interesting, when people talk about computers, for instance. I find seeing that one page on a screen very limiting. I've lost the context of the five pages before and the five pages afterwards—that whole scope.

DM I can't see things on that screen. I need my own messy bits of paper and the ink and everything. I need it like you need your own body smell, to know whose this is. Once I see it all distanced like that on the screen, I just don't know whose work it is. This is old-fashioned, no doubt. I suppose there are people who feel the same kind of personal sense with regard to the screen.

MO I find that there's something in my mind, a tone or something, that's the only thing I can cling to—apart from that thing you described, that piece of thread you're following and you're not quite sure where it's going or what it's coming from. So I'm collecting and writing, and working on a reconnaissance of a story…for me it takes about three years to find what the story is. But it does fit into that kind of a pitch, or tone.

DM I find that too. If you hit the right tone, that kind of book will write itself because you can always go back to that. You only have to read a paragraph of it and it will put you back into the tone. That's what I meant about not having found that until that third draft of *Johnno*, when I went to a poem which had that and realized that there was the tone; as long as I stuck with that, the book could be written.

There's another thing with me. Each of the books has a kind of atmosphere, a light, that's either clear or murky or oppressive, or something like that. I also need to go back into that atmospheric quality. It's a landscape that I'm seeing there. What I know will give the book unity is that light as it is in my mind. I can't tell whether that gets re-created in the book or not, but I know that for me I'm in a particular kind of landscape.

MO   Now you live in two places, you live in Italy and you live in Australia.

DM   I tend to live mostly in Sydney. But frequently I've carried manuscripts from Sydney to Italy. You fly and then the next day you get up and you go in and there's the manuscript on a different desk in a different place. But in your head it's exactly the same.

MO   Was Patrick White a great influence on your generation of writers?

DM   Yes, I think so. Sometimes, of course, a negative one. There he was, like this great cathedral you had to find your way around, if you know what I mean! Around the outside of, to find another bit of the landscape where you might put up a little hut. But he also, in Australia, offered a wonderful example in that he took the matter of Australia and revealed that you could make big works out of it that could stand in the world fiction. Writing about Australian experience didn't mean that you were writing yourself out of the world. Before that, I think a lot of Australian writing had seen itself as directing its attention only to local readers. I think he was somebody who revealed to us that you could take a big Australian subject and if it was big enough people elsewhere ought to be interested in it. He didn't write to catch their eye, but if it was big enough then …. In fact, what you were really saying is that all great writing is first of all local and specific to a particular kind of place, but if it creates that with real density and richness then other people can enter into it.

After all, that's what we've always done. If I'm reading Balzac I just have to enter into a world which is utterly a French world but it's a world that welcomes me, that I can walk into, and when I walk into it it seems to express the whole of life as I understand it while I'm inside that book. That's what all writing has to do. But in some ways because he did it he made it possible.

MO   So he was more of an influence as an example than as a stylist?

DM   Yes. The style as you know is so peculiar and so mannered. It's a very highly mannered style that derives in some ways from somebody like Faulkner.

MO   I can't think of anybody else apart from Faulkner. When you think of the kind of scope he had, compared to say the twentieth-century English novel, I can't think of too many people who wrote in his style.

DM   I think also Lawrence was a huge influence on him. In a way there ought to be no temptation to reproduce that manner. But nevertheless he too is one of those people who wrote about Australian life as if there was something very rich going on in the interior of those people as well as in the exterior. That certainly to me has been an example.

MO   Which of White's books do you like most or admire most?

DM   Maybe *The Solid Mandala* is one. Another one would be *Riders in the Chariot*. It's flawed, a lot of his books are, but a lot of great books are flawed. That doesn't make them any less great. There were wonderful things in *Riders in the Chariot*.

MO   If we're talking about English literature, in England, are there writers you find, say since the time of Lawrence and others, you are close to?

DM   I suppose not. I think Golding did some fabulous things. I think he did some great things. I've never been much taken with many other of the English writers. I've never been able to read Anthony Powell, for example. It's just not my thing. When I was young I was a great reader — as everybody was — of Joyce Carey. I think *The Horse's Mouth* is still a tour de force of a book. But none of those people do I feel very close to. Of the writers in English I've admired always, Faulkner would be absolutely tops.

MO   Yes, me too.

DM   Faulkner is just fabulously head and shoulders above everybody else. There are other books I really love. I really love *Seize the Day*, that short novel—the best of all—of Saul Bellow, because it's the one that does what he does. He tends to be terribly repetitive. Any book seems to me to be the same book only different. But *Seize the Day* is a wonderful little book. He's a very good writer. I think *Beloved* by Toni Morrison is a great book. I think Coetzee's a great writer. Do you read Coetzee?

MO   Yes, I'm reading *Age of Iron* right now, which is wonderful.

DM   I haven't read that one, but I thought that *In the Heart of the Country* is an amazing book. And *The Life and Times of Michael K.*, just in terms of the quality of the prose. I've recently been bowled over by Stevenson.

MO   I've just been reading Turgenev, whom I hadn't read.

DM   He's a joy. I read loads of Turgenev when I was young. He's the one that in mood and tone I feel closest to. Who are the writers you admire most?

MO   Faulkner. Strangely enough, he was the one who made me want to write prose. The book that still really gets to me is the one with Joe Christmas.

DM   *Light in August*. Isn't that an astonishing book! I read that when I was nineteen or twenty and I've such a vivid memory of it, I feel I could write it all down from beginning to end. But I've not wanted to read it again, not because I'm afraid I mightn't like it so much, but I don't want it to have the same kind of strong effect on me that it had then. It's taken me forty years to fight it off!

MO   I'll tell you what happened to me. I read it at university and was knocked out by it. It was the one I loved the best. That and *Absalom, Absalom!* Then I was going to teach it about ten years ago. I had just begun to wear glasses, and it was the first book I read with glasses. Suddenly, I could see the page was porous and full of fibres, the type was huge, and I found myself weeping constantly. I didn't know if it was a new intimacy with the book or what. There's that one scene when Joe is talking to the woman in his hut and I had no idea why I was crying and why I was so moved. It's a very quiet unemotional conversation. And then I realized it's because it is practically the only time he talks in the book, which is about halfway through. It's a remarkable book.

DM   I like loads of things. I've recently re-read—it's about the third time—*Sanctuary*. It's a much-despised book, but it's wonderful! I too love *Absalom, Absalom!* but I've never dared read that one again.

MO   No, I haven't either.

DM   You don't dare read them again because they had such an explosive effect on you that you want to say, can I afford to have this happen to me at this moment?

London, England, August 11, 1993

FALL OF THE WINTER PALACE

MELORA WOLFF

KERENSKY, rumour had it, once lived in seclusion on the top floor of The Mansion, hiding from the horrors of memory, revolution, and failure many, many years ago. In 1927, he arrived in Manhattan in a long coat and with a lowered head, his hat's brim turned down to cast his face in shadow, as if someone might recognize him and shout out his name across Times Square above the bustle of nameless masses — *hey, you there, Alexander Fyodorovich! Do you think it's so easy? You! Come back here!* — and he gripped the handle of a wicker suitcase that was still swollen with the few possessions he had gathered in haste in Paris, his former retreat. In Paris, land of the exiled, he had grown a beard, become decadent, and pushed himself beyond his fatal moderacy to cloak himself in volume and extravagance. But Kerensky could not exile Kerensky from himself. And so he had bundled into his suitcase his half-dozen sweat-stained shirts, a portfolio of papers and letters, woollen trousers and a pair of linen, three photographs (a lost wife, a beloved dog, a demolished street), and a dozen dog-eared books with indecipherable notes scribbled in the margins of each page (his intellectual, late-night musings, his undelivered speeches, and other revolutions of his brandy-sodden mind). He carried a cigarette case, empty of course, and a rolled sketch of the Winter Palace in fall under a charcoal sky, smudged somewhat aggressively by the thumb of an artist who was, finally, shot in the head on a narrow street beside the Neva. Kerensky also kept folded in his left coat pocket an unexpected invitation, which offered a room, privacy, meals, rest, and endless hours of solitude in an Upper East Side residence to dream, to forget, to revise himself. It would cost him little to nestle into the upper rooms of the Manhattan home of Mr. and Mrs. Simpson, and to purchase his obscurity or peace.

IN 1970, Mrs. Simpson's granddaughter Cynthia and I became best friends at the Brearley School for Girls on the city's Upper East Side, where even the fourth-graders are considered exceptional young ladies gathered together to blossom in bright rooms overlooking the East River. The school authorities had labelled me, like Cynthia, "a difficult child." Exceptionally difficult: moody, uncommunicative, prone to hiding under desks, or to bouts of tears, or to running away through the lobby of the school and out the gold and glass doors toward fresher air beside the river. Once, Cynthia threw her desk in a rage at another student, and afterwards, while the teachers searched the halls for us, I hid with Cynthia in a stall in the bathroom, the lights off, for the rest of the day. We spent long hours after school at each other's small apartments where — for fun — we imitated our wealthier classmates. We imagined that chauffeurs drove us to Carl Schurz Park to play, and that on weekends when uniforms were not required, we wore glamorous fur jackets like Tessa, Sidney, Missy, Martine, Kristina, Kyle, Alissa, Sasha, and the others.

Cynthia's mother and my own mother came for the two of us after school in shabby coats, their hair blown every which way by the fall wind. They leaned awkwardly up against the

Brearley's lobby wall, apart from the waiting drivers and the more elegant mothers who gathered and tapped the toes of their high-heeled shoes impatiently, their faces exquisite and their hair coiffed. Sometimes our two mothers talked to each other, although they weren't friends. Rather, they seemed drawn to each other against their own wills and they chatted almost angrily together, as though each saw more of themselves in the other than they had ever hoped to see. My mother was a secretary and did not earn enough money. She tried hard to avoid the subject of money, but really there was no avoiding it when I announced that my class would be taking a trip to Russia to study history and monarchs and buildings and things. The atmosphere went gloomy. I was a scholarship student at the Brearley School, and I would not—no, I would certainly not!—be going to Russia.

"*Russia!*" my mother said and laughed. "Are they joking? What happened to camping trips on Bear Mountain? Canoeing in the Adirondacks? A day trip to the Central Park Zoo? Why can't you study the buildings on your block like a normal kid? There are so many flakes over at that school!"

Only Cynthia understood. She wouldn't be going to Russia either. Instead, we would be hanging out in Cynthia's bedroom, listening to *Sgt. Pepper's Lonely Hearts Club Band* and creating fantasies of our future fortunes. "My grandmother is rich," Cynthia confided in me. "She lives in a mansion. Would you like to go there with me sometime?"

I would. And if our mothers would not let us go with our class, they must at least allow us a visit to The Mansion, right there on the city's East Side. Maybe our mothers arranged it, coolly, together in the lobby of the school. Maybe they spoke longingly about Bear Mountain, or about the Adirondacks, or about what to do with their exceptionally difficult chil-

dren while everyone else under the age of twelve went off to Russia. Or maybe they wondered where two still-attractive though frazzled young women might get a drink and practise their charm, and forget their troubles, and what they feared it would all one day come to, this work and frustration, and forget the cost of this exclusive New York City education for girls, and the despair they saw in each other's eyes. Who knows what they spoke of then? But at 3:15 when Cynthia and I crossed the lobby to meet our mothers, mine looked deeply relieved and Cynthia's began to rummage through her cloth handbag with obvious annoyance at whatever was lost.

"Thank goodness you showed up," my mother said to me later as we walked home along the boardwalk beside the river. "*That woman is such a flake.*"

KERENSKY, WE HEARD, had always been friends with the beautiful widow Mrs. Simpson. She guarded his privacy loyally, allowing no one to intrude on his meals, his studies, or his morning and evening appearances in the library of The Mansion, where he read his trashy romance novels and sniggered and snorted to himself over racy passages he loved and twirled the fringe of a frivolous lampshade. The Mansion was filled with guests and several other boarders as well, all of them transient types privileged with some funds or some other resources, but all of them more forthcoming, of course, than Kerensky. Boarders socialized and toured the city together, but Kerensky remained in solitude and devoted himself to his writings, his revisions of unpublished articles in Russian, and his watercolours. His rooms were strewn with finished and unfinished chapters of his imaginary memoir and with his canvases of incomplete paintings of—imagine!—little kittens and bubbling brooks and holiday picnics, pastoral scenes he longed for in his shuttered rooms, although his head was filled—no one knew this for a fact but Kerensky—with other, darker visions. How could he paint what he saw or what he had seen? The streets behind the palace were swarming with fools. The Nevsky was littered with bodies. Grieving families clung to him, pulled at his arms, pursued him, and demanded apology. The lights of the Winter Palace were extinguished and he could hear betrayers and murderers sliding on their bellies across the Malachite Hall, rolling back the rugs, hunting him down.

He would gather up a little case of paints, pull his hat's brim low, and hurry from The Mansion just before dawn as the city started up its reassuring hum and the beautiful, irrelevant crowds swarmed around him. He would head to the East River, up toward Gracie Mansion (a humble government), and find his favourite bench, beside which he would set up his easel and paint. He painted the dull, grey currents of an ordinary American river into which no one else he knew had looked for relief or memory, and he could feel his own blood flowing backward, toward home, toward the Neva, still flowing beneath the ice of his last provisional day.

IN MY own memory, The Mansion is unearthly, suspended in a visible dust that held its rooms outside of time. And the rooms I came to know well each had a distinct voice. Some voices were dark murmurs that persisted in my ear, as with the downstairs parlour, its velvet curtains drawn. Other rooms, like the vast green-carpeted Music Gallery, wailed in thin siren pitches that were unnerving, as though a soprano could not release her highest note but held it through the century as guests departed and there was no one left to listen. The dining room—all locked, arched windows surrounding a glass banquet table fit for thirty diners, but with a setting for one that faced the view of a garden of stones—sounded to me like a stifled yawn. Walking from room to room, I had the eerie feeling that the voices I was hearing, these whis-

pers and wails and exhalations, were the voices of vanished boarders, guests, devotees who lingered on in the rooms even after their deaths. There was so much volume in such an empty place. The Mansion was surely haunted. Every creak and groan of the old elevator, rising from floor to desolate floor, signalled a ghostly presence. Who would be in the elevator, going to the fifth floor of locked suites and boxed memorabilia? Who would be descending to the basement to study the wines or to admire the cans of fruits and pickles and sauces? Who was playing the piano in the gallery after dinner when Mrs. Simpson had retired to her rooms and the servants, Hank and An-Mei, were bustling about in the kitchen? Somebody, or a whole host of phantoms, exercised their rights and claimed their domain.

Cynthia helped me sometimes to climb into The Mansion's dumbwaiter, and she would pull the cord that sent me from floor to floor, to listen and spy. I was a terrible spy and discovered nothing. Once, the dumbwaiter got stuck between floors, and I hung suspended in darkness, determined not to cry out to the ghosts to release me. An-Mei, pear-shaped and grey-haired, with apologetic eyes, finally brought me back to the light of the kitchen, where she scolded us gently for our mischief. But we persisted in our investigations. We scaled the crumbling stone fountain. We peered over the wall into another barren garden. We hid in a hundred different corners of The Mansion, tried them all. Cynthia's favourite spot to hide was under the piano in the Music Gallery—the white piano, near the window. We were both too frightened to approach the black grand piano at the opposite end of the room, but we waited patiently, solemnly, for an explosion of Bach, or Mozart, to mysteriously seize its keys. Sometimes, we heard a television in the study on the second floor and pressed our ears against the oak door. We recognized a familiar theme song playing on the set inside.

What was the ghost watching?

"*The Brady Bunch!*" Cynthia whispered.

We nodded in amazement.

"Who watches the TV upstairs?" Cynthia asked An-Mei one afternoon at The Mansion as we lounged in the dirty laundry piled up in Hank and An-Mei's quarters behind the kitchen. Unlike the rest of the rooms in The Mansion, these quarters were steamy, comfortable, littered with belongings and books and stacks of paper and magazines. Mobiles hung from the overhead light bulbs, lampshades tilted at angles convenient for reading, pillows were scattered all over the place—in chairs, on sofas, on the floor—and all the furniture was covered with ragged bedspreads and worn tapestries. An-Mei worked at an ironing board she kept stationed in the centre of the largest room, and she looked up, shaking her head.

"Who lives on the fifth floor then?" Cynthia demanded.

An-Mei folded a sleeve, steamed it.

"Tell us the truth, An-Mei!"

She shrugged.

"Who plays the piano then?"

An-Mei beamed. "Betty plays piano! Betty is gonna be famous."

Betty was the teenage daughter of An-Mei and Hank. She was a longhaired beauty who we heard studied piano at a prestigious city music school—the Juilliard School, maybe, or Diller-Quaile. She would flounce in on some afternoons, throw down her school books and her sheet music, shove crackers into her mouth, spit crumbs, and curse, "Goddamn homework!"

"So messy!" An-Mei scolded her. "So rude!"

"I'm an American teenager," Betty snapped, tossing her hair. "Defiant behaviour is natural."

Betty had been born after An-Mei and Hank moved from China to America and she had lived in The Mansion her whole life, wandering restlessly back and forth between the elegant maze of rooms that were Mrs. Simpson's realm and the toasty, cramped rooms behind the kitchen. I think An-Mei and Hank tried to rein Betty in, to keep her from appearing too often in the outer halls as though she owned them, but Betty was incapable of meekness. As a child, she announced, she had purposely spilled all her marbles on the marble floor of the Grand Parlour and screamed with delight as they rolled every which way, invading the corners, scattering themselves brightly until An-Mei ran after them—sixty-five loose marbles—and put them back in their place in a bucket once used for soapy water to scrub the floors. An-Mei shooed toddler Betty out of sight and locked her in the pantry. At seventeen, Betty seemed to think very poorly of both her parents—"those poor blind mice," she called them—and sometimes she would imitate An-Mei, cast her glance toward the floor with lowered head, round her shoulders, and take small, mincing steps in circles. She also thought poorly of "that mindless aristocrat," and of just about everyone and everything related to The Mansion. Betty read thick books she carried home from the public library; she despised order and disorder equally, which kept her in constant motion, rearranging objects and furniture and thoughts. She paced around Cynthia and me, sometimes trying to recruit us to more mischief with her charm, sometimes lecturing us angrily on our complicity in "Mrs. Simpson's oppressive regime." She demanded to know whose side we were on, what sort of food we preferred, what our goals were for the future, what function we thought art and politics should play in the domestic routines of a household, what tasks we were willing to attend to for ourselves and what tasks we expected others to attend to for us, and if we believed elitism was the result of education, or wealth, or influence, or the conspiracy of all three.

What could we say? Cynthia and I just wanted to collect paper clips from Hank's pocket, eat grape Kool-pops, and maybe get a glimpse of The Mansion's ghost. Aside from her beauty, Betty made no sense to us at all. Even music seemed, in her hands, a potent weapon. There was a small upright piano shoved up against a wall opposite the ironing board, and there Betty raged, her hands moving furiously over the keys. Sometimes she slammed down the lid after the crescendo of music, and the piano would shake with a discord of its own.

"Do you play the pianos in the Music Gallery?" Cynthia asked Betty.

"Are you kidding? Those pianos are just open caskets. Didn't you see all the dead music inside?"

According to Betty, souls were lost and loose as marbles in The Mansion. And we knew they conjured tricks, paced the upper floors, competed with human restlessness, watched *The Brady Bunch*, and set the cold pianos on fire with their ghostly sonatas.

WHEN DINNER was served on Fridays at The Mansion, daisies floated on the surface of the water in blue china bowls at each place, silver rings engraved with *S* held the embroidered cloth napkins, eight flames swayed in lit candelabra at the table's centre, and wide, gleaming platters of food were rolled in on carts by An-Mei in her apron. Mrs. Simpson, close to a hundred I was sure, was rolled into the dining room in her wheelchair by Hank. "How do you, how do you do, children!" Mrs. Simpson screeched, tapping on her hearing aid, and then holding out a gnarled hand for us to kiss before we took our places. She kept her hair piled high in a beehive. Cynthia, educated in the manners of The Mansion, curtsied elegantly, mouthing, "Good evening, Grandmère!" and then she introduced me, mouthing my first, middle, and last name without sound, and I too curtsied, less elegantly, and we stood side by side, while Mrs. Simpson inspected the tidiness of our school uniforms, our hair, and the laces of our oxfords. She cautioned us vehemently to keep our knee socks raised above the knee.

"I don't want any Oonas running around the place," she said, concerned that Oona O'Neill Chaplin had been enrolled at the Brearley School in 1941 before running off with Charlie. "Thirty-six years her senior! Appalling! I won't have it!" Mrs. Simpson cried. She directed Hank to keep an eye out for us, and Hank, from behind her wheelchair, answered loudly, "Yes, Mrs. Simpson," and never once said more than that in the year I shared the rituals of The Mansion. Hank seemed in private conversation only with himself, or with the elegant rooms, and in perpetual disagreement with the furniture, the rugs, and the lamps. He was never pleased, never flustered, and never anything but silent and thorough. Caught unaware as he was checking the dining table or composing an agenda in his notebook, his eyes would flash briefly, his intelligence bubbling up to his cracked lips, but he would adjust his coat hem and shrug his words away.

"The insides of Grandmère's ears are blue," Cynthia said as we sat down at the table. "Be sure to look when you can."

Mrs. Simpson presided at one end of the table, facing the long expanse of empty places. Cynthia sat at her right side, and I to her left, both of us balanced on embroidered pillows that An-Mei had slipped onto our chairs before the bell summoned us to dine. Children were not permitted to speak except when spoken to, and even then our comments had to be written down on small pads of paper beside our place setting and passed over to Mrs. Simpson, who did not read lips but would read our notes out loud with drama and delight. "'Yes I do like carrots, Grandmère.' Good! Good!" She folded the little note and put it aside. "And what about school, girls? Do you like school?"

Cynthia would look at me, nod, and it was my turn to take up a pencil and scribble back and pass my note, while she got in a few bites of food. "'School is fine. Math is hard.'

Oh dear, math is hard!" The dinner went on in this way, with Cynthia and me eating between notes, and a small stack of papers accumulating beside Mrs. Simpson's finger bowl. An-Mei showed us no signs of affection or interest as she carried each platter to us, then stood waiting on our left while we helped ourselves to potatoes, creamed meats, piping vegetables in sauce. I remember looking up at her once, helplessly, while I pursued with a spoon the last of the potatoes that rolled around the enormous platter she held for me, but she kept her eyes downcast, even when I picked the potato up with my hand and placed it as elegantly as possible onto my plate. I glanced over at Hank, who stayed beside the wall, his hands folded behind him, and I hoped that I saw assurance in his gaze. Dinner was a lonely, tiring event that demanded complete concentration as well as skill at selecting the proper fork, cleansing appropriately between courses, and remaining composed in the presence of so many beautiful plates. I thought, sometimes, of my mother as I had discovered her one afternoon in our little kitchen at home, shattering one plate after another in systematic order on the squares of our linoleum floor and sobbing. "What are you doing to all our plates, Mom?" I had asked cautiously and she had paused briefly in her work to cry, "*I broke my heirloom crystal bowl! It should have been all of these! These are nothing!*" She resumed her smashing until there was nothing left.

I wished she could see all of the crystal at The Mansion.

One evening, someone else besides Mrs. Simpson sat with us at The Mansion's dinner table—an old, boisterous priest who ate his food vigorously and wiped his mouth several times between each mouthful of food. He passed more notes to Mrs. Simpson than I could have written in an afternoon, and he told jokes to Cynthia, nudged her repeatedly with an elbow. He wanted to know what we girls did around The Mansion, how we entertained ourselves.

"We play," Cynthia said, giving him a condescending stare. She hated jokes and idle conversation.

"Ah!" He clapped his hands and gasped. "Play! Yes! The interactive possibilities are limitless! We are social creatures, aren't we? Always in pursuit of our pleasure principle, our own expressive system of survival! I envy you girls. I myself no longer play, except of course in the dispensing of spiritual advice." He winked and nudged Cynthia, who glared. We found all his talk hard to follow, especially his conversation with Mrs. Simpson, as it was part written, part spoken, part screeched, but it was the priest, I believe, who first mentioned Kerensky's name.

"I do miss that communal atmosphere, that is to say, *seeing* others," he said, "but times change, they must, and so must the social contracts. Perhaps that's best. But it was a comfort back then to know so many boarders and guests, to hear the sounds of company, even from the quiet ones, in my view. The foreigners were so polite, weren't they? The Czech? Those sweet Danish sisters? Am I the only one left living? I think I am! A remarkable feat! Should we consider Donavetsky? He keeps to himself, poor soul. And my God—forgive me!—but Kerensky! Notorious fellow. I admit he might have had a certain vigour in his youth, a certain inevitable foreign maverick appeal, for ladies, that is," the old priest concluded, wiping his mouth, then coughing. "But I suppose he had good cause to keep quiet when he pleased, didn't he? He surely did."

"What?" Mrs. Simpson shouted.

The priest reached for his notepad and began to scribble his words.

"KERENSKY WAS a Russian king, or maybe some sort of general. He was very handsome and powerful. He lived in a huge Winter Palace that all the people admired, until one winter it fell down—probably because there was so much snow—it just collapsed! And then there was a revolution or a war and everyone in the land was murdered. Then Kerensky wandered all over the world looking for someplace to live, and then he came here and fell in love with my grandmother. I think that's what happened."

"Did he die here in The Mansion?" I asked Cynthia, the keeper of secrets.

She nodded wisely. "He must've. Or else—" she breathed, "he's still here!"

We determined to find Alexander Kerensky.

That evening the elevator popped and whirred as Cynthia pushed the heavy handle and took us up through the many storeys of The Mansion to the fifth floor. There were no lights, no windows, the doors to all four suites of rooms were locked, and faced one another across the elegant hall, blankly. We tiptoed toward a particularly ornate door on the left, then knelt and pressed our faces against the floor so we might peer underneath. Death, we assumed, was everywhere—leaning up against us in the stillness, breathing down our collars, scurrying with a wayward ball of dust toward our open mouths. There was a cough. A chair scraped. We heard a footstep, a distinctly foreign footstep! We leapt to our feet and pounded on the button for the elevator that had departed, leaving us alone with the dead. Panicked, Cynthia yanked at a door that led to the servants' stairwell, and we raced down the five flights and then a sixth, toward the cheerful yellow rooms of the canning cellar, and it was there that we discovered the paintings we knew must be Kerensky's, his paintings of the Horses of the Revolution.

The horses were prancing on the walls in fabulous, glorious watercolours, one horse beside every step, rearing, snorting, and pawing the invisible earth, galloping toward some unknown victory or battle. Cynthia was breathing loudly, my heart was fluttering away in my chest, but we were silent and in awe as we studied the paintings we had stumbled on in our fear. Who had stood there brush in hand in the cellar alone, day after day, painting these fierce animals? We exchanged a glance. Some of the horses had riders, wild-eyed men in black fur and tall hats, with moustaches curling up as they yanked on the reins of their stallions. The walls were alive. Surely this was Kerensky's lonely frenzy of art hidden in a canning cellar.

MY MOTHER came for me at The Mansion after dark. I remember that she seemed always reluctant to set foot in The Mansion, although she never forbade me going there. I could not understand her reticence. Wasn't The Mansion so much better than our own tiny apartment, a fourth-floor walkup, with peeling paint and bars on all the windows? Wasn't it a relief to move through the wide spaces of The Mansion and to know that if you got bored of one room, you could choose from fifty others? Wasn't it wonderful to have meals served to you and to have a gold elevator carry you whenever you were tired, and to have bells in every room to summon company or help? After the doorbell rang announcing through the halls my mother's arrival, Cynthia and I would sit together on the marble steps in the front foyer and watch my mother pace back and forth between the glass doors and the front gate. She must have noticed us there, watching her, not running to greet her, but she pretended not to notice. She was polite to An-Mei, who opened the doors, but she would never step across the threshold onto the polished floor. "Are you ready to leave?" she would ask me routinely, and I'd say, "No," and Cynthia would put in a good word for me, suggesting that I be allowed to stay just a little longer, but my mother's thin mouth told me I wouldn't be staying and that she only tolerated Cynthia in my life because we were exceptionally difficult children and needed her tolerance.

"Have you said your goodbye to Mrs. Simpson? And thanked her?" Why did my mother look so wrong, so awkward standing there, so very out of place? She seemed to have come from a completely different world, which of course she had, and she knew it, and she drew the line clearly and literally between herself and those things she knew she would never have. I sensed then that there were things that I *could* have, places I could go that my mother could not, and the knowledge made me feel powerful and embarrassed for us both and eager to flaunt my wealth of possibility in her face. She kept her hands in her pockets; she stomped snow impatiently from her boots onto the black welcome mat; she thanked An-Mei for all her trouble and asked, "How is your daughter, An-Mei?" To which An-Mei would reply, blushing, "She's a good girl," and my mother's glad nod to An-Mei seemed to incriminate me as she pushed her own child out the door into the winter and bracing air of another world. Her world.

"The Mansion is haunted, Mother."

"Mm?"

"There's a ghost. From Russia," I told her. But my remark received only cold silence until she said, "*We're going home*" and took my hand, not looking at me at all.

KERENSKY DID not haunt The Mansion, but us. He followed us through the rooms, whispering in our ears all the secrets that bore us through our ordinary days. Cynthia and I were his only contacts in the visible world, we believed, which is why Alexander Fyodorovich Kerensky's actual appearance in the flesh on a cold, quiet day in winter was so unexpected. We might have imagined him, but I think we did not. A terrible scene had erupted shortly before we discovered him, so we assumed he had manifested because he was stirred by all the music and the shouting. Perhaps he was bothered, as we knew spirits often are, by too much noise. Or, more likely, Kerensky wanted to watch us.

Cynthia and I knelt on the floor of the Grand Parlour.

We could hear Betty shrieking in the back rooms, as if she had, indeed, seen a ghost. Then she banged wildly on the keys of her piano, creating a terrific, violent dirge. And we could hear that An-Mei was crying, pleading unintelligible words to her daughter beneath the torrent of music. Betty slammed shut the lid of the piano and screamed, "I hate this awful place! You can't tell me I'm not going! It's my first tour! You just want to keep me here because you're afraid I won't come back! You're afraid of the whole world! You're afraid of me! You want me to die without seeing anything! I'd rather die than live like this, like a parasite. Why can't you get it? Things have changed!"

Cynthia and I stood up as Betty moved past us, finally a loose marble herself, unseeing, her bulging book bag slung over her shoulder as though in it were all her most beloved possessions gathered for her final exit. An-Mei scurried along behind her daughter, wringing a dishtowel in her hands and still weeping for her good girl, her Betty. We had never seen An-Mei like this, so undone, so bereft. The scene was unbearable to watch. Betty let the iron gate slam shut in An-Mei's face, and An-Mei was left standing alone, everything changed. Cynthia and I slipped quietly up the stairs and out of sight, mortified.

Then, as we continued our ascent, we heard, over An-Mei's weeping and diminishing footsteps, the mutterings of the television. The doors to the second-floor study stood wide open. And there he was. Or, there *someone* was, an old man, slumped over in an armchair, dozing, then lifting his head, then dozing once more. Kerensky? Kerensky!

"Oh, come in, children! Little ones!" Kerensky snorted to life. He wore old leather bedroom slippers and grey woollen socks that were gathered around his ankles, and he held a tattered cardigan tightly around himself. He smiled, but he was seemingly half-blind and unable to focus precisely on us. His teeth were yellow and pointed at various angles inside his mouth, and his hair hung in a wayward lock across his cheek.

His gestures were quick and approachable, like a child's, and he pointed to the rug and said in a thick and halting English, "Have a seat, this is a good show of television, I think you must like it," so we entered the study and sat beside him.

Our new friend was all alone, he confided to us sadly, and disliked by his grown children — two boys, one an architect, the other a literary man — who had apartments of their own that they did not allow him to enter. He had no place to go; he kept to himself. He had no friends except for Mrs. Simpson, who had taken him in some time ago, and he stayed on, finding solace only in his music, his drawings, his memoirs (several volumes, he anticipated, and which were taking almost all of the energy that he had left), and in letters to friends who were no longer living but lived in his mind's eye in the homeland from which he had exiled himself so many years before. Perhaps we two children would now become his friends? How he longed for a decent conversation! He liked chocolate, *General Hospital,* his walks beside the East River on brisk fall days, though not so much in winter, which brought him pain in his heart and knees, and he liked also backgammon. Did we know backgammon? We did not, but he taught us slowly, kindly, and for hours that afternoon the three of us played tournaments of backgammon, laughing, claiming victories, shaking hands, and never speaking of the past, or of revolutions, or of the extinguished Winter Palace we knew had once been the home of all his power and greatness. There was no need to speak of that, or to remind our friend of his old sorrows. He giggled with us until dusk.

"How was it," Cynthia asked him bravely, "where you used to live?"

"Very cold," he said and we knew not to ask him anything else.

We told no one, not even An-Mei or Hank, of our new and secret alliance. We had made promises, we had made plans. We had agreed to meet Kerensky whenever we could so that he might instruct us in more elaborate strategies for backgammon. When he fell asleep smiling in his armchair as though he was pleased to have taught us so well, we had even kissed his chapped face, lovingly. Certainly we never thought that on the whim that belongs only to those who have already departed, Kerensky would suddenly vanish — as would Betty, and An-Mei, and Hank, and even, one day, my mother — without a word goodbye.

ALEXANDER FYODOROVICH Kerensky, I have read, arrived in Manhattan on a dark and bitter day of winter, February 3, 1927, ten years after the end of the Revolution, his torn ticket for the SS *Olympic* crumpled in his pocket and his breath quick as his ship approached New York Harbor. He was still a young man. Jostled along in the arriving crowds, tripping once on the steep walkway that stretched toward foreign land, he searched the waiting faces and hoped for one friend, one ally onshore. He could speak no English. He was scheduled to give a lecture — but what could he say? — to the New York community gathered at the Century Theater, and he feared how he might be translated and received. With cheers? Hisses? He spotted the faces of those who would become his friends in those exiled years and also later, when he returned to Manhattan an old blind man in his eighties. There was Vinner, a bespectacled professor of Russian at Columbia University and Vinner's broad wife, Ludmila; and the Strunksys, a couple of gregarious journalists; and, I have read, Kerensky saw one Kenneth F. Simpson, an assistant U.S. Attorney, who stood holding the hand of a tall and beautiful woman, Simpson's soon-to-be-widowed wife.

That is a different story, made of someone else's facts and fictions — a story I learned only when The Mansion had sunk into my past. But The Mansion is hardly less vivid to me now than on what I believe was the last evening I saw it and the world I believed would be mine. My mother had come for me, as usual, but perhaps she was suffering a little bit more than usual. The New York winter was long, her burden of financial responsibility was heavy, and she had taken another job that year as a receptionist, working late hours. She was beaten, tired, and in no mood for a difficult child, or to stand any more on the line between what she had and what she did not. Inspired, maybe, by her defeated look, I resisted her eagerness to get my coat and to force me from The Mansion I loved. I stood with my shoulder against Cynthia's and my feet firmly planted. I refused to go. "I'm not going with you," I told my mother. I had An-Mei, Hank, Cynthia, and a new addition to my family of cherished refugees, Kerensky. I did not speak his name. His name was in my blood. I was ready to claim my new life.

We battled it out in the parlour of The Mansion. My mother wrenched my hand out of Cynthia's. I started screaming, "*No!*" She shoved my arms through the sleeves of my coat and when I screamed louder, she shook me back and forth. "It's time to go and that's the end of it." I twisted and tried to squirm out of my coat and when I couldn't free myself, I cried, "I don't want to go! I want to stay here forever! I hate it at home! I hate you! You're hurting me!" My mother stepped away from me and gazed at me, her face suddenly blank. She didn't need to hold me to own me, that much was clear to me then. "Can you hear me?" she said. "*This is the end.*"

I gave a look to Cynthia, and to An-Mei, who turned away from me, or from all daughters, and with my mother I exited The Mansion and the gate closed permanently behind us.

I have looked for The Mansion a few times when I have been back in Manhattan for work or errands. The buildings in that part of town look plain and blank and undistinguished to me. Every gate looks both familiar and wrong — close, but not the iron gate I think I am looking for. Cynthia became a therapist somewhere in the Northwest, I have heard. Mrs. Simpson has long been dead — her obituary ran in the city papers in the early 1980s I believe, alongside a picture of her in her youth, with a wide and generous smile. An-Mei's death and Hank's I can only imagine: An-Mei nodding off as she rested beside a pile of laundry and failing to wake, and years later, Hank clutching his chest in the canning cellar and covering his mouth to stifle his own cry. And I imagine Betty too — that she heard about her parents' deaths from Toronto, or from Paris, or London, or maybe from just across town where she lived in a one-room apartment with two cats and an upright piano she never played. And the lonely foreign tenant I knew only as my friend, the ghost Alexander Fyodorovich Kerensky, one day departed The Mansion and was taken in by a forgiving son, the architect.

I would not have believed any of this as my mother and I marched away from what we both longed for, leaving our footprints in the snow. I looked around at the white world. *So many flakes.* I thought I was hearing Betty play a wild, dramatic music, the music of tirade and escape, and I saw, in my mind's eye, Kerensky's Winter Palace, its hundred spires reflecting back the moon and then toppling, pitching downward to the earth. The windows shattered, a storm of glass fell on the square, and the stones crumbled, slowly at first, and then each stone crushed the other stones beneath it and everything cascaded in dust and quaking slabs, sending up white waves of snow. The Neva River overflowed its shores, and our palace was covered by darkness.

PERSIMMONS

ROO BORSON

WE HAD been driving in the hills in a borrowed car for the day when the road took a steep downhill curve, and we entered into a small vale. Houses stood here and there closed in by trees, many of which were fruit trees and had kept their leaves longer than any I'd noticed in the hills that day, or in the city. Neither the wind nor the strong autumn light seemed able to penetrate this place, though it had rained: there were bright damp yellows and a few flaps of red against the black trunks. It couldn't have taken more than a few seconds to round the last narrow curve up and out, yet what flashed past at that moment is still with me. It was nothing more than a house, with a persimmon tree in front of it.

The tree was huge, and entirely bare of leaves, but there were still a hundred or so fruits hung like glowing lanterns from the slender boughs. Behind it stood a house of two or three storeys, a discoloured white stucco with lead-light windows which would have looked out onto the tree and the road. The tree had been regularly pruned and the small bulb garden recently attended to, yet the house gave off such a sensation of abandonment—though under what circumstances it had been abandoned, it was impossible to tell.

The gloom, the empty house, the persimmons glowing under their stretched skins though no one was there to pick them—it was an image of death for me, not of my own but of my mother's, and of the life I had always lived up until her death. It brought to mind Tanizaki's story "Arrowroot," which I'd read some years earlier. In the story, the narrator accompanies a friend upriver to his mother's ancestral village; nearby, they visit the head of a poor family whose only treasures are the possibly faked antiquities which have brought a modicum of prestige to the area over the years, among them a scroll and a fox-skin drum. The drum was the more famous of the two, and for good reason: the skins originally used to cover it were said to have come from two foxes that had once been people—or so, at least, went the story as I remembered it. In the mythology of the region, the white fox Myobu-no-shin is associated with the harvest god Inari, and can be summoned at will by those with the talent for it. Like the Lady Shizuka in the play *The Thousand Cherry Trees*—though in that case it is the presence of the drum, and his desire to be near his parents, that draws the fox Tadanobu on, and brings him into proximity with humans. As I recall it, the friend finds in the course of conversation with the villagers that his mother's father, whom some reversal of fortune no longer recorded had forced to sell his daughter into bondage in the pleasure quarters of Osaka, had once "summoned foxes." Shortly after my father's death, on an isolated sandspit along the far northwest coast, a red fox had trotted nonchalantly past, as if to mimic the Hiroshige print my father had hung on the wall of his consulting room. The story of the fox skins had been haunting me ever since my mother too had died, and the world, without my parents, had become a hollow place.

For most of my adult life, even in the midst of the busiest public market, I've had to turn away, with a ridiculous anguish, from the sight of persimmons. Two persimmon trees had grown in my mother's garden. But it was through the description of the persimmons offered by the villagers as an autumn refreshment in Tanizaki's story that I'd recognized the ones I'd eaten as a child. They too must have been of the Mino variety.

It's hardly worth describing these trees in any season other than autumn. It's against autumn's enamelled blue skies that the oval leaves begin to turn, first leathery, then increasingly brittle, as if glazed with egg-white, while beneath the polished surface a variegated gleam, almost like that of fire opals, rises. And the fruits, the dull green of young bamboo when small, grow slowly until they are of a size to sit squarely in the palm. It's at this point that they should be picked: a frosty orange colour, with the blush of powder still on them. The tree furthest from the house always set fruit earlier and bore the most, the nearer tree presumably hampered by the extra hour of shade under the gaze of the back bedroom, where my mother would sometimes nap of an afternoon, overlooking the garden.

It was my job to check the picked ones day by day, and to select and serve them to family and guests in persimmon season, but it was my mother's gardener, George, who looked after picking them. George came on Wednesdays. It was my parents' day off, and though my father would always have patients to attend to in the hospital, my mother could spend all morning with her hair undone at the dining table, idling through the newspaper. Her patients were women, and apart from the occasional call to deliver a child, most surgery, as well as regular appointments, could be scheduled for other days.

Mid-morning, George would knock on the glass door of the plant room, which was adjacent to the dining room, and my mother would rise in her kimono-sleeved dressing gown to accompany him on their weekly rounds of the garden. Together they'd lean in consultation over a bonsai, or some other to-others-invisible problem, or they'd inspect the fishpond from a distance, all the while delicately colluding, sorting out priorities for the day or the season. Despite her profession, my mother was naturally so shy as to appear aloof, and to compensate spoke in loud imperious tones. Yet here she was a gentler person, more herself. Her voice was audible, if not her words — though not once was I able to catch a hint of George's replies, which were apparently so understated that even the breeze failed to carry them for any distance. They moved as one around the garden, propelled through a world apart from us, an extra-familial world, where she relied without question on his expertise. He was originally from Japan, and perhaps didn't know English all that well to speak, or perhaps because they communicated only about such topics as they both had intimate knowledge of, little explanation was needed — as though a tendril of ivy were itself a sentence, or a flower a burst of sentient feeling. Neither old nor young, with his slight stoop, he seemed a scrupulously modest man, noiselessly moving the wooden ladder around, weeding tirelessly, tying the spent irises into knots, or twisting persimmons from overladen branches.

I was not yet twelve when, one July, playing "grass fairies" under the sprinklers, I slipped on the slick lawn. The wind knocked out of me, an ankle twisted under me, I could neither move nor breathe. The glittering veils I'd skipped through only a moment before now passed over me mechanically. The next moment the water was shut off. George appeared, looking quickly into my pained face, though we'd never so much as exchanged a word. And then my parents were there, carrying me into the house. I spent the rest of the summer in a cast up to my knee. It was about this time that I began to feel queasy about boys, and that autumn my body began to change.

Most days, standing on the ladder, George would find only a few fruits to his liking; these he could fit into the pockets of his khakis. But as the season wore on, he'd have to descend several times to empty them onto a canvas tarp. Then he'd carry them to the plant room — really an enclosed porch glassed-in on two sides — which on a sunny day had the enervating atmosphere of a hothouse. Here my mother grew orchids and staghorn ferns and bromeliads; here too the smaller garden tools were kept, shears and trowels and diggers of various sorts, adding a metallic note to the fragrance of pebbles and peat moss. At the height of persimmon season as many as nine crates might be stacked in sets of three on the plant room floor. But the fruits, which bruise easily, could only be accommodated in a single layer, necessitating much movement of crates as well as of individual fruits, which would ripen unpredictably, and therefore had to be examined each day.

At the early stages it is possible to gauge the ripeness of a persimmon by sight, but once the skin begins to turn translucent all finer judgement must rely on touch. I had taken it upon myself to remember who, among the members of my family, preferred them just "gelled" — translucent but still firm and buttery — and who liked them fully ripened, with a blowsy fragrance and clear orange-flecked water which would seep from the fruit the instant it was touched by a knife. But that fall, sent to the plant room to select dessert for a number of guests seated at the dining table, all of whom could see me through the French doors as I crouched, palpating the persimmons, I felt myself flush, and turned my back to them.

About this time too I began to go to a rarely used place to be alone. The area under the wooden staircase at the front of the house was a narrow enclosure, tall at one end, and there was a rickety door you could pull to. Hoses were stored here, and faucets could be turned on or off for watering various parts of the garden. It smelled of dirt and concrete, snails sometimes strayed in, and sunlight and shadow alternated in severe stripes cast by the slatted stairs. At a younger age I'd been afraid of this place: monstrous bees lived there, a fiction of the slatted light, reaching out their spindly arms as I and my playmates raced up the stairs and into the house. Now the damp half-darkness seemed a haven. I did nothing much — hugged my knees, or watched for spiders. It didn't occur to me until the moment the door opened that this would be one of George's places too: from here he could enter the basement to get the larger shovels or the long-handled cherry-picker, and in fact it must have been from here that he'd shut off the water when I'd slipped on the lawn. We might have exchanged a nod or a smile, glossed over our mutual startlement, but instead, instantly and somehow admirably, without a word, he backed off and shut the door.

Not long afterwards George returned to Japan. Maybe there were ailing relatives, or an opportunity for work now that the economy had recovered somewhat after the war. It could have been sheer homesickness. In any case, it took my mother some time to reconcile herself to the loss. For a few years occasional handyman-gardeners drifted in and out, having advertised their services on telephone poles around the neighbourhood. The garden languished, as did my mother's mood and bearing, one always reflecting the other. It was only when I returned home from college for a visit that I found the garden, and my mother, restored to something like their earlier state. The new gardener was from Mexico. "Whore-hey — " my mother would call after him, screwing her mouth into a hideous grimace in the conscientious attempt to pronounce his name — and so Jorge too, at his own insistence, became "George." Once he had been a high school Spanish teacher; now he was a gardener, and carver. Whistling buoyantly wherever he went, he added coriander and tomatillo to beds that had once held only irises and quince.

There comes a point in the lifetime of any garden when the garden is at its peak — and this point arrived just as my mother's life was waning. Since the death of my father she had ventured outdoors less and less, finally turning away even from the windows. She died in a long purple nightgown, the purple of a clematis that had once climbed the front of the house. She died on my father's side of the bed, where she'd been sleeping since his death.

"These nights, to get to sleep, I imagine a bullet entering the back of my head," reads the start of a diary I kept at the time. The first night I spent alone in that house it was full of such abandonment it seemed no one should try to sleep there ever again. I spent the days burning stacks of old magazines in the fireplace, carting out troves of glass jars and newspapers. But the worst part was clearing out the fridge: the bits of food she was no longer there to eat. Several dozen containers of coffee-flavoured yogurt, practically the only thing she'd been able to get down for months. Two Brown 'N' Serve sausages, by now covered in hoarfrost, at one end of a near-empty package that had very likely been there for years. I fried them up and choked them down straight from the pan, burning my mouth. And in the months that followed what hurt most were the simple things: coming across a brand of bread she would have liked, or an imported fruit she'd never be able to taste. I felt stranded here, a remnant pair of eyes and ears, awash with sights and sounds.

After she was cremated we held a simple ceremony in the garden, planting her ashes with my father's beneath the redwood trees. A week or so afterwards a hand-carved cross appeared there, and we knew who had made it. I wished George too could have stood with us once more, in the garden he helped create. The first person to disappear from one's life, having been there from at least as far back as memory is able to reach, always occupies a special place, just as a first lover does. The disappearance remains eerie, a foretaste, inexplicable. Still, in

hindsight, George's disappearance is not nearly so eerie as the fact that he had once been there: that a grown man, and one with such skills as he had, would be forced by circumstance to leave behind everything he had known—land, language, family—and to replace all of it, even his name, merely to work in my mother's garden. For "George" was of course no more his name than it was Jorge's. Once the property had been sold and my brothers had divided up the ashes and buried them elsewhere, the cross remained.

And then, years on, we came across the house in the little glade, with its tree full of ripe persimmons, and its echoes. "After three days one eats again; after three months one washes again; after a year one wears raw silk again under the garment of mourning." So Confucius is said to have said. It's only now, another two years after passing through that dark persimmon glade, that I can look on persimmons—ridiculous as it sounds—with equanimity. It seems a shame that such fruit, of which there was once such an abundance, and for free, is now to be bought only at great cost, and that the fruits are not only expensive but inferior, picked too soon, scarred by shipping. I would like to go back and look at the house in the little glade, but it isn't mine, and people may be living in it after all. Neither have I gone back to my ancestral home in all these years: though I've lost all rights to that place, I would rather not have to see others living there. I suppose it would have been no different had I ventured upriver with Tanizaki in autumn. Foxskin drums, persimmons. Either would have been shown up for what it was: overvalued, esteemed only by villagers who have no other object of their pride, and by the odd traveller or two, seeking refreshment, who discover, not entirely by accident, some deep familial connection to the place.

AN INSIDE LOOK AT DONALD WESTLAKE

ALBERT NUSSBAUM, 81332-132

ALBERT NUSSBAUM conducted the following interview with Donald Westlake (in writing) from the U.S. Penitentiary in Marion, Illinois, where he was serving a forty-year sentence. His charge: making a series of "unauthorized withdrawals" from federal banks with his partner, Bobby Wilcoxson. Once one of the FBI's Ten Most Wanted, he was captured in Buffalo, N.Y., after a 100-mile-per-hour car chase when a police K-9 unit rammed his car. As Inmate 81332-132, he published some two hundred book reviews in newspapers across the U.S. and contributed over fifty short stories and articles to a range of publications including Alfred Hitchcock's *Mystery Magazine*, *The American Scholar*, *Cinéaste*, and *Harper's Magazine*. He published as Al Nussbaum, or under any one of a half-dozen different pseudonyms. After he was paroled in the 1970s, he wrote several novels and television scripts, and conducted mystery-writing workshops at the University of Southern California. Nussbaum's introduction suggests his correspondence with Westlake was more a meeting of minds than a standard author interview. The resulting exchange was originally published in *Take One*, a Montreal-based film magazine, in May 1975.

—*Tara Quinn*

I WAS LOOKING *around for a suitable subject. Donald E. Westlake seemed like a winner. His* Help I Am Being Held Prisoner *pointed in that direction. Westlake's "hero" was a compulsive practical joker, and his most recent joke consisted of parking a car near an expressway interchange with a realistically painted naked female mannequin draped across its hood. The resultant seventeen-car pileup earned him a prison sentence.*

Fortunately (or unfortunately), some of the convicts had a private tunnel to the outside. They used it not to escape, but to go out and commit crimes for which they were sure they would never be suspected. What better base of operations could they have than a prison? Westlake's man was taken into their confidence and reluctantly joined their schemes. Sent out to commit what was his first real crime, he thought, "It is bad companions, by God: Our mothers were right." That's the kind of mind he had. Westlake had given it to him.

I knew that Westlake had written at least thirty books in the last fifteen years and that a fair percentage of them had made it to the screen. He was also the holder of one of the Mystery Writers of America's annual Edgar Awards for Best Novel. His output and accomplishment weren't because writing was "easy" for him. That's never the reason for success. More likely, he was one of those people who works his ass off. Perhaps I could coax him into writing three-fourths (or more!) of an article.

I wrote him a letter, modestly explaining that I was probably the person best qualified to interview him: "I'm in prison, and the consensus is that you should be. You have a far too devious mind to be allowed to run free."

But it was other bait he snapped at. "Yes! I am interested in becoming an overnight sensation!" he replied, and the interview was on. I told him I would begin with easy questions so he'd know what to expect, and could get used to my coldly objective style. Then I launched my first missile:

AN   Now that you have seen several of your creations transferred to film, do you subscribe to the auteur theory, or are you one of those wise-ass scribblers who refuses to acknowledge the artistic superiority and creative transcendence of the director? (Answer by mentioning two American and two foreign directors, one of whom must be French; and relate their work to the young Orson Welles and the imitative product of Peter Bogdanovich. Use more than one sentence if necessary.)

DW   I love your question. Remember the scene in *The Third Man* where Joseph Cotten, the writer of Westerns, is posing as a literary-type lecturer? He's asked a question about James Joyce. If you can find a still of Cotten's face when he's reacting to the question, you'll have my answer to you, sir. But I might have some additional things to say, so why not start a new paragraph and see?

I subscribe basically to the theory that a movie is not the book it came from, and in almost every case it shouldn't be the book it came from. I have never adapted one of my own novels to the screen. Movies are a different form, they require different solutions. A new head will see the necessary changes a lot faster. I have written three original screenplays, one of which actually became a movie — *Cops and Robbers* — and which in the movie biz is a damn good percentage. After the *C & R* screenplay was finished, I filled it out and made a novel out of it, but I have never wanted to go the other way. Screenplays are very confined, limited to the surface of things, limited in a thousand ways. A screenplay is just an outline with dialogue.

The responsibility for a movie is not as easy to define as the responsibility for a novel; I am responsible for the novel *Cops and Robbers* in a way I could never be responsible for the movie version. The auteur theory is simplism for eggheads. There are two kinds of people in the world: the dummies who think the actors make up their own lines and the sophisticates who know the director did it. In *C & R*, I am responsible for most, but not all, of the storyline; however, I wind up responsible for very, very few of the details along the way.

Let me give you one small example. In one scene in *C & R*, two mobsters are being interrogated by cops at typewriters. The emphasis was on one of the mobsters, who was being introduced as a major character; however, the other mobster and the cop interviewing him were not ordinary actors; no, sir. The cop was a real honest-to-god New York City plainclothes detective, and the guy playing the mobster was a real-life Cadillac dealer and no stranger to the bent life. They brought a choreography to that scene that I couldn't have invented and the director couldn't have invented either. And it was somebody else entirely who thought to have the mobster give his occupation as "wholesale meat," so the cop could look at him and say, "A butcher?" And I'm talking here about the secondary characters in the scene; so, in that three-minute segment, who's the auteur?

There are directors who write their own scripts, and who have a total inner vision of the movie from in front, plus the strength to make it happen the way they see it. Bergman, Fellini, probably Woody Allen. There are directors who enforce their own craziness, or determination, or whatever on other people's material (and who consistently choose the same type of material) like Hitchcock. But if I told you you were about to see a Richard Fleischer film, what would you expect to see? How about Robert Wise? William Dieterle? Norman Jewison? Tony Richardson?

No one individual is ever totally responsible for a movie. Auteur theory people, frightened by complexity, wind up singing the praises of a lot of traffic cops. The director, because he's there when the thing is being shot and is in charge of filming and editing, has a chance to be responsible to a greater extent than the screenwriter, if he has the strength and desire.

AN With all the books you've written, you must really burn up your word machine. What do you consider a good day's output?

DW I have no sensible way to define my output. *Pity Him Afterwards* was written in eleven days. The last book I did, which really should have been easier, took five months. When I was writing the books about which I will not speak, I had a set schedule of fifteen pages or five thousand words a day for ten days, at which time the book was finished no matter what the characters thought. If I work every day from the beginning of a book till the end, my production rate is probably three to five thousand words a day—unless I hit a snag, which can throw me off for a week or two. But if I work every day, I don't do anything else, because everything else involves alcohol; and I don't try to work with any drink in me, so in the last few years I've tended to work four or five days a week. But that louses up the production two ways: first in the days I don't work, and second because I do almost nothing the first day back on the job. This week, for instance, I did one or two pages Monday, five pages Tuesday, five pages Wednesday, fourteen Thursday, and three so far today.

AN When do you write?

DW During my second marriage I used to yell, "I'm sick of working one day in a row!" But you can't yell that at a girlfriend. I work afternoons and nights, with no schedule, no set time, no set output, no discipline of any kind. Sometimes it works and sometimes it doesn't. Today it didn't.

AN Your Westlake books are (except for early work) well known for their humour, and Richard Stark's Parker series is every bit as violent and kinky as the Bible. Why do you think they're popular?

DW I'll tell you a funny thing. In the early sixties, when the first Parkers came out in paperback, Richard Stark got a bunch of fan mail. (The Westlake books had gotten practically none.) And almost all of that fan mail was from inner-city urban black males. I think what they liked about Parker was that he had chosen to reject society, rather than the other way around. He was the prowling outsider, but it hadn't been forced on him. Or maybe not. The fan mail trickled out in the late sixties, by the way, and now all I get are sheriff's assistants in Nebraska telling me I got the guns wrong.

AN What was/is your problem with Godard? Don't you feel a little sheepish for causing trouble for an internationally acclaimed cinematic genius? Have you no respect for your betters? Or do you think fingers should be slapped whenever Fate or Justice decrees?

DW My problem with Godard was/is that he let himself be put in the middle. A French producer named Beauregard wrote my agent, asking to buy movie rights to a Richard Stark "Parker" novel called *The Jugger*, which happens to be the worst book I ever wrote under any name. Maybe the French version was different. Anyway, we sold it to him for $16,000, in eight monthly instalments of two grand, and one failure to pay would revert the rights to me. Meantime, Beauregard had put all his money into a movie either about a whore becoming a nun or a nun becoming a whore, I'm not sure which, and when he was finished the French government told him he couldn't (a) show it in France or (b) export it. Which didn't leave much of a market. He didn't say anything to us, ask for extensions or anything; he just disappeared after making three payments.

Time passed. A girl I know who was living in Paris wrote to say she'd seen my movie. What-what? Correspondence ensued, and here was this movie called *Made in USA*, and Godard had said in an interview in a French cinema magazine that it was based on a thriller by Richard Stark. What had happened was, Godard had been making *Two or Three Things I Know About Her*, and to help out his old friend Beauregard, who was financially strapped, Godard took my book—which he thought was Beauregard's property—and in twelve afternoons made *Made in USA*. (If you see it, you'll wonder what he did the last three afternoons.) Godard had changed things around so much that Beauregard may have figured the film could be considered an original, but he didn't tell Godard, who innocently blabbed. By the way, in *Made in USA*, Parker was played by Anna Karina. A friend of mine, referring to this and Lee Marvin (*Point Blank*) and Jim Brown (*The Split*), said, "So far, Parker has been played by a white man, a black man, and a woman. I think the character lacks definition."

Now comes the lawsuit. An intercontinental lawsuit, taking three and a half years, at which I win, hands down. Absolutely. Because Beauregard is still broke, there's no financial restitution possible, so we hold out for North American distribution rights. (We'd blocked the film's showing in the United States for just that reason.) Fine. The French court awards it to us. However, the film is partly Godard's copyright. The movie can't be shown without my permission, but it can't be shown without his permission either. And he won't sign. He isn't holding out for money or anything like that; he just doesn't like those fat American capitalists dumping on his sweet friend Beauregard.

AN   Besides *Cops and Robbers*, Elliott Kastner put together some very successful projects. In discussing the picture, you didn't characterize Kastner. Was this because you fear a slander suit? Love him like a brother and don't want to bandy his name about? Or think you may be able to swindle him again if you keep your cool?

DW   Elliott Kastner is a living legend. Seriously. When producers sit around to shoptalk they tell Elliott Kastner stories. I will tell you about him. I was here one day, at my typewriter, and the phone rang. "Hello, I'm Elliott Kastner, calling you from my office in London. I think the world is ready for another *Rififi*, and you're the man to write it. Why don't you send me a letter with an idea 'or two."

I had never written anything for the movies, not really, and I had no idea who this nut was. I asked around, and found out he had produced *Harper* among other movies, and I know Bill Goldman, who wrote the screenplay for *Harper*. I called Bill and asked him about Kastner, and he said, "Did anybody else call you like that?" "No," I said, "he's the first." "That's Elliott," Goldman said. "You're about to be hot, and he'll know it before anybody else." Goldman also told me that Elliott was not a movie producer, but that he was a packager, and that his projects got made.

In writing books, of course, what you do is more important than how often you've done it, but in writing screenplays a credit is better than no credit at all. That you've written a piece of shit that got made is one up for you; that you've written three beauties that have not been made is three down for you. If a producer gets his projects made, what more can you want from the man? So I put together a story idea and sent it to Kastner, and he phoned and said no.

Then he said an associate of his, Jerry Bick, was coming to New York, so why didn't we talk. So Jerry Bick and I met, and we talked about how New York looked worse to Bick every time he came back from London, and the idea of *Cops and Robbers* was born.

At first Michael Winner was going to direct — Winner co-produces his films, and thus Kastner wouldn't have to pay him anything in front — but Winner's prior commitments elsewhere got in the way, and Kastner scrounged around and came up with Aram Avakian, who had had a reputation for being difficult just long enough to be hungry enough not to be difficult. (I'll wait for you to work your way through that sentence. Ready? Onward.) So he got Aram on the cheapo, and meanwhile United Artists — whose pocket Elliott was picking this time — had bought *Lenny* for Dustin Hoffman, leaving the Broadway star of *Lenny*, Cliff Gorman, up for grabs. Why not get Gorman too? Since he wasn't coming with *Lenny*, he, too, was cheap, a Tony winner cheap. (Do you suppose the pyramids were made this way?) I don't know how Joe Bologna got into it, maybe it was the first time his wife let him out of the house alone. Elliott, having assembled this square-wheeled package, disappeared, returning the night of final shooting to pat everybody's back, smile nervously, and depart again.

I heard this exchange of dialogue between Elliott and another producer at dinner one night. Other producer: "You ever get that tax problem straightened out?" Kastner: "All but a hundred fifty thousand of it." I wish I could write dialogue like that.

Early in our relationship, Kastner said these two sentences to me in a row, very earnestly and seriously: "I've made seventeen pictures in six years. I've never made a picture I didn't care deeply about." St. Francis of Assisi couldn't care about seventeen pictures in six years.

One last thing about Elliott: I like him.

AN What do you want to be remembered for ten years after you're dead that you haven't achieved yet? Take your time with this one. You have a full minute to answer.

DW Several years ago David Susskind was allegedly going to buy movie rights to one of my books. It didn't work out, but in the course of it he told me he'd checked into my other movie deals, including an option that Bill Cosby had taken on *God Save the Mark*. Susskind had wanted to know why the movie hadn't been made, and when he'd questioned Cosby's business partner, the fella said, "Bill decided he only wants to make posterity pictures." Susskind told me this, and we both laughed and then I said something like, "It's tough enough writing for the people alive now."

DEPARTMENT OF STATE
WASHINGTON

In reply refer to
FG 859A.00/6-1247

September 5, 1947

CONFIDENTIAL

To: J. Edgar Hoover, Esquire,
        Director,
        Federal Bureau of Investigation.

From: Jack D. Neal,
        Chief, Division of
        Foreign Activity Correlation.

Subject: Halldor Kiljan LAXNESS

   The subject named above is a prominent Icelandic author living
in Reykjavik, who is also a leading member of the Communist Party in
Iceland. We have been informed that Mr. Laxness' book, "Independent
People," was a Book of the Month Club selection for 1946. The book
is reported to have sold some 428,000 copies from which Laxness obviously received a considerable amount of income.

   Our legation in Iceland has requested us to inform them of the
average monthly remittances Mr. Laxness has received in 1946 and thus
far in 1947 from the sale of his book in the United States through
the Book of the Month Club. This information would be extremely useful in order to find out how much support is being given to the Communist
Party in Iceland from funds originating in the United States.

   For your further information, Mr. Laxness was granted a State
Artists Award for the current year and has stated that he would in turn
give away this award as a prize for the best essay on "The Surrender
of Sovereign Rights in the Fall of 1946." The competition for this
prize will close December 31, 1947. Entries are to be submitted to
the Reverend Sigurbjorn Einarsson, Chairman of the Landvorn (Society
for the Defense of our Nation) and fellow traveller lecturer on theology
at the University of Iceland. Landvorn is an organization founded under
Communist auspicies at the time of the United States-Icelandic negotiations concerning our use of air bases in Iceland, and the obvious
purpose of the essay contest is to produce further propaganda to the
effect that Iceland has surrendered its sovereign rights in permitting
the United States to use air bases there.

RECORDED   1/00-   35273
INDEXED

YOKED IN GOWANUS

JONATHAN LETHEM

IN EACH of the three decades of my more-or-less adult life I've moved away from the neighbourhood of Gowanus in Brooklyn, where I was raised and where I kept returning. At eighteen I embarked for college in Vermont; at twenty-two I ran away to California; just now, at thirty-six, I've emigrated to Toronto. Here the question has surfaced again, as it did twice before. It's a question which comes at nervous moments, a nervous question, though often tossed-off, jocular: *Ever been mugged?* The question's asker is usually a little breathless, despite himself, wanting that confirmation or consolation for his fantasies and prejudices.

Now, New Yorkers away from New York slowly grasp how pervasive, how penetrating, a certain image of New York City life has become, one derived from television and film and a half-decade of *New Yorker* cartoons. Recall Jack Benny's famous reply to "Your money or your life?": fifteen seconds of thoughtful silence. Picture a man with a gun emerging from an alley (never mind that New York mostly hasn't alleys) to interrupt a single man or a couple on their way home from a night's entertainment, and you've pictured New York City. That's how Batman's parents lost their lives, for crying out loud, and we all know that Gotham City is actually New York. Add the name "Brooklyn" — which like "Harlem" or "Hell's Kitchen" evokes a Jimmy Cagney–Barbara Stanwyk blue-collar or ethnic underside — and you've begged the question that much harder.

My old neighbourhood is now fashionable, mostly white, and renamed: Boerum Hill. In the early seventies, though, it was a weird patchwork, middle class and welfare class, black,

Hispanic, and an early wave of gentrifying whites, housing projects and historically landmarked brownstones side by side. In the public schools I attended I was part of a tiny minority, and, well, stuff happened to me, stuff I wouldn't wish on those asking me that curious question, or anyone.

But as to that question I lacked an answer, a clear yes or no. Like my questioners, I was slave to the archetype — the grown-up, gun-brandishing bandit who'd stand toe-to-toe and ask his victims to raise their hands. I knew that that unnamed script was what they had in mind, and that it hadn't happened to me. But I couldn't say *no* either. My real experiences drifted in a hinterland of childhood and were troubled on every side by racial guilt and apprehension. The fact that these moments, the ones which I might be tempted to call mugging, had instead no clear name — or that the name they had would be meaningless to my questioner — wasn't incidental. The odd unnameability which gave these experiences such a transitory quality was an essential part of their nature.

In a recent manuscript I've been reaching for this material, from the point of view of a kid like myself:

Sixth grade. The year of the headlock, the year of the yoke, Dylan's heat-flushed cheeks wedged into one or another black kid's elbow, bookbag skidding to the gutter, pockets rapidly, easily frisked for lunch money or a bus pass. "Yoke him, man," they'd say, exhorting. He was the object, the occasion, it was irrelevant what he overheard. "Yoke the white boy. Do it, nigger."

He might be yoked low, bent over, hugged to someone's hip then spun on release like a human top, legs buckling, crossing at the ankles. Or from behind, never sure by who once the headlock popped loose and three or four guys stood around, witnesses with hard eyes, shaking their heads at the sheer dumb luck of being white. It was routine as laughter. Yoking erupted spontaneously, a joke of fear, a piece of kidding.

He was dismissed from it as from an episode of light street theater. "Nobody hurt you, man. It ain't for real. You know we was just fooling with you, right?" They'd spring away, leave him tottering, hyperventilating,

while they high-fived, more like amazed spectators than anything else. If Dylan choked or whined they were perplexed and slightly disappointed at the white boy's too-ready hysteria. Dylan didn't quite get it, hadn't learned his role. On those occasions they'd pick up his books or hat and press them on him, tuck him back together. A ghost of fondness lived in a headlock's shadow. Yoker and yokee had forged a funny secret.

You regularly promised your enemies that what you did together had no name.

And so on.

Now, I suppose my answer to the question could have been, "No, not mugged. Only yoked, but that a few dozen times at least." It's odd to think where that conversation might have led, but shame and confusion along with ordinary reticence made it impossible. The shame was at being such a routine victim of racial hazing, as though it would be a racist act to ever mention it — perhaps even retroactive confirmation that the difference between me and my tormentors did matter, a possibility I struggled against and still do. These questions are too big to take up here, as they would have been and continue to be in the circumstances when I've found myself asked the question. I'm writing a novel now in an attempt to contend with this material, and I only hope I get it right enough in the hundreds of pages the attempt demands.

Something I learned recently, though, casts a funny side-light on the question which had always stymied me. Strangely, the clue came by way of Humphrey Bogart. In Nicholas Ray's *In A Lonely Place*, Bogart is suspected of a murder by a chief of police. Bogart plays a WWII veteran who's something of a connoisseur of violence, and he takes an unseemly pleasure in taunting the police with the possibility he may be the killer. During an interrogation the cop asks Bogart if he's heard how the girl was killed — in fact she was choked, then thrown into a ravine. Bogart grins, then makes a fist and curls his arm so that his elbow is thrust forward in emphasis. "Sure," he says, "mugged."

Unmistakably, Bogart has mimed a *yoking* — the grasping of a neck in a vise of forearm and bicep. And equally unmistakably, the urban lingo of the time—1953—regards this act as synonymous with the word *mugging*.

I wasn't surprised, though, that Bogart hadn't said the word *yoked*. I'd always thought, wrongly it turned out, that yoking was a term both local to Gowanus and pretty new. It seemed specifically black because I associated it with the word *Yo* (I also associated it, weirdly, with the raw eggs which were thrown with tremendous force on Halloween, as though everything wrong with my life at that point could be summed up as *various "yo's" yoking and yolking me*). But Bogart's pantomime sent me scurrying to a reference shelf.

From the *Encyclopedia of Word and Phrase Origins*, by Robert Hendrickson (Facts on File, 1997):

> *Mugging seems first to have been New York City slang for what was called "yoking" in other parts of the country, that is, robbery committed by two*
>
> *holdup men, one clasping the victim around the neck from behind while the other ransacks his pockets. The term either derives from the "mugs" who commit such crimes or the expression on the victim's face as he is brutally yoked, which can appear as if he is mugging, grimacing, or making a funny face. The term is now well-known throughout the country. As often as not the mugger acts alone today, and mugging has become a synonym for holding someone up. The spelling "mugg" seems to be yielding to mug. The word "mug," for "a grimace" was introduced to England by gypsies and may derive from the Sanskrit word "mukka," a face.*

From the *Dictionary of American Slang*, by Robert Chapman (HarperCollins, 1995):

> *To assault and injure someone in the course of a robbery (probably from drinking mugs made to resemble grotesque human faces); the sense of the violent assault comes from mid-1800s British specialization of the term "to rob with strangulation," probably from "mug-hunter," "a thief who seeks out victims who are mugs" (easy targets).*

And from *The City in Slang: New York Life and Popular Speech*, by Irving Lewis Allen (Oxford University Press, 1993):

> *An early pugilistic sense of the verb to mug was "to strike in the face." Mug, in the nounal sense of a person's face but more proximately in the verbal sense of hitting someone in the face, is the source for the 1840s term mugging—the act of criminal assault and robbery in city streets. Mugging then originally meant the act of striking a victim in the face or mug. Thus, street criminals, sometimes working in small gangs and who robbed people with violence or with the threat of violence, came to be called muggers, regardless of exactly how they did it. An alternative technique of mugging, grasping the victim from behind and around the neck in an armlock, or sometimes using a rope or a stick, and choking him into submission, was in other cities called yoking.*

You see the irony: my hesitation to call my experience mugging concealed a divorce of the word from its origins, and a crucial one, I think. Mugging was something that happened to adults and involved a gun and was incontrovertibly crime; I'd only been yoked and had nothing to complain about or even confidently describe. A mugging you reported to Kojak or Batman; a yoking you didn't even mention to your parents. One was the city on television and in the *New Yorker* cartoons, the other the dystopian racial miasma of real experience. But, go figure, that question had an answer all along: I've never been robbed at gunpoint or punched in the face, but mugged? You bet, a few dozen times at least. It's easier than it looks.

GETTING INTO THE CABRI LAKE AREA

TIM LILBURN

I

Go to Leader and stay at the hotel across from the elevators if it's too cold to sleep on the river flat just north of the Estuary townsite. Estuary is west and north of Leader—you'll have to pass by it eventually: only five houses or so left, two last summer with trucks parked in the yard, another one, a white bungalow set off to the west, nearer the river, owned, rumour has it, by an American hunter who turns up every fall or so. Anyway the Leader hotel. It's old, smells of cigarette smoke climbing through the ceiling from the small bar below; you could read the paper through the sheets. On the weekends, they have a buffet in the evening and morning. The town is doing well; a number of people there work at the Petro-Canada plant at Burstall, a forty-five-minute drive southwest. If you arrive on a Friday night, visit the Swiss men's store owner the next morning before you set out: lots of stories and some interesting merchandise aimed at the Hutterite colonies in the area.

COME DOWN into the river valley past the old Estuary cemetery and the abandoned town: the large cement rectangle rising out of the grass with the square hole is the old safe of the Standard Bank. To the west is Bull's Head, an odd-shaped bluff facing the confluence of the Red Deer and the South Saskatchewan rivers, deep water at the base of it, good for fishing. The ferry runs irregularly; if the man is on the other side when you get there, he'll see you and come over. Turn right when you've risen out of the valley and the valley's elm thicket and follow that crooked road east into the sun—just as it bends north you might see some clouds of white dust heaving up in the distance, winds coming off a large alkaline plain. That's where you're headed, Cabri Lake. You'll have to walk from the road, a long walk, cropped land, pasture, marsh, then a stretch no one seems to be doing anything with—I saw a large coyote there last year: its head made me think at first it was a sheep. If you do manage to get into the land around the lake and talk to anyone about this, keep your directions to the place as vague as these.

2

THE ASCESIS of staying where you are: your cell will teach you everything. I don't know anything right now. The land is there and I am here and I don't know anything. I keep lifting my mind to the light and peering in: nothing. My sort of people have always been moving through—Alberta looks good these days, they say, maybe B.C.—tuned to the anarchic flux of capitalism, a little too bright, a touch off plumb, with eagerness.

3

THE ACME of speech is language that carries the knowledge of its inevitable failure inside it: the word cannot be circumscription; it cannot name; it can't even confess with accuracy. But it still loves—helplessly—the world and so walks alongside it; it says what it loves is a red, red rose, says it's a sunset, dusk over a river, and names nothing with this, misspeaks what it points at but hears and reports a moan far inside the speaker. Such language can't identify what it wishes to name but it somehow manages to achieve a greater proximity to that thing by opening a reaching emptiness in the one who uses it. This is desire's speech of course: beauty makes you lonely; beauty gives you a sweat of plans; thick, multi-layered beauty makes you homeless. You must have close to nothing for any of this to happen, though, it seems. Lyric language is a companion along this way—it doesn't know what it's saying. The highest theology, pseudo-Dionysius says, is not definitional but hymnal: praise and wait for something to take you in.

4

ANOTHER INTERESTING place to go is the sandhills around Senlac, half a day north—sleep in the truck at the regional park there, close to the Alberta border, or take a room at the Sunset Motel, fifteen dollars a night the last time I was a guest. There's a large Manitou Lake at the north end of the huge range of treed-in dunes a little south of Neilburg, strange mounds surrounding it; there's abandoned towns scattered throughout the area, Artland, Winter, lots of community pasture and dirt roads, a place that could rub away a large part of your name. Most of the pasture is contiguous; once the cows are off, you could walk, you sense, forever.

5

LANGUAGE THAT doesn't know what it's doing; desire that doesn't know where it's headed: I spend most of my time listening and hear pretty well nothing. Maybe I've run out of gas, maybe (against all odds) I'm being obedient to the last real thing I've heard. A nice place to go for breakfast is the Senlac cafe. In the beer parlour at night: oil workers and long-time drinking buddies, some just returning from a brief retirement from the booze. The Anglican church in town is definitely unused; it looks as if they might open the United church for funerals. All of the names of the streets have a British ring, Hastings, William; the cenotaph at the centre of town has a plaque for The Great War with eleven names on it.

6

THIS IS what I can tell you about Cabri Lake: a large salt flat surrounded by high brown hills. My guess, based on the size of the alkaline clouds the wind was lifting, is that it would take a day to walk from the south to the north end—likely you wouldn't find any water as you went along: grass, grass, grass, then the big salt pan, then more of the same toward the horizon. I didn't get any further than the hills to the south of the white flat; that's where I saw the coyote ambling along, tilting its nose now and then until its nostrils were parallel with the wind; it didn't see us, didn't even appear to be wary—who comes into these parts anyway?

cranberry root   water

The Glade: Four foot stone boy in
                    the brook
                 on green, grey +
                      charcoal

carrying a large snail?

KIDS: "what's in there?"
        "Wa-er" (vawe)

THE WESTERN contemplative tradition, Plato to Weil, and from even before Plato, his Odyssean, shamanic precursors, is a simple story: desire and having nothing; being scrapped down until you can see beauty; beauty itself scrapping you down. The idea is to get to positionless responsivity: utter permeability guarded by the temple dogs of collection and division: this, say the dogs, is genuine advance, that is plain cleverness. This pair comes toward you out of anamnesis, an experience of beauty so strong it makes you half crazy and gives you the strange sense that you remember now some early, perfect time when you simply *knew*. Such an experience both ruins you—you will be ever unlike—and is the way home. They will come up to you, the two dogs of discernment, friendly but not domesticated, animals out of the forest, and snuffle your hand. This in itself will be disconcerting.

BE AS available to the right sort of daemonic exigence, says John Cassian, as a bit of down is to wind: the pure state is erotic nomadism: take this position as, at least, heuristic, and let it work you down.

YOU WILL find water, though, as you approach the southern hills, a couple of ponds, a stream and a salt marsh: take the east hill side of the stream as you move north: the west shore just leads you deeper into the marsh and that sort of mud can be unforgiving. I saw a godwit in one of the ponds you pass as you come toward the marsh.

THERE IS a story that a large human effigy rests in the grass flats around the empty lake, or possibly in the surrounding hills, well hung, ecstatic; someone saw it from a small plane thirty years or so ago; there was a newspaper report I vaguely remember. Your chances of finding it on foot are about nil. Or maybe it was seen further east in the Great Sandhills; I haven't heard any mention of it in a long time.

8

TWO OTHER good places to get into are the valley of the Frenchman River, east and south of the Cypress Hills, and Rock Creek valley in the East Block of Grasslands National Park, both on the northern limit of the Missouri drainage. Go in winter if you can; you will be able to walk the river: the ice is thick enough except where beaver chew protrudes and has made a small rapids; there you'll find open water even in the coldest weather. Listen to the river and you will be able to make out these places, current gurgle, current splash against ice, or simply follow the trail animals have made, mule deer, coyote, fox: cougar, people say, are moving east along all the river valleys, tracking an explosion in the white tail population.

DON MCKAY and I came in here three or so winters ago, mid-February, and spent one day slogging through waist-deep drifts down the coulees along the valley sides, having left our snowshoes in the truck: the valley top had no more than half a foot of snow on it and we thought we could safely forget the shoes. The next day we walked east along the river, coyotes crying in sequence along one side of the valley, across the flats and up and along the other side in the afternoon. We found the odd kill site but not too much else appeared to be happening in the wide white place. When you come you can stay either at the ranchers' bar in Val Marie or the re-fitted convent on the southern edge of town. The bar in Mankota is a good place to eat if you are coming in late from the east.

IT WOULD be difficult to get into the East Block in winter; there's only a track from the gravel road and, of course, it's not ploughed; few people go there so no trail would be broken. You might make it if the snow cover is very light; close all gates after you pass through: someone is wintering cattle here and would appreciate your courtesy.

BUT IF you can't get into the East Block in winter, try late summer after the golden eagle brood has fledged on the bluff where Rock Creek bends south. Come in from the north; that's the route everyone takes, but maps show there's an entry on the west though I've never felt eager to try it. In the winter, that way wouldn't be worth the risk; people don't seem to live out there, and there simply would be no way in; you could get stuck in drifts and freeze. A sudden rain in summer would strand you in gumbo. But it might be worth a try in dry weather. Do a little shopping in Rockglen before you come down this way and plan to spend a few days. The hills around are badlands, clay with rich grassy drainage clefts;

there are antelope through here, some impressive rubbing stones. Camp anywhere.

9

BEING IN a place demands a practice: it isn't tourism or Romanticism: things aren't laid on, nor are they occultly given: here the practice is putting yourself out there and walking. There is almost always a wall of fear to pass through as you undertake an exercise like this, the temptation to turn the truck back at Rockglen or Wood Mountain, to stay not so long, to forget the whole thing. It's nervousness around being *atopos*, I think, being culpably away from others, wasting time: maybe what comes up to you won't be friendly. Push a little on it and the blockage yields somewhat. Do what you can; walk and see where it gets you. The walking, though, is not an instrument, not a means to arrive at some autochthonic accord; as you walk, you are already as there as you're going to get, though you hardly feel this: the reeling, toppling condition of always wanting is as close as anyone gets to grace.

10

THE CABRI Lake area—I think I'll go back there this spring, or maybe I'll curve up to Gronlid and Arborfield at the edge of the Pasquia Hills Wilderness, thick aspen bush on the border of the northern forest—I've been wanting to stop in at Arborfield for years. I don't know what I'm doing, and when I listen I hear nothing, my ear embedded in a blank on the band. I'll go where this not-speaking, not-hearing urges: it's a thin road but little else is on offer. Ruby Rosedale community pasture, West Montrose community pasture: walking in the fall is best when the light is exhausted, one of the last hawks circling overhead, too high for hunting, and the distance seems to drink you a bit at a time.

A MINOR MISTAKE
IN THE EVIN PRISON

REZA BARAHENI

The following is the story of one of my nights in the Evin Prison of Iran toward the end of the year 1981 or the beginning of the following year.

I STAYED IN prison most of the fall of 1981 and the first month of 1982. At first I was kept in the corridor of the Joint Committee, an old torture station of the Shah's regime that had been reactivated by the Islamic Republic of Iran. There were many women in the cells of the ward where I was being kept. So, the men were kept in the corridor, with blindfolds covering our eyes, sleeping there, having the ration of the prison as food and waiting. I stayed in this condition for twenty-two days. Then I was removed to a solitary confinement in the upper floor where the blindfold was removed for the first time. Other people were brought into this cell, mostly leftist students who had been tortured and were waiting for their destiny. After a month, I was blindfolded, taken out into a car and removed to the Evin prison. Here is the exact story of that particular night:

As usual, I sat in the interrogation room, facing the wall.

It was late in the afternoon. My share of interrogation for the day had ended. I was waiting for them to come and put the blindfold on my eyes from behind me, hold my hand and take me out, raise my arm in the corridor, put it on the shoulder of someone ahead of me, then put someone else's hand on my shoulder. Then they would lead our column down through the stairs into the big lobby of the courthouse, then out into the open, up into a minibus, and then they would drive us up the hill to our cells.

It was already dark when they came. They were working very fast. The blindfold was on my eyes in a minute. I could feel that there was someone else besides the guard. The two of us were taken into the corridor and the hand of the man at the back was placed on my shoulder. Then my arm was lifted and my hand was placed on the shoulder of the man ahead of me. I don't know how many of us were there. From downstairs, I could hear the scattered but loud voices of bullying of the guards and authorities. Sometimes from the small cleft of the blindfold pressing on my nose and cheek, I could see wheelchairs passing by with swollen, bloody feet hanging from them. I could hear whispers, sighs, and painful breathing. Then we were ordered to move, but the bustle and jostle around us was too heavy to allow us to go down the stairs. I kept gripping hard on the shoulder of the man ahead of me and felt the firm grip of the man behind me, and going down was utterly laborious. The night seemed to be different from the other nights.

Finally we were downstairs. There were so many people that I felt there were perhaps a million of them whirling around my blindfolded eyes. The hand on my shoulder shook hysterically; my own hand on the shoulder of the man ahead of me was no longer under my control. We stood there, as if there were only the three of us, with all those people jam-packed around us, jeering at us. Now, every whisper, every scream, every smell and movement had a thousand meanings. Then suddenly I felt the shaking hand on my shoulder was no longer there. We had been staying there for a long time.

There were only the two of us, connected to each other by my arm, disconnected from the rest of the world behind the thick wall of the blindfold. I could no longer hold my arm straight and the grip of my hand strong on the shoulder of the unknown man ahead of me. It dropped by the volition of its natural inertia. And I stood alone and blind in a hostile world.

Was the audience forgetting the man on the stage? Was this the last scene, where was my stick, and was the blinded Oedipus leaving the stage in utter ignominy? I don't know how long I stood there, but suddenly I heard the voice of authority: "Put your hand on the shoulder of the person ahead of you and walk!" What a relief! What a moment of bliss! I would be in my cell in less than twenty minutes. I had felt at the end of the interrogation during the day that the interrogator was convinced that I hadn't done anything that would be considered treason. And now, in a few minutes, I could sum up in my mind the pros and cons of the situation and prepare myself for the next round of the interrogation. I raised my hand briskly and put it on the

shoulder of the man ahead of me, and almost simultaneously felt the hand of the man behind me on my shoulder, and we set out and emerged in the open air. The cold weather did not hurt at all. There must be stars up in the freezing sky. If only the blindfold were removed! We were ordered to walk, and walk we did, slowly and precariously, hunched-up subhuman beings, each with the hope in mind of one day straightening his back and looking up at the sky with free, open eyes. But this is not normal! Where are the minibuses? We seem to be walking on rough ground, going up, sometimes down, feeling sometimes the craggy and dangerous earth under our feet, and still going on with the hell in our eyes. We are not supposed to say anything. There is silence and dark and sometimes the dim streaks of something like flashlights, or rather like meteorites in the sky. But these are mere guesses. I whisper before I can think:

"Where are they taking us?"

I feel a strange pressure from the hand of the man behind me on my shoulder. But I cannot stop talking:

"Where! Where are they taking us?"

Others don't speak. Sometimes I can hear the barking of a dog in the distance or the coughing of someone nearby. And then the man from behind me says:

"Don't you know?"

"I was always taken to my cell after the interrogation. We never walked to our cells. They took us in the minibus."

"We were in the court. We're being taken to be shot."

"What!"

"You mean you weren't in the court with us?"

"No! I wasn't in any court."

"I must have put my hand on the shoulder of the wrong man in the confusion. You must have done the same. There were too many people there."

I don't know what to do. My whole mind is a vegetable. I try to shout and call out to the guards. I have no voice. Cold sweat is running down all over me.

"Have they marked the soles of your feet?"

"What!"

"Have they marked the soles of your feet?"

"No!"

"They've marked the soles of our feet with a marker that we're to be shot."

"I've no such things on the soles of my feet."

"What are you waiting for? Just shout and tell them."

This time I am shouting at the top of my voice: "Guard! Brother Passdar! There's been a mistake! I wasn't in the court! Come and look at the soles of my feet!"

"Shut up, you bastard infidel!" It is the voice of the Passdar all right.

The man from behind says: "Keep screaming. Tell them to come and look at the soles of your feet."

I scream. I don't know what I am saying, but I know I am fighting for my life. I can hear my scream reflected everywhere. My hand is still on the shoulder of the man walking ahead of me.

"Take off your shoes and scream. Tell them about the soles." The man from behind me is the only one who speaks. He doesn't think of himself at all. What kind of a human being is he?

"Come and look at the soles of my feet!" I scream, trying to take off my shoe, but it is impossible with my hand on someone's shoulder and someone else's hand on my shoulder. And then, how can I show the soles of my feet to anyone in the dark?

"It's impossible! It's impossible!" I whisper.

"Do what you can to stay alive. We lost our lives, perhaps for a reason. But why should you lose yours?"

I scream, thinking that it would be an honour to die by the side of this man.

"You godless bastard! You think you can save your skin by screaming. I'll show you when I shoot you myself in ten minutes!"

"But come and look at the soles of my feet. See for yourself. I wasn't in the court. I was being interrogated by Hadji-Agha Hosseini the whole day. The interrogation isn't finished yet! Why don't you believe me?"

"Don't tire! Scream!" the man whispers.

And I scream, no matter what. And the guard swears. And we reach the final destination.

We are all panting. There are many flashlights. There are many people, speaking in whispers. Some of them ought to make the firing squad. Others are there too, perhaps as spectators, to see what would happen to them if they didn't recant by betraying their friends. They have to see the face of death to make up their mind.

"Brother Passdar, please come and take a look at the soles of my feet! You will see that I was not condemned to death."

"Shut up!" A voice louder than anything heard before reverberates in the silence.

Someone says: "I want to ask you to remove the blindfold before shooting me. I want to see the night of Tehran once more before I die."

"Shut up! That's all." There are two men crying in the distance. One of them keeps saying: "God, is this the end of my life?"

Someone walks up toward us and we are told to walk, and then we are separated. As soon as I am alone, I take off my shoes and stand barefoot, waiting.

Someone asks: "Eight or nine?"

Someone answers: "Nine."

"Take off my blindfold! It is the voice of the man who wanted to see the night of Tehran.

Someone says: "Go and remove his blindfold."

Someone walks a few yards away. I don't speak any more. Barefoot, I wait. Then I feel from behind the blindfold the hurried streaking of the flashlights. Perhaps it is not the fear of death that is so horrible. It is the waiting itself, for death. The flashlight moves closer, spreading its light on the ground. The man is taking off his shoes. I can hear that. Then someone tells him to put his shoes on. I can hear him wearing his shoes. Then it is my turn. I tell the Passdar bending before me to examine the soles of my feet to see for himself that there has been a mistake.

But he doesn't let me go on. He calls out: "Hassan, come

and take this man to the courthouse and have them mark the soles of his feet."

I put my shoes on. Someone grabs my hand and pulls me away. He keeps me blindfolded, but starts to run, making me run blindly. And we are going downhill all the while. He doesn't ask questions, but I keep telling him while I am running with him that I am innocent, and I keep thinking that this kind of running might even be an earlier death before the one by the firing squad. Scribbling something on the sole of my foot equals death. How dangerous writing can be!

The man pulling me through the craggy path doesn't say anything. How long does it take to get there? I no longer say anything. When we finally stop and get into the courthouse, my head goes dizzy and I am about to throw up. What is this? They are having soup. I remember having had that soup once when we were delayed in the interrogation room. I also remember the jokes made about the soup said to have been made by the chief cook of the Hilton Hotel who had been arrested. But I begin to shout at the top of my voice that I hadn't been to the court and I was innocent.

Hassan calls out to someone else, asking him to come with the marker and mark my foot. The man comes. The first thing he asks me is my name. I tell him my name. I can hear him going through something like a file.

"Hold him right here," he says and departs. In a minute, there is chaos in the lobby of the courthouse. They have ordered everyone to take off their shoes. Then I hear a clapping of hands. No, it is a slap on someone's face. Now, I can feel that someone is being beaten up, and there are people running, and suddenly someone is pushed up before my very nose.

"Let go of him! Take this one up!"

The grip on my wrist loosens. I would like very much to see the face of the man who is going to be taken up the craggy path. He is breathing hard. His mouth smells of the soup he has eaten. We stand only for a minute, facing each other in the dark, with the smell reaching my nostrils from his mouth. Then they depart. I stand there. A few minutes later, someone takes my hand and leads me to a corner and tells me to sit down. I sit down. I see through the cleft underneath the blindfold a half-eaten bowl of soup with an aluminum spoon in it. I can hear others eating.

The man stands by me for some time; then he says: "Eat!" I take the spoon, and when I am about to raise it to my mouth, I hear the shots, loud and clear. I put the spoon back in the bowl.

FIELDING DAWSON REMEMBERED

Fee-Fi-Fo-Fum

ROBERT CREELEY

L OTS OF people talk about being writers and some even are, but now and again there's someone who seems peculiarly destined for that function — "to tell what subsequently I saw and what heard," as W.C. Williams puts it. I've never met anyone who was more particularly determined by his or her being a writer than was Fielding Dawson. It's said that his wife, Susan Maldovan, having gone out briefly the afternoon of his death to get something or other, came back to find him sitting at his typewriter, a sheet in the carriage, about to revise a story, just sadly and irrevocably gone. *On the job* — because that was the one and only thing he finally did, far beyond any wish or choice on his own part. He *had* to. It was like his literal life.

Despite not seeing each other at all in the last few years, we nonetheless went back to Fee's time at Black Mountain, and then in the army, in the early fifties. That's when we first connected — I was living in Mallorca about to head to Black Mountain, thanks to Olson and the faculty — and, as I can now recall, Fee had sent me possible work for the fledgling *Black Mountain Review*. It was wonderful the way he wrote — a wild blend of absolutely common phrasing and language in an utterly shifting, often surreal context of statement. Stephen King is the only one who comes close to it, although he does not move with either such speed or such "heroic" proposal (which adjective I take from a Gale *Contemporary Authors* article with its quotation of an old friend of Fee's, the critic Donald Phelps: "Phelps noted that Dawson's short stories have a number of distinguishing characteristics. They are written in a heroic mode and in a style similar to that of an artist, for Dawson 'enlists the process-rhythms of painting and choreography in the rippling, guileless complexity of his typical prose.'"). Fee loved prose like Raymond Chandler's, John O'Hara's *Butterfield Eight*, and used the last (plus the movie) as base for his own terrific story of the same name, or so I now recall — the whispering voice, the obliquely echoing phone number. One might well emphasize that Fee thought of writing as a completely engaged human activity, not as a privileged or obscurely isolated "literary art." His altogether practical use of writing in his prison work of the last years is an excellent example. He took on all the possible responsibilities, representing prisoners' needs to PEN's administration and the world at large, doing weekly workshops, you name it, focusing always on the fact of *their* writing, a completely common denominator between him and them.

He could be a hard friend, call it. He used to accuse me of coming to New York for a reading and then not getting in touch. My saying I was an industrial package period on such occasions was no excuse. Why didn't I have time for him? In like sense, one blurred night in Boulder, he was telling me he'd gone that afternoon to see Ed Dorn, who had opened the door, looked at him, and then closed it. Fee felt attacked and rejected, and couldn't understand why. The next day at a Naropa panel where I was being discussed and fêted, Fielding, a participant, began to propose emphatically that I "had never known love," that I was incapable of the emotion. It was an odd and grating experience, like being roasted all too literally. So I backed off after that, and whether or not we intended it, that was, to the best of my memory, the last time we ever met.

Writers are by definition totalists. They have to make a whole world and everything in it each time they write. This was especially true for Fee. "But isn't what he writes about still out there, it's just a world he describes or refers to," I can hear someone saying. "It's not really for real?" Not only is it for real but it's often the only reality, certainly at the time of writing. Fielding Dawson went all the way into his work and lived there as specifically and articulately as any writer ever has. The "I" of his characteristic narratives is not at all a usual agency or prop. It's always *I*, Fielding, here *and* there at one and the same time.

So when Fee writes of Teddy Wilson playing piano with his son accompanying on drums, or the quick, almost gestured conversation he has with Miles Davis, you are there too. It's the only place you can be, reading. Once, Fee said that at the start of writing a story, it's when the persons in it make a move you'd not thought of—*a turn on their own* was his phrase—that's when the story really begins and you, the writer now reader, are following them too, waiting to see what can happen, what will come of it, who these people are. Even when the material is a memoir—*Tiger Lilies* is the classic instance—it is still a necessarily opening world for both reader and writer alike.

John Martin's Black Sparrow Press was for years the most consistent and inclusive publisher of Fee's work. Fee was also able to provide the art on occasion, collages for covers and the like. He might well have been just an artist, like they say, and made his mark. I loved the early drawings in particular: the great ink portrait of Charles Olson, and another wonderful drawing of an old Royal typewriter. Perhaps it means something that Black Sparrow got sold not long after Fee died.

All that's now necessarily nostalgia, but Fee wouldn't mind. He was the master of that emotion. He was also happy, as fellow writer Steve Emerson says in Fee's *Independent* (U.K.) obituary: "He was different in that he came across as happy a lot of the time, notwithstanding all kinds of things. I think of a guy with a big smile saying THAT'S TERRIFIC with stress on both words, and doing that twitchy thing with his eyes." That seems enough.

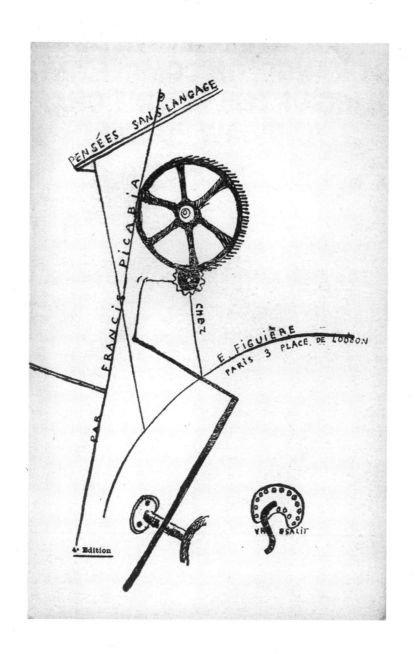

AN INTERVIEW WITH JOHN ORANGE, ON COMPLETING THE CEILING OF THE SISTINE CHAPEL, A JIGSAW PUZZLE

MICHELLE ORANGE

MO Hi Dad. Have you heard from the Spaniards yet?

JO No.

MO Nothing?

JO Nada.

MO I jumped ahead a bit there. Now, it took Michelangelo three years to complete the ceiling of the Sistine Chapel. How long did it take you to finish the jigsaw puzzle version?

JO Two and a half years.

MO What are its dimensions, now that it's done?

JO The dimensions are 272 centimetres by 96 centimetres.

MO And what's that in Yankee?

JO About three feet by ten feet.

MO How did you come into possession of such a thing?

JO [*laughs*] I was given the puzzle by my precious daughter, who was trying to drive me insane so I would commit suicide.

MO Right. Why did you decide to take it on?

JO Well, because we'd done a puzzle every Christmas for the last five or six Christmases and *we were all going to do it*.

MO I know, but how come you kept on doing it after we left?

JO Well, because it was a challenge. A nine-thousand-piece puzzle? I wanted to see if it could be done.

MO From what I remember, all we could do that Christmas was sort out the border pieces. What was your first line of attack?

JO Well, *you* started working on one end and you actually got details down, by looking at that dark blue of the stained glass, with the yellow running through it. When you got about ten square inches of it done, I was amazed that you could sort them out that way, and I decided I would work from one side to the other, because the right-hand side of the puzzle has brighter colours than the left-hand side.

MO Yes. That was a slightly controversial move, if I may say, because you finished the section that's closest to the altar first, while Michelangelo actually worked from the other end toward the altar.

JO Oh, really? I think they just took this picture for the puzzle before they were done restoring it, because the one half definitely has brighter colours than the other.

MO No, because when I saw it this year, you can see that his style evolved into much more intricate, brighter compositions as he moved across the ceiling over time.

JO Oh. Well, suffice it to say that it's easier to sort the puzzle pieces by colour when you have bright colours for one end and duller colours for the other. When I sorted the colours, it became clear that it would be easier to do the brighter side first.

MO I'm smart, right?

JO The side that was in the den.

MO When did you realize that the whole puzzle wouldn't fit on the family room floor?

JO Well, when I got into it about a month after that, I realized that you couldn't look at the whole thing at once, so I had to get each half into a more manageable space. Half in the family room and the other half down the hall in the den.

MO And when did you put the cardboard under it, from our refrigerator box?

JO At the very beginning, I cut that cardboard up.

MO Did any of your strategies progress organically?

JO What do you mean?

MO I don't know.

JO Well, by "organically" do you mean "changing strategies as I go along"?

MO I honestly don't know.

JO What I realized was that the arches containing the sibyls and prophets could actually be put in more easily than I thought they could, because they're all of a slightly different colour, and design, and the pieces of the arches would tell me what colour I needed inside that lunette. They formed the most important part, the central frame, because that holds the whole central panel; if I could get that in, then that would tell me exactly where things end and where things begin. So I spent lots of time putting in the central frame first in one half and then in the other, and once I had the central frame, that established the overall design, and once you have that…

MO So what you're saying is that the central frame is pretty much useless as far as strategies go.

JO [silence]

MO Were you on sabbatical the year I gave you the puzzle?

JO I was on sabbatical the following year.

MO And did the puzzle get extra attention during that year?

JO In a way, since I was at home, and when I got tired of doing the work I was doing, it was a way of distracting myself without having to, you know, go out.

MO Did you ever ignore the phone, doorbell, or shower when you were working?

JO No, I wouldn't say so. You're the one who ignores the phone.

MO Oh-ho! If I ignore the phone, you positively snub it.

JO Hmmm.

MO What about the puzzle reward system that developed when you were marking essays?

JO Well, that was the next year, when I had to mark essays again. Yeah, I would mark—I would say, "If I can get through these two essays, I'll give myself half an hour with the puzzle."

MO I thought it was you got to put one piece in, inconsiderate of duration.

JO Oh, well, sometimes I would say, "I'll put in one or two pieces and then go back to work." Again, it's the same kind of distraction.

MO Do you think any of your students benefited; say if you had a particularly satisfying go of it between essays, and you came back fresh, that the next student got the benefit of that?

JO Oh, I don't think so.

MO I mean, if you were really on fire, and locked a piece that you'd been looking for for months, you don't think that would bias you when you picked up the pencil again? Or maybe you'd whip through one so you could get back to the puzzle?

JO No. Well, it would affect my mood but not my marking. But I must say, it does give one a sense of satisfaction to get a couple pieces in over the course of the day.

MO More satisfaction than correcting it's/its over and over again?

JO Surely. The interesting thing about that is that at night, I trained myself to remember the pieces I had put in, or sometimes they would just occur to me—the pieces I had put in that day—and that would give me such a feeling of satisfaction that I could fall asleep at night.

MO   [*laughing pretty hard*] Would you count down the puzzle pieces, like sheep, to get to sleep?

JO   It depends on how much I did that day, but I'd go over in my mind how I found the piece and realized where it went. I'd rarely get past four or five. I could certainly reconstruct the more difficult pieces. The ones that I could remember the best were the ones that I'd been looking for for months — that would give me a real satisfaction. In fact, there were two pieces I could not find for the whole two years and I only found them when I was almost finished the puzzle.

MO   Why, did you have them in the wrong spot?

JO   No, they were just of a monochrome colour, and the shapes are all pretty much the same so I always assumed these pieces went someplace else. It never occurred to me they'd be back where I was before. Then when I found them, man, when I found them I jumped up and down and whooped and yelled and twirled —

MO   You did?

JO   Yeah.

MO   You twirled?

JO   Yes, I twirled.

MO   [*reflective pause*] Um, how many Ziploc bags were enlisted for this project?

JO   A whole package.

MO   How many bags did you have going at the height of it?

JO   Well, I didn't count but my guess would be, probably thirty-five.

MO   And what sort of a system did you come up with?

JO   It started out with colours — one bag of colours, one bag of body parts, one bag of just white pieces, browns, and then gradually the whites got divided into off-white, bright-white, yellow-white, grey-white, blue-white…

MO   Did you ever have a problem with Michelangelo's handling of the female body? I mean, did it ever confuse you, since his women tend to be built like linebackers, where you'd look at a piece and think that that big biceps belonged in the "man" bag and it would end up belonging to a woman

JO   The way they cut the puzzle you could hardly tell tha body parts were body parts, the pieces were too small. Wha struck me when I was going through it is that there are s few women in it.

MO   And aren't only the men nude?

JO   Eve is about the only nude woman in it, which surprise me — I thought there were more than that — but it turn out, when you look closely, those figures are not wome they're just…funny-shaped men.

MO   Did you get the equivalent of a Christian theology cours in studying the scenes for so long?

JO   I learned that I don't know who these people are. I don know what they're doing. I know they're sibyls but I don know why he chose to put them in there. I don't know wh he put Judith and Holofernes where they are, and Jonah. the one that says Jonah makes no sense to me. There's a fis but no whale; and Jonah's not even an old man, he look like a young man.

MO   When were the puzzle hiatus periods?

JO   I got very busy when I went back to work last year, so fo about five months I didn't work on it.

MO   What about the emotional setback you had?

JO   That was when J.B. and Nadia were coming to live her in the summer of 2000, and I was going on vacation. Th question was, would the kids and the dog upset the pu zle? And that was a real concern, so I tried to transfer th other half of the puzzle into the den so we could close th door and they could still use the family room. The puzzle i wider than the door and I turned the cardboard and it slan ed and then the whole thing just slid into itself, and half o it came apart. It took three weeks to put most of those bi sections back where they belonged, and it took me a goo two months after I got back from vacation to put the othe 150 or so pieces back in.

MO   Did you cry?

JO   No, I cursed.

MO   Did you twirl angrily?

JO   No, I cursed and I stamped and I pounded my fists on the ground.

MO   Ah. Did that help?

JO   No. It dislodged two other pieces.

MO   Was there a golden puzzling hour?

JO   When I first started in the morning, or if I'd just come to the puzzle fresh, all of a sudden pieces fell into place that I couldn't find for hours the day before. But you come to it fresh and you see things that, when your eyes tire, you don't see. There comes a point, I think, after about forty-five minutes, when you're not doing anything very productively any more and you have to stop.

MO   Was it a big moment when you connected God's finger with Adam's?

JO   The way the puzzle is made, that doesn't happen.

MO   Bastards! They deprive you of that?

JO   It's all cut in such a way that it takes four or fives pieces and then you see, "Oh, that's what that is."

MO   Do you now have a favourite scene from the chapel?

JO   Yeah, 'cause I've looked at it so long, and I took a real interest in some of it, because I didn't know what those scenes were. I guess the scene that I like the best was the picking of the apples from the tree and the banishing of Adam and Eve from the garden.

MO   Did you have any weird rituals or swearwords to get you through the tough times?

JO   I didn't find the puzzle frustrating…

MO   I wonder why I found it so frustrating.

JO   Well, you were doing it with time limits, but I didn't care how long it took me to do. I was just doing it as a hobby, and if it took me ten years that would be all right, too.

MO   How many pieces did you fear would be missing when you finished it?

JO   Oh, I thought as many as thirty pieces would be missing. I was very careful, but I figured, with nine thousand pieces…. Toward the end, the last, say, four or five days, there were so few pieces left in the box, and what seemed to be so much puzzle, that I thought, "Here I go, there's going to be a whole bunch missing." But it turned out there were only two.

MO   How did the two sections of the puzzle come together?

JO   Beautifully.

MO   But, I mean, how did you actually get them back together?

JO   Your brother and I found a way of moving the section in the den into the family room without tilting it: we plastered something against it really tight. Once I got that in, it came together so well that it was no problem at all.

MO   And how long after that did you put the final piece in?

JO   Three weeks.

MO   Were you alone when that happened?

JO   Yes.

MO   How did you celebrate?

JO   I didn't, because I'm still waiting for the other two pieces.

MO   You didn't get drunk?

JO   [scoffingly] I don't get drunk!

MO   Michelangelo probably got drunk.

JO   Ah?

MO   Okay, I'd like to take this opportunity to have you on record as saying you've only been drunk once in your life.

JO   Maybe twice.

MO   Maybe twice. When was the second time?

JO   When I was a teenager.

MO   But the main time was at Uncle Carroll's in 1971?

JO   Yeah.

MO   So you insist on this hoary legend? When you stood on the table and called Uncle Bob, whom some called Robin, "a Robbin' bastard"?

JO   Yeah.

MO   Bourbon?

JO   Apparently.

MO   Why do people call it getting "tight"? Is that just an F. Scott Fitzgerald thing?

JO   My dad used to say that too.

MO   What gets tighter? Your pants?

JO   No, I think it must come from getting tight with people.

MO   Like close-talker tight?

JO   Yeah, "those two are really tight"—drunks sort of get intimate with each other.

MO   Okay, now, how are you going to get the two missing pieces?

JO   There's an order form in the puzzle box and it tells you how to count the number of pieces up and across, and then put down what pieces you need and send it off. Which I did.

MO   To Spain.

JO   Yeah. But that was more than six weeks ago. Eight weeks ago.

MO   Will you ever forgive me for giving you the puzzle?

JO   No.

MO   What are you going to do with it now?

JO   That's the big question. I don't know what to do with it.

MO   Are you going to shellac it all together? Give it to me?

JO   I could…but there's no way of transporting it. You mean you want me to break it up in the box and give it to you?

MO   No, no! Nooooo! I just think it needs to go somewhere.

JO   What could you ever do with it?

MO   I'd put it on the wall…. Would you say you have a predilection for puzzles now?

JO   No, I did before. I've done all the puzzles I want to do because I did this one. The mother of all puzzles.

MO   Have you ever felt the urge to lie down—is it *lie* down or *lay* down?—

JO   *Lie* down.

MO   Lie down on the puzzle and roll around on it?

JO   No. I wouldn't…wreck it. It's too pretty.

MO   Did you know that…that I rolled around on it?

JO   [*laughs*]

MO   It's very smooth!

JO   [*still laughing*] Well, you dusted it anyway, that's good.

MO   So when I went to Rome this spring and visited the Sistine Chapel, I looked up and saw all those familiar toes and folds and faces, and got a case of the giggles that almost got me kicked out. You're going to go next year—what do you think your reaction will be looking at the ceiling?

JO   What interests me are how accurate these colours are; I want to see if they are as bright on the ceiling.

MO   I think you might giggle. You'll have an unexpected reaction.

JO   Yeah, I imagine.

MO   You may even twirl. Just watch out for those guards.

JO   The last time I saw it, the only time I ever saw it, it was so dark and full of soot that you couldn't make out much of anything. Adam and Eve—you couldn't see bugger all. It must be spectacular if it's like the puzzle.

MO   It is…. You used to make me feel guilty about being away from the puzzle by saying it called out my name at night. Did it?

JO   No, it kept calling *my* name.

MO   In Italian?

JO   You had abandoned it and given up on it and it mourned your loss and then moved on.

MO   Well, it did well by itself to do that.

Note: Two days after this interview was conducted, the missing puzzle pieces arrived from Spain. The fit was a little tight.

A CONVERSATION WITH GABRIELLE BUFFET-PICABIA

PAULE ANGLIM

OVER THE COURSE of her very long life, Gabrielle Buffet-Picabia was an avant-garde musician, a central cultural figure in Paris, and a member of the French Resistance. She married Francis Picabia in 1909, and the two of them, along with Marcel Duchamp, were among the founders of Dadaism. Among her numerous publications are essays on Guillaume Apollinaire, Alexander Calder, Marcel Duchamp (who, incidentally, fell madly in love with her), Arthur Cravan, and the books *Aires abstracts* and *Jean Arp*. A true revolutionary, during the Second World War she was active, with Samuel Beckett, in the Gloria network, participating in heroic "adventures," as she called them, such as ferrying microfilmed documents out of Paris.

In September 1976, Paule Anglim interviewed Mme. Buffet-Picabia, who was then in her nineties, at her home in Paris. Their conversation was conducted entirely in French and translated into English by Paule Anglim.

— *Nadia Szilvassy*

PA I understand you knew Beckett. Can you please tell me about him?

GBP Yes, I knew him very well. He was a mysterious figure. We were very close friends. And my daughter was in the Resistance with him. He worked in her network for a number of years. He participated in the Resistance in a very active fashion and had extraordinary adventures. The Gestapo caught my daughter but he was able to escape. As an Irishman I suppose he had special papers. He wasn't English, and that protected him somewhat. He and his wife hid in the centre of France, I don't remember exactly where — they tried to be forgotten by the whole world. Very prudent.

PA And of course you know his work very well.

GBP Yes, indeed, I know it very well. I don't know everything, but I know quite a bit, and all of that was of great interest to me.

PA Do you still see him from time to time?

GBP I haven't seen him for some time now. I used to see him fairly often, and I did him some favours. He is very kind; he translated an article I wrote on Apollinaire that appeared in an important American review, which no longer exists. It was a very respectable review. In any case, it appeared in America, and it was Beckett who did the translation. He found it interesting enough. Besides, he never told me anything. Essentially, he was interested only in himself. In fact, I know that he wouldn't have translated it unless he found it interesting.

PA Did you like his theatre, his plays?

GBP Well, his plays are very curious; that is perhaps what I

understand about them the most, that they are difficult to understand. The translations don't give that impression at all. My English is good enough to tell the difference between the translation and the original text. It's rather surprising and extraordinary. *Waiting for Godot* was a success that no one really understood. So it is that the paths to success can be quite unusual…. We wondered how he could attract such a diverse audience. It was a success throughout America. And so all of a sudden he became a millionaire.

PA   I like Beckett's plays very much.

GBP   I myself very much admired the person with whom he lived. Her name escapes me. She was extremely devoted to him. She did everything for him. She made all his clothes. She even made his shoes. Everything, absolutely everything. She was entirely at his command. A beautiful love, very inspiring, for sure.

PA   Did you also know Beckett's editor?

GBP   Indeed, but I did not know him very well. Beckett and I were much closer and I often went to his home for lunch. He usually did the cooking. One day I arrived a little late and his companion was quite irritated—yes, because they had made scrambled eggs and by then they were overcooked.

They didn't have much money. After all, it was the Great Depression. It was different for me, because I had connections. In time I was able to get him some work at *Reader's Digest*. Someone there, whose name I do not recall, gave him something to translate, which was extremely difficult and complex in order to test him, and they thought he did it very well, naturally. But they were not too enthusiastic about having Beckett at *Reader's Digest*. Fortunately he had other means. Fairly quickly Roger Blin, the actor, became interested in him and right away introduced him to his publisher, Les Editions de Minuit, who helped him monetarily.

And there were extraordinary adventures. When he was part of the Resistance, he had to register all the *péniches* [barges] that travelled from Paris to Marseille along the Rhône. I was in the Resistance, too, and we were always on the brink of danger. I have a rather amusing story to tell you. There were two girls in the same network as my daughter, and they had a cat. There was a courtyard in between their house and another house, and the cat jumped from one window to another. One day the window of the house next door was closed, and the cat fell and broke two paws. So do you know who took him in and took care of him? Beckett.

Later on someone sent me a message that the cat had completely recovered and could be taken back to its home. I was in the area that day and I heard the news. I was at a friend of mine's, Mary Reynolds, and Beckett's wife [Suzanne Dechevaux-Dumesnil], an extremely nice person, was also there. I told them that I was on my way home, which was toward St. Germain, and I would tell them that they could come collect their cat. Suzanne said to me, "It is not worth your taking a detour—you have the metro just a few steps away, and I myself must go home so I will go by there."

When she entered the apartment building of these two girls, the concierge seemed timid but told her that the girls were home. As she approached the apartment, she found that the Gestapo were there. The girls had been arrested and the Gestapo were staying there to catch anyone who might come in. There was someone at the concierge who was observing everything that the concierge would say. All of this was very dangerous indeed, but Suzanne did not lose her head. The Gestapo asked her, "Why do you come here, miss? Do you know these ladies?" "No, I do not know them, but I am coming here because of their cat. It was at my house and we were caring for it, and now it is recovered and I came to tell them that they could pick up their cat." One of the officers said, "Well, then let us go see the cat." His car was downstairs.

Fortunately there was a cat, but what was much more serious was that all of the records and documents regarding the *péniches* were in a book on the table. They did not pay attention to them. The officer looked at a book now and then, but not at the book on the table. The cat was there and the explanation was good. And then Suzanne said, "I must go to the station to pick up my mother." "Then we will take you to the station," because they were thinking she was going to meet someone other than her mother. She was indeed meeting her mother. So everything was in order and the officer had not noticed what was on the table since it was all pell-mell and couldn't be dangerous. It appeared that the officer was from Wehrmacht, and he said, "Miss, I am very happy that we did not find anything at your home." So there it is, she came back to Mary Reynolds's, and there she found herself very faint. She had been able to hold firm until the last minute.

PA   Let me hear a little about your experience in America at the time of Stieglitz and all that.

GBP   The first time I was very charmed, enchanted even, and perhaps not in the same fashion as they would have wanted me to be enchanted. I was enchanted first of all by the extraordinary welcome of the people. There were no complications of etiquette or proper introductions as there are in France. We are not very hospitable in France; at that time especially we did not like foreigners. We did not like the Americans. But in the United States we were received as friends. Everything was easy.

PA   What was the date of your first visit?

GBP   In 1913 we came to New York for the Armory Show. Picabia had been invited to show many paintings. At first we hesitated because it was such a long trip at the time. We had an extraordinarily difficult crossing. It was in an almost historical storm. But the boat held firm. We met another boat, one of the large boats from the Cunard, the large English company. Our boat's name was *La Lorraine*. It was a luxury ship, but we had taken the third class.

PA   Who were the first people you met in America?

GBP   I had an amusing encounter on the boat immediately as we were arriving in the port. There were journalists who asked me, "Mme. Picabia, what do you think of American women?" "I don't know them yet. Wait until I meet them and then I will tell you." It was a rather strange entry to America. I spoke very little English at the time.

Immediately we went to a French hotel, where we were very warmly greeted. It was not a brilliant hotel, the service was not so good, but there was extraordinary activity and lots of people everywhere. There was a very good restaurant, and there was an extreme cordiality among everyone there. No sooner had we entered our hotel room than there was a telephone call asking for Mr. Picabia! But as Francis did not speak a word of English — he did not want to speak English — it was I who answered the call. They asked when they could come do an interview. There were telephone calls like this all the time, and what amazed me especially was the ease with which everyone knew what was going on while we didn't know anyone.

When we arrived at the Armory Show, it was at night. All the women were in extravagant costume, and what a crowd! It was at the base of a cavernous space. All of the walls were covered with paintings, at least twelve hundred paintings. They had hung Marcel and Picabia's paintings next to each other. These were set back in a small theatre-like space. This was the corner of the revolutionaries. A director came onto the balcony, where he spoke about the history of the exhibition, saying, "Here we are. We have quite some paintings, this all cost us a lot of money. And now, have a look and educate yourselves." So then there was a sort of procession around this large hall, everyone making their way around, and then they would stop

in front of Duchamp and Picabia. Duchamp had this one painting *Le Nu descendant l'escalier*. That provided quite an important reception for him in the paper. He had even more success than Picabia.

PA   Your first stay, how long did it last?

GBP   We had left for fifteen days, and we stayed almost six months.

PA   When did you meet Stieglitz?

GBP   The same week that we arrived we received a visit from a charming French man named Haviland. He was a representative of the large Limoges porcelain company. This charming young man was very well informed about painting and art in general. The first thing he did was take us to Stieglitz because he was part of Stieglitz's trusted circle. Stieglitz had a small gallery. It was an apartment with many small rooms, and it is there that he received

everyone and that he created such a reputation. There was de Zayas, another very good draftsman, and Haviland, and connecting all of this was a certain Mrs. Meyer, a very tall and beautiful American with lovely legs, an extraordinary allure, and a great cordiality. And she was also very wealthy. At that time she was the owner of a lovely estate in the country where we were invited. These people whom we hardly knew received us as if we were old friends. Stieglitz had a very important presence and influence. He was born in America, but he had studied in Europe and he was of Austrian origin. His Austrian school was the school of revolutionary painting and ideas, and all of this had significant ramifications for him. At that time Austria was in an extraordinary époque.

PA   Did you know his wife? And O'Keeffe?

GBP   I knew his wife, and I also knew O'Keeffe very well. She is still living. O'Keeffe was fairly particular and fairly difficult. But we still exchange messages now and again through friends who come here.

PA   Did you like her painting?

GBP   She had talent and a certain personality. It was difficult to have a personality at that time. But I felt sorry for poor Mrs. Stieglitz; she was not the wife that Stieglitz should have had. But that's how life is, isn't it?

PA   And John Marin, you knew him?

GBP   Yes, he had very little to do with us from the point of view of painting. You see, he wasn't at all avant-garde, but he was very nice. And whom else did I know? An Italian, a tall, good man, and he was sweet as anything.

PA   An Italian by birth?

GBP   Yes, he was in New York and was quite frequently at Stieglitz's. He was not specifically avant-garde but was quite interested by all of the figures of the avant-garde.

PA   So all this was during your first visit in 1913?

GBP   Yes. There is a little anecdote not very often talked about, but it is quite amusing. Among the people who interviewed the important painters there was an editor of one of the main newspapers whose name I don't recall, but it was one of the big ones, and he suggested that we visit his newspaper. This amused me greatly and I accepted his invitation. We entered a large room with piles of drawers. It was the room of the archives. He pulled out one of the drawers and showed me a photograph of myself with Picabia. It was quite fantastic because the photograph was from before we were married and we were completely sure that no one knew we were together at that time. It is quite amusing, isn't it; all of a sudden to find a photograph, while we were thinking that our being together was a secret and that no one could have observed us. But thinking back, we recalled seeing such a journalist. This photograph had been taken at Cassis on the Midi Canal where we were living clandestinely. No one in our family knew, but there was a journalist who came and took a photo because Picabia of course was very well known.

PA   I would also like to speak with you about Calder…didn't you review his first show in Paris?

GBP   Yes. That is the root of an old friendship with Calder. As it happens, I was enormously interested in all of these inventions, things that were so new, and an anti-painting invention is something that interests me because I don't like painting. Everyone laughs when I say this, but it is the truth. I did not like painting. I always hated museums and everything seductive, which is the point of the anti-painting, the anti-classical. When I first met Picabia, then later on with other friends, and with Marcel Duchamp, who was a great friend of Picabia and mine, we created an anti-painting movement, which became more important and which incorporated more and more friends. I was very privileged to be among the group of the first anti-painters, whose careers I followed very closely. I always had the impression that it was they who had discovered it all,

and that makes it become less and less personal, less and less interesting, in reality. In my opinion, the lessons of the machine are now part of society; everyone is making machines.

PA   Did you see the show *Machines Célibataires*? I myself did not see it. When I arrived it had already closed.

GBP   Is it already finished? No, I did not see it but I know very well the background of the *Machines Célibataires* and especially the story of Marcel Duchamp's *Large Glass*. I saw him do it.

PA   Would you speak to me a bit about this? And how it related to your trip in the Jura.

GBP   This trip in the Jura took on great importance. I am from the mountains myself and was very out of touch with everything that is official in the world of art. I was enormously interested in music in particular, but after I married Picabia there was no question that I could be interested in anything besides what Picabia was doing. But naturally I always remained in contact with music.

Later on, [the composer] Edgar Varèse found us in America. Varèse would always talk about extraordinary things that took place—when he was in France, when he was in Germany—but in the end really nothing had happened. Varèse was very schizophrenic, completely off-centre, but he was a rather amazing personality. He would start to work, then he could not. He would write a line and everything was over, he could not go any further. I was very close to him, to this type of personality, this difficulty of concentration, which created a barrier that separated him from realizing his work. At the same time he was very intelligent, very intriguing, and he used his intrigue to give the impression that he was a great genius and that no one around him could produce anything.

When he arrived in the United States, I was not at all happy to see him because he arrived with the idea that we could help him. If he had not had such a good relationship with Picabia, I would never have seen him. But he and Picabia used to have a great time, going out every night, going to all the bars in New York. They never stopped making puns and they used to amuse each other enormously. One night they came back to their hotel and they still had a lot of energy left, so they started to wrestle and Francis broke his wrist. It was not very serious, fortunately. And he was also very lucky another time. One day, while walking on Fifth Avenue, there was a taxi that was out of control, that went up onto the sidewalk and crushed his feet. That brought him a lot of money, and then he had to be cared for in the hospital. There were a lot of people around then, and Varèse was beginning to tell stories. Really it's quite interesting, the ease with which he told stories about things that he had never really experienced. But there was always some element of truth, just enough to keep you listening.

PA   Perhaps we could speak about your first meeting with Calder?

GBP   Well, the first meeting was completely by chance, in a small gallery directed by a fairly well-known figure, politically, Mme. Cetobu. She had quite a bit of money and amused herself with this gallery. She was very interested in all that was new, and it was she who discovered Calder and launched his career. And so I entered this very small gallery, and saw these boxes of large toys and under them some apparatus of wires, bits of wood, bits of wire; these sorry things, really contrary to all that is precious, all sorts of eclectic materials. There was also a small scenario for each of the objects, the boxes, the strings. And there was movement among the interlacing of the strings. A white ball and a black ball. Everything was in movement. It was very amusing, like an invention from toys. This was a very interesting investigation. The plastic arts set in motion, that is to say an investigation with rather pathetic materials which all of a sudden became characters—this was very significant. Calder played with the way movement occurred, the way things shifted. Essentially, this was more complex than anyone thought—being strictly contemporary. It was a way of explaining movement with things, in an environment that shouldn't be in motion. So Calder tried to explain movement—he found small motors that actuated these objects. It was quite curious.

At one point he left for America, and he left his studio with my children. At the time my son was quite young and had a passion for research. One day he brought all of the toys from Calder's studio and he locked himself up with these objects. When Calder came back he found all of these little toys broken, all of the apparatuses broken. So I ran to the electrician to see what could be done. The electrician did something and everything started working. However, we spent an uneasy time at the Calders's.

PA   Did they know each other, Calder and Duchamp?

GBP   No, they actually didn't like each other very much. That is to say, they both had an enormous audience, but it wasn't the same audience. They didn't have an enormous sympathy for each other, but they were good-enough friends. However, Marcel liked Louisa Calder very much. Louisa was very charming, and always has been. She was more demanding than she is now, but that didn't prevent her from having the same grace and hospitality. She is very generous. But in this small gallery I saw astonishing things, for me, everything was new. It was in 1932, I believe, that I wrote an article on his work.

And when I knew Calder, he was having great success in Paris with his "Circus." He was magnificent, the way he spoke French and how he himself was part of the circus—you couldn't really separate the two. His was a very sophisticated success, in the art world and in certain social circles. It was very fashionable to see the *Cirque Calder* (I didn't see it until much later). Calder made important things insofar as he was an engineer, that is to say he made his caricatures with such precision. He had such a good sense for forms and articulations; the mobiles in his circus were ingenious. It was necessary that he work with his materials until they were no longer so precious, so shiny. To make art with no matter what…the essence of artistic creation.

PA   But Duchamp felt the same way about materials, didn't he? Isn't it true that he wasn't partial to any material?

GBP   Quite the contrary; he wanted only undesirable materials, common, like the things that he chose for his ready-mades—like a bottle holder made from iron wires. That's something that Calder shared as well—he produced everything with iron and iron wire. He was called the king of iron wire. In his circus, everything was made from iron wire—there is a magnificent piece made from a long, serpentine piece of iron.

PA   Yes, his Josephine Baker in the circus is just marvellous.

GBP   When I met Marcel, he was a fine draftsman, but he was very much influenced by his brothers. His family was quite provincial and they had very particular values, while he on the other hand had the air of being a very sophisticated young man. I knew his brothers, Jacques Villon, who was a painter, and Raymond Duchamp-Villon, who had done sculpture but abandoned it. This was at the very beginning of Raymond's evolution. It seemed that he could have taken it up again and would have been able to develop quite a bit, but he died quite young, during the war in 1914. It's really a shame. When Marcel came upon Picabia, it was a remarkable meeting for the both of them. They really helped each other out of a rut, though Picabia was much further along than Marcel. Marcel inherited many of his brothers' talents as far as painting is concerned, but what distinguished him is that his mind was open to all of the evolutions, the revolutions. Picabia had been making a rather successful career as an impressionist, but one day he decided to abandon all of that, and it was quite a drama. He became estranged from many of the dealers. All of a sudden we found ourselves with a large number of his paintings. Picabia didn't want to work any more. He didn't want to do anything. He put everything up in a hall where everything was sold for a very low price. He wasn't so much of a businessman, but he really made a lot of money. He had thus done away with it all, all of the sordid details and intrigues with the dealers.

PA   Yes, I know the circuit well.

GBP   And so, what was remarkable about Picabia was his imagination, an insatiable imagination. He had been greatly influenced by his grandfather, who was a good friend of Daguerre, who had invented photography. Anyhow, Francis's grandfather told him, "It's stupid for you to be painting. In a few years, painting will be done with. It's been done, they've copied nature, but no one has copied the forms that exist in the mind." Immediately this meant something for him. He had lost his popularity, that is for sure. No one understood anything; everyone was against Picabia — all of the newspapers that had generally been supportive no longer had any compliments. All of a sudden, they became enemies; it was quite crazy. And naturally, I found it amusing, this change that occurred among the journalists. Very curious. But in truth, with Picabia, his creative force cannot be analyzed. He didn't have a rational, analytical mind like Marcel, for example. It was something very spontaneous, a type of power, a force of creation. But of course there were difficult times…the dealers were quite cruel with him.

However, the youth were interested in the general evolution; after all, this evolution was an everyday problem, for everyone, concerning the way of living, concerning how one is amorous. Moral principles were being completely overturned, and it was the beginning of the complete liberty that we enjoy today. It's not always perfect, that's certain, but it's still quite extraordinary if we consider that in the Middle Ages when a woman cheated on her husband, one had the right to take her life. I myself was born a revolutionary, into one of the strictest families that you could imagine, with values of the old nobility. I left — it was really madness.

PA You had told me a bit about Sophie Taeuber-Arp.

GBP Indeed, she was a great artist. And she immediately joined the revolutionary spirit of the epoch. I'd like to say something about this: one doesn't seem to realize that when we speak about these particular figures and all that is interesting about them, in actuality this evolution of painting was a revolution that came simply from the general evolution of the world. The young people don't seem to realize that only a hundred years ago there was no electricity, telephone, or material things; it was a completely different life and moral principles remained

very important. There was an evolution of painting which took place and it occurred in all the states of mind and life…at the same time the manner of thinking, the manner of feeling, and the manner of living all transformed along with the transformations of science. The evolution of painting is integrated with evolution in general. This is all part of the evolution of the mind, the evolution of values, and the evolution of politics in general.

And there was one thing that really had a huge influence on painting, and that is photography. Painters didn't like to hear you say that, but it's true. Photography surpassed painting in one of its reasons for being, that is to say, for the purpose of recording certain aspects of life, recording events…in that sense painting became something of history; but the advancement of photography brought about the television, and then the tradition of painting battle scenes and important figures changed completely. Essentially, painting no longer had a reason to exist. The art of painting took refuge in the spirit. This is especially meaningful for the visual arts. One doesn't often think about it, but it's something that I insist on enormously. This way of being for influential figures is simply the idea, the evolution of life itself.

PA Was their way of being influenced by the epoch or was it they who influenced the epoch?

GBP No, neither one or the other. They were all influenced by the epoch; it could not be otherwise; they were influenced by light, by communication, by the rapidity of occurrences.

PA You spoke briefly about Sophie Taeuber-Arp. She had a mind that has always interested me profoundly, both as a companion to Arp and as an individual.

GBP Yes, as a companion she had a great influence. She was very much her own person, so detached from the painting of the time; that is, in the nineteenth century where the painters were extremely skilled, but not really of very much interest. For example, there was a painter named Ziam who painted only views of Venice. He was very skilled but not really of very much interest. He depicted Venice at five o'clock in the morning, at ten o'clock in the morning, and at four o'clock in the afternoon. However, this articulation was much more commercial than artistic. It was for people who could not travel because it was too expensive at the time; they could have an idea of Venice, they could dream of this town. I find that completely idiotic. I have never had any interest for this kind of painting that depicted laces and very elaborate dresses. Sophie Taeuber-Arp was outside all of this. She understood that there were investigations and visual forms besides the depiction of nature. It was a spiritual investigation, just as much as vision, that one saw. She surpassed mere copies of nature; for her it was all instinctive and pure. She searched. She was interested in the lines of useless forms, forms that weren't representational but instead imaginary forms. She met the Dadaists, Arp among others, who were about to disrupt all of the theories on painting and vision. So she was immediately attracted to all of this, and there she developed and began to do these very remarkable watercolours, remarkable for the time and for herself especially. It was within herself that she had these desires — to give more visual freedom, and that had nothing to do with utilitarianism.

PA   She had quite an influence on Arp, didn't she?

GBP   Arp had a magnificent imagination, in my opinion. I admire more his poetic gift than his sculptures; but it was with his sculptures that he made quite a bit of money. Yes, he was a delicious person, a delightful person. I met him in Ascona, I spent a day at his home, and at that time, Marguerite Hagenbach was there. She was very much in love with him and she had a lot of money. Neither Sophie nor Arp had any money, and Sophie had

no sense to push herself to the forefront or to bring her husband forward, so it was Marguerite who arranged the household. She tried, however, to destroy Sophie's influence, but Sophie had already been taken by Dadaism. This was in 1916, in Zurich, and this was very significant I feel. Dada was born during the war. It was a revolution against the war, this absurd war, this imbecilic massacre. A society planning to sacrifice the best of its youth for a goal that had no good reason to exist. Surely this was a youth that was sacrificed like some toy. That is what is most ridiculous.

PA   Could we speak about Margaret Anderson?

GBP   Listen, I don't have anything important to say about her. Naturally, she had the courage to defend many works that seemed very immoral for the time, such as Joyce. Were you aware that she had been imprisoned? It is she who publicized Joyce, who had been refused by the censors.

PA   We spoke of Duchamp, and of *L'Archange aux Pieds Forchus.*

GBP   No, let us not speak about that. It could be misinterpreted.

PA   Did you know Herbert Read, the English critic?

GBP   Yes, very well. I met him in London during the Resistance. At one point the Gestapo located me, but I was able to escape by another route, and then I left for England. I crossed the Pyrenees with the officials of the Char and then I arrived at Gibraltar. It was interesting. It was the moment of the great campaign in Italy, and at the time one could not risk crossing by boat. I recounted this to Calder when talking about his plane [the *Braniff Airlines Plane*, 1975]. I said, "What is your plane when you consider that I saw the whole English fleet completely camouflaged." What an extraordinary memory, all of these boats covered up, completely brown and red, remarkable. I have never seen an exhibition quite so interesting as that.

AU HASARD SUICIDE

FANNY HOWE

I have always had a weakness for donkeys.
—Robert Bresson

Two years ago I completed a series of short novels that I had begun thirty years before.
These books were failures on the marketplace, so in fact their fates mimicked the fates of their subjects.

I can't say that they were experiments but chops and grabs at moments in time, attempts at discovering emotional sequence—that is, the rhythm that flows between the arrival of a moment and its disappearance. They were like notes for another genre.

Because of the accidents of when and where I grew up, some of the first movies I saw were made by Bergman, Visconti, Rossellini, Fellini, and the French New Wave. Janus Films were premiered at the Brattle Theatre in Cambridge. They were all foreign and subtitled.
Black and white and speckled with stars and radiant dust.

They were the remnants of the War, barely separable from the news that was broadcast in movie theatres along with the main feature, and the cartoons.
The blurry subtitles, white on white, oddly selected from the conversation taking place on screen, would come to me as a kind of poetry, scraps fallen from the divine table of babbling tongues.

These half-understood movies were the model of a contemporary fiction because the future inherent in my own stories was always at night.

Weirdly I didn't realize this. Instead I relentlessly pursued a written fiction that had as its model something foreign, half-expressed, and highly visual, without ever asking: Is this an outline for something else?

My novels were failures undoubtedly because they were not novels. Airy and incomplete, they were like people dying on purpose but full of doubt.

Years before I had read two books, *Film Form* and *The Film Sense*, by Sergei Eisenstein, and these helped me legitimize the process I was already engaged in. In his chapter on montage he determined that the tonality of a work is established by a rhythmic relationship between its segments.

He noted that in music the distance of separation between intervals can be so great that it leads to a collapse inside the organic body of sound. However, its irregularity usually becomes its dynamism. Like a healthy human heartbeat, which has an intrinsic irregular system, the body of an artwork gets its vitality from a rhythm based in uncertainty. (Sick hearts have a dull regular thump.)

Eisenstein believed that there is a social mission for artists — that is, the purpose of any work is to "make manifest the contradictions of Being" and this way to harmonize them, if only temporarily, in the single mind of the viewer/reader.

His notes on juxtaposition and composition reassured me, because I was working already out of the very far and very near. I was aware of the galactic loneliness that lay outside the circle of my stories and the strange nature of choice in the construction of a narrative. I used to spread the final draft, sheet by sheet, on floors all over the house and move them around. This way an eruption of action became a self-contained section. But of course the floors and the air were bigger than all those papers.

Conventional (and wonderful) narrative that knows where it is going is like a farmer setting out for the daily tread. It is a form of lifting and carrying to a pre-determined destination.

My kind of story always had an uncertain goal, and it discovered itself only by shedding what it already knew. It ran without memory, recklessly monitored by chance influences. No one learned from experience.

In this sense each book was seeking a state of innocence, a capitulation to freedom.

———

Suicide is usually a reaction to one's own idea of a future. A person can be crushed by a self-made vision of oncoming fate. A night without gravity. Rather than running and shedding the present in a state of blind hope, you falter and feel the rest coming at you. Suicide is the answer to one question; religion the answer to many. In the fifties existentialism put suicide as the only logical outcome of a life of pure freedom. Suicide for Catholics remained a renunciation of hope; it was a collapse into despair. It was triggered by the separation from divine love.

The novelist Georges Bernanos wrote, "People generally think that suicide is an act like any other, the last link in a chain of reflections, or at least of mental images, the conclusion of a supreme debate between the instinct to live and another, more mysterious instinct of renouncement and refusal. But it is not like that. Apart from certain abnormal exceptions, suicide is an inexplicable and frighteningly sudden event, rather like that kind of rapid chemical decomposition which currently fashionable science can only explain with absurd or contradictory hypotheses."

One is seized by suicide as one is seized by love. The Prince of the World prepares you for this collapse in small doses. Back-turning, bad luck, poverty, illness, verbal cruelty, changes of heart, betrayal, slander: all of these are anti-love. Suicide is less common during times of revolution because there is a surge of hope for a better future. Suicide is a surge of unhope.

It is more common to commit suicide when you are abandoned by your lover than when your lover dies.

The barn door creaks on its hinges. A prolonged rasping like the one you hear in working machinery. It is as if the use it is being put to is giving it a taste of suffering.

The depressive sound of a buzz saw or an electric lawnmower.
A refrigerator groaning at night.
Or something like the bare winter trees forming a syntax that looks like new sheet music.

It isn't a barn door creaking after all. It is a donkey's mechanistic bray.
Then the donkey comes out into the light and stands aside while the children play nearby.
And this is the beginning of *Au Hasard, Balthazar.*

About this film the director Robert Bresson remarked in an interview, "It is the life of a donkey going through the same steps that you find in a human life — infancy with its caresses, maturity, work, talent, the donkey who is put in a circus and then some time before dying has a dreamy period, and then he does die from the weight of human sins, having transported the gold all the way to the final frontier."

Au Hasard, Balthazar was one of Bresson's last two black-and-white films (the other was *Mouchette*). A luminous pallor surges out of the screen, spreads over every face and form in the picture; it is the colour of consciousness. The subtitles are ghostly and easily submerged in the background light.
Squalor bleeds into this whiteness. Blends.

The plot follows an erratic lifeline until it is swallowed in bells and pale sheep.

(Bresson chose the name Balthazar because of the way it rhymed with *au hasard*. And in French *au hasard* is a phrase that means more than "by chance"; it suggests a kind of errancy, a path formed and interrupted according to external influences. Certain people, like animals, live *au hasard*. They can't learn from experience because experience for them never repeats itself exactly.)
Balthazar and *Mouchette* were made in the days when the poverty of resources in filmmaking were complicit in the stories of human poverty and petty crime. There was no separation between equipment and intent.

The sudden shifts in scene, the unschooled acting, and the engagement in a religious view that carries consent to its last point replicate the donkey's experience.

That is, the whole movie—its message, its method, its tools—functions as a whole instrument. The donkey is the hero. He is the film. He seems as blind as chance. Only once is there a scene where the donkey is put in a circus to perform with other long-suffering animals and there is an unblinking exchange of glances among them.

Otherwise the film is at the end what it was at the beginning—image without illusion.

Mouchette was made immediately after *Au Hasard, Balthazar*, before Bresson used colour, and it was the first of his movies that end in suicide. The tale shimmers and leaps into the wasteland of space. No more chances or choices are possible for the writer or the character. The novel, *La Nouvelle Histoire de Mouchette*, was written by Georges Bernanos, who also wrote *The Diary of a Country Priest*, which Bresson turned into a movie.

Georges Bernanos wrote his major fiction during twelve years of an intensely thoughtful and politically active life. He was a monarchist, served in the military, and then worked for an insurance company. His royalist beliefs collapsed in the late 1920s and he denounced Franco, appeasement in Munich, France's armistice with Germany, and the French middle class. He was embraced by both the extreme left and the extreme right, as many Catholics are.

Fourteen-year-old Mouchette (little fly) is a social reject among beaten-down peasants. Her parents are alcoholics; the whole town drinks gin. She is a sullen schoolgirl who has had little or no love in her life. She wears dirty clothes and has a bad attitude. Her mother dies, leaving behind an infant who is screaming with hunger. Mouchette hides in the raining woods and is taken home by an alcoholic, epileptic poacher. In the novel she has had her eye on him for some time, aware of his degradation as a revolt against the convention and cruelty of their town. He has an epileptic seizure in the shack, she comforts him, he violates her, she assents, and off he goes, in a state of paranoia about a crime he didn't commit, to the next town. When asked by the authorities what her relationship to him was,

Mouchette replies, "He is my lover."

Arsène's paranoia about having murdered someone is the symptom of his self-loathing. What Mouchette feels in him is this soft spot, this place of ruin and fear. Her love for him is indistinguishable from God's love for him, if one has a universe structured in the mystery of love, which Bernanos did. Her unexpected consent and tenderness is a blessing that he then abuses, slashing his way through the rain to escape payment for a crime he in fact did not commit.

The book is 127 pages long. It is a perfect short novel, written with the sense of bitter detail that is also characteristic of Balzac, and with full understanding of the despair that grabs Mouchette in the end. The novel gives a deeper sense of Mouchette's emotions, her reasons for calling Arsène her lover; it hovers longer over their time together than Bresson does in his film. It is fuller than the film. The film is like a shadow of the book, but a divine, transparent shadow; it is like a second image of Balthazar.

The beast doesn't know despair but has nobility of spirit. He consents to his mechanism, his purpose. The child knows despair and therefore has a soul to lose. Her obedience becomes suicide. The soul is made of choices.

Each receives the same battering from people.
Each has had very pale and swift encounters with love—a touch here, a slap there. Unintended good is what is called grace. It can be the yellow lights like a fishbone on a wall in a squat or something that splashes out of a human without thought.

"It had happened one holiday-time at Trémières. She was taking back to Dumont's café the fish which the old man had caught during the day—a basketful of eels. On the way a big fair-haired girl had bumped into her, and turned round and asked her her name. Mouchette had not answered and the girl had gently and absent-mindedly stroked her cheek. At first Mouchette had thought nothing of it, and indeed the memory had been painful until evening, and she had pushed it out of her mind. It had returned suddenly, changed and almost unrecognizable, just before dawn when she was asleep on the ragged mattress which Madame Dumont, on events when the café was full, put down for her in a narrow corridor littered with empty bottles and cans and smelling sharply of sour wine and heavily and greasily of paraffin. In some strange way, while she was half-asleep, she felt herself cushion her face in the crook of her arm and smell the imperceptible perfume of that warm hand, and indeed she seemed to feel the hand itself, so near and so real and living that without thinking she raised her head and put up her lips to be kissed."

Later Mouchette looks at her own swarthy, calloused hand and is horrified. It is the sight of this hand that drives her into the blur of suicide. There is nothing in her drowning that is joyful or gives a feeling of spiritual liberation. But there is excitement and, once the inevitability has sunk in, a mild consciousness that "grace is everywhere." Bernanos, like Bresson, exhibits *sang froid* to the end. "The smell of the grave itself rose to her nostrils."

Suicide, like little else, makes people aware of chance. If only, if only.
The dreadful thought that suicide could have been prevented by a phone call, a plan, a tender word, haunts the loss forever. One feels that it could have been prevented because it has the force of an accident (but whose?) in the trajectory of the person's life. The whole plot got derailed. Someone lost the storyline. Who? The others around the suicide or the suicide herself?

Bresson was preoccupied with suicide. In his first colour film, *Une Femme Douce*, the young woman, nearly a girl, kills herself. In *The Devil, Probably* the boy wants to kill himself and gets what he wants.
Bernanos was attacked by critics and the public for the cruel story of Mouchette. How can a story show a child choosing to die when this act fundamentally interrupts the passage of time and time is the pulse of plot? Suicide is detachment beyond recognition.
No one who has survived affliction can understand and believe it.

It is a scandal to simply chart the miseries in a child's life that lead to her suicide. Where is the lesson?
If suicide is seen to be a sin and the suicidal character is the most sympathetic in the story, what is the moral judgement being made? Is it possible that suicide is a movement toward God? Not if God is indifferent. There would be no gravity behind indifference.

Most traditional stories end in the same state where they begin: "Now I have what I need to live." In this case the story ends, "I can't live because I don't have what I need."

The moral burden is shoved onto the question of need in the world. (At least one of three criteria has to be met for a person to survive: one needs to be useful, to be loved, to be safe. Old people, like the children of the poor, are often deprived of all three.)
This is what the story of Mouchette is out to discover. What we need in order to live.

The mystery of the story is that Mouchette loved the destroyed Arsène and claimed him as her lover. In the movie, these moments fly by almost too quickly. For Bernanos they are central to his Catholic vision, which includes a large portion of despair. Mouchette is both redeemed and made weak by the emergence of love into her soul. Her suicide is her way of ending her own story before it is finished in the long, human, exhausting way. She ends it where it has found its meaning.

Her love for Arsène has a little history but it is essentially not chosen but delivered. It is automatic. *Au hasard.* She loves and cares for him at his most reduced moment, while he is frothing and twisting in a fit. (Simone Weil said she loved animals because they were born by accident.)

Bresson's Arsène is ugly, brutish, middle aged. He shows no tenderness for the child whose hands wrap around his shoulders during the rape, and there is hesitation and deliberation in the girl's suicide at the end of the story. The shift of attention from her strength to her consent are reversed between book and film.

Bresson doesn't hover over the problem of love, whereas he does over the act of suicide.
Bernanos sees that she has been set up to die by experiencing love and that her consent to suicide is as natural as Arsène's epileptic fit. She just steps into the water. ("Her sins, which are many, are forgiven; for she loved much." [Luke 7:47])

Bresson, who made films from stories by Dostoevsky as well as from Bernanos, also confirms — through his nearly robotic models who serve as characters in his film — the belief of Simone Weil that necessity, gravity, and labour are all of a piece. The imperceptible hesitation in each gesture in his films signifies gravity as a weight against which faith is in continual struggle. Just to take a step is an act of faith. You don't need to go further than that. The hand, the transaction. The step, the agreement.

"What is necessity without labour? Necessity must be regarded as being that which imposes conditions." This and other remarks from Weil's notebooks underlie Bresson's method. They also underlie the questions many artists and thinkers were concerned with after the Second World War. Suicide is the single act of freedom available to a person in the act of becoming.

Mouchette was a part of the existentialist problem, just as so many of the neo-realist movies coming out after the war were. How Catholic is it. Its incarnational sensibility is what makes it Catholic. That is, the forging of a soul takes place on earth in time through suffering and pleasure, through choice and degradation.

"If we behold ourselves at a particular instant—the present instant, severed from the past and the future—we are innocent. We cannot be at this instant anything other than what we are; all progress implies a duration. It forms part of the order of the world, at this instant, that we should be such as we are. All problems come back to the question of
time." (Weil)

At any time a story can seem complete enough.

JACK SPICER'S "POETRY AS MAGIC" WORKSHOP

This questionnaire is in no sense designed to indicate whether you can write poetry. Since the workshop is limited to 15 people, I must have some guide as to which of you would most benefit from a workshop of this particular content. Some of the questions will seem bizarre or pointless, but it would be useful if you would answer all of them as precisely as possible.

A list of those selected will be posted on Thursday, February 21, on the main bulletin board of the Library and at the Poetry Center, S. F. State College, Juniper 4-2300 Ext. 251.

I. POLITICS

1. What is your favorite political song?

   _____

2. If you had a chance to eliminate three political figures in the world, which would you choose?

   1._____

   2._____

   3._____

3. What political group, slogan, or idea in the world today has the most to do with Magic?

   _____

   _____ With Poetry?_____

   _____

4. Who were the Lovestoneites?

   _____

II. RELIGION

1. Which one of these figures had or represented religious views nearest to your own religious views? Which furthest? Jesus, Emperor Julian, Diogenes, Buddha, Confucius, Marcus Aurelius, Lao Tse, Socrates. Dionysus, Apollo, Hermes, Trismegistus, Li Po, Heraclitus, Epicurus, Apollonius of Tyana, Simon Magus, Zoroaster, Mohammed, the White Goddess, Cicero.

Nearest_____ Furthest_____

2. Classify this set of figures in the same way. Calvin, Kierkegaard, Suzuki, Schweitzer, Marx, Russell, St. Thomas Aquinas, Luther, St. Augustine, Santayana, the Mad Bomber, Marquis de Sade, Yeats, Gandhi, William James, Hitler, C. S. Lewis, Proust.

Nearest_____ Furthest_____

3. What is your favorite book of the Bible?_____

III. HISTORY

1. Give the approximate date of the following people or events:

Plato_____ Buddha_____ The Battle of Waterloo_____ Dante_____

The invention of printing_____ Nero_____ Chaucer _____

The unification of Italy_____ Joan of Arc_____

2. Write a paragraph about how the fall of Rome affected modern poetry.

_____

_____

_____

_____

IV. POETRY

1. If you were editing a magazine and had an unlimited budget, which poets would you first ask for contributions?

_____

_____

_____

V. PERSONAL

1. Name:_____ Address:_____

Age:_____ Sex:_____ City:_____ Phone:_____

Height:_____ Weight:_____ Married or unmarried:_____

2. What animal do you most resemble?_____

3. What insect do you most resemble?_____

4. What star do you most resemble?_____

5. What card of the ordinary playing-card deck (or Tarot deck) represents

the absolute of your desires?_____

the absolute of your fears?_____

6. Write the funniest joke that you know;_____

_____

SWIMMING POOL

A. L. KENNEDY

THE HUMAN body, we rarely see it as it is—those internal miles of vessels, restless with beaten blood for as long as we live: the humdrum usefulness of feet: the weirdly tranquil beauty of the brain. And, beyond the brain, the body has a memory of its own. If, for example, you open up the abdomen of any corpse, you will discover the fine web of veins that nourished it before its birth, still tucked away behind the navel after no matter how many years. And just to the right of our navels each of us has a ligament, a remnant of our umbilicus, another ghost of the womb. We carry as our substance our own recording angel: flesh and bones responding to every force: our habits, good and bad: the pressures of our professions: the legacies of forebears far out of reach.

And how well it can work, the body: the lining of our hips smoother than glass and yet wonderfully calibrated to give us at least a chance of walking as we intend while balanced between a pair of miracles. The lacework of nerves and tendons in our hands allows us to play the harpsichord, pick pockets, applaud, caress, and generally hang on for dear life. A cunning mesh of feedback loops and electro-chemical checks is fixed in us to keep us stable and nourished and feeling with the minimum conscious effort on our part.

But even the loveliest things can fail us and, taking the long view, all any person on earth can guarantee is that the body they trust like no other will betray them fatally. The fact that we think of this so seldom only goes to show how beguiling flesh and blood can be, how permanent they make us feel, how seamlessly they interpret our personalities and intentions.

My particular trouble, my body's fault, is my back. Of course, a damaged back is by no means the worst of the very, very many bad options, but it is enough to force an alteration in everything.

The spine is a splendid idea in theory, keeping all those nerve impulses cozy inside a flexing protection of bone—except that the bone itself can be a problem—and the disks between the bone—and the layers of muscle surrounding—and we aren't really designed to stand upright, evolution lagging somewhat since our days in the trees—and your vertebrae can suddenly feel so fragile when you consider that *everything passes through them, this is how you keep moving and how you keep breathing and how you keep swallowing—so why put it all in one place? I mean, isn't it simply reckless of Someone to build us this way, if not intentionally sadistic?*

When you mention *back* to anyone, they will tell you how they slipped a disk by coughing, or sneezing, or bending over incautiously to pick up an envelope—they will talk about torn muscles, pincered nerves, collapsed cartilage, bone grinding against bone—they will impress upon you how stupidly frail your whole spine truly is—they will make you walk around as if you were balancing all of your self on a stack of cracked porcelain cups, because *you might as well be.* Anyone with half a brain must realize that your back is perpetually creeping up behind you, just waiting to pick its moment and ruin your life.

Me, I was born with two of my lower vertebrae fused—not too much of a problem, but I do have to guard against repeated twisting and I can expect to enjoy arthritis there (if not everywhere else) in later life and to suffer all the other unpredictable effects of that extra, constant burden of motion displaced above and below.

Then add in the skull fracture when I was seven — either wisely or rashly choosing to jump from a bolting horse as it pelted along the wrong side of a road. I had no confidence in the beast's ability to dodge oncoming cars. On or near the ground, I was kicked in the side of the head, quite close to the thin bone at the temple, and was therefore lucky to avoid Death by Riding Lesson — the sudden exit reserved almost exclusively for middle-class schoolgirls. I was left alive, but my cervical vertebrae remember the impact, they snuggle it tight against my neck, an irretrievable lump of fear.

Then at thirteen I slip, implausibly overexcited, on the wooden floor of a church hall at the Lea Brook Methodist Chapel Christmas Party. I fall and land squarely on the bones of my (now-redundant) tail. The pain is almost transcendental and I am tended with cushions and long soaks in the bath, during which my grandmother (chapel stalwart and a woman with no understanding of embarrassment) invites members of the congregation to nip in and wish me well through the steam. I am just old enough to find this discomfiting, but still too young to say so. X-rays many years later revealed that I broke my sacrum when I fell and that it subsequently healed back together without making proper reference to *Gray's Anatomy* — or, indeed, mine.

All of which meant that any additional tension would ratchet me into serious disarray — especially if I stored any excess stress along my spine and round my neck — which, quite naturally, I did. And my worst possible career choices would include pyramid building, exotic dancing, or anything that involves clattering at an unergonomic keyboard for hour after hour, shoulders slumped, wrists locked, pounds of fairly useless head held unhealthily immobile, with the soft mind inside it grinding on in semi-lunatic and apparently impermeable isolation.

It was only a matter of time.

But, because God is nothing if not humorous and fond of dramatic gestures, the collapse of my physical well-being did not arrive alone. It was joined by the dissolution of what passed for my personal life and the guarantee of an infinite elongation of sexual famine, along with a mystery virus, the construction of a stupidly long novel, a financial crisis, and a good head of loathing directed toward typing — the only career for which my paucity of skills makes me suited — the career which, by then, had kept me in a clean but under-financed box for almost ten years. Apart from anything else, I was simultaneously heading for a number of personal train wrecks and a kind of writer's shell shock, a physical disability when it came to hitting those keys, an absolute mental horror of going near the interior spaces necessary to make fiction.

There are, of course, painkillers — which make you blitzed and nauseous, to say nothing of rendering you unable to restart the unwilling fight with your novel and equally unable to remember your own name. So you don't take the pills. So then you are in pain. Your metabolism alters. You are permanently cold, shivering cold, unless the room is at ninety degrees. A drink with ice in it can seize up your neck for the day. You cannot sleep and therefore have plenty of time to review your disastrous life, which, in its jolly turn, keeps you awake. You watch videotapes of comedians late into the night in case you go insane, or because you've gone insane. You start to lose your voice. You cannot travel. You cannot believe in sensuality. You cannot carry shopping, raise your arms, stand without feeling sick, tie your shoes, bear to wait in queues, avoid losing your temper with strangers, avoid losing weight. You drop forty pounds in three months, give or take who cares how much — your clothes no longer fit and you cannot afford, or be bothered, to buy any more. You are self-employed and not earning and at the mercy of brain-dead general practitioners and flirtations with Accident & Emergency and the good, the bad, the brutal, the mad and frankly sleazy, amongst the varied ranks of osteopaths, masseurs, chiropractors, acupuncturists, reflexologists, physiotherapists, occupational therapists, practitioners of both Bowen and Alexander Techniques and hot packs and electric shocks and ointments, oils and prayers and lying on your back with your skull propped against the skirting board and pushing as hard as you can in the hope you can rip off your head.

ALTHOUGH, SOME of the help actually helps. Slowly, over months, you can sleep again, lift bags again, walk on a beach again. And by the time you are almost better you are thirty-six instead of thirty-three and you have been irrationally angry with a great many people whom you cannot recall and there are numberless other details that you don't remember—cities, pages, arguments—and you cry very easily now and you are a different shape and a different temperature permanently.

I'm not saying it wasn't also funny, from time to time. It was, for example, fantastically amusing when I was told that swimming would be the best possible exercise for my back. As a Scot, I have no illusions about swimming: it always involves being truly, penetratingly cold. Given my new constitution, it was obvious I'd require—as a minimum—water temperatures best reserved for cooking eggs—something unlikely both indoors and out. Meanwhile, what my ideas about swimming lacked in associations with happily baking childhood beaches, they made up for with decades of wildlife-movie paranoia: the customary hidden predators and dangers at large in all waters deeper than a teaspoon.

And water, in itself, is dangerous. As a child, I learned to swim late. At first I was very happy, splashing hither and yon and, being told to relax, take off my rubber ring, and paddle off, I did so—only to sink like a lead-covered stone. I sank in a relaxed manner, but kept right on sinking and then began breathing water, something for which I am not designed.

Needless to say, I did eventually learn how to keep myself afloat, but never found I was truly happy when out of my depth. Now, as an almost immobile, unbuoyantly scrawny,

and semi-hypothermic person, I was told that I had to get back into the water after having found it completely unnecessary to swim more than two or three times since leaving school. Beyond that, I was informed that I had to make all of my efforts on my back—any other position would be out of the question and cause further gloomily unspecified damage, if not death. I had never, ever swum on my back.

So, to summarize, I was supposed to relieve a condition caused by stress and buried fear by taking part in an activity the simple thought of which could render me hysterical. If I got cold—and I was bound to—my neck would seize, followed by the rest of my body, causing me to drown: this fear of drowning adding to my burden of terror and driving me to tense pre-emptively, possibly to the point of non-cold-related sinking, which I might conceivably escape, but only by flailing into a drowning-by-basic-panic scenario as I lurched out blindly, face to the roof, unaware of my direction, the possibly imminent impacts of other, far heartier swimmers and the, albeit unlikely, advent of piranhas and hungry squid.

But, naturally, as a Calvinist I couldn't truly convince myself that any or all of these experiences would not be the best I should expect. So I started to take lessons at a local pool.

A broad-thighed instructress attempted to teach me a racing start until I pushed off backward into a snout full of water once too often and she suggested that I should just float up, like any other lump of flotsam, into some kind of stability and then push myself off from the side as hard as I could. This allowed me to shudder and kick a yard or more before chlorinated water would once again roar down both nostrils and choke me.

After a while this grew discouraging—especially as there were always gaggles of observing pensioners in the shallow end, ready to advise me on the many inadequacies of my technique. I had also realized that the weakness and lack of rotation in my left shoulder meant my course across the water's surface was wildly inaccurate and, given a large enough pool, I would eventually batter round to complete a full circle. Still, I persevered and eventually made it deep into the deep end—before loosing all power entirely and simply bobbing about like a helpless beetle, too exhausted to scream. Only by resorting to a burst of the forbidden breaststroke did I finally make it to the relative security of the side, drag myself along toward the steps, and then flounder out, whimpering.

Weeks passed and my ability to cover any distance actually managed to shrivel, along with my pretensions to buoyancy. My horror of the backstroke was dragging my head and neck into much the same frozen arch associated with the terminal stages of tetanus. Weighing my alternatives, I discovered that I had completely forgotten how to do the crawl and was tempted again to the breaststroke which, as promised, hurt my neck like nothing else and lured me into zigzag bursts across the length of the pool, muscles tightened to such an extent that one morning's session would leave me virtually immobilized for days.

It seemed that swimming was possibly not for me.

Until the hotels.

Because, with the return of my health came the return of that portion of the writer's life which insists on grisly travel, involuntary sleep deprivation, whole days of meals involving nothing but stolen canapés and crisps and the wonderful chance to meet people you might really like if you were ever going to see them again—only you're not.

There are always a few lunatics who want to break the writerly spirit by making us comfortable and there is always the possibility of putting in the sly request—"If there's a cheap place with a pool…I have a bad back…wouldn't want to end up paraplegic on your watch…are you insured…?"

(There is, apparently, a widespread belief that running fresh water, running hot water, closing windows, completed flooring, sheets without cigarette burns and the pubic hairs of others, peace and quiet after 3 a.m., properly locking

doors, showers with curtains not giving directly on to public corridors and/or kitchens, and a lack of mysterious smells reminiscent of decomposition are all things that writers are delighted to forego. This is the only explanation for many of the accommodation options offered to us.)

So the pools began as a simple device, a way for me to get clean sheets, but my last two years of occasionally generous accommodation have allowed me to discover that they are also the perfect place for even the most terrified to teach themselves to swim.

This unexpected process began in Montreal, where I duly trotted myself up to the hotel's tiny leisure area, disrobed, and eased myself into my first dip. Which is when I discovered the wonderful truth that hotel pools are usually toasty. No one can be bothered with flustered businessmen bringing lawsuits for head colds and the pulling of unwarmed muscles, or the hospitalization of vacationing pensioners who snap something vital taking their first plunge or while shivering without due care and attention. The air and water temperatures in hotel pools will, therefore, be more than adequate, even for me. Guests who end up floating, lifeless and blue after hideous accidents, are also not good for business. But lifeguards cost money and probably flirt a lot, so hotel pools are almost always rather casually attended, but are also, for safety's sake, less than adult drowning depth. They tend to be clearly and reassuringly marked as unable to pass the chin of a person who is five feet, six inches. Hot and shallow—ideal.

Not that chin-depth water wasn't a worry at first. In Montreal I could feel myself starting to panic as soon as it held me, swaying and clinging to the side like an evicted whelk. At which point another quality of these pools came into play—they aren't exactly huge. This means that, if the pool has prior occupants, a great deal of sociable nodding and smiling has to be gone through when you enter, and darting straight out again just as soon as you are in will be looked on with some curiosity, if not concern. Hotel pools also attract people who might even be slightly less fit and confident than me. Which means the pools play on both my desperate avoidance of humiliation and the nastier parts of my competitive nature — I can't chicken out without feeling foolish and (when pitted against the scared, infantile, elderly, and otherwise infirm) I feel compelled to make some show of aquatic prowess.

The able swimmers of a sporting pool simply reduce me to spasms, shame, and sinking. Whereas on my first, Canadian outing, I ended up grinning helplessly over at a shy and nervy Japanese grandmother and two toddler-sized individuals who may well have been her grandchildren — just the kind of competition I had a chance of taking. Needless to say, my clumsy flailing quickly emptied the water of other swimmers and brought in an attendant, checking for signs of impending death. But by the end of fifteen minutes, I wasn't in pain, or imagining anacondas, or so scared of dying that I couldn't punch out the ten or so strokes that took me from one side to another. I felt exhausted and pathetically flushed with victory.

In fact, I spent the whole of my week there making twice-daily exertions in the pool and then performing literary readings and attending business meetings while proudly reeking of chlorine. I was swimming before breakfast, for heaven's sake — I don't normally stand before breakfast, or indeed lunch.

And my progress continued at each suitably equipped hotel. There are few things nicer than trudging out in a summer sleet, leaving the tents of a book festival and knowing you are on your way to a Turkish bath in a tiny steam cupboard, a sauna in a yet tinier wooden closet, and then a nice thrash about until you're tired.

By this time I had learned a few of the other features of hotel pools — there will always be a fat and hairy man in the water, if not when you arrive, then before you leave. He will always plod methodically through miniature length after length, his back hairs rippling in time as he goes. Also, in

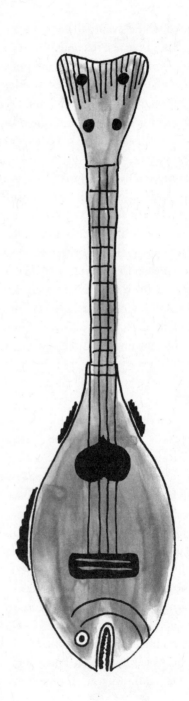

basement pools without natural light—and there are such places—young women will feel compelled to lounge in their towels and costumes on the recliners provided, as if there were some possibility of their somehow getting a tan. They will sleep and read magazines, going nowhere near the water and, I can only presume, awaiting the arrival of their masculine equivalent. And there will, naturally, be nice mothers or nice fathers who flop through the wavelets apologetically while their unpleasant daughters and sons spit, break wind, and impersonate hooked marlin fighting for their lives while laughing.

Despite the marlins, I was, slowly, slowly, beginning to be able to swim in a straight line. I had bought a nose clip which, albeit absurd, meant that my choking days were over and I could proceed in relative tranquility. The length of my efforts extended and I finally touched, in a small way, the idea that I might be able to make physical improvements without any increase in pain.

On occasions, I was even spoiled—for instance, that time in Budapest when the hotel was within walking distance of the famous Gellert thermal baths. I can recommend sharing changing and bathing facilities with fellow delegates from an English literature conference—the elbowing chaos of communal cubicles and the pleasant humility and calm of academics in swimming attire are a splendid icebreaker. And then you can patter off (in your modest costume and compulsory, hygiene-related, absurd shower cap) and wallow in eighty-five-plus-degree ponds inhabited by massive, naked, Hungarian women who seem to have become entirely aquatic and more than slightly territorial. It is possible (while wondering what is so awful about head hair in the water when yards of pubic hair is wafting in the shallows on every side) to picture these ladies, marvellously graceful underwater, being fed with sprats when the evening comes and the baths are closed to the public. (I believe there are similar phenomena at liberty on the gentlemen's side of the baths.)

Better yet was the little spa town of Leukerbad, with its festival and its thermal springs and its trilingual, designated hotel with one long, roasting mineral pool indoors and another, equally heated, outside in the Swiss fresh air. In Leukerbad, I swam three and four times a day and wondered why so few people still shunt off into Switzerland in search of health. Meanwhile, I seemed to have slipped into a Chekhov story—the author regaining vigour while taking the waters. Although, of course, I met no mysteriously bitter men, took no group excursions in the meadows, said nothing witty or beautiful, had no affair, fell into no love.

Love is probably the final common feature of the pools—couples appearing shyly and then slipping into the water with a sense of increased privacy. The last couple I saw was in 2002's final hotel—a monstrous building devoted to golf: a game which is not so much a good walk spoiled as an ecological holocaust combined with nauseating boredom and illegal knitwear. Still, inside the dreadful place, I was able to enjoy a massive pool with accompanying Jacuzzis. As the time passed, I was joined by a young man and woman who were inevitably fond of each other, then two children, then a fat and hairy man, and then two women. The women, I suppose, may have been other-halves—the facilities being provided, no doubt, to placate non-golfing spouses, although most of them seemed to have chosen to stay away, perhaps looking blankly out of their bedroom windows at the clipped and luminously dyed grass surrounding them and wondering if they ought to buy a gun.

In 2003 it's not inconceivable that I may try a full-scale pool. Equally, I may not. Whatever I do, I will be back in the hotel pools whenever I can. I will focus on trusting the strength of water, its support, the possibilities for movement that it offers and that I don't know how to take. And I will like the movement of it against my skin and also its heat. And I will try not to think this is all that my body and I will ever have.

SOME NOTES ON INFINITY

SEMI CHELLAS

Debauchery is perhaps an act of despair in the face of infinity.
—Edmond de Goncourt

I
s IT just me or can everyone remember the first time she came across infinity? The childhood infinity of infinite regress—Why? Then why? Then why? For me it was learning to count, a sudden grasp of the *system* of counting, and I remember sitting under the poker table my parents used for eating, and counting, as long as I could—it seemed like all day—and then my mother setting the table with me under it, realizing that I would have to stop counting to eat dinner, and if not then, even if I counted through the pork chops, there would still be more numbers, that I was never going to finish, there would always be more numbers than me.

My parents were the kind who read terribly frightening books out loud to me at bedtime, like *Pride and Prejudice* and *Treasure Island* (I thought till quite late in life that those were books for kids). I told my father about the counting and he—as he would at all momentous moments of our relationship, including when I decided to go to college and when he explained to me that he was terminally ill—pulled out a sheet of paper.

He proceeded to illustrate for me Zeno of Elea's paradox, which you probably know. The tortoise and Achilles are racing, and all the other nonsense about slow and steady aside, no one's gonna win, because each of them has to get halfway to the finish line, and then half of what's left, and then half of that, and half of that…to infinity, and never quite there. The exhaustion! The pointlessness of racing, whether speedy and arrogant or humble and committed! The horror of the asymptote, and I must have been five! I remember this so clearly: my mother was making fudge (unlike her, and possibly in order to comfort me) and I was rooted to my chair, because what, after that, was the point of getting up out of it, of trying to go anywhere? The exhaustion, like the dream you have where you're moving through syrup. I could feel my heart beat in my eyes, too much light coming in.

My father was a philosopher and so I can forgive him.

I'm not alone in my anxiety of infinity. There is a capital-R Romantic tradition of infinity the Great and Terrible. Edmund Burke's my favourite—he wrote, "Infinity has a tendency to fill the mind with that sort of delightful horror which is the most genuine effect and the truest test of the sublime."

"Delightful horror" is it. I take pleasure in poking around in infinity the way you might have pleasure in biting a nail too close to the flesh. "Infinity" meaning, literally, never to finish.

But I think it is worse for me because I was raised without faith. I was raised by the most committed atheists I've ever met. I have no capacity for faith, and this is, pragmatically speaking, a difficult way to live.

Aristotle had some ideas about infinity. He thought it was an imperfection, the absence of limits. Debauched. Infinity has always been controversial.

There was Brahmagupta, who tried to put zero into the number system and drove himself mad.

There was Nicholas of Cusa, who argued in the fifteenth century that the universe was infinite and the stars were all suns. (He was right.)

Giordano Bruno, who argued for the infinity of the universe and was tortured by the Inquisition for nine years.

Then Galileo. He noticed something weird. If you take all the numbers, to infinity, and remove half of them, the remainder is as large a set of numbers as you had in the first place. His conclusion was basically that infinity has its own rules, that unlike in our finite understanding, infinite quantities cannot be one greater or less than one another. It's anti-intuitive, because our intuition is mostly based in a finite understanding of the world. What is outside that takes a leap of faith.

This sort of thinking was banned by Rome.

We know what happened to Galileo. Bruno was burned at the stake in the year of our Lord 1600.

Some thinkers have taken the idea of infinity to mean that if the universe is infinite, it must have every possibility in it. The absurdist version of this is to imagine that this would mean an infinite number of planets with an infinite number of possibilities, and therefore, somewhere, a planet with all of us on it, except we are in our underwear, and one even closer where everything is the same except that only I am in my underwear. Infinity the nightmare. An infinite number of girls like me on an infinite number of planets all with only a small difference—they are probably a little bit better; they don't, for instance, get up and sing Patsy Cline out of tune in bars or bite their nails. Is it me or is this not the greatest fear that everyone has? An infinity of people just like you and nothing to set you apart.

So it was spring and my heart was broken. My father was ill and my mother was travelling; I went home to care for him. This was an uneasy reversal, as I was often sick as a child, and he used to stay home to take care of me sometimes. He would give me logic puzzles to do, of the kind where Mrs. A can't sit with Mr. B at dinner and the woman in the blue dress is sitting next to the man who won't take off his hat and if the table is round, who is at the left of the hostess? Such rude guests, why didn't they just sit where they were told?

My father was ill and it should have been frightening, but it was boring, in fact. I had left all the storm and tragedy of my real life, and I would lock myself in the bathroom and cry, and sneak bourbon from the liquor cabinet. (The vodka was still watered down, from a party I had in high school. Fifteen years and my parents never noticed.) Debauchery in the face of despair.

My father, on the topic of heartbreak, had nothing to say. On the topic of my heart, nothing to say. Except the fatherly things—how could he leave you? Being my father, and thinking that there was only me like me. I was feeling rather acutely that there were in fact many potential mes. I was feeling sorry for myself. I told my father my theory, that whatever he might say, there was proof, mathematically, that there were an infinite number of girls like me.

He was in bed, I remember, and he had pneumonia. His lungs were weak from the operations and there was the difficulty of helping him urinate into a jar. He said, "There are things outside of infinity."

"No, there's not," I said. "The infinite contains everything; that's the point of it."

Never argue with a philosopher. "Get me a piece of paper," he said.

He started writing down numbers and symbols. He made a grid and filled it with fractions, and then he threw that aside and filled it with ones and zeroes. Simpler that way. I was tired and there was bourbon in my frontal lobe; I could feel it there. I was tired of being wronged and being sad and being an adult in my childhood home caring for an adult as if I had never been a child. But because he was weak and focused and because he is my father, I tried to concentrate. He was drawing diagonal lines and alephs and subsets and talking about set theory, and I was trying to concentrate, and then there was a moment, just a moment, a sublime moment where I got it.

I understood for a second that there can be different sizes of infinity.

It was sublime.

Suppose you didn't know how to count to five. Suppose you were from some planet where they had only the numbers one, two, and three, and you wanted to know whether you had the same number of fingers on each hand.

How would you do it?

You would put your fingertips against each other and realize there was a one-to-one correspondence.

So you can count something and you don't necessarily need to know all the numbers. In this way, we know we can count anything with the natural numbers, which are infinite, because we know how to generate them infinitely even when we cannot imagine to what they might correspond.

For instance, we could make an infinite string of *even* numbers

2   4   6   8   10   12   14 . . .

and we could count them by doing this:

1   2   3   4   5   6   7 . . .
2   4   6   8   10   12   14 . . .

The even numbers are an example of what is called the *countably infinite.*

The question is whether there is a collection of things that are *not* countable.

This question was answered by Georg Cantor, a nice Russian boy who ended up in Germany in the 1860s. He played a lot with infinity and he changed mathematics forever. He was wildly attacked back when people attacked you for proposing that infinity comes in shapes and sizes. It made him very depressed. Suicidal even.

First, you have to play a parlour game that my father showed me. You begin with a three-by-three grid and fill it with any combination of Xs and Os. Such a grid might look like this:

	Item 1	Item 2	Item 3
Sequence 1	X	O	X
Sequence 2	O	X	X
Sequence 3	X	O	O

What we're interested in, in this game, is the composition of the horizontal sequences themselves (that is, the rows in the grid). We can now create a fourth sequence in an entirely mechanical fashion, and know for sure that the new sequence is different from the ones preceding it. To do this, we take the opposites of the quantities in Sequence 1, Item 1; Sequence 2, Item 2; and Sequence 3, Item 3 (where the opposite of X is O, and vice versa). By doing this automatic operation, we get a sequence that looks like this:

	Item 1	Item 2	Item 3
Sequence 4	O	O	X

The reason we know Sequence 4 does not appear among the horizontal sequences in the grid is because we've made sure that it is different from each of those sequences in at least one place.

Now, what if we made each sequence extend to infinity? For example:

X   O   X   O   X   O   X . . .

And then we made a list of *all of the possible* infinite strings of Xs and Os:

```
X   O   X   O   X   O   X...
O   X   X   X   X   X   X...
X   O   O   O   O   O   X...
O   O   O   X   X   X   X...
O   X   O   X   X   X   X...
O   O   O   X   X   O   O...
```
.
.
.

And then we counted these sequences using our conventional set of natural numbers. How many would we have?

```
1   X   O   X   O   X   O   X...
2   O   X   X   X   X   X   X...
3   X   O   O   O   O   O   X...
4   O   O   O   X   X   X   X...
5   O   X   O   X   X   X   X...
6   O   O   O   X   X   O   O...
```
.   .
.   .
.   .

Clearly, the number of possible infinite strings of Xs and Os is infinite.

Now, however, as in the parlour game, we can make a *new* sequence by taking the opposite of the first item in the first sequence, the opposite of the second item in the second sequence, and so on.

But by the reasoning of the game, the new sequence *cannot* be in the set of sequences it came out of, because it is different in at least one place from every string in that set. So even though we have created an infinite set of sequences of infinite Xs and Os, now we have a new sequence that is *not* in that infinite set.

Therefore, the collection of all the sequences of Xs and Os is of an infinity that is *larger* than the infinity we can reach with the set of natural numbers we use for counting. Which means—

There are different sizes of infinity.

"That woulda showed Aristotle," my dad said.

He would have explained it better.

The understanding left me. I disputed with my father whether I could take comfort in what he'd said or whether it was all set theory that had no analogies in the real world, the world of wayward boyfriends and crying in pillows.

I still have the piece of paper my father used when we calculated how my parents would help me pay for college.

I still have the piece of paper my father used to show me how his heart was coming apart. He labelled the valves.

I lost the piece of paper he used to show me that there are different sizes of infinity.

Cantor became obsessed with the idea that Francis Bacon wrote Shakespeare's plays. He demanded to be allowed to lecture in philosophy instead of math, and all he talked about was that. He didn't even really speak English.

I read recently that someone put a finite number of monkeys at a finite number of typewriters. Actually it was computers. The monkeys defecated on them at first, and the alpha chimp broke his. But after a while they started typing.

They didn't come up with any Shakespeare. (But they're publishing a book.)

I guess that woulda showed Francis Bacon.

Georg Cantor died at age seventy-two in an insane asylum, after a long period of depression and despair. "That delightful horror."

In 1997 my father retired from philosophy to become a fulltime jazz guitarist. He is still alive.

COUNTERPOINT
Three Movies, a Book, and an Old Photograph

DON DELILLO

I

THE FIRST FILM begins with a scene that lasts some forty seconds, a distant figure in a glacial landscape, alone with a pack of wailing dogs.

Then the scene becomes a crowded enclosure, an igloo, night, maybe a dozen adults and several small children, with oil lamps lighting the face of a boy named Atanarjuat, three months old.

There are many tight shots of people's faces in the film—individuals in brief separation from the enveloping world of ice and sky. Midway through, Atanarjuat, now a grown man, is running for his life. Three men are in pursuit, armed with spears and knives. The fleeing man is naked, filmed at a distance, then in close-up, then wide-angle from above as he runs on rocky shoreline and across the sea ice, bloody and freezing, and this is the remarkably stark heart of *The Fast Runner*, the contemporary film version of a five-hundred-year-old Inuit legend, passed orally through the generations.

THE SECOND FILM begins in near monochrome, with a figure approaching from the deep distance across a vast expanse of ice.

He is not Atanarjuat, the naked runner, but Glenn Gould, the classical pianist.

Thirty Two Short Films About Glenn Gould is a ninety-three-minute movie, each independent episode, or variation, preceded by a title. This is not a documentary. There is an actor playing Gould but there are also interviews with people who knew him, including the violinist Yehudi Menuhin, and these individuals serve as counterweight to the intentional lightness of the film, a disembodied quality that issues from the episodic scheme and elusive subject.

The film shows us an intense and humorous man, his mind and body flooded with music, his hands in motion (in fingerless gloves at times) even when he is nowhere near a piano. He is a Canadian, of course, emotionally engaged with the rigorous north. This is a film of distances. The artist is an adept of solitude living at the edge of that psychic immensity, the otherworld of ice and time and wintry introspection.

This is also a movie about sound. In a busy diner, there are voices in layers and zones, some folded over others, in counterpoint, and there is music throughout, or sounds arranged in time, coming from radios, phonographs, a chamber group, and studio playback. People speak to others from a distance, into telephones and microphones. There are footsteps, applause, the screek of tapes rewinding. People in interviews speak French, English, and accented English, and Gould interviews himself, pointing out that the relationship of audience to artist is one to zero.

He is the remote artist, the one of elliptic disposition, leading a life, Menuhin says, to the exclusion of the rest of the world, wearing layers of clothing in dead of summer, avoiding the touch of others. He is also a performing artist who stops performing at the age of thirty-one, becoming involved with the technology of recorded music.

Several episodes in the movie seem forcibly imposed, but then again, if the film were called *Twenty Nine Short Films About Glenn Gould*, we'd lose the title's resonating link to Bach's *Goldberg Variations*, which number thirty-two, counting theme and reprise.

There is an eccentric clarity to the movie and, always, something stirring in the distance. This is Glenn Gould himself. In an enterprise less responsive to its subject, the writer and director would attempt to compress the distance, find some trace of the tangible man, something familiar to us all, a subplot concerning his inner rage, his will toward total control, his sexual persona, a sense of the man's paranoia and hypochondria, his roster of doctors and medications, the obsessive readings he did of his blood pressure and pulse rate—whatever ravel of terror might coexist with the high designs of the spectral artist.

This does not happen here, to the film's credit and effectiveness. Here is the artist in idiosyncrasy and seclusion. It is his film on his terms, even if made by others, eleven years after his death. We don't have to know everything about the man. Less-than-everything may be the man.

IN THE NOVELS of Thomas Bernhard, the human mind in isolation is the final spiralling subject. Trained as a musician, he imagines in *The Loser* that Glenn Gould is a friend of his, a fellow student under Horowitz and a man so compulsively preoccupied with his art that this quality must inevitably destroy him. It has to be understood that Bernhard himself writes a prose so unrelenting in its intensity toward a fixed idea that it sometimes approaches a level of self-destructive delirium. He is frequently funny at this level.

The Glenn Gould of the novel is not the same man one sees in *Thirty Two Short Films*. He is robust and occasionally loutish, hurling a champagne bottle at a piece of sculpture. Bernhard insists that his Glenn Gould is more interesting than the phantom figure so widely admired.

But to what extent is Bernhard himself speaking to the reader? The narrator, who is nameless, maintains in the course of his book-length monologue that Gould's interpretation of the *Goldberg Variations* is to blame for the suicide of their mutual friend, Wertheimer. Not only Wertheimer's death but also Wertheimer's life, much of it disastrous, can be traced to Glenn Gould's genius, one day in Salzburg, in the service of Bach. Wertheimer is the loser of the book's title.

"If Wertheimer hadn't walked past room thirty-three on the second floor of the Mozarteum twenty-eight years ago, precisely at four in the afternoon, he wouldn't have hanged himself twenty-eight years later.... Wertheimer's fate was to have walked past room thirty-three in the Mozarteum at the precise moment when Glenn Gould was playing the so-called aria in that room. Regarding this event Wertheimer reported to me that he stopped at the door of room thirty-three, listening to Glenn play until the end of the aria.... In 1953 Glenn Gould destroyed Wertheimer."

This is what genius does. It shrinks the will of others. But it can also produce an odd wistfulness on the part of an admirer, a yearning to blend environments. Bernhard refers to the pianist most frequently as Glenn, and he works a transference, lesser musician to greater. He alludes to Glenn's lung disease, but in fact it was Bernhard who suffered gravely from this condition. In the novel, Glenn dies at fifty-one (instead of fifty), maybe because Bernhard turned fifty-one the year Glenn died.

There are shadings of identity among author, narrator, and character. There is the doubling of Bernhard/Gould and also the split between Bernhard the pianist and Bernhard the novelist.

But where is the novelist? He is sitting in a room in Vienna or Salzburg writing lines for a narrator who is not him, but is him, but isn't. In the end the narrator is an uncredited actor playing Thomas Bernhard in much the same way that a flesh-and-blood actor plays Glenn Gould in *Thirty Two Short Films*.

I USED TO THINK I was one of ten people in the world who knew that Thelonious Monk's middle name was Sphere. In the documentary film *Straight, No Chaser*, Sphere is the third word spoken. The first is Thelonious. So is the second.

The words come after the music, an opening sequence that has Monk onstage—on his feet and spinning—as the band performs behind him. He wears a snug cap, Central Asian, and then hustles to the piano before the set ends without him.

Monk does this spin several times in the course of the film, a meditative whirl that may be a bop variation on mystical dervish dance. He wears a dozen hats—beret, fedora, plaid cap, skullcap, modified fez—and at the piano he sweats and gleams, most notably in the handsome high-contrast black-and-white segments, in which he sits in the phosphorescent foreground, with solid dark behind.

At one point he wears a hat in bed in his hotel room, sheets drawn up to his beard. This is somewhere in northern Europe and he is ordering room service from a waiter who happens to be in the room, writing down Monk's puzzling request for chicken liver. The waiter can take action on chicken, he can execute an order for liver, but he can't seem to place these items in the same edible context. Maybe it's a language problem.

Monk uses language in an expressionistic manner, making speech sounds through much of the movie, levels of utterance that rarely glide above a mutter. Glenn Gould used to hum while he played. Monk hums while he talks. He is smart and complex but tends to regard speech as some weary subgenre of music. He has a funny exchange with one of his sidemen on technical matters involving G-flat. And when he is given a pen for signing autographs he makes an effort to employ a proper sheet of paper.

"I'll do it etiquettely," he says.

There are other moments not so light in tone. He suffered periods of depression and deep introversion. There were periods when he'd pace a room for days before lapsing into exhaustion. He spent time in hospitals and his son remarks, "It's a startling thing when you look your father in the eye and you know that he doesn't exactly know who you are."

On film he spins, inscrutably, eyes shut, while the drummer plays behind him.

The filmmakers are not circumspect on the subject of Monk's difficulties so much as they are faithful to their method, which is to collect archival footage, shoot new footage, and let the film spring directly from time, space, and chance, with a few interviews and old photographs to provide historical background.

This is jazz, after all, and the movie has the improvised and staticky look of late-fifties cinema, Cassavetes and *Shadows*, with Mingus on the soundtrack, or Robert Frank and *Pull My Daisy*, with Kerouac doing narration. This was the period of Monk's emergence as a force in music, at the Five Spot in New York, and the film offers excerpts from nearly thirty tunes. Then there is Monk himself, at the piano, bobbing and stomping, an ecstatic in his natural state, under a spell, in disconnection.

Is there something of the north in Monk's music? The word *cool* is not incidental to the era. His work has a self-contained quality. He composed nearly one hundred pieces of music, many becoming jazz classics, and his playing is spare and distant at times, oblique, free of hybrid influence—spaced notes, off notes, missing notes, notes in conflict, and then, after a pause, maybe a vibrant little leap, like a spike on the heart monitor.

He is making modern art, edgy and spattered, in the manner of Pollock or Godard.

Monk does full spins in a crowded airline terminal and again in a hotel room. He is the jazzman on perennial tour, dislocated in more ways than one, and these rotations imply a need to make his own geography. The world has collapsed to a single square metre of paved earth but it is spinning, still, and he is spinning with it.

In mid-film, in colour, there is a brief tight beautiful close-up of Monk at the piano. He is playing "Crepuscule with Nellie," his face in profile showing a wispy whitish beard. He wears a pinkie ring the size of a walnut and one of his more solemn hats, a silky piece of headgear, midnight blue, suited to an aging Chinese sage.

2

MONK WITHDREW, mysteriously, not putting a hand to the keyboard, publicly or privately, in the six years before he died in 1982. Glenn Gould died later the same year, long after abandoning the concert stage, although he continued to record.

Thomas Bernhard writes, "I met Glenn on Monk's Mountain."

Gould has been called the musical equivalent of Brando and Dean. He worked on the scores for a couple of films.

Bernhard's film is anti-cinematic. There is almost nothing to *see* in his work. It is all personal history and tossing emotion, all voice—no faces, rooms, rainy days. There are references to streets and cities but no sense of place, and the novels I've read have no paragraphing, no divisions of text or accommodating space breaks. Bernhard's prose has a rapid and clamorous pulse rate. The narrator delivers eloquent chronicles of misery, illness, madness, isolation, and death. There are points at which the narration amasses such compressed layerings of loathing and self-loathing that it becomes rackingly comic. And weaving bleakly through it all is a sense of themes and patterns that ride recurrently in the mind.

Glenn Gould's discomfort before an audience made him want to master the culture of the recording studio.

What did he say about this?

He said, "Technology has the capability to create a climate of anonymity." He developed ideas about non-linear radio and did a documentary called *The Idea of North*, in which five people speak in counterpoint about the power and isolation of remote Canada, one voice yielding to another and sometimes overlapping at length, with train rhythms and ambient noise

adding texture to the appealing fugal quality of the piece.

Monk added texture in more immediate and startling ways. In clubs he sometimes began playing one tune and then switched to another, leaving his bass, horn, and drums marooned in space.

Bernhard was a solitary who knew many people. He never knew his father, however, and felt the sting of this predicament all his life. His work and public statements caused loud controversy and scandal. His farmhouse was off-limits—even, at times, to invited guests. His long-term companion was a woman thirty-seven years older than he was. He did not marry, had no children. Why have children? What is a child? People who produce what is called a child, he said, are actually creating "a sweaty disgusting beer-bellied innkeeper or mass murderer.... That's whom they bring into the world."

Gould's second recording of the *Goldberg Variations* was made twenty-six years after his first rendition and is sombre and slower, far more contemplative. He is not only re-imagining Bach but engaging in a form of dialogue with his own mortality.

Monk wrote a tune called "Introspection." Two minutes twelve seconds (or more, or less, depending on which recording you listen to). But what happens when introspection develops a density that obliterates the world around it?

Gould in his coat, scarf, gloves, and touring cap, whatever the season. Monk in his astrakhans and white panamas.

Monk's hats were famous. But when he stopped playing, he put away his hats. He'd stand in a room and grind his teeth, or stare at a wall, or walk from wall to wall, refusing to speak.

Damage and deficit and malfunction of the central nervous system, according to one doctor, and probably caused by long-term dependence on drugs.

Long before he retired from public life, there were periods of disturbance. At a club in Boston, he sat motionless at the piano, pressing the keys down, soundlessly, for such an unremitting length of time that his sidemen finally left the stage. He was hearing something they could not.

After a long silence he'd say, "Monk know, Monk know."

The prisoner is thrown into solitary. He is alone, confined, sequestered. This is the harshest punishment the state allows, short of outright execution.

Bernhard believed that his art depended on two things, his disease and his madness. He suffered from an abnormality of the immune system resulting in pulmonary problems that were complicated by a heart condition. This amounted to a long-running terminal illness, which he said he "cherished and exploited" in his work.

Where was his madness?

In his atlas of contempt, madness was a function of geography. To be Austrian was to carry an unsparing historical memory, a narrative of fascism and anti-Semitism that struck him as the moral equivalent of madness.

Between sets, in one city or another, Monk liked to go into the street and direct traffic for a while.

Glenn Gould said, "Isolation is the indispensable component of human happiness."

It was also, he thought, the only way for him to experience ecstasy. He travelled by train as far as northern Manitoba but never reached arctic Canada, his idea of north, because he feared flying and was unwilling or unable to travel long distances by boat.

In *The Fast Runner*, Atanarjuat, racing, naked, is a man reacting to a primal danger; there are other men who want to kill him. But he may also resemble an individual trying to re-establish his sense of isolation, his natural place in the landscape. Life in the winter dwelling built of snow blocks gets crowded and complicated, and even introspection becomes a group dynamic. The man is running, eyes wild, into the arctic sky.

The Greek and Latin roots of the word *ecstasy* include a sense of terror, derangement, displacement.

In a documentary film, Gould performs the *Goldberg Variations* in a studio, curled on his low bench, the camera at times barely locating his head between the piano's raised lid and the lid stick. His mother played the piano often when she was pregnant and here he is a near-fetal presence—the fetus as genius. He is shot from high angle and low, this side and that, the camera tight on his hands and then his face as he hums and sings and seems to chatter, conducting occasionally with his free hand. It isn't until the reprise, the last bare minutes, head at keyboard level, body subdued, that he begins to detach himself from the audio devices and image gathering, melting into the music, into Bach and into Gould.

Some people thought Monk had a regal bearing. Others saw a large black man who stood so impenetrably still in a room, behind dark glasses with bamboo rims, outside every conversational lure, that they took him to be blind, or mute, or simply intimidating.

In his last will, Bernhard cut off an entire country, his own, stipulating that "nothing I published during my lifetime, or any of my papers wherever they may be after my death, or anything I wrote in whatever form, shall be produced, printed, or even just recited within the borders of the Austrian state...."

This includes scrawled words on scraps of paper.

In Delaware, Monk was arrested and beaten by police for entering a segregated motel and asking for a drink of water.

Glenn's family name was originally Gold. He was nine years old when the name was changed and he never discussed it, apparently, with anyone.

When Thomas Bernhard was a child, he liked to play dead. It suited him to scare his mother. Later he would write extensively for theatre and in some ways tried to organize his life (and death) as pieces of performance art.

The idea of eating frightened Gould. So at times did the idea of people, being trapped with others, talking to them, dealing with them. At the same time, he pointed out, he had

"certain exhibitionist tendencies" and liked to appear on TV wearing comic outfits and speaking in funny accents to ridicule various figures in the music world.

One of these figures was Vladimir Horowitz, his fictional teacher in Salzburg in Bernhard's novel.

In older cultures, the solitary is a malignant figure. He threatens the well-being of the group. But we know him because we encounter him, in ourselves and others. He lives in counterpoint, a figure in the faint distance. This is who he is, lastingly alone.

There is an element in *The Fast Runner* that seems responsive to the nature of film itself. This is the image of a lone figure in a hazardous landscape. The purest moments in film may be those of solitude and danger. During the end credits, footage appears, unexpectedly, of the cast and crew at work, men in sunglasses, cameras mounted on sleds, and the effect is a little heartbreaking. Here is the fiction exposed, the filmcraft in plain sight, and two levels of isolation are shattered, the character's and the moviegoer's both.

Bernhard writes of Gould: "He had *barricaded* himself in his house. For life. All our lives the three of us have shared the desire to barricade ourselves from the world. All three of us were born barricade fanatics."

The fictional Wertheimer is the third member of the barricade cult, and Monk makes four.

First there is the gradation of language, a sense of deepening threat played out in the terms themselves. Introspection, solitude, isolation, anxiety, phobia, depression, hallucination, schizophrenia. Then there are the human referents. He is free from convention; or there is something scanted in his humanity; or he is trapped in a modern context, bearing some taint of estrangement that makes him uneasy in the world; or it's a result of upbringing maybe; or he's a goddamn genius—leave him alone; or the matter is strictly clinical, a question of brain chemistry; or it's a natural state in fact, some dread that lingers in the early brain, the snake brain, outside the slanted limits

of all the things he has shored against it.

If we know the answer, then this is the question: How close to the self can we get without losing everything?

MONK'S MOUNTAIN, in Bernhard's novel, is also called Suicide Mountain. Every week, three or four suicides.

"Their smashed remains on the street have always fascinated me and I personally (like Wertheimer by the way!) have often climbed or ridden the elevator to the top of Monk's Mountain with the intention of hurling myself into the void, but I didn't throw myself off (nor did Wertheimer!). Several times I had already prepared myself to jump (like Wertheimer!) but didn't jump, like Wertheimer."

What Wertheimer did was put a rope around his neck and jump out of a tree.

There is a doubling between Gould and Bernhard that the novelist did not have to invent. In *Thirty Two Short Films*, Glenn speaks of his fear of dying. He does this, typically, on the telephone, standing in a public booth talking to a cousin about the occult bearing that certain numbers have on human affairs. When the digits comprising one's age, a seven and a six, say (in Schönberg's case), add up to thirteen, the implication is ominous. Schönberg died in fact at seventy-six.

Gould, as he speaks, is about to turn forty-nine. He says into the phone, "Schönberg's still talking to me."

This is the power of numbers to a consciousness that funnels the world endlessly inward. The world is a set of assumptions designed to accommodate one's introversion. Gould would escape the baleful effects of that *four* and that *nine* but only technically. He suffered a stroke two days after turning fifty and died a week later.

Bernhard, his wishful soulmate of the keyboard, would eventually become Glenn's numerological double, fixed to digits that total thirteen. He died later in the decade, two days after turning fifty-eight.

In Bernhard's novel, Glenn dies romantically, playing

the *Goldberg Variations*, as if to balance the toll exacted by genius. One fictional suicide, Wertheimer; one fatal stroke, Glenn Gould.

Another victim of a stroke is seen on film as he lies in state at Saint Peter's in New York, the jazz church, with mourners filing slowly past. Here is Thelonious Sphere Monk, stopped spinning at last.

3

A LARGE PHOTOGRAPH hangs on a wall in this room, where I work. It is a picture taken in 1953, black-and-white, showing a jazz group in performance at a club in Greenwich Village. For the inspired chronicler, this is a photograph that might easily elicit a book-length meditation on the men and their era. But let this bare rendering suffice:

Monk, foreground, hatless, in a striped suit, mouth open, hands on keyboard. At extreme left, Mingus, head down, lower face in shadow, hands working the strings of his bass. Deep background, Roy Haynes on drums, wide-eyed, face floating above the elevated cymbal. Just to his left, a mural of a reclining woman, naked, a figure out of the old bohemian Village. And far right, facing away from the group and looking out of the frame, white-suited, with sax, there is Charlie Parker, vivid as a blizzard in July.

It is the legend inserted above the saxophonist's head that finally defines the photograph — two words handwritten on the print itself in chalky white letters that match the colour of Charlie Parker's suit.

Bird lives.

This epitaph, written in chalk and paint on sidewalks and in subway tunnels after Bird died, at thirty-four, has the ancient emotional grain of a mouldering Roman wall inscription. It is a classic human cry against finality. What might we leave behind that will cling to earthly memory? The Bird

graffiti was first employed by a Beat poet named Ted Joans, who himself died recently. Three of the men in the photograph are dead, all but Roy Haynes, still working in his late seventies, but all share an afterlife, of course, on compact disc, audiotape, and old vinyl, and in the minds and musical sensibilities of unnumbered people, alone, in a room, listening.

Where Glenn Gould lies, a small headstone is engraved with the marks of another kind of permanence, in granite — the first three measures of the theme from the *Goldberg Variations*.

Thomas Bernhard was buried in secret, in Vienna, one hour ahead of schedule, to secure the terms of his privacy.

Charles Mingus is pure mineral matter in the sacred river, the Ganges, his ashes scattered by his widow, before dawn, to ready the way for reincarnation.

4

AT THE END of *Thirty Two Short Films*, a figure moves across the permafrost, away from the camera and toward the icy horizon. The sky is slate blue and faded rose and the image is the idea of north.

Voyager 1 and *2* were launched in 1977, a pair of U.S. spacecraft now at the far frontier of the solar system, eight billion miles from Earth, the first man-made objects to enter deep space. Aboard, among other artifacts, is a recording of Glenn Gould playing a short prelude of Bach.

We are intelligent beings, versed in mathematics and capable of organizing a coherent sequence of sounds in time to produce a unified composition, called music, a form of art whose truth, craft, originality, and other indefinable properties bring a quality of transcendent delight, called beauty, to the mind and senses of the listener.

This is the message to those who are out there, at a distance only death can measure.

HOW SCIENTISTS PARTY

ALASTAIR BLAND

EVERY YEAR around finals time, scientists from San Francisco State University gather at the house I was raised in for the Holiday Physics and Astronomy Party. My father, Dr. Roger Bland, a veteran physicist at the university, has hosted this event for the past fifteen years, and I've attended nearly every time. The party, which has achieved near-legend status among the faculty, is a rare opportunity for brilliant scientists and their burnt-out students to mingle, to revel in the underlying silliness of their field, to loosen their neckties after the long semester, to have a few drinks, and to light up the night with electricity and fire.

The first group of guests this year arrived at 7 p.m., tromping in the front door with a spark-generating Tesla coil, a pot of liquid nitrogen, some blowtorches, and a case of Heineken. By 8:30 the alcohol was flowing, the music was thumping, and the whole place was swarming with nerds. There was hardly room to move, yet the throngs parted gracefully for my dad as he made his way from the kitchen to the living room to announce the first event.

He clinked his wineglass with a fork and hollered, "Now begins the Equation-Editing Shootout!"

There were a few cheers, but many of the students looked puzzled. They'd heard about this annual gathering from the old-timers, about how their professors historically got drunk, set things on fire, and acted like delinquents, and they wondered if the party, like an aging rock band, had finally lost its edge.

It was certainly a slow beginning to the famous fete. A Microsoft Word window was projected onto the living room wall as the first contestant, a professor, took a seat at the computer desk. A man with a stopwatch said, "Go!" and the professor began to type. Her goal was to transcribe from a textbook a long and tedious quantum mechanical wave function—and to do it in the least time possible. As a configuration of numbers and Greek lettering began to unfold on the wall, the grad students paid close attention. They sipped their beers and nodded in approval as the equation filled out. It took a full six minutes for the professor to finish, and when she did, there was a round of applause, and a voice shouted, "Yeah! That's what I'm talkin' about!"

I looked up at the screen, but all I saw was this:

$$\Psi_{nlm}(r,\theta,\phi) = \left(\frac{2\mu Z}{m_r a_0}\right)^{3/2} e^{-\frac{r}{a_0}} \sum_{m=0}^{n-l-1} \sqrt{\frac{2n+1}{4\pi}\frac{(n-m)!}{(n+m)!}} \left(1-x^2\right)^{m/2} e^{im\phi}$$

In past years at the Physics and Astronomy Party, I've seen Ph.D.'s get high on helium, vacuum-sealed oil drums collapse under the weight of our atmosphere, a giant weather balloon expand across the living room, and balloons full of propane go up in flames in the backyard, so this new event did seem a bit tame. I spotted my father hovering near a huge bowl of tamales, waved him over, and suggested that we get a new act in motion for the laymen in the crowd: "I think they're hoping to see something explode."

"Yeah," he said through a mouthful of pork and cornmeal, "I'd say it's about time for the liquid nitrogen."

From behind the Christmas tree, my father produced a vat of super-subfreezing liquid, a common light bulb, and a half-dozen safety goggles. While the next contestant in the Shootout stationed himself at the keyboard, Dr. Bland plugged in some wires, handed out the glasses, and prepared to lower the glowing bulb into the steaming pot. "This," he said, "is what happens when three thousand Fahrenheit meets seventy-seven kelvin! Fire in the hole!"

The bulb dropped, and the crowd collectively held its breath — but nothing happened. The light bulb remained lit for three seconds in the vat, then fizzled. Dr. Bland furrowed his brow like a man immersed in thought; synapses in his brain fired and sent off electrical currents this way and that to retrieve notes and textbooks from the cerebral shelves, to check the facts and figures related to the matter, to try to understand what had — or had not — happened.

But the semester was over, and it didn't really matter. He shrugged and grabbed a carrot from a nearby vegetable platter. I saw what was coming — the Liquid Nitrogen Smash-Out, a foolproof, tested-and-true crowd-pleaser. He dunked the carrot for ten seconds and then shattered it like glass over the coffee table. "Anyone else want to try?" he asked as he set the bubbling vat on the floor.

Everyone did, of course, and frozen shrapnel began to fly. When the vegetables ran out, the participants went for napkins, tamale husks, flowers from the vase, and branches from the Christmas tree. Almost everything except fingers became fodder for the smashing, and the carpet was soon littered with debris.

It has long been a tradition at the Physics and Astronomy Party to plug wires into a dill pickle and set it aglow. It's a simple trick that takes place on the back-deck table, and at this year's gathering, a student was given the job of sinking the wires into either end of the vegetable. "The tough part," my father joked, "is not to get electrocuted." The young lady set down her beer, securely lodged the wires, then plugged in the cord. The pickle turned an alien yellow, began to hum like a spaceship, and started cooking from the inside out. For thirty minutes, the students played this game, laughing and rearranging the wires, adding more pickles, pouring beer over them, and somehow managing not to fry one another.

In the living room, an astronomy professor took his place in the Equation-Editing Shootout, but it was nearing Saturday morning by now, and few were watching. Wine and beer had numbed senses, and even the most respectable Ph.D.'s had taken to sipping liquid nitrogen and then gargling it like mouthwash. They giggled and cheered as clouds of vapour blasted from their mouths. Bystanders covered their eyes, fearing that someone's tongue would crack and fall off, but there were no such accidents.

Actually, surprisingly, no one has ever filed an official complaint over the Physics and Astronomy Party. Like an experienced rock band, my father and his colleagues know how to put on a show *and* keep things in order.

But one incident from four years ago deserves mention. After a long and happy night, Dad and company goaded me into dumping a gallon of liquid nitrogen onto a hot barbecue. A violent mushroom cloud of burning ash enveloped me while twenty drunken guests went diving over chairs and tumbling into the doorway for shelter. The insulated vat dropped from my hands and shattered while I fell backward. I bumped my head on the wall, landed on shards of glass, and was temporarily blinded by dust. I might have had grounds for a lawsuit, but even in America, a fellow can't sue his parents and still expect a room to stay in.

This year, it had been my level-headed father's plan to ignite rocket fuel on the back porch as the grand finale, but only one of the required ingredients — pressurized nitrous oxide purchased from a novelty shop in the Castro — had been located. "We won't be going to the moon tonight," my father apologized to the half-dozen remaining students, "but this stuff will still burn." He lit up a blowtorch while a student opened an N_2O cartridge and filled a large red balloon with the gas. One student forced the nitrous oxide through a length of PVC piping while another ignited the gas on its way out the opposite end. It was true, nobody went to the moon; but the gas flared brilliantly like a miniature space shuttle for several seconds.

"This guy's so rad," a student said quietly to me. "He's such a cool professor."

"I know," I told him. "He's my dad."

MANOS DE PIEDRA

DIONNE BRAND

WHAT MAKES me remember Roberto Duran? They called him "Manos de Piedra" (hands of stone) because legend has it that at fifteen he knocked a mule out with his fist. Why is another question. That legend was surpassed by another during his last fight with Sugar Ray Leonard, when he turned away from the fight saying, "¡No más!" and got labelled as a quitter. But anyone who ever saw Duran fight knows otherwise. What didn't get wide attention was that he had stomach problems that caused him such distress that he had to quit.

I loved Roberto Duran and I hated Roberto Duran. I was always torn in those fights he had with Sugar Ray Leonard and Thomas Hearns, just like I was torn between Hearns and Sugar Ray. Duran had a face like an axe, a sharp axe. Around this face he grew a bristly, black beard and moustache that made him seem even more dangerous.

"I am not an animal in my personal life," Duran once said, "but in the ring there is an animal inside me. Sometimes it roars when the first bell rings. Sometimes it springs out later in the fight. But I can always feel it there driving me and pushing me forward." What writer cannot relate to that doubleness? That in-and-outness? That being and

non-being? That thing driving and pushing you forward out of your diffident self? Well, let me not speak for everyone. I can relate. So I loved to watch Roberto Duran moving forward with something lethal in his hands. The boxing ring became a kind of electric square when he was in it, his body the magnetic centre—even in his fights against Sugar Ray Leonard, who floated and danced and alighted for dazzlingly quick combinations; even in his fight with Tommy Hearns, who cornered and marked him like an assassin. Duran was always on the brink of causing a casualty.

So why do I remember Roberto Duran when I'm sitting in the crowd at Sully's gym, above a garage off Lansdowne Avenue on a June Sunday in Toronto, watching a card of women boxers? Maybe it's the workmanlike grittiness of the fighters. Maybe I recognize that thing inside them roaring at the first bell or waiting to spring out later in the fight. Anyway, the event's billed as "Fight Factory 101—a herstoric event—Toronto's 2nd ever all-female boxing card," presented by the Toronto Newsgirls Boxing Club, which trains out of Sully's.

Now first of all—Sully's. Somehow that name suits the fight game and the space. There must be a Sully's in every

town in the Americas. There's certainly a Sully's in every American movie about boxing. Sully must be this ubiquitous guy who stalks every city just to put his name on a boxing gym above a garage or down an alleyway, so that would-be, itinerant, and hopeful boxers can go there to jump rope, beat the heavy bag, and spar — and then come out and look down sweltering or wintering streets, convinced that they're going to leave all this behind someday.

Well, this Sully's does not disappoint. I go in with my "crew," and whom do I run into there but another writer, Rachel Zolf. She's been working out with the Newsgirls herself, and she tells me that her nickname in the ring is "Poet." (You'd have to know the four manifestations of the poet in Chinese culture to appreciate that name. Or simply read Sonia Sanchez and Anna Akhmatova.) If you're a fighter, you have to have a nickname. It's laid down as a template and it comes to define you: it's a sign telling your opponent how scared of you they need to be. It can be as tricky as "Poet" or as clear as "Scorpion," my partner's nickname. Scorpion has run a few laps and sparred a few rounds with the Newsgirls too. When Scorpion comes home one day and suggests that she might try a fight, I hear my plaintive and desperate voice say, "What about your face?!" How shallow of me. But Scorpion has a beautiful face and I convince her, for the time being, that it would be sacrilegious to ruin any element of it with a punch.

I do not have a nickname. I am only a fan, a fanatic, an aficionado of boxing matches great and small. Where was I when Muhammad Ali fought Joe Frazier or George Foreman? At Maple Leaf Gardens, watching on closed-circuit. Where was I when Roy Jones Jr. first met Antonio Tarver? In my very dingy neighbourhood bar, watching on satellite.

Where was I when Oscar de la Hoya met Félix Trinidad on Saturday, September 18, 1999? In a bar on Commercial Drive in Vancouver, watching via satellite. (And I was there at some peril to myself, among a crowd that consisted mostly of men who wanted de la Hoya to win. So I had to keep it to myself and walk away quietly when Trinidad whupped the "Golden Boy.") I consider these satellite attendances as good as being there. I recount them to friends as if I had been. At Sully's, I am actually there.

The ring takes up most of Sully's. On the walls are photos of Ali, Ken Norton, George Chuvalo, and others. Local legend has it that Ali sparred here for his Toronto fight with Chuvalo.

The crowd is a little more subdued than your typical boxing crowd—at first. It is a multicultural sketch of the people who live in this city. So are the fighters. The boxers are warming up on the sides of the ring; the sound of their fists hitting their trainers' pads with combinations they hope to execute later is ominous. The promoter is Savoy Howe, and the ringmaster is Boo "Fabulous" Watson. She takes the mike, welcoming the crowd to this historic event and announcing the sponsors. One of the sponsors is Sensual Sensations and, between the rounds to come, a well-endowed male model will display more than necessary in microfibre boxers and jockeys as he sashays the ring with the round card. But first a woman on electric violin plays the boxers' anthem: the theme from the movie *Rocky*. Then we are ready to rumble.

THE FIRST fight on the card is in the forty-eight-to-fifty-kilogram class. It's between Vilesloshani "Knuckles" Reddy and Mandy "the Bomb" Bujold. Knuckles is obviously less experienced, but she's quick and earnest. Her fans are calling out instructions to her, but the Bomb eventually gets the better of her and wins by unanimous decision. Vilesloshani doesn't look discouraged though—"Good fight, good fight," her fans tell her and she tucks the experience away for the next time. When I ask Mandy how it feels to fight and win, she tells me that her hard work has paid off. She says, "Only one person comes out of the ring, and you want to make sure it's you."

The second bout is between Johanna "Razzamataz" Bollozos and Wolven Heart. Wolven Heart is so integrated with her boxer personality that her birth name is not recorded. The crowd is behind Wolven Heart because she's from the Newsgirls, but Razzamataz Bollozos overwhelms her with punches. Wolven Heart moves too slowly and is an open target for Bollozos, who is pitiless, easily evading Wolven Heart's punches and delivering all she has to the head of her opponent. After the fight, wearing a red bandana, a muscle shirt, and jeans, Bollozos is bright-eyed with victory and tells me she feels great; she's been fighting for less than a year, out of Mississauga. "I didn't plan not to win," she says, laughing, and looks at me as if she thinks I'm an idiot when I ask if she thought she would win when she entered the ring.

Before the third fight, I talk to glove man Carlos Varelo Jr. He's got all the gloves laid out on a table, and he examines the fighters' hands before they put on the gloves. He makes sure there's no tampering—no hidden weapons. As I'm talking to him, a woman comes over to me and says that she won a ticket to come to the fight through the Toronto Women's Bookstore. She says that she didn't think she'd enjoy boxing, because it's violent, but she's having a good time. Sounding like a veteran, I say, "Sure it's violent, but you have a fair chance in there—you win, you lose, it's all up to you and your hands and your movement, your reflexes. You know yourself in a deep place there." She looks at me, still conflicted, and I shrug my shoulders, walking away.

IT'S ONE of those things you have to work out for yourself. Take the time I watched Sugar Ray Leonard and Roberto Duran fight in 1980, at Olympic Stadium in Montreal. I was sitting in this massive crowd in Maple Leaf Gardens. A couple of boxers on the undercard were fighting. That fight didn't interest me much, so I wasn't paying attention and I don't remember who the boxers were. Suddenly, about three seats away from me, a woman jumped up and started screaming at the screen, "Knock his head off, knock his fucking head off!" Well, I froze. The woman's face was so angry, so awful, that something like horror passed through me. I thought, Whoa, who the hell am I sitting here with? What kind of people are these and what did they come to see? And then of course the declensions on those questions: What kind of person am I? Well, not the kind that wants to see the guy's head knocked off, but the kind, possibly, that wants to see a certain physical play, a risking of corporeal integrity. The kind that deduces an honesty and clarity in the sort of aggression one finds in a boxing ring. Hidden aggressions and hidden intentions bother me more, as does the strong over the weak, and there's a difference between cunning and deceit…Oh, oh, now who's screaming? Obviously the referee should have stopped the fight two rounds ago—the guy had been in trouble since then but wanted to go on. Why this woman wanted this man's head knocked off only she can say, but I'm sure that she surprised herself as she surprised me and at least four rows of fans—her voice several octaves too high for her screaming to be anything other than strictly about her life. See, boxing is not a sport about excesses, and it's not about anger, which boxers will tell you makes you weak and vulnerable. It's much more precise, calculating, measured.

Fight crowds are strange, different from, say, literary-event crowds or jazz-concert crowds. You might think this is stating the obvious. You're thinking high-brow and low-brow. That's not what I mean. They're different too from rock-concert crowds or basketball crowds or even hockey-game crowds. Fight crowds actually have elements of all those. They have a deep and unparalleled appreciation of the grace and cleverness—the endurance and innovation and imagination—of boxers, of their virtuosity, and of the way they play with chaos.

A good match is as multidirectional and contrapuntal as, say, John Coltrane and Rashied Ali playing "Venus." It requires that kind of physical and lyrical virtuosity, that liminal combination of improvisation and composition.

THE CROWD at Sully's is a family crowd; there are teenagers and babies, mothers and fathers, lovers, prowlers.…The noise level rises and falls throughout each round. Fans urge their favourite boxers and trainers call out instructions. There's a ragged line of women who stand up at the front, one with a baby on her side, yelling things like, "Back her up now! Do it now—stick, stick! You got her! Come on!" The fight doctor visits the ring several times to check cuts and concussions.

I catch Heather Hopkins after she has beaten Vanessa Francis in a rematch of their fight from some months ago. Heather fights out of the Cabbagetown Boxing Club and is lean and rapier-like. She tells me it's her tenth fight and that fighting is exhilarating; she feels on top of the world and there's nothing like it.

In the next bout, a man in the audience yells to his fighter in the blue corner, "She's older and slower, girl. You can get her!" The audience groans disapproval—after all, whether they're men or women, it's a women's liberation audience—and this seems to motivate the fighter in the red corner. She might be older, and she does look a little "beat-up," but that only makes her more cunning, and the insult from the spectator is enough to doom his fighter and propel the other boxer to victory.

We're building up to the two last fights, and for those who care to notice, the model's briefs are becoming briefer as the fights go by. For the bout between Rita "Piranha" Lwanga and Lina Barkas, he wears a tiny blue strip of shorts as he hoists the round cards.

With a nickname like "Piranha," you'd expect a kind of deadly industriousness, with hardly any blood in the water. And so gravely does Rita Piranha go about her task that at

the merciful end there's little sign of life from the taller Barkas. Lwanga's great skill, my friend Virma says in my ear, is ring generalship. Lwanga manages the ring, moving Barkas about, cutting off all her exits, and working the body until the head falls.

FABULOUS WATSON announces the last fight of the afternoon. "In the red corner, Joyce 'the Furious' Findlay," she bellows. "And in the blue corner, Canadian Champion Amanda 'Bambam' Beaulieu!"

I'm standing with my friend Virma for this one. Virma has fought Joyce the Furious before, and lost. Virma says that when Joyce hit her it was stunning and terrible. Joyce has been sitting grimly in the front row through all the bouts so far, with her hands taped, and a blue bandana and a hoodie over her head to keep warm. She and Razzamataz Bollozos fight out of the Chris Johnson Fighting Alliance. When Razzamataz Bollozos fought earlier, Joyce yelled instructions to help her to victory. Joyce is nervous and pumped, and you can tell that she is deadly serious about winning. At the bell, she turns

into Roberto Duran coming forward—that thing inside her propelling her toward Amanda Beaulieu. But Beaulieu is more crafty, more experienced, and holds her off. The noise of the crowd crests higher and higher. I hear Virma yelling to Joyce, "Back her up, back her up; out of the corner, out of the corner. Good left. Slip! Slip! Now body, body! Work the body when you're in there! Her left side is open! Upper cut, upper cut! Move! Move!"

I join in. "To the body, Joyce, to the body! She's there, Joyce, she's there!" To no avail. Joyce is a valiant fighter, but Amanda Beaulieu is a finesse boxer, and boxer invariably beats fighter. Why? Because it's hard to arrive at the nexus of improvisation and composition.

Joyce is inconsolable. No amount of "Good job, Joyce; good fight, Joyce," will do. Her eyes are red, her mouth rigid, and the heat off her body incendiary; she is still in that moment—the roaring in her head, the lethal possibilities of her hands—when that fight had to do with her life and something that would have changed if she'd won.

AN INTERVIEW WITH DAVID SEDARIS

ESTA SPALDING

ESSAYIST AND *short-story writer David Sedaris first leaped into the popular consciousness with a story he read on* NPR's Morning Edition. *That story, called "The SantaLand Diaries," told of his brief Christmas stint as a Macy's elf. It led to a book contract for his first collection,* Barrel Fever, *and then to four more collections:* Naked, Holidays on Ice, Me Talk Pretty One Day, *and* Dress Your Family in Corduroy and Denim, *each of which has sold millions of copies. A regular contributor to* NPR *and* The New Yorker, *David Sedaris was recently dubbed by the* New York Times *"America's pre-eminent humorist."*

Sedaris's latest project is an anthology of short stories, the proceeds of which will go to 826NYC, a non-profit literacy group. Titled Children Playing Before a Statue of Hercules, *the anthology was selected, edited, and introduced by Sedaris. In his introduction, he gives a brief, comic overview of his twenty-year romance with the short story. (In one memorable passage, he recounts how he once typed a page from an Alice Munro story and left it in his typewriter, in the hopes that a burglar would find it and think he had written Munro's words.) I spoke to Sedaris by phone in August 2005. He was in his home in Normandy, France, and I was in Ontario; it was the middle of the afternoon for me, and it was only as we finished talking that I realized it was nearly midnight on his end.*

ES   Can you tell me about the title *Children Playing Before a Statue of Hercules?*

DS   Well, I had to come up with a title, and I didn't want to use the word "I." I mean, basically, the title would be *My Favourite Short Stories*, but I didn't want to suggest that the only thing that was worthy about, say, a Richard Yates story was that it's my favourite. So I was searching for a title, and I was in a museum in Munich and I saw a painting called *Children Playing Before a Statue of Hercules*, and I thought, Oh, that's a good title. I think I probably would have found any way to justify it. But I thought, well, these writers are huge to me, and I thought of myself as like a child, you know, just sort of scratching around in their shadows.

ES   In the introduction to the anthology, you describe your younger self, saying, "Having spent a life trying to fit the will of others, I was unable to distinguish between what I enjoyed and what I thought I should enjoy." I think that's just such a lovely encapsulation of what so many of us feel when we're young.

DS   Developing an opinion, developing our own tastes, comes from reading a lot—in isolation. If I had gone to a school that had a writing program, I don't know that I would have become so confident in my tastes, because there would have been other people who had read the same book, who said, "Oh, that's crap" or "That's completely derivative." But I didn't really have a fellowship; I was on my own.

ES   So you had to actually think about what measured up for you.

DS   Yes, without fear of anybody having read the same book.

ES   And why did the short-story form appeal to you so much?

DS   I loved how you could read a short story and it could just sort of colour the rest of your day. That something so short can have such a profound effect is amazing. I go to the movies just about every day, and I'm always hoping that the same thing will happen, and half the time I forget the movie while I'm watching it. But once in a while when you leave the theatre, you're kind of in a daze, and you go to the grocery store and nothing makes sense. It doesn't make sense that people are walking around with baskets in their hands. It doesn't make sense that there's food piled in the produce section and there are cans that are sealed shut. Nothing makes sense. I guess that's the way I feel after I read a really good story. I don't recognize the world anymore.

ES   In those first moments of really falling into the reading of short stories, who were the writers that you discovered you liked?

DS   Flannery O'Connor was one. When I read her, it was a real shock to me. I'd never read anything like it. I mean, we had to read certain things in high school, but I'd never read anything so funny. I like how her stories make me feel very careful, like you laugh at a character and then you realize that that character is yourself, and then you finish the story and you say, "Well, I'm not going to be like that anymore." Two days later you're back to yourself. But she could at least sort of change somebody or make them think for two days; that's saying something.

ES   You grew up in the South. Was it also seeing the South depicted in a way that was true to your own experience?

DS   I think part of it was reading good dialect, having read bad dialect for so many years. I could hear the people—I could just hear them off the page. So when I first started reading O'Connor it was just so exciting, and it was the same way when I first read Tobias Wolff. He had a story in *The New Yorker* a few weeks ago, and I had to clean the house, I had to get everything just so before I read it. I was so excited. I like how his stories are abstract but not abstract. The characters seem completely real to me.

ES   I loved that the anthology ends with Wolff's story about a literary critic being shot to death. It's about the last seconds of a literary critic's life. At the start of the story, this man—the critic—has lost his love for literature, but in the final moments of his life, he returns to the moment in childhood when he first fell in love with the sound of words. What an extraordinary ending—to his life, to the story, to the anthology.

DS   Isn't that such a good story? I love how it starts off funny. I mean, you laugh out loud.

ES   So for you, what's the ideal shape of a story? I know that's an amorphous question, but I want to understand something about the form of the stories that appeal to you.

DS   One of my teachers, a poet named Susan Wheeler, once asked me what stories I liked, and I told her about this Tobias Wolff story called "Hunters in the Snow." She asked me to go through the story and tell her how it was put together. So I went through the story and I said, "A person is introduced and we see what his face looks like, and then he says three lines, and then somebody else is introduced, and then they say two lines…" I mean, I was looking at it in the same way that I paint. When my boyfriend paints, he paints everything at the same time; he sees the whole, and he can put the whole together out of brush strokes. Whereas if I'm painting, let's say, a leaf, I don't know that I ever really look at the leaf. It's just an idea of a leaf. I paint every vein—and it's painstaking—but when I finish, it doesn't look like a leaf.

It's the same with reading. I read something I really love and I think, Gosh, what is it? Is there some secret here? Is there some code? But I can't decode it. But I guess one thing

I like, which I notice in Flannery O'Connor, and which I notice in Tobias Wolff, is that when you laugh at things and then something happens, that laughter sort of turns on you. You feel bad for ever laughing.

The story that I wrote that comes closest to what I feel like a story should be is called "Repeat After Me." It's about visiting my older sister, and it actually feels grown-up to me. It's the kind of story I always wanted to write when I decided that I wanted to write. I don't know that I could do it again or that I could break it down into a formula, but I know that when I read that story it feels complete. It starts off funny, and then at the end it's not so funny any more. I think that is the only thing I ever wrote and looked at and thought, That's not bad.

ES   Were there writers that were hard to leave out of the anthology? I mean, there are some obvious omissions — Raymond Carver and Richard Ford, for instance.

DS   Oh, there were a lot of people who were hard to leave out. Like Mavis Gallant — I just started reading her last year and I had that feeling that's like, "What have I been doing with my life?" But for the anthology I wanted stories that had stood some test of time for me, so I had to leave her out and that was difficult. Joy Williams is somebody whom I like a lot, and I had to leave her out. Raymond Carver is a writer who was such an inspiration when I first started writing. He made it look so easy; his sentences were so simple that I thought, I can do that. Then, of course, you realize that you can't. But when I went back and reread him, I thought, the thing that had stuck with me from those stories was that they had made me feel hopeful, but the most I can say about them now is that they're good for a young person to read. For instance the story about the baker —

ES   "A Small, Good Thing."

DS   Yeah. I reread that and I just wanted it to be rewritten. I suppose I wished that he was still around and that he could have rewritten that story. Not for me — I mean, I think that

it's too bad that he died so young. The last story he published, about Kafka, was really so different from the stories he wrote in his first collection.

ES   So many of the stories in the anthology are self-conscious about how we tell stories or about how we use other people as material for our storytelling. The Richard Yates story is filled with observations about how other people are being described by the character who is the storyteller. In the Lorrie Moore story, there's a mother who's a writer and her baby gets cancer. The mother and father in the story keep talking about how the mother's going to have to take notes about what's happening so she can write the story of the baby's cancer in order to pay the doctor's bills. In Alice Munro's story "Half a Grapefruit," the character Rose takes the people that she meets at school — their lives, their foibles, their troubles — and she turns those people into characters for her tales. I guess I wondered if you were conscious of choosing stories that are about that writerly experience of storytelling?

DS   Oh, it's completely unconscious. But it's interesting to me because it's something that preoccupies me. "Half a Grapefruit" is something I read for the first time so long ago, and the Richard Yates story — I wasn't really writing when I first read that. I mean, I was just keeping a diary. So I guess that question was preoccupying me before I even started writing stories.

ES   You must have dealt with that question in your own experience as a writer.

DS   Sure. And I can understand a reader's desire to know whether something is true or not. Like it was interesting for me to read the biography of Richard Yates that came out last year and to realize that he was basically writing non-fiction. In real life his mother's name is Dookie, and in the story in the anthology her name is Pookie. And she was a failed artist, and they lived in a number of apartments, and they moved from this place to that, just like in the story. One of my favourite novels by Yates is *The Easter Parade*—it includes a letter that a sister writes to her brother from a sanatorium, and it is verbatim a letter his sister wrote to him. Or that Lorrie Moore story…I know that when I met her, I wanted to ask, "Do you have any children?" But I didn't ask.

When I'm doing a reading, people will often ask me, "How much of that story is true?" And I always feel like saying, "None of your business." When I read stories—for instance the stories in the anthology—I think a great number of them could be true, and then I think, so it must be easy to take true things and turn them into fiction, and I read those stories over and over again for clues. Or I'll sit down and think, okay, I'll write about myself, and I'll just disguise it. I'll say that I'm a father and that I have two children, but I'll still be myself. But then one of the children is in the oven and it just gets out of hand. I don't know how to do what those authors do; I'm incapable of it, and so I'm in awe of it.

ES   Okay, but you describe your mother in one of your pieces, you say, "She played the ringleader blowing the whistle and charming the crowd with her jokes and exaggerated stories. Her observations would be collected and delivered as part of a routine that bore little resemblance to our lives." And that makes me wonder if your mother's storytelling shaped your approach to writing in some way.

DS   Oh, definitely. I mean, I tell stories in the same way that she did: something happens and you tell one person and it's changed a little bit, and then you tell another person and another person, and after a while…Sometimes when people say to me, "That's not true," I think, What does it matter? It's a story.

ES   I know what you mean. I come from a household of writers, and there's great respect for the well-exaggerated tale in our family.

DS   It's different if you're telling a story and you're talking about your brother and you say your brother went to jail for five days, and your brother never went to jail. Then I can

see that is important, because someone's not going to hire your brother because they think he's been in jail. So, in that sense, I need to be factual. There was a story of mine in *The New Yorker* last week, and before it was published I gave it to everyone who was in the story and I said, "If there's anything you want me to change or get rid of, I'll do it. I don't think I've said anything that would cast you in a bad light, but if you think I've said something that casts you in a bad light, tell me and I'll get rid of it." For myself, I don't care.

ES   Well, if this exaggerating was something your mother did, it must be something that your family understands.

DS   Yes, but sometimes you read something about yourself and you laugh and you say, "Oh, that's funny. I remember when I said that or did that." But when somebody else says, "Can you believe what your brother wrote about you?" it's not so funny any more. People will often say to me, "How can your family stand you?" But I haven't told any of their secrets.

ES   I have a mother who wrote a non-fiction story about me being locked in an outhouse by an orangutan.

DS   [*laughs*]

ES   That was telling a secret. Is there anything that you won't write about from your life?

DS   I don't write about sex. I'm always sort of amazed when people do write about sex in a non-fiction way. For instance, there's a story of mine in an anthology called *Scoot Over, Skinny*, which is all stories about obesity. This guy who weighed four hundred pounds wrote about meeting women in the newspaper, and about how he met this one woman and she said she wouldn't let him fuck her, but he could eat her out. And then he ate her out and then he ate her ass. I read that and I thought, I couldn't write that. I couldn't. He's very honest, and that's great, but I just couldn't write that. And I don't think that anybody would necessarily want me to. I don't think I'm depriving anybody of anything. [*laughs*] Just in terms of myself, there's certain things you don't write about just because it doesn't look good. Or let's say, maybe from time to time I do a good thing, but I won't write about that either. It would negate it to write about it.

ES   So you can only write about yourself in a way that's demeaning or self-mocking?

DS   Pretty much, yeah.

ES   You often write as an outsider. Is that hard now that you're so successful?

DS   No, because I live in Europe. More than anything, I'm an outsider, a foreigner. That's the number-one thing that I am.

ES   Do you like that? Are you more comfortable feeling like an outsider?

DS   Yeah. I like kind of not quite understanding what's going on. For instance, I went to the supermarket yesterday and in the garden section they were selling a life-sized black slave girl with a rag tied around her head. She's lifting a pot as if she's offering it to her master, and there was a sign on it that said, "This is a plant holder, not a trash can." [laughs] In the United States, I think that sign would read differently. You know, "This is garbage, but not a garbage can," or, "This is a racial stereotype, not a plant holder." I can think about something like that for hours.

ES   One of the articles I read about you said that you're writing a novel.

DS   Well, I'm supposed to, but I don't know how to. You know, now and then you read about somebody who wrote a novel in three weeks, and I guess every day when I wake up, I hope that's going to happen to me. But I don't know … maybe people just kind of write what they write and that's

their thing. This year I took the fall off. So I don't have any deadlines, I don't have any assignments, I don't have anything I have to do. I still work every day. Normally when I'm scheduled to do a reading tour, I think to myself, I have to finish this story by Wednesday. But now I don't have to necessarily finish it by any time. I still sit at my desk every day, but it's just kind of with a different spirit. There was an article in *The New Yorker* a few weeks ago about leeches, and apparently there are leeches that live in the anuses of hippopotamuses. So yesterday I wrote a story about a leech that lives in the asshole of a hippo. It's like a fable. The leech lives in the hippo's ass, and the hippo won't talk to it because it doesn't want this deadbeat living for free. The hippo says, "If you gave me a little money every month, that would be different, but as it is, no, I'm not talking to you. I don't want anything to do with you." It goes on from there. And it's fun because it's completely made up. I mean, there are some elements, some things that are going on in my own life that got incorporated into it, but just in an abstract way. It isn't like the leech goes on a book tour. If I read that story out loud, nobody will say, "How much of that is true?"

ES   [laughs] Many of the stories in the anthology have a sense of nostalgia about them. Do you think your own writing is nostalgic, or do these stories carry some kind of mood or tone that you yourself have trouble getting down on the page?

DS   I think that's more it. I'm a nostalgic person. I think I definitely am, but I'm not sure what I'm nostalgic for. Maybe I'm nostalgic for experiences that I didn't have.

THE CHORUS IS IN OUR HEADS

or, Pier Paolo Pasolini

JOHN BERGER

If I say he was like an angel, I can't imagine anything more stupid being said about him. An angel painted by Cosimo Tura? No. There's a St. George by Tura which is his speaking likeness! He abhorred official saints and beatific angels. So why say it? Because his habitual and immense sadness allowed him to share jokes, and the look on his distressed face distributed laughter, guessing exactly who needed it most. And the more intimate his touch, the more lucid it became! He could whisper to people softly about the worst that was happening to them and they somehow suffered a little less. "For we never have despair without some small hope." "*Disperazione senza un po' di speranza.*" Pier Paolo Pasolini (1922–1975).

I THINK he doubted many things about himself, but never his gift of prophesy which was, perhaps, the one thing he would have liked to have doubted. Yet, since he was prophetic, he comes to our aid in what we are living today. I have just watched a film made in 1963. Astonishingly it was never publicly shown. It arrives like the proverbial message put in a bottle and washed up forty years later on our beach.

At that earlier time many people followed world events by watching not the TV news but newsreels in cinemas. In 1962, G. Ferranti, an Italian producer of such reels, had a bright idea. He would give the already-notorious Pasolini access to his news archives from 1945 to 1962, in order to answer the question Why was there everywhere in the world a fear of war? He could edit whatever material he chose, and write a voice-over commentary. The resulting one-hour film would hopefully boost the newsreel company's prestige. The question was "hot" because, at that moment, the fear of yet another world war was indeed widespread. The nuclear warhead crisis between Cuba, the U.S., and the U.S.S.R. erupted in October 1962.

Pasolini, who had already made *Accattone*, *Mamma Roma*, and "La Ricotta," accepted for his own reasons, because he was in love with and at war with History. He made the film, and entitled it *La Rabbia* (Rage).

When the producers saw it, they got cold feet and insisted that a second filmmaker, a notoriously right-wing

journalist called Giovanni Guareschi, should now make a second part and that the two films be presented as one. As things turned out, neither was shown.

La Rabbia, I would say, is a film inspired by a fierce sense of endurance, not anger. Pasolini looks at what happens in the world with unflinching lucidity. (There are angels drawn by Rembrandt who have the same gaze.) And he does so because reality is all we have to love. There's nothing else.

His dismissal of the hypocrisies, half-truths, and pretenses of the greedy and powerful is total because they breed and foster ignorance, which is a form of blindness toward reality. Also because they shit on memory, including the memory of language itself, which is our first heritage.

Yet the reality he loved could not be simply endorsed, for at that moment it represented a too-deep historical disappointment. The ancient hopes which flowered and opened out in 1945, after the defeat of Fascism, had been betrayed.

The U.S.S.R. had invaded Hungary. France had begun its cowardly war against Algeria. The coming to independence of the former African colonies was a macabre charade. Lumumba had been liquidated by the puppets of the CIA. Neo-capitalism was already planning its global takeover.

Yet despite this, what had been bequeathed was far too precious and too tough to abandon. Or, to put it another way, the unspoken ubiquitous demands of reality were impossible to ignore. The demand in a way a shawl was worn. In a young man's face. In a street full of people demanding less injustice. In the laughter of their expectations and the recklessness of their jokes. From this came his rage of endurance.

PASOLINI'S ANSWER to the original question was simple: the class struggle explains war.

The film ends with an imaginary soliloquy by Gagarin, after he has seen the planet from outer space, in which he observes that all men, seen from that distance away, are brothers who should renounce the planet's bloody practices.

Essentially, however, the film is about experiences which both the question and answer leave aside. About the coldness of winter for the homeless. About the warmth that the remembering of revolutionary heroes can offer, about the irreconcilability of freedom and hate, about the peasant flair of Pope John XXII whose eyes smile like a tortoise, about Stalin's faults which were our faults, about the devilish temptation of thinking any struggle is over, about the death of Marilyn Monroe and how beauty is all that remains from the stupidity of the past and the savagery of the future, about how Nature and Wealth are the same thing for the possessing classes, about our mothers and their hereditary tears, about the children of children of children, about the injustices that follow even a noble victory, about the little panic in the eyes of Sophia Loren when she watches a fisherman's hands cutting open an eel....

The commentary over the black-and-white film is spoken by two anonymous voices; in fact the voices of two of his friends: the painter Renato Guttuso and the writer Giorgio Bassani. One is like the voice of an urgent commentator, and the other the voice of someone who is half-historian and half-poet, a soothsayer's voice. Among the major news items covered are the Hungarian revolution of 1956, Eisenhower running a second time for president, the coronation of Queen Elizabeth, Castro's victory in Cuba.

The first voice informs us and the second one reminds us. Of what? Not exactly of the forgotten (it is more cunning), but rather of what we have chosen to forget, and such choices often begin in childhood. Pasolini forgot nothing from his childhood—hence the constant coexistence in what he seeks of pain and fun. We are made ashamed of our forgetting.

The two voices function like a Greek chorus. They cannot affect the outcome of what is being shown. They do not interpret. They question, listen, observe, and then give voice to what the viewer may, more or less inarticulately, be feeling.

And they achieve this because they are aware that the language being shared by actors, chorus, and viewer is a depot of an age-long common experience. The language itself is complicit with our reactions. It cannot be cheated. The voices speak out not to cap an argument, but because it would be shameful, given the length of human experience and pain, if what they had to say was not said. Should it go unsaid, the capacity for being human would be slightly diminished.

In ancient Greece the chorus was made up not of actors, but of male citizens, chosen for that year by the chorus-master, the *choragus*. They represented the city, they came from the agora, the forum. Yet as chorus they became the voices of several generations. When they spoke of what the public had already recognized, they were grandparents. When they gave voice to what the public felt but had been unable to articulate, they were the unborn.

All this Pasolini does single-handed with his two voices as he paces, enraged, between the ancient world, which will disappear with the last peasant, and the future world of ferocious calculation.

At several moments the film reminds us of the limits of rational explanation, and of the frequent vulgarity of terms like *optimism* and *pessimism*.

The best brains of Europe and the U.S., it announces, are theoretically explaining what it means to die (fighting with Castro) in Cuba. Yet what it really means to die in Cuba—or Naples or Seville—can only be told with pity, in the light of a song and in the light of tears.

At another moment it proposes that all of us dream of the right to be like some of our ancestors were! And then it adds: only revolution can save the past.

LA RABBIA is a film of love. Yet its lucidity is comparable to that in Kafka's aphorism: "The Good is, in a certain sense, comfortless."

That is why I say Pasolini was like an angel.

The film lasts only an hour, an hour that was fashioned, measured, edited forty years ago. And it is in such contrast to the news commentaries we watch and the information fed to us now that, when the hour is over, you tell yourself that it is not only animal and plant species which are being destroyed or made extinct today, but also set after set of our human priorities. The latter are systematically sprayed day and night by the mass news media.

The ethicides are perhaps less effective, less speedy than the controllers hoped, but they have succeeded in burying and covering up the imaginative space that any central public forum represents and requires. (Our forums are everywhere, but for the moment they are marginal.) And on the wasteland of the covered-over forums (reminiscent of the wasteland on which he was assassinated by the Fascists), Pasolini joins us with his Rabbia, and his enduring example of how to carry the chorus in our heads.

WHY I RIDE A BICYCLE

SARMISHTA SUBRAMANIAN

ON MY first birthday, with all the guests assembled in my grandparents' Calcutta home eating cake from Fleury's, I walked for the first time. Actually, I'm told, I ran—at breakneck speed. I rose shakily from the polished concrete floor at my mother's feet and raced to a pair of legs that loomed like twin water towers across the room. For the next hour, I sped madly from one set of legs to the next. In the part of the story my mother loves best, it became so harrowing for the people watching that thereafter when I entered a room, all the adults would immediately sit down. There had been no foreshadowing of this milestone—no assisted walking, no wobbly attempts. If the Jesuits are to be believed, temperament exerts itself early in life, and I must have been reluctant even then to try and fail. My parents surely puzzled over why their first-born, aged one, was still crawling. I'd bloomed early when it came to exercising my tongue, babble quickly giving way to words, which clustered into proto-sentences. But I didn't so much as stand on my own—until, presumably, I decided in my one-year-old mind that this was all going to work out, and then I didn't walk; I ran.

In this way, I waited thirty-two years before I rode a bicycle for the first time, down a tree-lined street in Toronto. I had barely sat on one before, so there were a few false starts as my boyfriend, Stephen, called out instructions beside me—*Relax your arms*; *don't think about the steering*; *the weight of your body is all on your bum*; *think about your bum* (which made me laugh so much, I almost did fall). But then I found I was moving. And since I, more than most objects, seem to obey Newton's first law of motion—an object in motion will remain in motion until

acted upon by an external force (the converse is, sadly, equally true)—off I went, whizzing downhill, weaving like a drunk, and smiling idiotically, all of life seeming like an Edith Piaf song. I didn't stop until three blocks later, where a car was speeding toward the intersection. I'd not yet learned to brake (I hadn't had to), so I just dropped both feet to the ground inelegantly. Then I got back on the bicycle and did the whole thing again.

I don't know why I'd never learned to ride before—a rite of passage that most people experience somewhere around age six. Clearly, not all middle-class parents in India teach their children to ride bicycles. Mine certainly didn't. I had singing lessons and, briefly, dancing lessons, during which I (always happier on one side of the mind-body divide) elected instead to sing. I had math tutors and physics tutors. I even had swimming lessons. No bicycles.

Later in life, some combination of fear, embarrassment, busyness, and inertia kept me from learning to ride. But desires, like terrors, can surface in the pillowy comfort of semi-consciousness, and I rode for years in my dreams—through hilly pastures and on dark, iridescent asphalt, dodging traffic. On those mornings, I would wake up with a real pang: *Oh, that didn't really happen.*

It's strange to come to this mysterious activity as an adult. Most people my age have been riding for so long they give little thought to an act that is nothing short of miraculous. But getting on a bike for the first time at thirty-three reveals the triumph of physics and human will that is cycling. Five hundred years ago, someone (the tireless Leonardo da Vinci, it was thought) drew a sketch of what was meant to be the world's first bicycle, though both sketch and artist are now disputed. Since then we've had the "walking machine" (Baron von Drais of Sauerbrun's wooden two-wheeled contraption without pedals, designed to aid walkers — a bicycle even I could have ridden), velocipedes, ordinaries, high-wheel tricycles. Each is a marvel of engineering and machine-age design, but also of something more intangible.

To operate a bicycle is to balance upon two tubes of rubber and wire, connected by a frame, and to propel them forward with no more than a little foot power and the conviction that you can. We think bicycles carry us forward, but they don't: we carry them. It is largely human will that keeps bicycle and rider in motion, as well as that law of Newton's, which can be adapted into an exhortation — *Move, because if you are moving, you will keep moving.* How much of our lives are lived like this.

FEAR CAN breed a strange attraction, and I loved bicycling for years before I could do it. Maybe "fear" is too strong a word, but it seems the right foil to that careless confidence it takes to ride, one best developed in childhood. Minus the confidence, one sees a panopticon of minor tragedies. There is no reason one should be able to balance 112 pounds on a bicycle's delicate frame. There is no reason one should be able to turn sleek curving corners, slanting like an italic into the wind, or trace a perfect line on the road, untrembling, sure-footed. Why, in the face of so many distractions, probabilities, mechanical failures, should anything happen so flawlessly? And how in life do so many things, in fact, happen flawlessly — dancers executing stunning arabesques each night for a season; singers climbing notes like staircases with never a missed step; auricles and ventricles pumping blood, minute after minute after minute, whole systems working in unison?

Perfection, even in its mundane forms, is mystifying when you stop to think about it. Are some people simply better suited to infallibility than others? Popes, I suppose. I am a well-employed editor. I sing and play guitar and I knit and cook, all rea-

sonably well. But infallibility? I don't think I can do one thing flawlessly — not even sleep. You may have to believe in infallibility to be infallible. Or maybe it just takes practice — that bridge between the swamp of incapacity and the pristine surface of proficiency. Maybe all one needs in order to ride a bicycle is this smoothing of wrinkles, the extermination of mistakes.

Exactly the opposite is true. Riding a bicycle depends upon — no, *is* — a series of mistakes and corrections. A free-standing bicycle is unstable unless its centre of gravity stays constant — which in an object so slender is an impossibility. In reality, that point moves, and the bicycle must follow. Only in motion is balance achieved and human will supplanted by the even mightier force of forward momentum. Until then, we ride, chasing this centre of gravity, attempting to keep the metaphorical broom balanced on the tip of a finger. That single, unswerving line is in fact a zigzag, a sequence of right turns and left turns made by the bicycle unbeknownst to the rider, continual adjustments so minuscule as to be unseen but there nonetheless. Each is a correction that itself eventually becomes a mistake to be adjusted by another eventual mistake. Such flawed motions propel us forward. A bicycle ride is an homage to the sublime beauty of failures.

Bicycle physics is full of such moments. Here's another: to turn a bicycle to the right, you must first actually turn the handlebars slightly to the left. (It's true; we all do it, even without thinking.) Otherwise, the centrifugal force would throw you off the bicycle the other way. Thinking of going in exactly the opposite direction gets you closer to where you want to go.

Bicycle sociology is the individual multiplied exponentially. David Gordon Wilson writes in his book *Bicycling Science* that cycling is the pinnacle of human power generation, our most efficient energy use. So much goes into producing these revolutions of the wheel: breathing rates, oxygen rates, pedal torque, gyroscopic action. And in Beijing, in Amsterdam, and, more recently, in Havana — true bicycle cities — the sheer numbers of *those* revolutions intimate other revolutions. One recalls iconic images of suffragists on bikes, or of dress-reform activists who, with bicycles as tools, altered women's fashions irrevocably near the turn of the twentieth century—imagine those flared art nouveau–era skirts (complete with several pounds of underwear) behind handlebars! And cyclists organized as The League of American Wheelmen brought good roads (and, yes, eventually, the automobile) to Kansas, Delaware, California. The bicycle remains an icon of proletarians, workers, citizens: roles that in North America these days are often subsumed into other roles—tourist, consumer, recreational athlete—though even here, the bicycle is inherently egalitarian. We all—Lance Armstrong, you, I—ride the same bike, more or less. The machine that distinguishes his performance from ours is really one of flesh and bone, which he has forged with patience, training and will.

BICYCLING, ONE could argue, is the opposite of writing (and, I suppose, of editing). To ride well, it is imperative not to think, not to consider the possibilities or the impossibilities. There are far too many of each. To write well—I paraphrase Arnold Bennett—one must think and feel more, infinitely more. I internalized Bennett's advice twenty years before I encountered it. I thought and felt deeply, as often as I could. I reasoned; I brooded. And my not riding was equally the story of a profound attraction to those activities, and of a profound lack of interest in that other machine you need in order to ride a bicycle.

The problem was the body. I had no time for its thirsts, its crass demands, its sulking threats. It bored and occasionally annoyed me, and through years of limiting the attention I gave it, I came to forget I had one. Other people I knew were like the active boys and girls who swam and surfed and played basketball in science-textbook illustrations—all muscle and sinew and blood vessels, enveloped in taut, healthy skin. Me, I was outside the laws of simple biology.

The literature of my youth was full of models for my approach: consumptive English heroines who lived despite their bodies, well-mannered Victorians who hid their physical aspects behind corsets and baroque social rituals, and intellectual and spiritual figures from both the West and East whose days were spent in the stratosphere of the mind. They spelled out in unambiguous terms the dynamics of mind-body dualism. I saw the armies laid out on the battlefield, and there was no question on which side I was fighting. As a child, I read Austen and Dickens and wrote doggerel, and, most tragically, conducted with a pencil the New York Philharmonic playing Bernstein on my parents' stereo. When I moved to this country as a teenager, I managed the impossible: I had the compulsory physical-education requirement lifted on grounds of the huge cultural transition I was making. At fifteen, influenced by a precocious friend, I plunged into Sartre, who is no model of any kind for a fifteen-year-old. Ronald Hayman wrote of Sartre, "To reassure his mind that it had nothing to fear from sibling rivalry with his maltreated body he constantly ignored all messages it sent out.... He resented the time he had to spend on washing, shaving, cleaning his teeth, taking a bath, excreting and he would economize by carrying on conversations through the bathroom door." Some of that described me, too, though the comparison with Sartre ends there.

I recovered, eventually, from the weight of all this. Sarah Vowell writes in her collection of essays *The Partly Cloudy Patriot* of being so serious as a child that growing up in fact entailed becoming *less* mature. My development took a similar path. I have a fondness these days for just the kinds of sparkly trinkets and toys and colourful frocks I turned my nose up at so many years ago. My speech, for better or worse, would now fit better on a teen TV drama than in a Victorian novel. And I am no longer immune to the charms of corporeal existence these days. Walking is a miracle almost on par with riding; swimming is, well, like walking on water; and tennis has a poetry that only a few writers, notably David Foster Wallace, have explored.

But it took a long time to come to this. In the intervening years, I never felt the ill effects of indolence or of recklessly ignoring hunger, thirst, sleep. I was healthy; my weight seldom fluctuated. Apparently, even my body had no time for base appetites. As an adult, I came to view it more as a house for my thinking parts. No, not a house—that suggests too much a feeling of being at home. A shop. A shop that is a front for other operations. No transactions really take place here, but we have to keep it open to allow the real work upstairs to take place.

Bicycling, of course, is all about the business downstairs. Trying to turn it into upstairs work, I've learned over the years, only makes it more challenging. One cannot enjoy the blur of motion by deconstructing it into a series of stationary poses; movement wilts under such intense focus. A bicycle ride is better viewed like a flipbook than like a slide under a microscope. Slow it down, and—well, you stop.

IT'S A linguistic tic of our times to describe the simplicity of a task by comparing it with riding a bicycle. Yes, hmm, I've always nodded. Like riding a bicycle—really, *that* easy? My inability to ride seemed to go hand in hand with my deficiency in carrying out other simple tasks—the scattered quotidian requisites of adulthood, say, which nearly everyone else of my generation seems to have mastered: regular doctor's appointments, paying bills, returning library books, filing taxes on time. Not riding could even have been a symbol for why I felt ill at ease in that stage of my life cycle. Stephen and I had remained agnostic on the question of marriage, content to keep our lives joined in a Venn-diagram unit, as we had for six years. I couldn't contemplate children, in part because I myself still felt like a child. I'd

see young parents urging on tots on bikes with training wheels and fantasize—not about little ones of my own, but about those training wheels for myself!

My bicycle, a blue Raleigh mountain bike, was a birthday present from Stephen six months after we met. I declined the gift at first—it was too expensive; it was too soon. But I knew even then that it was an extraordinary present, because it was a promise—a promise, if you will, of training wheels.

In that first year, Stephen and I saw all the usual ups and downs of any new relationship—maybe more. Stephen is an exquisitely still and gentle person, but my path through life is more like a very healthy EKG chart. I wondered during some of the more tenuous periods about that bike. Would it outlive this nascent union? Was it in fact a sign that, whatever we thought during those uncertain moments, something greater bound us together? Or would I one day be explaining to a new partner why I had a bike I'd never used? Sometimes, in my most fearful, or selfish, moments (are those the same?), I thought to myself that I should learn to ride that bike soon, because who knew about the future? Romantic partners enter our lives with their particular enthusiasms, their foreign rituals of eating and sleeping and brushing teeth, which merge with our own—until one day, suddenly, with no real warning, they, and their worlds, are gone.

But I didn't learn to ride. I moved the bike in and out of apartments and houses. Stephen and I took it out exactly twice in six years. My greatest stride was in being able to mount it and then walk it home without handling it as though it was a sidecar on a spaceship, or a mule on a leash.

And then, one day I got on the bike and began to ride. The real surprise is that this didn't surprise me. The catalyst was Stephen's purchase of a new bicycle for himself. But I had just a day earlier had one of those bicycle dreams; I was riding down a steep incline amid a parade of cars, terrified—but I kept riding, and I realized I was going to make it. When I later rode my bicycle past those stop signs on that afternoon in May, the sensation was quite familiar; the physical world was merely catching up.

There were few things I wanted to do over the next few months other than ride. Each day brought a minor milestone — how often in life is it that way? By the time one is thirty-three, milestones are spaced so widely the fearful person learns to avoid them, along with everything else. Now there were dozens. I learned to brake. I crossed a major street without dismounting. I rode on grass, careening up and down the slopes of an out-of-the-way park. Each day was new: hands-free, riding alone, the first ride after dark, *the first ride after dark!* — the city around me an alternate geography, its outlines sleepy and relenting, its avenues and alleys dissolving into Edward Hopper shadows, the scent of lilac and viburnum drifting through the velvet night.

Riding a bike in the city uncovers a new overlay of stories. It is like reading very fast (though not too fast; the bicycle is that rare model of technology in which the dog still wags the tail) — you see the sharp outlines of progress, rather than the fuss of details. Suddenly the houses drop away, and you are surprised by a periscope view of the skyline, a bridge you've never seen before, a cemetery from another era wreathed in ivy, the majesty of modernist apartment buildings seen from a valley. Some of my most cherished moments that spring took place on parallel sets of bicycle wheels with Stephen, as huge saucer magnolias dropped silently from bare branches and forsythia bloomed in golden streaks.

Bicycles, from their invention, have led riders down new and unknown roads, and it cannot be entirely accidental that my first bicycle ride was accompanied by other milestones. Four months after that first bike ride, Stephen and I got married. I had left a desperately unhappy job in the fall and chose now to edit part-time and to write more. I found the time, and the inclination, to try cross-country skiing and to swim. I made doctor's appointments and paid my taxes. I'd felt for years that I had been trying, unsuccessfully, to catch up to my own life. Now at last I stood a chance.

Having time to think can be a mixed blessing. Lives are buoyed by busyness. Jobs, deadlines, and the daily to and fro form a kind of padding around a person; they constrain you from some things and protect you from others. And when they retreat, you absorb every shock on your own. A low that may have faded into the other peaks and valleys in a week's interactions can suddenly seem much more dramatic. And so, gloriously, can a high.

In some respects, I am a textbook late bloomer, the thirty-something who learns to ride a bike twenty-five years after everyone else and stands on the rooftop to proclaim, *Hey, this is fun!* I still don't entirely understand why this has happened now, or why it didn't happen before. (There are people living who have read Sartre *and* learned to ride a bike. In fact, Sartre himself is known to have loved cycling!) Is late blooming a phenomenon of procrastination? Does it speak to an inherent optimism about tomorrow, a time when everything will come to fruition, or a nihilist's romanticism, a belief that possibilities exceed realities and that the dream is always better? Or maybe it is a kind of spiritual hoarding — socking away aspirations, the way squirrels do nuts, in fear of the unlikely event that you one day run out of them.

But perhaps this is not about blooming late at all. It's hard to know why we don't get around to things. I suppose we are just too busy doing other things. But what other things, and how did we come to be doing them instead? Are they the things that we are meant to be doing? Or perhaps the buzzing, noble sense of being busy is alone more valuable than any of the things we should or shouldn't be doing. The accidental pathways of our lives bring some of our deepest and most unexpected pleasures. But they can also be terrifying reminders of the millions of unexplored worlds, of the utterly haphazard way in which we choose, and of how brief it all really is. So maybe all of this is why I ride. Because I didn't before; because inertia guides us and I cannot stop; and because I have found this one thing, or it has found me, and the view as I hang on for dear life is quite nice.

Oxford, Miss.
17 September, 1935.

Dear Mr Dean:

        The mss. are being returned
by express today. I think the reason why
they have not been accepted is as follows.

BLACK ORCHID

It is too long. It is too episodic; a string
of episodes continuous enough but some of
which are not necessary, and the unnecessary
ones not interesting enough in themselves
to warrant the extra printing. It is not
tight enough. It is not built around one single scene of dramatic value.

FOOTS

It is too long. It is just a strung-out
short story, all of which might have been
told in the court room.

        I could stop there and take no
chance of offending you, but I shant. I hold
the profession of writing in too high regard
for that, and I think too highly of anyone
who will voluntarily accept the travail and
worry of doing it.

        I was disappointed in BLACK
ORCHID. The story you told me about that
family was damn good. But you didn't write
it. You wrote something which has been written so often that it is now hokum: of the
hybrid who escapes. I thou ht you were going
to do the other thing, write about the hybrid
 or family of hybrids) who had inherited so
much character from the white side which
fought the War Between the States that they
refused to escape, but on the contrary stuck
it out and beat a lot of people who had no
blemish of blood. That's the story. If you
dont want to write it, how about giving it
to me?

That answers one part of the
question. (Remember, it is a writer/talking
to some one who is trying to write now)
The second part is your method, your con-
ception and telling of the story which you
yourself know well and which you are trying
to put on paper in a way that will move anybody that reads it just as it moved you.

I dont think you have read e-
nough. I dont mean research, facts: who in
the hell cares for facts. But you have not
read enough novels and stories of people
who have told their stories well. My advice is, read the following books, see how
they are all built about one single dramatic
idea or situation, then rewrite BLACK OR-
CHID from beginnging to end.

The Brothers Karamazov. Dostoievsky.

Buddenbrooks. Thomas Mann.

Tess of the d'Urbervilles. Thomas Hardy

Any other Hardy you would like to read.

This may offend you. If it does,
you have no business trying to write at
all. If it does not, and you fol ow this
advice, you may get somewhere someday. I
cant say when nor how long because I couldn't
in my own case. But no writing that was worth
doing was ever done the first time nor in
one day or one year, somethmes, oftentimes,
not in one decade.

Yours sincerely,

William Faulkner

A DELAYED DISCLOSURE

CLARK BLAISE

MY MOTHER was nearly forty years old in the bleak, pre-wartime spring of 1940 when I was born. I assume it was bleak because it was Fargo, North Dakota, in early April, and I know it was pre-war America because my parents had just left Canada to escape the war. After my birth, my mother had other pregnancies, but none were carried to term. Doctors said she was too old. They said I had survived—barely—because I was the first pregnancy, and was born before my mother had built up mysterious antibodies against my father. What that meant, exactly, was never fully explained, but in my childhood, incompatible Rh-positive and Rh-negative blood factors were popular explanations for the problem.

The idea of inimical antibodies preventing further pregnancies seemed plausible; it even carried a whiff of censure for the late-in-life, beneath-her-class, and what was generally termed "interracial" status of my mother's marriage. There was something culturally, as well as genetically, incompatible between my parents. My father was an uneducated village Quebecer and a lapsed Catholic; my mother was a Manitoba-born Anglo, and anti-Catholic in an almost Northern Irish way; and the city in which they'd met and married was Dark Ages, 1930s Montreal. (In reality, my father's anti-Catholicism, based on first-hand suffering at the hands of priests and up-close experience in the seminary he'd been sent to as a *donné*, was far more visceral than my mother's. He just didn't express it.) My mother took the doctors' admonitions to heart. She'd been vain and perhaps a little loose. She'd defied her destiny as a "bachelorette," and there was something trashy about carrying a baby at a grandmother's age. Hers was a poisoned womb.

In those years, doctors operated on the Sherlock Holmes principle: once you've eliminated the impossible, what is left, however improbable, is the answer. I was a weak, impoverished thing; I didn't walk, didn't talk, didn't sit up. My parents were extraordinarily strong, athletic "physical specimens": I should have been a eugenic marvel. I should have benefited from hybrid hardiness, like Manitoba wheat; instead, I was, at best, a weed. Sixty years ago, there were no tools for genetic inquiry. And so, there must have been a psychological component to my physical symptoms. Psychoanalysis was in the air.

Sixty years ago, women—those frigid, castrating, smothering wives and mothers—were blamed for most inexplicable and insidious family disasters. Fathers might be ne'er-do-wells or alcoholics or abusers, but those failings were known, pre-absolved ones with predictable outcomes, especially in Dark Ages Montreal.

"Failure to thrive," as we'd say today, however, required a more subtle analysis. How to explain bedwetting? Spastic colon? Sissiness? Juvenile delinquency? The answer, in the words of bestselling pop-essayist Philip Wylie, was middle-class, American "Momism." Freudian analysis of the problem added heft to Wylie's argument. "Moms" were modern witches. Obviously, all the kinks and quirks of American dysfunction were the fault of mothers who'd been too withholding—or too dominating; who'd denied a breast, or exposed it; who'd enforced potty training too early, or neglected it too long; who'd picked up squalling babies too quickly, or let them scream incessantly; who'd permitted too much, or not enough, of just about anything in their secretive and exclusive control of their children. (Fathers in the 1940s weren't around enough to be much of an influence on anything.)

Since perfect physical specimens like my parents were obviously able to conceive—why couldn't *she* carry them to term? My father had been a Golden Gloves champion in two countries; my mother was an avid ice-skater and field-hockey player. My father had the arms, shoulders, and barrel chest of a middleweight, in a short-legged bantamweight's frame. Even in her mid-fifties, my mother could kick her legs far over her head. She could thrum her fingers on a tabletop with the force of small hammers. What was wrong with

them together, or with her?

Maybe she didn't *really* want children. Perhaps unconsciously (that sophisticated, all-explaining European word) she'd been fighting against the role, or definition, of motherhood. She'd had a European life, she was educated, she was an artist, she felt superior to her husband and everyone in his furniture-salesman's life; *unconsciously*, she must have felt she'd made a terrible mistake. During her first pregnancy, she'd taken all the proper steps, as they were understood in 1940. She still smoked, but she gave up driving. My birth was uneventful. She went up to Winnipeg a few months after I was born to be assured by her father, a doctor. "Don't worry, Annie; he'll never be a boxer," her father said. (I was never a fighter, although throughout my childhood and high school years, I served as the classic schoolyard punching bag. I dreaded every day of school. If there had been today's high school culture of lethal vengeance, I might have made history.)

When I was about nine months old, I fell into a mysterious decline: my eyes grew dull, my body toneless; I flopped in my high chair as though I had no bones or spine. One morning, my mother found me with both legs wrapped around my neck, paddling with my hands like a self-propelled beach ball. I stayed physically and mentally undefined until I was three-and-a-half years old. By then we had moved to Cincinnati, the second of thirty towns and cities, north and south, Canadian and American, where we would live before my parents' inevitable breakup fifteen years later. My condition was diagnosed as *amytonia congenita*, a form of muscular dystrophy that was considered fatal. My mother didn't give up. She read to me, even though I didn't respond. She took me to doctors, finally finding one who prescribed a new wartime thyroid extract. At about the age of four, the pills—or something—kicked in; I sat up, I talked, and I walked.

Fifteen years later, in Pittsburgh, during the time of my parents' divorce, I asked our family doctor what was wrong with me: I was pudgy, slow, and uncoordinated. Soft. I have never been able to do a push-up. I don't know what it's like to launch a one-handed jump shot. In high school, I weighed a corky 230 pounds: a football lineman's weight, lacking only heft and bulk. Most of the moist-skinned, shiny-pants kids my size seemed to me stupid as well — genetic mistakes. Where would my weight gain end? Four hundred pounds? Five hundred? I could see a limitless, freak-show trajectory.

Was there a name for it, when people asked? "A form of dystrophy," the doctor said. "Amytonia?" I asked, and he said, "Probably not. Be grateful that it keeps you out of gym class." It got me out of gym in high school and college. Nothing more was said; given my love of spectator sports, an inability to compete was my own quiet form of disappointment.

Seven years after the Pittsburgh diagnosis, between college and entering the Writers' Workshop in Iowa City, I was called up for my army physical. I stood at attention in a line with nude young farmboys while someone tried to pass a single sheet of paper between my knees. The sheet of paper tore. My legs form a kind of geometry, like two letter *k*'s placed back to back. I would be unable to stand at attention without passing out. Knock-kneed, a congenital deformity: it afforded a respectable deferment.

A year later, I was married. Our first son was born while my wife and I were still in the Workshop. He was a beautiful, lusty, active baby, out of his crib at seven months, dark-haired and light-eyed with a peachy complexion born of my wife's genetic contribution. She is Calcutta-born, the daughter of three thousand years of obsessive marital supervision. Hybridization actually works, I thought.

MY MOTHER was one of those supremely rationalistic women of the 1920s, a Canadian version of one of Evelyn Waugh's Bright Young People or someone out of early Aldous Huxley. She could stand in for any number of Alice Munro or Carol Shields heroines; she was a Winnipeg college graduate in arts who'd left her father's stern Methodism and drifted far from her prairie origins into Eastern wisdom, theosophy, and atheism. She aspired to a career in design, against her father's inflexible will. So she taught for three years in rural Saskatchewan and Manitoba schools, saved her wages, and in the summer of 1929, took off for Europe.

She worked first in London, then, dissatisfied by the stodgy standards of local design, removed herself to the centre of modernism: Germany. She enrolled in an art school in Dresden, and then took classes in Dessau, at the Bauhaus. Following the closing of the school by the Nazis in 1932, she escaped to Prague, using her German, and stayed there till 1935, when friends suggested she leave. With a Canadian passport, she found herself suddenly desirable in the eyes of many older, interesting, accomplished men. She returned to London for a year, and then came home to Canada.

My parents met in Montreal in 1937. My mother was older, taller, heavier, and more educated; he was handsome, raw, ambitious, violent, and effectively illiterate.

My jolly grandmother Orienne Blais, four feet ten inches tall, undertaker to fourteen of her eighteen children, lived with my parents in Ste. Rose du Lac, Quebec, for the final two years of her life. She once asked my mother, "Why did a good woman like you marry a boy like Léo?" In the fateful month of September 1939, while my mother was pregnant with me, her mother-in-law died. His mother's death was the release my father had been waiting for. My parents left immediately for Winnipeg and then continued to North Dakota, and then the story gets interesting.

OVER THE years I have taken great comfort from my French-Canadian half identity. Montreal is the "hometown" (out of thirty contenders) that I claim. French Canadian is the identity I answer to. The happiest years of my life were spent in Montreal. Our younger son was born there (where, in those years of ethnic and religious identification, he was registered as "French Hindu"), and my wife and I taught there for a dozen years. The life and language of Quebec still delight me. The tenacity of that small, threatened culture is heroic. The suffering and poverty, the harsh conditions, the low self-esteem, and the tight little gene pool—in which, after four hundred years, everyone is related—have always told me everything I needed to know about myself. I've never met a fellow Quebecer anywhere in the world and not been able to discover a common ancestor—a Blais, a Chouinard, a Boucher, a Robert—after a dozen questions. I might have been an only child, but I have six million cousins.

After my parents' divorce, my father married two more times and suffered mightily for what he knew to be his sins. The wife he left my mother for tried to kill him on a beach in Mexico; the next one, in Manchester, succeeded. He was seventy-two, and is buried in *le petit coin du Canada*, in the old French-Canadian ghetto of now-gentrifying Manchester. By then my mother, who lived ten more years, did not recognize his name, or mine. She died of Alzheimer's at eighty-four, in a nursing home in Winnipeg, the city where she'd started.

IN MY growing up, the stories my mother told me of my various potential fathers fired me with nostalgia for a life I couldn't live. This was partial compensation for having an "old" mother in the rural south of my childhood where toothless grandmothers could be thirty years old, or even younger. My mother was in her mid-forties by the time I started school. For us, in Pittsburgh, or deep in Florida and Georgia, or back in Winnipeg, physical and economic life would always be a struggle. We'd always be renting backrooms in other people's houses or duplexes, and there would always be new schools twice a year with new bullies, each town worse than the one before. The few stories my mother told me about her earlier boyfriends—my *beaux*, she called them—made them seem like parachuters, dozens of father-insurrectionists landing behind family lines.

"Of course, you wouldn't be you," she'd say, easily detecting the calculations I was making. That was okay with me: I didn't much like the fate I'd been dealt. We wouldn't be in Florida or Georgia or Alabama; we wouldn't even be American. I would be Canadian, or European. I'd be cultured. I'd be lean, hard, and athletic. I would be English or German or Czech or Hungarian. I went to the atlas and looked up those countries. They were, by the faintest thread of imagination, mine. I'd be Jewish, an artist or intellectual, or some kind of deposed aristocrat. If my father had been the Toronto architect who figured prominently in many of my mother's London stories, whose old letters she sometimes took out and read, whose accomplishments she was able to trace through the Canadian magazines that followed us in her American exile, what might that have meant for me?

My father was the reason, obviously, that I wasn't taller or smarter or richer. I would have settled for some of his good looks and bullish strength, but he didn't pass them on, the selfish bastard. He was the reason we lived among violent people who spoke darkly of "traits." He was the one who lied about his origins, covered them up, lived a secret life with women, all known to my mother. She had to be friendly with his mistresses, she had to certify his bogus Paris childhood. He was the one terrified of being "discovered," the one who caused us to flee landlords and processors deep in the night. Without him, life wouldn't be so endlessly unfair, such an unwinnable struggle.

"Your father should be respected. He's had a lot to overcome," she'd say. "You have to admire what he's made of himself."

All of that was true. Many of my father's traits were admirable. He worked harder than any two men. He had to. He could read the baseball box scores, but little more. He kept up with the exploits of Lou Boudreau and Leo Durocher. He wrote numbers, not letters. Pencils and ballpoint pens snapped in his hands; their points ripped through the pages. His life—his constructed "French" life, with a Paris education, with vineyards in the countryside; the *e* he'd by then added to his last name to make it look more "French"—was an embarrassing lie; if we had moved in more sophisticated circles, he would have been easily exposed. He'd been born poor, Catholic, and French in a time and place that sent boys off to work or the priesthood as soon as they could toddle. To have transcended all of that was heroism enough, though he—and I—didn't honour it at the time.

"Architects make a lot of money, don't they?" I'd ask. They designed things, and I was busy filling up writing tablets with plans for future cars, planes, trains, and buildings. That famous Canadian architect who figured in my mother's Manitoba-girl-against-the-world London and Dresden and Montreal stories was still living in Toronto. Toronto was not an architectural triumph sixty or more years ago, but that hardly mattered. ("Toronto architect" still carries an oxymoronic ring to me, unfairly, even now.) Of course he was married, but he'd been married then, too, and studying in London when he met my mother. That didn't matter. My mother wasn't shy about the implications. "Gordon" was the love of her life, and she'd met my father on the rebound. My father hid his string of girlfriends; my mother's lovers were all embedded in history.

Many years after she was gone, I learned to appreciate the fact that a first-time, forty-year-old mother had had a full life; she had done her living and growing before I was born. She was always a fully formed individual; she seemed to me infallible. But our years together were numbered. Alzheimer's began claiming her by her mid-sixties—my age now. I was still in my mid-twenties. We would never be adults together. Her full life is one I'll never know, and the absence fills me with wonder and regret. What she gave me is the gift and the right to imagine alternate selves—what she, and I, might have been—and to frame her life as a rather dazzling young woman, free of cares, free of me. The cities she talked of, especially Montreal, became mine.

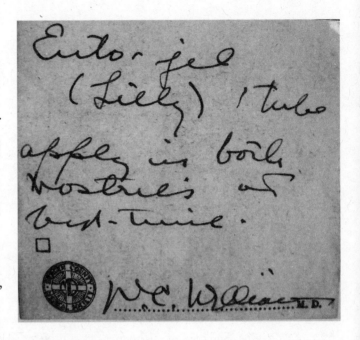

What she wanted from me was someone to listen to her, to understand her hard and embittering choices and to take from them a certain caution not to be so trusting. Her life had started on the Canadian frontier, and then it had leaped to pre-war Europe and to Montreal: she'd enjoyed as full a life as any possible in that time and place. Then she'd failed her promise; she'd panicked (today we'd talk of the biological clock). I became her only consolation, after the brutal years in the rural South, the empty years in northern cities, then back to a 1960s and 1970s Montreal more French and unforgiving than the English and European Montreal she'd known, before ending where she'd started, in Winnipeg. A shelf of history vanished with her memory; no other Canadian woman had lived a life like hers. She gave me life, she saved my life, she gave me a profession, and in her last years of clarity, she was able to pass her stories, with the same passion, on to my wife's and my children.

IT HAS taken many years for the mystery of my mother's poisoned womb to resolve itself. In the past few years, the old *amytonia congenita*—my mysterious dystrophy—has reappeared. It is now called myotonic dystrophy, one of the many forms of muscular dystrophy, and doctors have realized it is inherited, not congenital. As modern genetics has discovered, each of my children has a fifty-fifty chance of inheriting the trait. Half of our genetic makeup comes from each parent. I have two "good" alleles (the possible mutational forms of a gene) from my mother, and one good and one bad allele from my father. (My mere survival indicates that my father, not my mother, is the source.) I assume that many of my mother's pregnancies were spontaneously aborted because of myotonic dystrophy. It is the mysterious "antibody," the source of the poisoned womb.

In my marriage, my wife contributed two sturdy Bengali alleles. If a child inherits my good allele from my mother, and either of my wife's, he or she is entirely free of the problem; it will never occur—it is not part of his or her DNA. But if my father's bad allele shows up, it is dominant and will cause the victim to create huge numbers of genetic copies (in a kind of stutter), like zebra mussels clogging an intake pipe. The muscles are literally starved of sugar.

Myotonic dystrophy is almost the reverse phenomenon of that experienced by, say, Jerry Lewis's young chair-bound Duchenne's sufferers. Duchenne's presents in early childhood, attacking the muscles of the trunk, and moving outward to the limbs. Myotonic dystrophy is obviously the preferable of the two forms of dystrophic illness. It presents later in life—in adolescence—at about the time Duchenne's has claimed its victim. Myotonic dystrophy starts in the limbs, and migrates to the trunk. It moves slowly. Myotonic sufferers cannot relax their clenched muscles. They're subject

to apnea and cardiac arrhythmia. One by one, the muscles die: the little muscles of the ears, leading to deafness; the little muscles of the eyes and eyelids, bringing on blindness. Speech slurs. One of our sons noticed in high school—even as he ran high hurdles—that if he balled up his fist, he had to unfurl it, finger by finger, with the other hand. My wife and I never knew, and he thought nothing of it—not that anything could have been done. A couple of years ago, the effects became increasingly apparent; we did the modern thing and took DNA samples. My myotonic dystrophy is "mild," with sixty genetic replications. Sixty stutters. My older boy, the active little beauty in our family, is "classic," with three times as many.

It is strangely comforting to finally have a name for everything that can possibly go wrong, a new identity to go with all the others, and a certain fate. I wish only that I could have gone it alone.

Fortunately, says the medical literature, the "genetic drift" that causes the condition is limited mainly to isolated pockets, those small-population gene pools grown stagnant from long inbreeding. A classic outcropping is the Lac-Saint-Jean region of Quebec. Probably my father had no more than twenty replications, not enough to register a single complication on his magnificent physique. But it is the nature of this condition to increase the stutter, generation by generation, and for our dark, secret trait to grow more devastating, until nothing remains.

I still cherish my millions of cousins and the living fact that in Quebec we are all linked by fewer than six degrees of separation. On each visit to Montreal, I take new pride in my people's self-reinvention, even as I see them now in my dreams, robed and hooded, chanting prayers against a new enemy I know too well.

A VISIT FROM JEAN GENET

CLAYTON RUBY

I KNEW HE was a thief, of course. We all did. But I was still surprised when he stole my father's desert boots.

I had breezed into the office at the end of a day in criminal court, and as I passed the office of my secretary, she called out, "Masai Hewitt and Jean Genet are waiting for you in the library." Masai Hewitt I knew. He was a regular visitor. He was a representative of my long-standing client, the Black Panther Party, and often visited Canada with instructions for me. He was tall, sophisticated, with a master's degree in history from Harvard.

I spun to the left rather than to my office on the right, and as I walked down the hall I said to myself, "Hmm. Jean Genet (spelling it phonetically in my mind as John Jennet). That's a Black Panther I don't know." I arrived at the library. I hugged Hewitt. I noted an attractive black woman sitting next to him and then saw the iconic face of the short, white-haired Frenchman sitting nervously in an overstuffed chair. It was Jean Genet. Instantly recognizable.

First impressions are very important. Mine was not perfect. Like a fool, I blurted out, "You're Jean Genet!" "*Oui.*" He smiled beatifically.

Genet had been asked by the Black Panther Party to speak at a large political rally in Boston and then later to appear in New York. He had previously been refused entry to the United States because he had a criminal record — and because his politics were awfully subversive for the early 1970s. It had

seemed obvious to him from France that the world's longest undefended border would be easy to slip across and so he had flown to Toronto — our immigration people did not ask if he had a criminal record — to make his way into the United States. His presence here was secret. If the Americans found out, they would arrange for the Canadians to deport him.

The beautiful woman was the European representative of the Black Panther Party, based in Paris. She remained with Genet while Masai Hewitt went back to the United States. I thought it would be easy enough to keep them both in my apartment at Rochdale College on Bloor Street while they made what arrangements they could. Not so. In that druggy but literate subculture, Jean Genet was as instantly identifiable as Dwight Eisenhower or Colonel Sanders. We walked in the front doors, headed for the elevators, and three people identified my friend as Jean Genet within the first thirty feet. They stared. They pointed. They were not cool. This location would clearly not do as a hideout.

My parents had taken their extended winter vacation in Florida. Thus their Willowdale home was empty. We headed north on Bayview. Surely no one would find him there.

The house was large, a transplanted suburban California ranch style, ghostlike because each item of furniture (already covered in plastic that was removed only for guests) had been carefully wrapped in a sheet for the winter. My father's clothes were neatly laid out as usual, awaiting his return. We removed the sheets, raised the heat to a livable level, and left M. Genet and his beautiful keeper to make travel arrangements as best they could.

Days went by. It was not as easy as it had looked from the south of France. Each day Jean Genet trudged down the block in the spring snow in his socks and sandals to the pay phone, urging God-knows-who to get him across this border. He seemed never before to have encountered winter. He was amazed every time that snow this deep would inevitably cause his socks to become soaking wet and miserably cold.

The Black Panther Party's beautiful European representative waited impatiently with him. He was not an easy companion. As he was addicted to methamphetamine, her role included supplying it, calming the resulting rages, and performing translation duties. Immune to her charms — he was gay — he was a difficult charge.

The Black Panther Party, of course, could easily obtain passports. But none of them bore a photograph of an elderly, short white man. Their photos were all of young black males. The draft-dodger underground had access to counterfeit birth certificates and matching U.S. driver's licences that they used to funnel Americans who were fleeing the draft into Canada. But none of these identifications bore names that could match a man who spoke only French.

Canadian theatre director Jim Gerrard was prevailed upon for the use of his ancient Volvo. Off they went in an attempt to "run" the border. Alas, they were turned back to my father's vacant house. He was not a very plausible Canadian. More phone calls. Jean Genet was getting speedier and speedier, but going nowhere. His frustration increased.

Finally, nothing would do but a real assault on the border, but this time with a "real" driver. Juan Manuel Fangio, then the world's most famous race-car driver, was a close friend. He was to fly to Toronto from his home in Mexico City to do the job. I don't think Fangio ever arrived.

In the end, Jean Genet flew to Ottawa, where he had a for-mer lover who worked in the American embassy. That man issued him a U.S. visa, and with it firmly in hand, Jean Genet flew to the United States to serve the revolution. A week later, my father was looking for his desert boots. It didn't take long to figure out what happened to them: they'd left on Genet's feet.

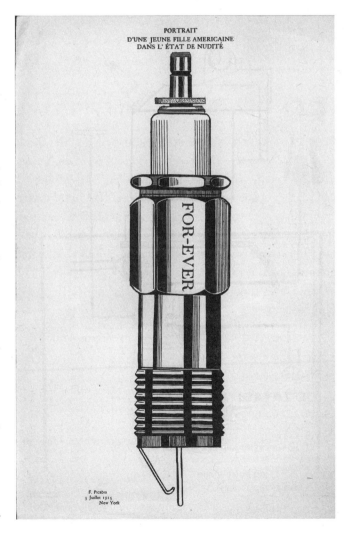

TOMAS TRANSTRÖMER: A TRIBUTE

ROBERT HASS

Tomas Tranströmer published his first book of poems — the stunning *17 dikter* — when he was twenty-three years old. Eight volumes have followed, each rather austere and beautifully made. The poems were, from the beginning, thick with the feel of life lived in a particular place: the dark, overpowering Swedish winters, the long thaws and brief paradisal summers in the Stockholm archipelago. But they were also piercing inward poems, full of strange and intense accuracies of perception. The most famous lines —

Awakening is a parachute jump from the dream.

or

December. Sweden is a hauled-up,
unrigged ship

— stay with one a long time. And there are whole passages equally indelible:

Daybreak slams and slams in
the sea's grey stone gateway, and the sun flashes

close to the world. Half-choked summer gods fumble in sea-mist.

And this:

The black-backed gull, the sun-skipper,
     steers his course.
Under him is wide water.
The world still sleeps like a
many-coloured stone in the water.
Undeciphered days. Days —
like Aztec hieroglyphs!

Hieroglyph is the right word. The brilliance of the metaphors, and their originality, was what most attracted the attention of other poets and made Tranströmer the most widely translated European poet of the post-war generation. His work has been translated into fifty languages, and as if each dialect required its own version, into English by English, Irish, Scottish, and American poets. This is remarkable at least in part because his work is not easy or immediately comforting. It was admired by poets first, and that is what the work in translation tells us.

His brilliance is very difficult to separate from the terseness and almost classical restraint of a style that makes almost all other poets seem garrulous, sociable, eager—even in their most rebellious attitudes—to please. Tranströmer's metaphors have a way of suggesting an uncannily alert imagination turned to an undeciphered, but not entirely undecipherable, world. Its meanings often come in hints, glimpses along the way, sometimes brutal and ancient, sometimes unnervingly fresh. Almost always this world is as peculiar, bald, and hermetic as the opening of a hand when we cannot say whose it is or what purpose it intends. And almost always in the poems, the everyday world, the one organized for the purposes of power, commerce, pleasure, and transportation, is not the one we need to read. This way of seeing gives one the feeling, reading him, that one ought to wake up from whatever one's previous idea of being awake was, and it has made him one of the most urgent imaginations of our time.

The later poems often occur in the moments between sleeping and waking, between work and home, as a commuter on the outskirts of cities, as a tourist at the edge of cultures. It wasn't without profit that Tranströmer the poet practised his profession as a psychologist in small cities outside Stockholm, working as a psychotherapist and counsellor in an institution for juvenile offenders and then as a psychologist for a labour organization. This immersion, or submersion, in the working world may be what gives his poems their intense sense of what it is like for consciousness to try to locate itself around the edges of the meanings—social, political, existential—it finds itself among. That must be why so many of the poems take place along the blurred seams of twentieth-century life, when the imagination has come unhinged a little and ceases to know what it thinks it knows about itself. These poems, more than any others I can think of, convey a sense of what it is like to be a private citizen in the second half of the twentieth century. Anywhere this private citizenship exists—among the people who read and write books, for

example—the phrase conveys the idea of a certain freedom, a certain level of comfort, and also some unease and isolation.

And this is another powerful feature of his art. It praises art, but it never claims any special privilege from the situation of the artist. Maybe it is in this way that Tranströmer's break with modernism is most complete. Other poets of his time and of his stature—one thinks of Zbigniew Herbert, Seamus Heaney, Joseph Brodsky—have faced the public world and the public horrors of their time with an art in their hands that served as both a hermeneutic of suspicion and an honourable tradition of dissent, but Tranströmer's poems don't seem to lay claim to that tradition. Art, especially the art of music, comes into his poems as other hieroglyphs, hopeful scents picked up from the world's unpromising winds. One of the most powerful of these images comes from his long poem *Baltics*, when he stumbles on a carved baptismal font in an old church:

In the half-dark corner of Gotland church,
    in the mildewed daylight
stands a sandstone baptismal font—12th century—
    the stonecutter's name
still there, shining
like a row of teeth in a mass grave:
              HEGWALDR
    the name still there. And his scenes
here and on the sides of other vessels crowded with
    people, figures on their
    way out of the stone.
The eyes' kernel of good and evil bursting there.
Herod at the table: the roasted cock flying up and
    crowing, "Christus natus est"—
    the servant executed—
close by the child born, under clumps of faces as worthy
    and helpless as young monkeys.
And the fleeing steps of the pious

drumming over the dragon scales of sewer mouths.

(The scenes stronger in memory than when you stand
    in front of them,
strongest when the font spins like a slow, rumbling
    carousel in the memory.)
Nowhere the lee-side. Everywhere risk.
As it was. As it is.
Only inside there is peace, in the water of the vessel
    that no one sees,
but on the outer walls the struggle rages.
And peace can come drop by drop, perhaps at night
when we don't know anything,
or as when we're taped to a drip in a hospital ward.

Reading this, one understands that part of Tranströmer's power is that, all along, he has been doing the work of a religious temperament in a secular and dangerous age and why he is, as the poet and critic Göran Printz-Påhlson has written, "one of the central and most original poets of our time."

Tomas suffered a stroke in 1990 that left him partially paralyzed on his right side and that affected his speech. His wife, Monica, is a nurse. I am told that, while he was recovering, she drove to Stockholm, found a music store, and bought all the piano literature for one hand she could locate, drove home, gave it to Tomas, and told him to get to work. It must have been an effective therapy. Tomas was already an accomplished pianist, and his publisher Bonniers has recently issued a CD that combines recordings of his poems with recordings of his work at the piano. The piano performances, like his late works—the remarkable "Sad Gondola," and the haiku, a few syllables like scratches in snow that make up most of *The Great Enigma*—feel like metaphors for his art. One hand finding its way, note by note, in a darkness it has made luminous.

- There was th   of the scream
- Doctors house
- money, Beatrice, Dorothy
- silk, door knob
- Paris warm - cotton trousers, suit

2nd draft — 3/3/11

Buying the house and   invest
Beatrice

21 - The Blue of Storms

*where to put
"The year he had th
house."   that year

The year that he had the house, the spring ~~of it~~,
the summer, was the happiest of his life. There hadn't
been the money to do much, even buy furniture, but in its
bareness, its simplicity, one was free, the spirit was free.
There was the embrace of the seasons coming full through the
windows, the trees, the tender grass sloping down to the
smooth ~~silver~~ or blue of the pond. The windows of the
doctor's house, a long way off, a house that seemed to have
been there before the even trees, were in the morning silver
too. Summer morning, with the light of all the world coming
in and the silence. It was a barefoot life, the cool of
the night on the ~~pale~~ floorboards. The ~~huge~~, burgeoning
trees if you stepped outside, the first faint birds. He
arrived in a suit and didn't put it on again until he went
back to the city, and How happy they were. ~~There was nothing to~~
~~disturb it~~. The doorknob on the kitchen ~~door~~ came loose.
The ~~window~~ sills were cracked by ~~the~~ weather and peeling.
~~One morning~~ he ~~tried~~ to scrape and fill several but never
got around to painting them. In the middle of the afternoon
there was a sudden scream. It was Anet. She had rolled over
on a wasp. Christine had come running up the stairs.
    -What is it?
The wasp had stung her on her sleepy haunch. The sting
had awakened her. She was terrified and weeping. It had been
so sudden and unexpected. Bowman ~~came up having heard the~~
~~crying~~. He held a washcloth under the cold water/tap.
    -You'll be all right, he said. Hold this against it.
Where did it go?
    -Where did what go?
    -The bee.
    -I don't know, Anet said, sobbing.
    -When they sting you, they lose their stinger. It tears
loose ~~and the bee dies~~. It has barbs on it. You should
always brush it free. Don't try and pull it. Where's the
sting?
    They weren't listening to him.. Anet/she had been sleeping
in shorts that were now half pulled down. I pulled up

CK.
P.
3

the house
couldn't
be locked

SILENT CINEMA:
AN AESTHETIC CALL TO ARMS

GEORGE TOLES

Now that mainstream movies have become as dull as theatre, where are cinephile pilgrims to go in search of pleasures untried and suitably raw? Silent film, the lost world of cinema's infancy and unbridled youth, may provide the best way out of our present listlessness, our habitual mood of diminished expectations. For many decades, silent movies commanded a dutiful respect that was seldom accompanied by passion. Rudolf Arnheim and Kevin Brownlow seemed merely quaint or contrarian when they contended that the silent era was "the richest in cinema history." At this remove, however, silent film has finally shed the stigma of obsolescence and the feel of embarrassing old-fashionedness.

Just as modernists once found the means of "making art new" by returning to the large, unruly texts of antiquity, we might similarly begin afresh by apprenticing ourselves to the grandeur and visionary excitement of the pioneers in the art of pure (well, almost pure) image. Encounters with silent film force a drastic reorientation of our viewing reflexes, shaking and shattering the amply conditioned moviegoer self. The overthrow of this Pavlovian dullard is, of course, what many of us claim to seek. Perhaps an even greater number of us crave such a remedy for our spectator malaise without fully realizing it. Even silent movies of no special distinction partake of the alien majesty of this abandoned expressive discipline. The silent screen, in part because of its deep, unshakeable alliance with death, reveals an invincible otherness.

The Passion of Joan of Arc seems to lay bare the quivering mortal roots — the death's head secret — of all silent film, and maybe this is why it appears to provide an awesome and alarming template for the entire haunted medium. Carl Dreyer's Joan (Maria Falconetti) is endlessly harrowed before being led to the stake. In every return of the camera's gaze to her afflicted countenance, the certainty of a torture that must be carried through to its appointed end seems engraved in the act of witnessing. But she also conveys to us a remoteness from the bleeding present tense in which she is held captive. She gives the impression of having already been through *this* death and consented to return to her ordeal—becoming visible for us so we can re-experience all the phases of it once more.

The human form in a silent film nearly always seems tethered to a ghostly counterpart, such as Buster Keaton's unflinching and unstoppable dream double in *Sherlock Jr.*, who dissolves limitations and boundaries as though external reality were a bright series of magic tricks. Or consider Norma Shearer at the beginning of *Lady of the Night*. A prostitute fresh from the penitentiary, venturing onto a lonely city street, Shearer is greeted by an old-fashioned hearse, with a glass window fronting the coffin. Keaton-style, Shearer uses the window as a mirror for herself and calmly adjusts her makeup. There is a kind of nimbus attending so many silent film faces that seems eerily wafted from the afterlife. Often actors confront the camera with what feels like unearthly awareness, as though they have been struck by the thought that they may already be dead and are momentarily transfixed by this possibility. Whether the ghosts are literal or submerged, the world of silence has the atmosphere of a rollicking graveyard, where, as in so many cautionary medieval paintings, skeletons peer unobtrusively through windows and doors at the deceptive feast of life. Because death is so tangibly hovering over these mimed shadow plays, human striving and doing acquire both a forlorn inconsequentiality and a lovely nobility that comes from meeting inconsequence head-on. "The set trap never tires of waiting," in Joy Williams's memorable phrase, but in silent film every human gesture, every risked connection in the fleeting time being, has an unlikely air of victory.

One of silent cinema's most powerful and ambiguous death-in-the-midst-of-life effects occurs at the conclusion of King Vidor's *The Crowd*. John Sims (James Murray) has persuaded his wife, Mary (Eleanor Boardman), who has all but given up on their marriage, to grant him one more reprieve. They attend a vaudeville program in a large New York theatre with their young son. (Their second child, a daughter, had been killed less than a year ago in a traffic accident.) John is barely employed. Earlier in the day he had nearly thrown himself off a bridge after being slapped by his wife during a quarrel of unprecedented savagery. He is restored to clear-headedness after an intense emotional reversal brought on by his son's unexpected expression of faith in him. John then manages to secure temporary employment, performing a task that he had once, long ago, laughed at as hopelessly demeaning: juggling in a clown outfit while wearing a restaurant promotion sandwich board. In his present mood, John is grateful for *any* chance to work and feels lucky that he has been asked to return for another day of juggling.

John, Mary, and their son unabashedly enjoy the vaudeville entertainment (perhaps out of relief that their family has withstood one more crisis). A group of mute clowns onstage inflict and receive various stylized forms of injury. Those who cheerfully administer kicks and blows are interchangeable with their resilient victims. In short order, the act promises, the tables will turn. Part of what makes this scene in *The Crowd* remarkable is that the irony of the clown show is not accentuated and seems to be of less concern to the director than the family's elated response to it. Vidor urges us to see the family's laughter, joined with that of an equally demonstrative surrounding audience, as spirited, un-self-pitying, even heroic. We have no reason to assume that John is blind to his kinship with the performers, or that he makes too much of it. Mary suddenly notices that an ad printed in the theatre program includes a slogan that John not too long ago had submitted to a contest and won a $500 prize: "Sleight o' Hand—The Magic Cleaner." He turns to a stranger sitting beside him and casually announces that he came up with it. In the easy camaraderie of the theatre crowd, the stranger warmly commends John for his accomplishment, and then the two of them return their attention to the stage, where another gag erupts that delights both of them. This is one of the few occasions in the film when anyone other than John's wife and child has found cause to praise him for something. The illustration in the Magic Cleaner ad also features an amiable juggling clown. As we register the import of the stranger's acknowledgement, a shadow overtakes the moment. John's prizewinning slogan was directly linked to circumstances that resulted in John's loss of his daughter.

The trajectory of *The Crowd* is sombre, and its documentation of John's many defeats, often brought on by weaknesses in his character, is sympathetic to his anguish. Yet Vidor crucially finds ways to infuse even the most comedy-resistant episodes with vitality and capricious sparks of exuberant sentiment. The film, overall, sustains a near-buoyant tragic atmosphere. Such an atmosphere is characteristic of silent film and has much to do with our different apprehension of the weight of things in silence — the lightened weight, with no reduction in visible suffering, of life itself.

The Crowd draws to a close with a crane shot of the theatre audience that startlingly removes us from John's and Mary's fragile but authentic joy in each other's company and in their viewing of the clowns' expertly choreographed misfortunes. As the camera pulls back from them, we lose our intimate proximity to the couple's present togetherness, to their son's rejoicing that things are good for now, and his palpable wish that his family may have the same gift of bravado and knockabout zest that the clowns exhibit. The camera movement does not cancel out the Sims's hard-won satisfaction or movingly rekindled hope. It simply pulls them away from us, severing our taken-for-granted contact with their lives. We can't locate their faces any longer in the mass of patrons that comprise the rest of the theatre audience. The crowd seems to be at one with the Sims in their hungry laughter at the stage show, seizing every morsel of pleasure that the slapstick mayhem affords them. When the camera moves to a certain height, however, the human dimension of the audience begins to dissipate. We see the paroxysms of bent-over spectators as suddenly mechanical, withdrawn (at this high vantage point) from the saving flow and energy of high spirits. Our last glimpse, from an even greater height, makes the audience into pure abstraction. Their movement

is now flickering, ghostly, unreal, as though they have passed without warning into that always close-at-hand death's country, where their actions are as unreachable and unburdened as fireflies at dusk. Vidor does not ask us either to scorn the apparitional crowd or embrace it as we find ourselves — in these final moments — bound over to its inclusive presence, from whatever movie theatre *our* crowd is watching from.

Just before abstraction puts its concluding seal on things, we have the salutary sense that this large, festive gathering, like so much of silent film reality, draws sustenance from natural, as yet undepleted, ties with ceremony and ritual. The very artlessness of testing, for a two-hour story, the meaning of crowds in relation to striving individuals suggests a condition where ceremonies haven't gone dry from overworking and smooth feats of ingenuity. Silent narratives, without pressing for it, never seem far from archaic rites, formal and casual bids to mingle religion with a more boisterous, earthbound magic. Bacchanal, swelling sentiment, tableaux of suffering, sublime vistas, peep-show unveilings, and feats of sustained looking all take on a quasi-sacred character, as though the new art would ideally emulate the mystery of a Catholic Mass, where death is transmuted into a redeemed life. But redemption here is not meant to hold. The proffered radiance dims as death in plain clothes returns by a back door.

Possibly because of their missing colour and sound dimensions, silent pictures can more readily induce in the viewer a state akin to trance. Roland Barthes has written in his meditation on the silent face of Garbo of the "deepest ecstasy" of losing oneself entirely in the contemplation of an image. The Garbo face represents an absolute of our fleshly incarnation, which can "neither be reached nor renounced." In the presence of so many similarly exalted forms and faces, palpably tenured to death without quite losing their hold on life, the viewer of silent films is often ushered to what feels like a threshold of immortality. The threshold opens to our gaze for brief instants, then we are required to draw back from it and descend to a (slightly) less ethereal plane. The screened reality, beheld in ever-deepening folds of silence with a cathedral-like musical accompaniment, tantalizes us steadily, and need I add erotically, with intimations of transcendence. The finest silent film actors — among them Gish, Gaynor, Chaplin, Keaton, Pickford, Brooks, Chaney, Jannings — use the dispensation of silence to release an almost superhuman expressiveness. Body and face unite to form one large communicative vessel, making luminously transparent every flicker of intention, everything shared with others and everything withheld from them. These dauntingly exposed creatures take us to the furthest reaches of privacy and divine ways to convey the heretofore inexpressible. What we are inclined, in our fear of untrammelled expressiveness, to call melodrama is, in fact, what Eric Bentley calls the "naturalism of the dream life." The actors bear witness to the frenzy and giddiness of the feelings we expend so much daylight energy holding in check. Only in the night gardens of our silent movie dreams do our starved bodies demand restitution for all the ways they have been cheated and denied.

In addition to faces that lead us, without effort, to empyrean reveries, silent film also abounds in Zolaesque earthbound faces that seem to have been hewn from rock or torn from the ground. Among these dry-land mugs, especially ones allied to comedy, are many that seem artfully constructed, as in a cartoonist's sketch, around a single feature — a mass of hair, a potato nose, a bristling beard, a Medusa grimace. Let us attend briefly to the strenuously ordinary but somehow transfixing demeanour of Harold Lloyd, whose only standout feature is a permanent prop, a pair of horn-rimmed spectacles. Lloyd, doomed to eternal third place in the silent comedy triumvirate of Chaplin, Keaton, and Lloyd, achieved enormous popularity early in his career with an eccentrically garbed character named Lonesome Luke. He was virtually the only major comedian of the era to risk losing his audience by doing a drastic overhaul of a firmly established comic persona. (Perhaps he understood that the idea of lonesomeness was not, in his case, a sustainable

proposition.) Lloyd's immense gamble can be boiled down to a decision to don glasses and to make his odd relation to them the core of his identity.

What do glasses, all by themselves, contribute to Lloyd's otherwise flapjack-bland Rotary Club features? By proclaiming defective sight, they put a much-needed flaw in plain view, mitigating Lloyd's natural facial drift toward smugness. They lend an air of the studious and almost bashful fellow to a full-tilt extrovert who seems to have been put on Earth to preside over jolly social gatherings. Spectacles are also a subtle dragline on Harold's celebrated speediness, marking — even when he is dangling from the iconic skyscraper clockface in *Safety Last!* — his ability to pause and reflect. These fractional, owlish pauses are the grace notes in his scrambles to save himself. The horn-rims also give his face a credible focus point in his bids for pathos, suggesting a fragility, a breakability that little else in his sturdy frame and well-guarded manner corroborate. (The camera never dwells on his missing fingers!) The Lloyd straw hat, separated from the glasses by a few critical inches, seems to be an overcompensating move by a small-town fantasist who longs to be mistaken for a dandy. But his glasses somehow expose the lie. (Perhaps Clark Kent in his original comic book incarnation was a conscious reworking of Harold Lloyd.)

In the haunting opening of Lloyd's best film, *The Kid Brother*, we are given a natural landscape that serves as a grand surrogate for the unplumbable surface of Lloyd's ordinary visage. A horse-drawn wagon of travelling players makes its way in long shot around a strangely confined body of water with a large, half-sunken vessel at its centre. The image feels like a visual riddle, an ornate but still trim and unassuming poem for Lloyd's well-locked temperament — the dream of the hidden man. This scene reminds us that even Harold Lloyd's face shares, at odd intervals, the silent film hankering for transcendence — a flesh-shedding spiritualization. We shall part company with Harold as he climbs higher and higher in a gratifyingly tall tree in *The Kid Brother*, trying to keep his beloved Jobena Ralston in sight as he extends his "goodbyes" to her with waves and hal-loos. After each fresh ascent, his face grows softer, more fervent and yielding, as though the very air at this altitude combines with his romantic dream to make him, save for his spectacles, a pure soul. Of course, what allows this momentary transfigur-ation to happen is our certain knowledge that Lloyd's face is overreaching and that this shoulder-to-the-wheel pragmatist is due for a pleasing fall.

Artifice and reality intermingle with much less strain in si-lent than sound film. Things are less cumbersomely grounded in the realm of silence, and our eyes do not require that a materi-al-world weightiness be maintained, or accounted for. Weight can be invoked when it serves an image's purposes, but it can also be whisked away when it proves too much of a hindrance. Life can play, untroubled, at a variety of speeds in silence, and the Newtonian universe becomes, in a phrase of Hugh Kenner's, "a great spinning toy" where machines and humans expand their capacities for velocity as need or the spirit of play dictate. The first decades of the twentieth century, recall, were a period when the simple fact of motoring—the process of picking up speed and watching familiar sights sail by—was an ample re-ward. Travel by Ford, by airplane, even by the well-established railway was not yet reduced to "an anxiety to be elsewhere." Motion all by itself could still enchant, even at moderate tem-pos. The mere sight of men and women shaking loose from old impediments and moving without encumbrance was a reliable intoxicant. All the animate and inanimate components of the silent world can move up and down the ladder of wakefulness and momentum, as Vertov's man with a movie camera discov-ered. At times a chair, a bush, a bench, a wagon, a hand, a shop window achieve a pitch of presence (of rapturous attunement) to the things around them that is like an explosion. And every-thing made of energy longs to dance.

Perhaps it is the partial victory over gravity and the resulting jubilant "lightness of being" in silent film that grants miracles of every sort a free-and-easy existence in this domain. I am

not only thinking of the marvels sanctioned by religion and the Gothic—say, Cecil B. DeMille's parting of the Red Sea in the original version of *The Ten Commandments*, the devil's ride through the El Greco skies of Murnau's *Faust*, and the spindly vampire emanations of *Nosferatu*. I am also taking into account actors regularly confronting the terrors and perils of barely manipulated nature—in arctic blizzards, rock slides, sky-high conflagrations, floods, desert treks—as though risking one's life for a few baubles of illusion were a matter of course, a devil-may-care continuation of child's play.

Finally, there are the lovers' miracles, which achieved their most rapturously beautiful expression in the films of Frank Borzage. In *Seventh Heaven*, a soldier (Charles Farrell) returns from a battlefield death that his lover's faith and will have not quite submitted to. He pushes his way, in a state of clairvoyant blindness, through a horde of people celebrating the end of conflict in the city streets, determined to arrive at the loft he once shared with his beloved (Janet Gaynor) by the exact hour he and she had long ago pledged to think of each other daily. By the same power that they so often conjured each other into shimmering presence in their twinned thoughts, he finds a route back to her, not entirely purged of wounds but neither held back by a death to which he remains oblivious. Finally he stands before her, weeping, "coated," in Ado Kyrou's lovely phrase about the surrealists, "with sleep and with dreams." In *Lucky Star*, another lover disabled by war (Charles Farrell again) finally regains the use of his long-crippled legs for a demand-ing snowscape run to prevent Janet Gaynor from leaving him, against her will, with an unworthy rival.

Such episodes are, of course, absurd to recount. They seem to rest on nothing but the faux-naive indulgence of antique conventions of romantic fantasy. But onscreen these Borzage images of miracles willed by love retain an astounding per-suasive force. The immaterial conditions bestowed by silence and an especially luminescent black-and-white ambience sup-port Borzage's wholehearted endorsement of a Platonic realm, straddling this life and the next, where the strength of lover's souls can be made manifest and their visionary hopes accomplished. Borzage specializes in lovers' slow awakening to the secret charms and cherishable eccentricities of each other's behaviour in upstairs hideaways — a few rooms crammed with homely details that appear to be floating mystically on the tide of the lovers' expanding feelings. Janet Gaynor, in her numerous Borzage pairings with Charles Farrell, is assigned the most demanding emotional work in her ever-modulating, exquisitely responsive close-ups, but Farrell knows how to convey the most crucial attributes of a supporting male partner: unwavering attentiveness and the sense that whatever she reveals of herself is not lost on him. Borzage couples are always imperilled when they depart their "seventh heaven" garrets to run earthly errands or keep pressing appointments elsewhere. But when they mount the stairway that leads to their private sanctuary — the site for deliriously sexy trysts for the pure at heart — nothing unsynchronized to the steady pulse of love remains clear or comprehensible.

Music, like visual artifice, is not obliged to fight for its right to exist *credibly* in silent movies. It does not tilt against other sounds (noises and voices) as a competing, possibly unwarranted presence — a calculating intruder. The silent film accompaniment — whether piano or orchestra — is summoned into being by the images. The music potentially gives voice to every shy signal and shaded window in the visual flux. It imbues the actors' speech and motion with the delicately responsive melody that they long for. Without it they must live in exile from the redemptive powers of sound. The music (often improvised) that anticipates the image and follows in its wake escapes the toils and cloddish approximations of the verbal. The world of sound is all of a piece — airborne and harmonious, the music drawing all sound desire together, as if through the eye of a needle.

The silent film camera, innocent of the requirements of television, tends to be placed farther back from the action than current convention dictates. This extra distance allows figures to be much of the time viewed in full and in concert with their physical circumstances. There is typically in silent film a high degree of integration of humans and their defining environment. The long view also makes it possible for performers to approach every scene as a "whole body" statement. It is assumed that every beat of the action must be creatively physicalized. Costumes, therefore, are designed with a realization that they must beautifully accentuate and enhance motion: they focus the actors' characteristic walk, way of holding themselves, and amplify their gestural resources. Clothing can never be taken for granted in silent films. Fabrics sculpt the body in a manner that seems sharply, thrillingly at variance with contemporary norms, and create another mystifying merger of naturalness and stylization. Clothes are themselves a form of architecture, making bold, supportive design statements within the lavish settings. It was a crucial concern of designers that the vast sets and ornate decor not overwhelm the costumes, but rather cause them to shimmer more eloquently.

A frequent architectural tug-of-war in silent films is conducted between immense interior spaces and cozily cramped ones. The grand sets, all built in the dream shadow cast by D. W. Griffith's *Babylon*, proclaim wealth in such surfeit and Charles Foster Kane vacancy that the human being can only seem stranded there. One can pass through these sets, as though in a formal procession, or one can display oneself opulently in a well-staged entrance, but never convincingly inhabit them. The tighter, Chaplinesque locales give the human presence a vivid, inviting security, a warm (if sometimes perilous) sense of being accommodated. The smaller spaces and shadowy grottoes, frequently suggestive of poverty or mental illness, almost hug the actors, putting every item that serves their needs within friendly arm's reach. The usual intimate texture of the "limited means" milieu gives a strong implicit endorsement of the human struggle for survival. A room that presses in tenderly toward its occupant is already a manifestation of community. The settings, on the other hand, that exist to support fantasies of magnificence are chill and recessive. Their dominant note is isolation, which magnifies with every step taken, alone or in company.

To conclude, it is well known that the grammar and narrative language of film were worked out in the silent era. The countless surviving movies and fragments are a sprawling flea market of forgotten experiments and audacious alternatives to contemporary storytelling practice. The star and studio systems were also consolidated in the silent period, in addition to the conventions and codes still operative in most film genres. The central creative role of the director was defined, in the public consciousness at least, by the grand, reckless, self-mythologizing work of D. W. Griffith. In the incredibly diverse written response to the new art form of silent pictures (these "bewitching mass séances in our midst"), there is intense, moving debate about what movie aesthetics and popularity could mean and be in relation to everything that came before. Surely there are sufficient reasons to pursue, with the zeal of an Antarctic adventurer, the lure, unsorted mysteries, and religious vertigo of the silent screen.

AN INTERVIEW WITH MAVIS GALLANT

STÉPHAN BUREAU
Translated by Wyley Powell

I MUST CONFESS *at the outset that I was rather terrified of interviewing Mavis Gallant.*

I had been a long-time admirer, knew the extreme rigour with which she undertook her work, and, most of all, from my research, sensed that she did not suffer fools gladly. In fact, I knew that she preferred to have her work speak for itself, and that she did not view literary criticism as an art form. Her choice has always been to concentrate uncompromisingly on her craft, to search for that perfect architectural form that lies in a great story. You have to come prepared: a great challenge … and a minor source of stress.

We agreed to meet at the apartment of one of Gallant's Parisian friends, for the author's apartment was her inner sanctum. A choice I of course respected, although I admit I wish we could have shown Contact's *viewers a glimpse of Gallant's private world.*

Very elegant in a green dress, Mavis Gallant was punctual as a Swiss clock and ready to start the minute she walked in. I was first struck by her smile—a radiant smile that I soon realized was also a way to punctuate what she was saying; a delicate but firm way to mark that we had reached the end of a topic. Her life, the fabric of which I believe is still at the core of her work, was often off-limits. That material is hers and not to be shared before it takes its full and complete form in her work. She was generous and forthcoming, but she firmly protects, and for good reasons, a certain core. For that truth, no interview can reveal what can only be found (if it can be found) by reading between her lines.

Our conversations took place in French over a period of two days in mid-December 2005. They were broadcast in April 2006 as part of the television documentary series Contact: The Encyclopaedia of Creation. *This interview was edited for* Brick *with the participation of Mavis Gallant.*

SB   Your destiny as a storyteller became apparent very early.

MG   Yes.

SB   Because, in the first place, you were very young when you started learning the alphabet and reading.

MG   Yes. It's very important for a child to read. I don't think there's ever been a writer who was not also an avid reader.

SB   Yes. Moreover, you've written: "Writing grows out of reading."

MG   Yes.

SB   Sometimes you were overheard reading or talking out loud, which was when you realized that the stories you liked to tell yourself were also being heard by the adults around you.

MG   No, I wasn't telling myself stories. I had an entire colony of characters. I was a little older—six or seven, or even eight years old. They were paper dolls, and I made their clothes, which I put on top of the dolls because they were lying on the floor. I had a little suitcase full of these dolls—of these characters. I would cut them out of newspapers and magazines.

SB There was also a bit of the director in you?

MG Well, I'd move the dolls with two fingers. I don't think you can move the people you're interviewing with a couple of fingers. [laughs]

SB That would be too easy?

MG This took place on the floor and I'd create their voices for the dialogue. Someone who was visiting my mother said, "Does she always talk to herself?" No, it was my mother who said that. The visitor said, "But what's she doing? Is she talking?" And my mother said, "Oh, she talks to herself all the time." You know—all the time. And I didn't know that people could hear me. It came as a surprise. That's all.

SB What fascinates me in what you're saying is how sharp the details are and how exact your recollections are. I imagine it's important for an author to be able to call up—

MG Certain things.

SB Yes.

MG Certain things and with an abundance of details. I remember what people were wearing. I remember my mother's clothes, for example. Not all of them, but there were certain things that struck me. I liked the way my parents looked, how they dressed. They were quite young, in their twenties. I thought they were better looking than other parents. I was proud of them. [laughs]

SB You notice things, write them down, remain constantly vigilant. Are you aware of this?

MG I think that's the way I am. There's nothing more to it than that. There are lots of things that I forget. If I didn't keep a diary, there are things I'd forget completely.

SB I was reading a piece of yours in which you said, "In my early teenage years—when I was fourteen or fifteen, my mother would find my journal and read it. If there

was anything I didn't want read I'd tear it up—I didn't really want people to read what I was writing."

MG Yes.

SB You also said: "From the time I was young I was haunted by the fear that I had inherited a vocation from my father but not the means to fulfill this vocation."

MG Yes, yes. My father would have liked to be a painter, an artist. He was a talented amateur. My great fear, for many years, was that I had inherited something of that from him.

SB A vocation without talent?

MG It's strange because I had every reason to feel reassured. I had sent a short story to The New Yorker. They didn't know who I was. I simply wrote my name and the address of my newspaper in the corner of a page. And they promptly replied that they couldn't use that particular story but asked whether I had anything else to show them. Their exact words were: "Have you anything else to show us?" So I quickly sent them something else, which they accepted.

SB But didn't you have every reason to think that your talent was up to the mark?

MG Maybe the editor couldn't see how worthless it was! [laughs] No, it wasn't all that bad. But all the writers I've known who have to talk about this have had the same doubts. They constantly need "reassurance."

SB You had seen your father's vocation for painting, but you weren't convinced that he had the talent?

MG Well, that's not what I thought when I was a child. As a child, I marvelled at everything my father did. But later I did come to see things in a more rational light.

SB Speaking of your father, he died at a very young age.

MG He died young.

SB You were ten years old?

MG It was on my tenth birthday that I saw him for the last time. I wasn't told a thing; everything was kept hidden from me. Since I've written on this subject, I can talk to you about it. I was told that he was in England—I wasn't told that he had died—and that he was going to come back for me. I waited for him from the time I was ten until I was thirteen. Then, when I was thirteen, somebody said, "You mean you still don't know that your father's dead?" It was brutal, you know. But that's how it was.

SB Having to wait must have been a horrible thing.

MG Well, children don't think about such things every day because they're busy growing up. Children aren't obsessed. Obsessions come at a later age.

SB Later?

MG How could people have been so stupid? But we have to remember how things were back then. Children weren't told very much.

SB And later, did you feel you'd been deceived because no one had given you—

MG Yes, in a crazy kind of way, I think. If people lie to you about such essential matters as life and death, especially when your close relations are involved, a trace of that shock stays with you.

SB I would suggest to you that there's more than just a trace.

MG Do I strike you as abnormal?

SB Oh, I didn't say you were abnormal.

MG No? Good! [*laughs*]

SB I said that there's a trace that remains and that it can be seen in your writing.

MG I don't want to give you the impression that I was a poor little orphan, etc., because my life wasn't like that.

SB That's not the impression you give.

MG Good.

SB After the death of your father, it was just your mother and you.

MG My mother remarried almost immediately. There were predictable consequences.

SB In what way predictable?

MG I didn't like the man who had taken the place of my father. No daughter likes the person who takes her father's place.

SB As a girl and soon-to-be young woman, did you feel somewhat rejected by your mother?

MG I was the one who left home. I wasn't rejected.

SB Was this a case of self-expulsion?

MG Why are you using such words?

SB Well, I don't know, I'm asking you.

MG I lived in New York from the age of thirteen to eighteen, and when I was eighteen, still legally a minor, I left New York and went back to Montreal.

SB Yes, and there's a Linnet Muir story that tells something about this episode.

MG Yes. My arrival in Montreal was the way it's described in the story. I arrived after spending the whole day on the train because, in those days, it was a very long journey. No one knew I was coming and there was no one waiting for me. I'd told just a few friends that I was leaving New York. I said, "If you want to tell my mother, give me twenty-four hours," because I was underage.

SB At the time, you needed to be twenty-one.

MG Yes. And I did something worse than that. I got married at twenty, with still a year to go. I could have been stopped because in Quebec at that time rules for minors were very strict.

SB There's nothing like that nowadays.

MG My husband knew nothing about any of this at the time. He wasn't from Quebec. He'd been born and brought up in Winnipeg. At this time, he was in the RCAF, training in Ontario. I wrote to an American friend, a woman who was older than I. She and her husband had been marvellous to me in my somewhat difficult teens. In fact, at one point I had moved in with them, with my mother's consent. The husband had known my grandmother, so there was a link.

At any rate, I wrote a letter, saying I needed consent to get married and could she give it to me. Well, she wrote a perfect answer, "To Whom It May Concern…" just saying that, as far as *she* was concerned, I could marry John Dominique Gallant. She didn't claim any relationship or legal authority. She said just that. And so I was married. I told him later about the letters. He said if he had known, he would have asked his favourite aunt to write it. But it wouldn't have worked. She might have written something like, "…permission to marry my beloved nephew, John etc…."

SB Today when you look back at the period that followed your father's death, does all that moving around now strike you as having been a difficult time?

MG Between the ages of ten and eighteen, let's just say that it wasn't much fun. But, as soon as I had found my freedom and was in Montreal and had hopes of staying there for a while, I was quite happy.

SB You're going to be quite annoyed with me, but, a little while ago, you took me to task for the words I chose—I believe I used the word *self-expulsion*.

MG Yes.

SB And just now you said, "When I found my freedom."

MG Yes.

SB I find that expression rather strong. Freedom from what? From that life? From your mother?

MG From my youth. I was eighteen and I found youth difficult because I had to depend on someone else; and I didn't like that. You know, there were all those constraints: "Do this, do that." I decided—and I remember this well—that never again would anyone tell me what to do. And that was in the taxi; I still remember it, when I arrived in Montreal.

SB In the taxi that was taking you to…?

MG That's about all I remember. I recall that extraordinary feeling of freedom.

SB You were eighteen and you were taking control of your life?

MG Yes. Yes. And I did it. I didn't have a penny.

SB You were leaving New York to return to Montreal.

MG Yes.

SB Where people thought you were dead?

MG Yes, but I didn't know that.

SB That was extreme freedom indeed—returning to a city where people thought you were dead.

MG Oh, I wasn't shocked. Later I looked up people who had known my parents, because I wanted to find out what had really happened. And they thought I was dead.

SB When thinking about your life, isn't *freedom* the keyword?

MG *Autonomy*. I was aware that we live in a society; and it's possible to be autonomous within a society. I had my autonomy and was determined to keep it.

SB And you still are?

MG *Freedom* would be the appropriate term if I had been in a Fascist country where people were oppressed and I was part of a freedom movement. That's something else. But, as for personal autonomy, I was enormously set on that. And I have kept it.

SB Proudly?

MG Essentially.

SB In the next few hours, semantics will be playing a big role. Essentially…

MG No, because we need to be specific.

SB Absolutely.

MG And don't forget that I don't speak French as I do English. That's why it's essential to have the right word.

SB Always.

MG Yes.

SB So, *autonomous* is the word.

Early 60s. Morning sunlight in
Montparnasse.
The apartment house was new + so was
my flat + everything in it. Now it is over-
run by books, like a plague. They're
piled on the floor. I don't know how one
gets rid of them. The picture was taken
by an American expat, Bob something,
who just drifted around earning bits of
money. I advised him to go home to
Chicago + get a job and so he did. Someone
told me he married a hospital nurse.
He must be over 70. Amazing. When he was
here he broke the heart of the ballet critic on
"Combat" by saying she was too old for him. She
cried so much that her eyes were damaged.
Once I introduced him to a beautiful but gloomy
Polish teacher. He said "You remind me of a
dancer I knew" + she said, "I know, I look
terrible." My name for her was "Olga-la-
Triste." She asked me one day for a very sharp
knife. I said, "Why?" She said, "To sharpen my
eyebrow pencil." I thought she meant to kill herself.

MG If we were speaking English, I'd say, "You know what I mean." That would be it.

SB But we have a very good idea of what you mean. For a young woman who was still underage, such autonomy—

MG I wasn't yet of age. I'd never done anything. And suddenly, here I was barely out of high school—

SB So, autonomy has to be earned?

MG Well, it's something you have to achieve. You mustn't let yourself be influenced. If you want your autonomy, you have to be really set on it. This can also be very irritating for other people. At the newspaper where I worked, there was one editor—the one who told us what to do—you know, the one who assigns you a story about four dogs that got run over, etc.

SB The one who gives the assignments.

MG Take a picture of this or don't take a picture of that. It was obvious that I didn't get along with him. I tried not to show it. One day, quite a bit later, I was visiting Montreal—that was about fifteen years ago—and I ran into him on the street. Back then, he'd had red hair, but now he was grey. We talked. He said, there in the street, "I know you never liked me, but you've forgotten what *you* were like. You never accepted an assignment without more or less saying, 'Why do I have to do that when I want to do this, or why do I have to do it that way when I want to do it this way?' And it would be better if I went to see such-and-such a person before going to see that other person." And he said, "It was like that all the time—all the time."

SB Strong-minded, weren't you?

MG Well, I didn't realize just how much I got on his nerves, but he was the one…I've written about this. I'd once gone up to the poor man and said, "Listen, this week Jean-Paul Sartre and Paul Hindemith, the composer, will be in Montreal. I'd like to cover them both. Each of them will be holding a press conference and I want to cover them and I want a photographer and I want…"

SB I want…I want…

MG *"I'd like to have."* Yes. [*laughs*]

SB "I'd like to have."

MG He was sitting down and I was standing up. Then he said, "Who?" I said, "Jean-Paul Sartre and Paul Hindemith." He said, "Listen, Mavis, I'm sick to death of these French-Canadian geniuses that you're always trying to cram down my throat."

SB Jean-Paul Sartre—now that's a good one!

MG Yes, and it was also appalling as far as Hindemith was concerned. And guess what I did. I did something one should never do at a newspaper: I went over his head to a much more senior editor.

SB Another authority?

MG That's something you should never do unless you want to make enemies. I'm warning young people not to do it. But that's just what I did. He was more reasonable and said, "Well, there's a press conference for Sartre. Yes, okay. But you'll have to cover Hindemith on your own time." I replied, "That's fine. He's going to give a lecture I'll be going to anyway."

SB You don't seem to have many regrets concerning the person you were at that time or for—

MG No, but I've always been amused by that "Who?" of his. Don't forget, however, that Sartre, as far as I know, had not been widely translated at that time. It was 1945. The war was over. A group of French reporters came to North America from France. The Americans brought them over. Jean-Paul Sartre was among them. You must know the story: they were shabbily dressed after four years of war and occupation. So, the first thing the American authorities did was to provide them with clothes. They took them shopping and bought them something to wear. But that's another story.

SB When you arrived in Paris, did you have any idea that you'd spend your life here?

MG   No, I had no idea what was in store for me. None what-soever. But I had a typewriter, so I started writing.

SB   In a rigorous and disciplined manner?

MG   Well, I made the time to write. I'd have been stupid not to. But after a month at the hotel, I was seeing too many Canadians because everybody wanted to come to Paris. There was Mordecai Richler, who was nineteen. I had met him in Montreal—John Sutherland introduced us. I met more Canadians in Paris, in 1950, than I've ever known since.

SB   It seems to me that throughout your career as a short-story writer, you've drawn on your experience as a reporter. That's rather curious. Because, to say the least, the use of words could be seen as a link between your earlier experi-ence as a reporter and your literary career. But bringing a reporter's eye to your way of writing strikes me as quite innovative.

MG   I've often been criticized—but nicely—for question-ing people in the way a reporter does. For instance: "Do you have any brothers or sisters?" I'm not even aware of doing this.

SB   Does the writer, the author, sometimes work as a re-porter?

MG   Oh yes! But unconsciously so. As a reporter you quickly feel the atmosphere of a house or of a place you've never been in before. It speaks as much as the person you're there to interview.

SB   And with a minimum of words?

MG   Oh, that's essential!

SB   It seems to me that this would also be true for the writer.

MG   Yes. I take a knife to what I write. I cut a lot, really a lot. And I've written only two novels. Some time ago, I started another novel; I then reread what I'd written and it struck me that this book had only three important things in it. So, what about all the rest? Why was it there? I removed those three things and they became three long

short stories—which you've read. Unfortunately, in the French translation, they were arranged in the wrong order, which must have made for difficult reading.

SB   But, in your view, does the short story go right to the heart of things? Does it immediately go to the most ur-gent aspect?

MG   It shows people in a given situation. And the tension either eases or it doesn't.

SB   Is tension important?

MG   Well, if you take a look at life or remember your own life, it's…it's…tension. I'm sorry, but I can't really explain.

SB   No need to apologize. We understand by reading your works. You don't need to talk about them.

MG   Good, because I'm not a teacher and I can't analyze what I do. I can be a critic. I've been asked to review books, but I can't analyze my own work. Other people tell me things that amount to clichés. For example: "All of your subjects are about exile." That's not true.

SB   People talk to you about exile?

MG   Constantly. And it's not true. I'm not in exile. You're in exile when there's a party in power in your country that you oppose; you then go off to live in Patagonia because you think you'd rather be in the company of horses than with your countrymen. That's what exile is. But when you leave on your own accord, with no bitterness…Absolutely no one was malicious toward me in Canada. Back then, people did talk about men's attitudes to women, but, I repeat, that was a sign of the times. It was the same else-where.

SB   It's my impression that your short stories deal more with fragility, with the loss of a beloved person, a lack. Often your characters seem to me to be in situations of this type.

MG   I don't know.

SB   You don't know?

MG   No. If I analyzed what I've written, I wouldn't amount

to much. I'd have nothing left. I read what other people write.

SB   Is what they write sometimes accurate?

MG   Sometimes—namely, when it coincides with my own thoughts—but sometimes it's off target. Even when it's kind, it's still off target. It couldn't be otherwise. I keep very few reviews, very few. One that I liked and did keep appeared in *El Pais*. I'd just published a translation in Spanish and the reviewer said, She came to Western Europe after the war; no one knew who she was and she didn't know anyone. She lived as anonymously as possible with an exercise book, a notebook and a pencil. She was like Kafka's invisible woman and the invisible woman took note of everything that Europeans thought was of no importance. And now people see that it was indeed important. I really liked that.

SB   Does a short story have a gestation period?

MG   The beginning of the story doesn't. That part comes very quickly and it can come at any time. You may be brushing your teeth when an idea strikes you. You drop whatever you're doing because if you don't immediately write down what comes into your head, you'll lose it. It's like a dream, you know—you'll forget it if you don't write it down at once.

SB   So, it's an idea that whizzes by at lightning speed?

MG   A flash. I've already compared it to a play when the curtain rises and you see the stage. You don't know what's going to happen, but you know somebody is going to come onstage. If it's a light comedy, somebody will walk on and answer a white telephone. But that's only the beginning, and you know nothing yet about these characters. The difference—when you're at the theatre, I mean—is that the characters walk onstage; and, if it's not a play that's been performed a million times, you don't know what's going to happen. So you wait to find out; you wait for someone to say something. But with a work of fiction, if nobody makes an appearance…I'm speaking from my experience. Other writers may tell you something different. John Updike sees the beginning of a novel—I read this somewhere—as a blob on the horizon. Not so for me. I see faces, the faces of living people, even though I've never actually laid eyes on these people. You may wonder where these faces come from. I don't know.

SB   So, it's always the characters who—

MG   It all starts with the characters. They are what make literature. That's how it begins—not with a sunset. You must avoid sunsets. If that's how a work starts, don't read it.

SB   If it starts with a sunset, stop reading immediately!

MG   Yes, right away. You can even burn it!

SB   Your dialogues are often extremely complex. There are times when a dialogue is taking place inside the head of a character at the same time he or she is also talking with another character. This use of multiple levels is quite a gymnastic feat. The dialogues are very significant.

MG   What's said is significant. What's being thought is also significant.

SB   When you make corrections—or, I should say, when you reread what you've written—you strike me as a very demanding reader as far as your own work is concerned.

MG   Yes. I have to be. I can't write just anything, especially in a brief piece like a story.

SB   Indeed, you don't seem very lenient on yourself.

MG   No. I don't know whether you've read a story called "La femme soumise" ("The Moslem Wife")…. Well, I saw a lot of myself in that woman but not until quite a bit later.

SB   She's a very modern and very autonomous woman. She may be like you.

MG   But that wasn't the issue. When the doctor asks Netta, after the war, to marry him, or to live with him—just as she chooses—she refuses. She's waiting for her husband to return. And he, the doctor, says, "Don't be too hard on Jack." Her answer is, "I'm hard on myself." When I reread that passage I thought, I could easily be the woman saying that.

SB Were you merciless with yourself?

MG No. Please don't say that. On the contrary, my life has been very pleasant compared to—

SB I'm talking about when you're rereading what you've written, when you're working.

MG In that case, yes. But it wasn't a case of forced labour for me—not at all. If that had been the case, I'd have made a mess of my life. I think you understand that. The American writer Elizabeth Spencer wrote in her memoir, "Get up in the morning, write and you'll see that you're happy." I agree with that.

SB You got up, you wrote, and you were happy?

MG Yes. One is not unhappy at such times. Sometimes things go badly and you tell yourself it's worthless and that you're making a mess of your life writing about people who don't exist. Because it's strange spending your life writing about people who've never existed. In a way, it makes no sense.

SB Have you ever been afraid that the characters will no longer appear in a flash, that there'll be no more characters who compel you to tell their stories?

MG No. But it's different as I grow older. You reject more than you accept because you can already see where you're headed. But I do prefer a little mystery all the same.

SB Because you know all the strings?

MG Well, I can see that either I myself have already written about such-and-such or that various other people have done so. I stop there. But at an earlier time, it didn't interest me whether someone else had already done it.

SB Are you now more critical about your work, about those flashes, at an earlier stage in the writing process?

MG Perhaps. I don't know.

SB When you decided to write fiction full-time and to come to Paris, you gave yourself two years.

MG Yes.

SB For you, what was the stage when you could say to yourself, I have what it takes to be a writer?

MG The desire. The desire to do it. That's all. The desire to live in a certain way…and I made the effort. You know, there's no point in wishing to live in such-and-such a way. You've got to try. And if it works, so much the better.

SB Have you ever had any regrets?

MG No, sincerely, no. You may look me in the eye and I will tell you that I have no regrets.

SB In those early days, did *The New Yorker* play a significant role?

MG A huge role! Huge! If it hadn't been for *The New Yorker*, I don't know what I would have done. My situation would have been difficult, even impossible…

SB …without this magazine. You also worked with an editor.

MG Yes, William Maxwell. He was a great writer whom I very much admired, but I didn't realize that the editor was the same William Maxwell. Though I finally did realize he was the same man.

SB So, if it hadn't been for *The New Yorker*, the path would have been very different?

MG It would have been very different.

SB Since you were probably well paid, did you find it hard to accept—if *accept* is the right word—the fact that it was the Americans, and not your fellow Canadians, who first opened their pages to you?

MG Oh, I was unknown in Canada. I was unknown or rejected for a long time. There was a time—especially in the 1970s, in the period 1960 to 1970—when Canadian nationalism became very intense. This was a stage that the country probably needed to go through at that time.

SB So much the better if you were fairly well paid. But were you affected by the fact that your initial good fortune led to publication in *The New Yorker* rather than at home?

MG You know, I slid into another life. There were no great

1953

Café des 2 Magots

St Germain - des - Prés

With a visit from Montreal,
DOYLE KLYN. An accomplished
Journalist (at The Standard, where we
met, then at Weekend, which replaced
The Standard.) She was women's editor
then after I left Canada (1950) had
a witty column, read all over Canada,
if one can judge by the mail she
received. A close friend. We never
lost touch until her death. St Germain-
des-Près was only just becoming touristy.
They (the tourists) sat around in Café Flore
+ the 2 Magots, looking in vain for J-P Sartre
+ Simone de Beauvoir.

revelations or extraordinary moments in which I said to myself, That's it! No, not at all; I was going in a certain direction, like a river. That's all.

SB But what about the fact that you found no immediate resonance at home?

MG Well, the immediate resonance was that I had very little money. Do you know who else was in the same situation? Anne Hébert. We were close friends. I had met her in France in 1955 and neither of us had a thing. Then we learned what it meant to be broke in post-war Europe. But one can't write on command. For the most part, I was writing short stories and usually had a novel in the works on the side—but I was never satisfied with it. *The New Yorker* was very generous toward its writers. It was a unique situation. I don't think there was anything really like it anywhere else in the world. So, I had money and spent it. And I had to pay for all the things I'd not paid for in the meantime, you know. It was harder for Anne, until she had an international reputation.

SB Does it bother you that you weren't published first in Canada?

MG No.

SB Are you completely indifferent to that?

MG Well, you know, there were very few publishers. It affected me later when that wave of nationalism was still going on. The same thing happened to Mordecai Richler because he was living in England with his family.

SB To some degree, you idealized life in Europe because of certain great English-speaking authors, such as Fitzgerald, Miller, and Hemingway, who had made Paris their home during an earlier time in the city's history.

MG Fitzgerald was the one I admired—admired a great deal. Not for the way he lived, because he wasted his life. He didn't waste his life in terms of his work, however, because *The Great Gatsby* is without peer as a novel. And he was a great, great writer! But people dared to judge him because he was a drunk. That's how it was. But they had no right to. Only the work matters.

SB The things that can be found on the other side of the book.

MG We need to separate the artist from the art. Visitors wouldn't look at anything in museums if they knew everything about all the painters. We're now living in an age that is extremely open, but, on the other hand, it is a puritanical age; and people want to know about the individual, his life, what the person does. More and more biographies of writers and artists are being written in an attempt to bring them down a notch. It is reassuring to a certain audience. I don't mean to every audience but to a certain audience.

SB That's not so bad either.

MG Well, it's worse if these people take drugs and have five wives at the same time. They're good-for-nothings. But you, on the other hand, are decent, clean, and noble and you brush your teeth five times a day. So, be happy.

SB And avoid being a dropout or an eccentric.

MG More importance is attached now to the biography of an author or painter than to the writer or artist. Just look at the frenzy surrounding Picasso—the women he married, the mothers of his children. What difference does any of that make? It's irrelevant.

SB Only the paintings matter?

MG Only the work life. That's the life that matters.

SB What is it that makes us prefer these famous people to what they do? There is more interest in the celebrities themselves than in knowing about their vision.

MG Well, people can stop doing this. They read or learn this and that and they can talk to you about these things, but they can't talk about the work itself. They read much less nowadays. But I know I'm not going to change anything by telling you this. That's my opinion.

SB In an ideal world, an author or painter would hand

over his or her works to the public and say, "Judge me on these."

MG Perhaps these works could have numbers on them rather than names. I might be, for example, number 16. People would then try to put a face to number 16 but wouldn't be able to. That's how it would be.

SB Would that be better?

MG No. I'm joking, of course.

SB But, at the same time, as soon as you begin to attract media attention by exercising your profession, you become less anonymous.

MG I lived in virtual anonymity for years. The work was translated late. I was reluctant. I felt that nothing would work in translation, that I wrote in English for English-speaking readers. When it began to happen I was afraid it would change my life in a way I'd regret.

SB Things were going to change?

MG Yes. It was in the 1980s. A writer friend in Paris said to me, "You're being coy about translations. As you get older, it seems absurd." But it's ridiculous!

SB Not to have achieved sufficient success or not to be translated?

MG Not to be translated is a form of coquettishness. But I wasn't…. We're going to avoid that.

SB Why?

MG Because! But here's what happened in Canada: a Scottish editor and publisher working in Canada wrote to me about a book, *From the Fifteenth District*, that had just been published in the United States, wanting to know if the Canadian firm could publish it under their own imprint. By this time, I had been published in New York and in London for some thirty years. It was the first offer or suggestion of its kind in Canada. After that, the same Scot wrote to ask about an idea of his he thought I'd refuse: a collection of stories set in Canada or with Canadian characters living abroad. I remember telling him that I

hoped his shirt was painted on his skin because otherwise he was bound to lose it. He didn't lose it, and the book, *Home Truths*, received a Governor General's Award for fiction. Since then—the early 1980s—everything has been smooth sailing in Canada.

SB I'm wondering just how well it serves you, as an author, not to be too much in the limelight, to keep your distance?

MG I'm fairly anonymous.

SB It's more—

MG It's more comfortable. Yes.

SB And the author has more freedom of action as well?

MG Yes. As for the journalist still living inside me, you know, it's a curious…a good thing, because I still observe things.

SB And I imagine that you don't want to spoil your material by talking too much about it?

MG Oh, as soon as you begin writing something, you mustn't talk about it when it's only half done because your own interest will fade. It's like something that's worn out, a half-smoked cigarette, you know, something like that.

SB We were talking about *Home Truths: Selected Canadian Stories* a little while ago and I recall an anecdote I read about Linnet Muir. What kind of name is Linnet?

MG A linnet is a bird. Just as Mavis is a bird—a thrush. I was looking for a name. There were two possibilities: Merle, which is a girl's name in English, or Linnet, which is a small bird no bigger than that. So I used Linnet, which I thought was a prettier name.

SB This cycle is very much about Montreal and is also fairly autobiographical.

MG Not the whole book.

SB Of course not, but some episodes are.

MG It's a cycle of about five short stories, I think. Four or five.

SB I recall an anecdote in which your editor once implied that these Montreal stories were perhaps less inspired than some of your other works.

MG   Oh! That was an editor at *The New Yorker*. Shall I tell you about that? I was stopped in my tracks. I had written four or maybe five Linnet Muir stories. William Maxwell had retired. He was forced to retire because of his age and really didn't want to. But he did. And then, a young editor—much younger—took over from him. I was completely absorbed in what I was doing, writing one story after the other. This young editor wrote to me, saying, "Some people around here have been saying they wish you would go back to writing real stories."

SB   As opposed to false ones, no doubt?

MG   That stopped me dead in my tracks. Dead in my tracks. I thought, But who are these people? No one had ever mentioned them to me. When William Maxwell was the editor, I didn't know that what I sent him was being read by other people. I thought it was only Maxwell and the magazine's legendary editor, William Shawn. I didn't know that just anybody could have a say.

SB   Especially if they didn't like it.

MG   No, it was perhaps the feeling of having been read by people I knew nothing about. But I was certainly stopped in my tracks.

SB   Was that hard on you?

MG   The whole Linnet sequence went dead in my mind. I tore up the one I was then working on and never wrote another.

SB   To preserve your memory of something, you may need to be at a distance from it and out of sight of the changes. Don't you find that an interesting idea?

MG   Yes, you're absolutely right. When I think of Montreal, when I have some particular reason to think about it, I see it the way it was when I was young. I can see the tall trees in the streets where they were chopped down long ago; when I go back, that's how it is now. But I quickly forget. By the time I'm on the plane, flying back to Paris, I've forgotten the present-day city.

About 1956

Menton–Garavan, close to the Italian border. I used to walk over the frontier to swim on a stony Italian beach. There was a steep path to Arturo's, a village sort of restaurant. I'm told there is a chic hotel there now. The house you see was my nearest neighbors', from when I rented an older + prettier cottage. When they had visitors from England they'd ask me over for drinks. Once there was a sort of dowager visiting who kept staring at me. She said, "Are you Mavis from Canada?" She was an aunt of my father's + had once seen me aged about seven in Montreal.

SB   It's the Montreal of your youth that stays with you?

MG   Especially Montreal as it was in the 1940s during the war and the post-war, when I was working at the *Standard*. You always have other, earlier memories of the days when you were very young because the trees looked huge and you were small. Things were different. There are also the well-known true stories about returning to see a house where you lived as a child. In your memory, it's like the Palace of Versailles. But it's a more or less ordinary house, like any house, with a door, a staircase, etc.

SB   For an author, childhood remains very fertile soil because of those first impressions.

MG   Yes. I even think that's what counts in terms of nationality—what's essential to memory. Everyone comes from somewhere. It's not so much from Daddy, Mummy,

Grandmother that very young schoolchildren learn to be the centre of the universe. This comes from sitting in class with their little ABC books. There are people all around you when you are a baby, when you are young. You're the centre of the universe—all children are—for better or for worse. It may be an unhappy universe if you're the child: an orphan in Bangladesh or a baby who will live only three months. In France, I've often been asked, "But why have you never taken out French citizenship?" One can't *become* something. That's my opinion. I'm Canadian, I was born Canadian, and I learned to read and write in Canada, in English and in French.

SB   I would put to you, moreover, that one's identity resides at a level even lower than the national level. Identity is linked to the neighbourhood where a person is brought up. It's the culture that has had a direct impact on us.

MG   It's culture in its very smallest incarnation. But I do think that where you learned to read and write and count, etc., is, in a certain way, very much related to a particular country.

SB   So, fifty-five years after you chose Europe and Paris, you're still, in a certain way, that young person who left New York at eighteen.

MG   Well, I'm going to tell you something: when I'm here in Europe, I'm Canadian. I'm asked what I am. I'm Canadian—that's all I say. I don't want a second passport or an American passport, which I could have had because I spent five of my teenaged years in America—and that's how many years you needed in those days. I could hold a British passport because I had the right grandparents. I could probably apply for a French passport considering the number of years I've been here, but I'd not be a real French person, nor a real American, and especially not a real British person. And I'd not want to show a passport and say, "That's not me." I don't know whether I'm making myself clear.

SB   Indeed you are. So, it means something.

MG   It has nothing to do with patriotism and nationalism, which I detest. I loathe that. I don't want to hear anything from anyone about any country. I can listen for five minutes, maybe six.

SB   I'm not even sure! I have the impression that you have a very visceral reaction when people talk about nationalism.

MG   Because, in my view, it leads directly to some very nasty consequences.

SB   The experience of the Second World War.

MG   Oh, the experience of the twentieth century. And this one isn't so pretty either.

SB   So, being Canadian does mean something?

MG   It's who I am.

TWO ENCOUNTERS WITH THE GREAT CHILEAN POET, NICANOR PARRA

ROBERTO BOLAÑO AND FORREST GANDER

1998

MY BUDDY Marcial Cortés-Monroy takes me to visit Nicanor Parra. For me, Parra's long been the best living poet in the Spanish language. So naturally the visit makes me nervous. You'd think it wouldn't be such a big deal, but the truth is that I *am* nervous, I'm finally going to meet the great man, the poet who sleeps sitting in his chair, although now and then his chair's a blasting pad, with jet propulsion, and sometimes it's a drilling bench, subterranean, but yes at last, I'm going to meet the author of *Poems and Antipoems,* the most definitive figure on that stretch of island over which they all stroll, from one point to another, searching for an exit, never to be found, those ghosts of Huidobro, Gabriel Mistral, Neruda, de Rokha, and Violeta Parra.

At our arrival, Corita opens the door. A bit suspicious, Corita, although she's clearly not a bad type. Then we sit down by our-selves and in a little while we hear footsteps approaching the living room. Nicanor appears. His first words, after greeting us, are in English. It's the welcome the peasants of Denmark offer to Hamlet. Afterwards, Nicanor talks about old age, about Shakespeare's destiny, about cats, about his first house in Las Cruces, which burned, about Ernesto Cardenal, about Paz, whom he admired more as an essayist than a poet, about his father who played various musical instruments and about his mother who was a seamstress and who made, with leftover thread, shirts for him and his brothers, about Huidobro whose tomb is visible from the balcony, at the far side of the bay, of a forest, a smudge white as bird shit, about his sister Violeta and his sister Colombina, about loneliness, about certain afternoons in New York, about car accidents, about India, about his dead friends, about his childhood in the south, about the choritos that Corita cooks and that are in fact really tasty, about the fish in purée that Corita cooks and that is also really good, about

Mexico, about Indian Flanders and the Mapuche who fight on the side of the Spanish crown, about Chilean university life, about Pinochet (Nicanor is prophetic with regard to the fall of the lords), about the new Chilean fiction (he praises Pablo Azócar and I'm in complete agreement), about his old friend Tomás Lago, about Gonzalo de Berceo, about Shakespeare's ghosts and Shakespeare's madness, always obvious, always circumstantial, and I hear him speaking live and in person and later I see him in a video talking about Luis Oyarzún and I feel like I'm falling into an asymmetrical well, the well of the great poets, where his voice goes on mixing, little by little, with the voices of others, and these others, I'm not sure who they are, and his footsteps can be heard echoing through the wooden house while Corita listens to the radio in the kitchen and laughs herself silly, and Nicanor goes up to the second floor and then comes down with a book for me (which I've had for years, the first edition, Nicanor gives me the sixth) and he signs it to me, and then I thank him for everything, for the book that I don't tell him I already have, for the food, for the sweet hours I've spent with him and with Marcial, and we say *see you later* although we know we won't see each other later, and then the best thing is to get the hell out of there, to look for a way out of the asymmetrical well and to split quick and in silence while Nicanor's footsteps reverberate up and down the hall.

—*Roberto Bolaño, translated by Forrest Gander*

2006

THE BUS stops in Isla Negra and I step out with my friend Kent Johnson. Classic comic scene: two travel-bedraggled strangers on a dusty road looking in either direction for a sign. Kent spots a restaurant to the north and we drag our luggage through the tawny dirt toward Restaurante Veinte Poemas de Amor. How, now that we've come all this way without his address or any contact information, are we going to find Nicanor Parra, the ninety-year-old poet? We order lunch and glance idly at the folk art on the wall. One painting, decorated with shells, is a simplified map of the island. Below a square house on the main road, the artist has scrawled *Neruda*. Not far off, in a little woods, another house is labelled *Parra*.

We discover ourselves to be the only guests at a hostel called La Casa Azul. The owner is gone, but her friend, an Argentine painter, shows us to our room and gives us a cursory tour of the kitchen where we can make coffee and find oranges. Yes, yes, he knows Nicanor Parra. In fact, Parra's writing studio is just up the road, he can show us. But Parra doesn't actually live on Isla Negra any more, he explains. He lives two towns away.

With flagging energy, we trudge back down to the main street to bargain with a taxi driver. Yes, yes, he knows Nicanor Parra, and of course he knows Parra's house. It's only a twenty-minute ride. When we get to Las Cruces, the taxi driver slows down to ask the first person he sees where Nicanor Parra lives. With fresh directions, he takes us straight to the house, butted against the sea. We leap out with books we hope Parra will sign, with a T-shirt from his U.S. publisher, New Directions, and with a note, in case he isn't there, explaining that we are admirers who have come this long way hoping just to meet him briefly and that if he feels like granting us a visit, he can leave a message for us at La Casa Azul in Isla Negra. The teenager who answers my knock sticks her head out from behind the wooden door and tells us that no, we cannot see Parra. Is she sure? Yes, she is sure. We ask if we can leave our gifts and the note. She takes them, closing the door in the same fluid gesture, and we go back to the taxi and wait, hoping that Parra, who Kent thinks he glimpsed as the door cracked open, might read the note and step out. We stay there for five stifling minutes. No luck. The taxi driver, commiserating, hauls us back to Isla Negra. At La Casa Azul, we tell the painter that we are expecting a call from Nicanor Parra. A call, he says, perplexed. We don't have a phone here.

Abandoning all hope, as it has been written, we decide we might as well have a look at Neruda's house before it closes, and we walk across the street and take the tour. Rooms of ship figureheads, collections of shells, an enormous narwhal tusk, African masks, stunning hand-carved furniture, and broad rafters carved with the names of his dead friends. It's all museum quality. *Lived well for a communist,* I'm thinking. When we get back to La Casa Azul, the darkness is absolute. The painter sees us making for our room. Oh, he says in Spanish, Parra came by to see you. He drove here by himself in that beat-up orange Volkswagen of his and he came to the door with some books.

Did he leave the books, a message, anything?

He just said, Tell them that I came.

There is a wonderful poem by Walter de la Mare about a man who gallops his horse to a ramshackle mansion on a dark night and, when no one responds to his pounding, shouts up at the shuttered windows, *Tell them that I came.* I wonder if Parra, who knows English poetry well, might have been quoting that poem. There are Chinese poems too, written by would-be disciples who hiked up mountains to visit a master and who waited and finally left without ever making contact. None of the literary precedents, which Kent and I recall to each other from our bunk beds in the cold, dark room, is quite comforting enough to let us sleep.

—*Forrest Gander*

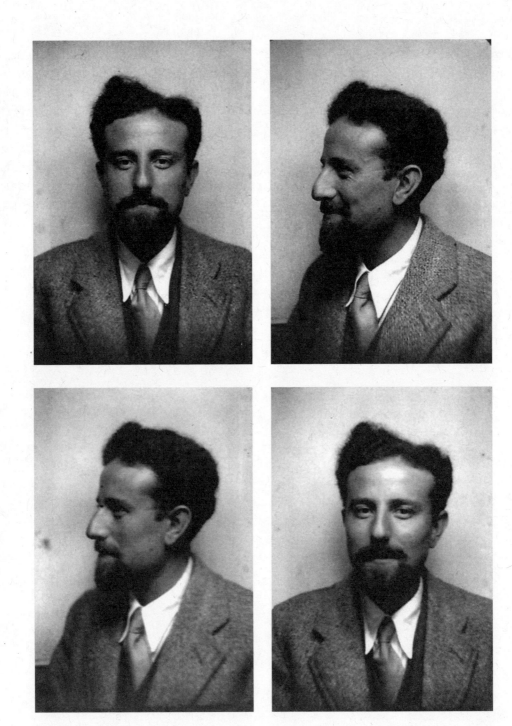

LEON EDEL AND G. BERNARD SHAW

CRAIG HOWES

IN 1928, Leon Edel was twenty-one years old, on scholarship in Paris, and planning to write about the plays of Henry James. Bernard Shaw was seventy-two. This account is taken from an interview I conducted with Edel on January 25, 1997, more than sixty-eight years later, as part of an extensive oral history. He died in September of that year, four days before his ninetieth birthday.

— *Craig Howes*

O N MY first day in London, I experienced a very amusing coincidence. I remember going to Trafalgar Square for the first time. I was walking past the National Portrait Gallery, which is at the curve there. I suddenly looked and walking toward me was unmistakably Bernard Shaw.

He had a beard, you know, that beard marked him out, a white beard, and I had a good glimpse of him. He had been my sort of idol at McGill University, and I'd been reading him a lot. He had an enormous attraction, I think, for late adolescents.

That was a glimpse of Shaw unexpectedly; in the same way that one day during one of my visits to Toronto, coming out of my hotel, I saw another bearded man walking toward me whom I recognized—I seem to specialize in that—and that was none other than what's his name. He died recently. Robertson Davies. That was the same kind of beard and so on. Many years later, you see. I was already an old man when I watched Robertson Davies walking up the street.

Some time after this first sighting of Shaw, Edel interviewed Theodora Bosanquet, Henry James's secretary. He asked whether she had any details about the composition of the plays.

I RECEIVED a sheet with a series of dates on it. She obviously got them out of her diary. One date was "James was dictating such-and-such a play on such-and-such a day, and he dictated another play, worked on another play at such-and-such a date." So on and so forth. And then one sentence: "On this day James received a letter from Bernard Shaw about a one-act play he had written, and he wrote a long letter to

Shaw in reply."

Having been an enthusiastic Shavian, I thought to myself, Goodness gracious. What shall I do with this? I was living in Chelsea, not far from Crosby Hall, and I remember thinking, Well, it was easy to find out where Shaw lived. I had his address because I had written a letter to him some time before. He had been one of the critics who attended the booing [of the James play *Guy Domville*]. So I'd written about that. I had asked him whether he thought the audience was anti-American. He wrote back and said no, he didn't think that was it at all. The audience just thought it had seen a bad play.

Shaw by that time was not signing letters, because everybody sold his letters. He had a secretary named Blanche Patch. Blanche Patch, I think, signed letters, writing, "Mr. Shaw asks me to say to you…"

I was working at the British Museum, where I was finding all kinds of stuff about James's playwriting. All kinds of reminiscences. People who had been present at the booing. It was my first great experience at the British Museum, and I was having a wonderful time. In those days you could order thirty or forty books and go out to breakfast, come back, and there they were, on a nice big work table. So I was having a gorgeous time. I was already full of enjoyment of the whole project, realizing that I did have a project. And with Shaw in it, that was even better.

I thought, What have I got to lose? I sat down and wrote: "Dear Mr. Shaw, I have just learned that you had correspondence with Henry James in such-and-such a year about a certain one-act play. I would like to know more about that one-act play, and what made you write a letter about it. And it would, of course, be wonderful if you happen to have James's response. And I wonder whether you might have, in your busy time…"

He had three plays running in London at that time. *Heartbreak House* was running, and *The Apple Cart* was the new play. That was all about the Labour Party. Ramsay Mac-Donald, I think, or at least a MacDonald type. I had been to see it, and there was one other that was playing.

And I wrote: "If you would have a few minutes so that I could talk to you about this…." I stated it very succinctly, in a note. I mailed it on my way to the British Museum.

Those were the days in London when there were eight or ten deliveries of mail a day. So when I got home that evening, I saw a letter from Blanche Patch. Something I hadn't expected. The postcard read: "Mr. Shaw will see you tomorrow at ten A.M. Blanche Patch."

Well, I had obviously pressed the right buttons. Newspapermen were knocking themselves out to interview Shaw, and never got to see him, but I had touched playwriting, apparently asked the right questions. And so the very next morning, instead of going to the British Museum, I remember I put on my best necktie, tidied myself up, and went.

Shaw lived right in the heart of London. He had a large flat (it looked large, at least; I only saw one room) just off Trafalgar Square. He had lived there for quite a few years, very easy for me to find the address. I walked across the square, arrived at ten o'clock sharp, rang the bell, and a maid came, opened the door, took my hat and coat, and brought me to a very long room with a big window at one end. And there was Blanche Patch, seated at a typewriter, writing a letter.

And Shaw. I looked at him. He had looked big when I saw him in Trafalgar, but he wasn't really a very tall man, rather slender. His beard was splendid. And he must have been astonished to see—I was, you know, young and rather boyish, and he looked puzzled. And he glanced at Blanche Patch, and she said, "Henry James."

"Oh yes! Tell me," said Shaw, "what do you want to write about Henry James?" I said I was writing about his playwriting. "I've read your review of *Guy Domville*," and I recited that I wanted to see the influences of his dramatic years on his fiction. I added, "I particularly want to know what you were corresponding about."

Shaw then sat me down and began to pace up and down. I don't think he saw me any more. He was busy, dictating in perfect sentences. An account. Yes.

He said, "I belong to the Stage Society."

I said, "Yes, I know about the Stage Society."

"Well," he said, "Good!"

The British censorship of plays still existed. The Lord Chamberlain had to read every play being produced in London and could veto any play. This had existed since the Restoration, and the British hadn't changed it. All of Shaw's plays were being censored, so naturally Shaw was an active member of the Stage Society.

Whenever they got a play that they thought should be produced, the Stage Society mounted a private production. You had to be a member of the Society in order to see it, and of course, some of the best actors in London were to give a reading of it.

Shaw said, "Mr. James's agent has submitted a one-act play which no one wants to produce. In this case, it has not been censored, but we were discussing whether we should produce it." He added, "I'm on the committee, and I voted against its production."

They also produced plays that were not likely to be financial successes. That's right. After all, censorship of plays was fairly rare, total censorship, so there would be occasionally a play that ran into trouble. So they'd extended the Society to produce plays that producers wouldn't touch. They would produce them for three or four performances, depending on how many seats were taken. It was a very active organization, and the plays would be reviewed by the press, and it was an active part of the theatre in London.

And Shaw said, "There we had this play of James's, about a young man who is a pacifist."

"Oh," I said, "'Owen Wingrave.'"

That was a story. Owen, as I later found out, means "the young soldier." It is Scots for "young soldier." I think it's Scots.

Owen is the young soldier. And "Wingrave"—the young soldier wins his grave. [The play itself was entitled *The Saloon*.]

"It's a ghost story," said Shaw. "Ghosts are difficult to produce on the stage anyhow."

Shaw was very expansive. He described how he and his committee had decided that it was not worth producing because—and then Shaw came to the crux of it—James has the ghost kill the young man. The man wants to show he's really brave. He's a pacifist. He doesn't want to go to whatever military school the family wanted him to go to. All their family was military. He had rebelled against it. He was interested in poetry. That's a short story that James had published and which he had dramatized. It's a rare short story, by the way, but it's a ghost story.

And so the young man shows how he isn't afraid by sleeping in the room in which the ghost of an ancestor, who had also rebelled against militarism, was killed. The young man had been killed, and Owen is found dead the next morning.

And Shaw said, "I wrote to James and said that he could give victory to one side as well as to the other. No reason why that young man should die. After all, he's fighting against war," and so on. And Shaw felt that this play was all wrong. And then came the really Shavian moment of this interview, when he said, "Well, the young man should kill the ghost, not the ghost the young man."

I said, "I'd love to see that letter you wrote, and James's reply."

He turned to Blanche Patch. "Did we find them?"

She said, "No, I haven't been able to find James's letters."

"Well," he said. "They may be gone. I don't know. My papers, as you may imagine, are immense."

I said, "May I ask you some questions about *Guy Domville*?" I asked him what he thought of James as a dramatist. He thought James was a very fine dramatist. His review had been favourable. He had attacked the audience for booing James, and said it was purely an audience that had expected a happy ending in the play or something of that sort, and they didn't get what they wanted, so they booed James. James should never have been brought out on the stage.

And he said probably Sir George Alexander, who was a popular actor and who loved the role that James had created, had been upset at the audience—there had been some out-cries while the play was being performed. There were already hints that the audience was restless. It was a first night, and the main part of the theatre was filled with the full-dress audience. The gallery was very uproarious, and Shaw re-de-scribed it to me pretty much as he had reviewed it.

What struck me as I listened to him was that he had seen so many plays. We were talking about 1895, and this was 1929, and he proceeded to describe this silly scene in *Guy Domville*, in which the two men try to get each other drunk but are really pouring their liquor into a flowerpot. He went through the gesture of it.

I felt I mustn't take any more of his time, and I stood up to go, and Shaw went on talking. He wouldn't stop. So I asked him more questions. We stood for a few more mo-ments, then he conducted me to the door, and at the door, he kept the door open and kept on talking. He proceeded to say, "Well, you know…"

I remember this little speech, which I later found he had delivered on many occasions: that James had been too much influenced by George Eliot. He said that to me at the door, and—how did he put it? The idea that this gloomy view of life…he as a socialist couldn't accept, because the future could be very bright. He would write about a socialist revolu-tion, and those in effect were the words that he was giving me.

The word *pessimism* was used by Shaw as he stood in the doorway. George Eliot's pessimism, which Shaw was using when he was still embroidering the idea that the young man should have killed the ghost.

Shaw did say at one point: "I reminded James that his father, who was a Swedenborgian, had a more optimistic view of life." He'd forgotten that it was a one-act play. I think he thought it was a two-act play or something, and he kept say-ing, "I wanted him to change that act." That was obviously why he'd received me, when I wrote to him and said I wanted to know about the correspondence. This touched the heart of something that he felt very deeply.

We shook hands, I think. I think he would have liked to go on talking. It had been a whole soliloquy. I'd spent half an hour with him.

Actually, he was quoting from the letter he had written to James. On the first day that I was given access to the James archive, prior to its being given to Harvard—it was still in the hands of the family, but it was in the basement at Har-vard—I found a folder in which there were two letters from Shaw. I copied them, and since Shaw was still alive, I sent him the copies and asked his permission to use them, and reminded him that several years before, we had talked about it.

In red ink he wrote: "Leon Edel is hereby given permis-sion to print these letters. But he must under no circum-stances call me George Bernard Shaw. I am G. Bernard Shaw. I don't need George from the pens of pirates." And he signed himself *G. Bernard Shaw*, and sent me that Shaw item which is at McGill now. So that was the end.

But the interesting thing, as I said, was that I mailed that letter in the morning, and got the summons in the evening, and the next morning I was seeing Shaw. And there I was, on my first real week in England to do my research: Shaw handed to me on a platter, thanks to a date given me by Theodora Bosanquet.

MUSIC

COLM TÓIBÍN

I T .WAS the Hay-on-Wye book festival in the early 1990s. I was wandering around the tents after my own event, wondering what else was on. The program that afternoon included a reading by two poets: one name I vaguely recognized, the other was new to me. As I passed that tent, I found that the poets were starting. I went and sat on my own at the back.

I know that I had not slept very well the night before and was slightly hungover; this may have meant that I was oddly more receptive to things, more open and vulnerable. But I am not sure. Whatever it was, the work of the poet whose name I had not known hit me with considerable emotional force. There was a mixture of playfulness and rhythmic intensity in the work, of an imagination held down by the discipline of stanza form and metre and fired up at the same time by the beauty of language and by life itself. The poet, I should add, was also very good-looking and had a soft American accent. He was fresh-faced and young, and seemed almost innocent. His name was Michael Donaghy.

One of his poems in particular had filled me with delight, especially a line in which "a nice distinction" had been changed by a saint "into an accordion." After the reading, when I was getting a book signed by him, I mentioned this poem and must have seemed disappointed that it was not in a published volume yet. He said if I waited he would write it out in longhand for me. I waited behind and he did so. Later, back home, when I read it over and over, I loved it as much as I had when I heard it for the first time. It was called "Irena of Alexandria":

Creator, thank You for humbling me.
Creator, who twice empowered me to change
a jackal to a saucer of milk,
a cloud of gnats into a chandelier,
and once, before the emperor's astrologers,
a nice distinction into an accordion,
and back again, thank You
for choosing Irena to eclipse me.

She changed a loaf of bread into a loaf of bread,
caused a river to flow downstream,
left the leper to limp home grinning and leprous,
because, the bishops say, Your will burns
bright about her as a flame about a wick.

Thank You, Creator, for taking the crowds away.
Not even the blind come here now.

I have one bowl, a stream too cold to squat in,
and the patience of a saint. Peace be,
in the meantime, upon her. And youth.
May sparrows continue to litter her shoulders,
children carpet her footsteps in lavender,
and may her martyrdom be beautiful and slow.

EITHER BECAUSE of things he said when he introduced some poems or because of poems in the two books of his I bought — *Shibboleth* (1988) and *Errata* (1993) — I realized that Michael Donaghy, who was born in New York in 1954, could play Irish traditional music and knew a great deal about it. This was not unusual, as some of the best Irish players had emigrated to New York or Boston or Chicago, and some of the best early recordings of Irish players were made in the United States. Many of the next generation, born in the United States, had learned to play the fiddle or the flute from their parents, some of them with skill and purity. Among the mythic figures from this world of traditional playing was one Daniel Francis O'Neill, who became the chief of police in Chicago at the beginning of the twentieth century and was responsible for collecting and writing down in notation the largest number of Irish traditional tunes ever, some of which he got from his colleagues.

The following week when I went back to Ireland I was able to call a few friends who knew about Chief O'Neill, or who cared about poetry, and tell them about Michael Donaghy's poem "A Reprieve," which dramatizes O'Neill at work both as a cop and as a collector of tunes:

> Here in Chicago it's almost dawn
> and quiet in the cell in Deering Street stationhouse
> apart from the first birds at the window and the milkwagon
> and the soft slap of the club in Chief O'Neil's palm.
> 'Think it over,' he says, 'but don't take all day.'
> Nolan's hands are brown with a Chinaman's blood.
> But if he agrees to play three jigs

> slowly, so O'Neil can take them down,
> he can walk home, change clothes,
> and disappear past the stockyards and across the tracks.

> Indiana is waiting. O'Neil lowers his eyes,
> knowing that the Chinaman's face will heal, the Great Lakes
> roll in their cold grey sheets and wake,
> picket lines will be charged, girls raped
> in the sweatshops, the clapboard tenements burn.
> And he knows that Nolan will be gone by then,
> the coppery stains wiped from the keys of the blackwood flute.

> Five thousand miles away Connaught sleeps.
> The coast lights dwindle out along the west.
> But there's music here in this lamplit cell,
> and O'Neil scratching in his manuscript like a monk
> at his illuminations, and Nolan's sweet tone breaking
> as he tries to phrase a jig the same way twice:
> 'The Limerick Rake' or 'Tell her I am' or 'My Darling Asleep.'

Over the next decade, as I continued to read him, I met Michael Donaghy twice. Once in London at a literary party, where he seemed the essence of charm and good humour, and where I noticed that he seemed at home, smiling and joking, in the company of many poets. The other time was at Cúirt, the literary festival in Galway in Ireland, where he was carrying around a small baby, his first, and seemed just as before, boyishly happy, immensely popular, wearing his huge talent and increasing reputation lightly and easily.

It came as an enormous shock to me when I read in September 2004 that he had died suddenly at the age of fifty. To those who knew him better than I did, and for those who loved him, it is not hard to imagine what his death meant.

Among the company at the literary party that evening in London was the poet Don Paterson, and I knew vaguely that he had at one point played in a band with Michael Donaghy and they were friends. Just as I paid attention those times when I met Donaghy, I tended to pay attention the few times I met Paterson because I had noticed something very special in his work, something that was deepening book by book, a way of handling emotion or even irony and then a way of disarming what he had been so dexterously handling. He had a way, too, of building up an unusual eloquence in a poem, and either trusting it and letting that tone soar or dismissing it and finding a way out of it. I treasured the idea that I would find myself reading both Donaghy and Paterson for many years to come, as they produced new work. It still seems immensely sad that there will be no new poems by Michael Donaghy.

FOR POETS since poetry began, the business of elegy is a daunting prospect. If each poet wrote an elegy to each person who died, the world would be awash with elegies. All death is sad. Some poets have made sure to maintain an elegiac note throughout their work, as, say, Keats did, or spent many poems writing dark elegies to themselves, as, say, Philip Larkin did. But there are elegies that stand apart. The elegies by Sir Thomas Wyatt for his friends who were executed by Henry VII; "Lycidas," written by Milton in 1637; "Adonais," written by Shelley for Keats in 1821; "In Memoriam A. H. H.," written by Tennyson in 1849; "In Memory of Major Robert Gregory," written by Yeats in 1919; "North Haven" by Elizabeth Bishop, written for Robert Lowell in 1978; the elegies for his friends who died of AIDS written by Thom Gunn and collected in the final section of *The Man with Night Sweats*, published in 1992.

Don Paterson, in "Phantom," his long poem for Michael Donaghy, has now entered that company. The poem is filled with lines of soaring beauty and is also tempered with irony and reason. It is language heightened and haunted, it is also language living with full knowledge on the dark earth and the ordinary universe. Some of the sections of "Phantom" are created with immense, slow reverence for things, for rhythm itself,

for the singing line in poetry, for mystery and the strangeness of our fate and for the *lacrimae rerum*:

> We come from nothing and return to it.
> It lends us out to time, and when we lie
> in silent contemplation of the void
> they say we feel it contemplating us.
> This is wrong, but who could bear the truth.
> We are ourselves the void in contemplation.

Other sections attempt to be faithful to a friendship, to the laddish relationship between two poets who were crazy about music and enjoyed the night:

> *Donno, I can't keep this bullshit up.*
> *I left this message planted in your head*
> *like a letter in a book you wouldn't find*
> *till I was long gone. Look — do this for me:*
> *just plot a course between the Orphic oak*
> *and fuck 'em all if they can't take a joke*
> *and stick to it. Avoid the fancy lies*
> *by which you would betray me worse than looking*
> *the jerk that you're obliged to now and then.*

All the time, as you read, you are aware that in a time when it is hard to be entirely serious in either poetry or prose, Paterson has created an atmosphere in "Phantom" that is serious beyond words but also, accurately and with a rooted and sensuous precision, within words. He has managed, by the risky, hushed careful tone he has taken and the way he has played one section of the poem against another, to keep solemnity at bay and sentimentality a hundred miles away as he has created a great public monument for his friend and one of the poems written in this new century that is likely to endure and deepen as time goes on.

PHANTOM

DON PATERSON

i

The night's surveillance. Its heavy breathing
even in the day it hides beneath.
Enough is enough for anyone, and so
you crossed your brilliant room, threw up the blind
to catch the night pressed hard against the glass,
threw up the sash and looked it in the eye.
Yet it did not stare you out of your own mind
or roll into the room like a black fog,
but sat there at the sill's edge, patiently,
like a priest into whose hearing you confessed
every earthly thing that tortured you.
While you spoke, it reached into the room
switching off the mirrors in their frames
and undeveloping your photographs;
it gently drew a knife across the threads
that tied your keepsakes to the things they kept;
it slipped into a thousand murmuring books
and laid a black leaf next to every white;
it turned your desk-lamp off, then lower still.
Soon there was nothing in that soundless dark
but, afloat on nothing, one white cup
which somehow had escaped your memory.
The night bent down, and as a final kindness
placed it in your hands, so you would know
to halt and stoop and drink when the time came
in that river whose name was now beyond you
as was, you found differently, your own.

ii

Zurbarán's *St Francis in Meditation*
is west-lit, hooded, kneeling, tight in his frame;
his hands are joined, both in supplication
and to clasp the old skull to his breast.
This he is at pains to hold along
the knit-line of the parietal bone
the better, I would say, to feel the teeth
of the upper jaw gnaw into his sternum.
His face is tilted upwards, heavenwards,
while the skull, in turn, beholds his upturned face.
I would say that Francis' eyes are closed
but this is guesswork, since they are occluded
wholly by the shadow of his cowl,
for which we read the larger dark he claims
beyond the local evening of his cell.
But I would say the fetish-point, the *punctum,*
is not the skull, the white cup of his hands
or the frayed hole in the elbow of his robe,
but the tiny batwing of his open mouth
and its vowel, the *ah* of revelation, grief
or agony, but in this case I would say
there is something in the care of its depiction
to prove that we arrest the saint mid-speech.
I would say something had passed between
the man and his interrogated night.
I would say his words are not his words.
I would say the skull is working him.

iii

(Or to put it otherwise: consider this
pinwheel of white linen, at its heart
a hollow, in the hollow a small hole.
We cannot say or see whether the hole
passes through the cloth, or if the cloth
darkens itself — by which I mean *gives rise*
to it, the black star at its heart,
and hosts it as a mere emergent trait
of its own intricate infolded structure.
Either way, towards the framing edge
something else is calling into question
the linen's own materiality
and the folds depicted are impossible.)

after Alison Watt: "Breath"

iv

Zurbarán knew he could guarantee
someone to faint or swoon at the unveiling
if he arranged the torch- or window-light
to echo what he'd painted in the frame.
This way, to those who first beheld the saint,
the light that fell on him seemed literal.
In the same way I might have you read these words
on a black moon, in a forest after midnight,
a thousand miles from anywhere your plea
for hearth or water might be understood
and have you strike one match, and then another —
not to light these rooms, or to augment
what little light they shed upon themselves
but to see the kind of dark I laid between them.

v

We come from nothing and return to it.
It lends us out to time, and when we lie
in silent contemplation of the void
they say we feel it contemplating us.
This is wrong, but who could bear the truth.
We are ourselves the void in contemplation.
We are its only nerve and hand and eye.
There is something vast and distant and enthroned
with which you are and continuous,
staring through your mind, staring and staring
like a black sun, constant, silent, radiant
with neither love nor hate nor apathy
as we have no human name for its regard.
Your thought is the bright shadows that it makes
as it plays across the objects of the earth
or such icons of them as your mind has forged.
The book in sunlight or the tree in rain
bursts at its touch into a blaze of signs.
But when the mind rests and the dark light stills,
the tree will rise untethered to its station
between earth and heaven, the open book
turn runic and unreadable again,
and if a word then rises to our lips
we speak it on behalf of everything.

vi

For one whole year, when I lay down, the eye
looked through my mind uninterruptedly
and I knew a peace like nothing breathing should.
I was the no one that I was in the dark womb.
One night when I was lying in meditation
the I-Am-That-I-Am-Not spoke to me
in silence from its black and ashless blaze
in the voice of Michael Donaghy the poet.
It had lost his lightness and his gentleness
and took on that plain cadence he would use
when he read out from the *Iliad* or the *Táin*,

Your eye is no eye but an exit wound.
Mind has fired through you into the world
the way a hired thug might unload his gun
through the silk-lined pocket of his overcoat.
And even yet the dying world maintains
its air of near-hysteric concern
like a stateroom on a doomed ship, every
table, chair and trinket nailed in place
against the rising storm of its unbeing.
If only you had known the storm was you.

Once this place was wholly free of you.
Before life there was a futureless event
and as the gases cooled and thinned and gathered,
time had nothing to regret its passing
and everywhere lay lightly upon space
as daylight on the world's manifest.

Then matter somehow wrenched itself around
to see — or rather just in time to miss —
the infinite laws collapse, and there behold
the perfect niche that had been carved for it.

It made an eye to look at its fine home,
but there, within its home, it saw its death;
and so it made a self to look at death,
but then within the self it saw its death;
and so it made a soul to look at self,
but then within the soul it saw its death
and so it made a god to look at soul,
and god could not see death within the soul
for god was *death, In making death its god*
the eye had lost its home in finding it.
We find this everywhere the eye appears.
Were there design, this would have been the flaw.

vii

The voice paused; and when it resumed
it had softened, and I heard the smile in it.

Donno, I can't keep this bullshit up.
I left this message planted in your head
like a letter in a book you wouldn't find
till I was long gone. Look — do this for me:
just plot a course between the Orphic oak
and fuck 'em all if they can't take a joke
and stick to it. Avoid the fancy lies
by which you would betray me worse than looking
the jerk that you're obliged to now and then.
A shame unfelt is no shame, so a man's
can't outlive him. Not that I ever worried.
Recall if you will that night in Earl's Court Square
with you, Maddy and Eva, when I found
those giant Xeroxed barcodes on the floor
and did my drunken hopscotch up and down them
while the artist watched in ashen disbelief…
Oh, I was always the first to jump; but just because
I never got it with the gravity.
I loved the living but I hated life.
I got sick of trying to make them all forgive me
when no one found a thing to be forgiven,
sick of my knee-jerk apologies
to every lampstand that I blundered into.
Just remember these three things for me:
always take a spoon — it might rain soup;
it's as strange to be here once as to return;

and there's nothing at all between the snow and the roses.
And don't let them misread those poems of mine
as the jeux d'esprit I had to dress them as
to get them past myself. And don't let pass
talk of my saintliness, or those attempts
to praise my average musicianship
beyond its own ambitions: music for dancers.
All I wanted to keep was the drum
so tight it was lost under their feet,
the downbeat I'd invisibly increased,
my silent augmentation of the One—
the cup I'd filled brimful…then even above the brim!
Nor you or I could read that line aloud
and still keep it together. But that's my point:
what kind of twisted ape ends up believing
the rushlight of his little human art
truer than the great sun on his back?
I knew the game was up for the day
I stood before my father's corpse and thought
If I can't get a poem out of this…
Did you think any differently with mine?

He went on with his speech, but soon the eye
had turned on him once more, and I'd no wish
to hear him take that tone with me again.
I closed my mouth and put out its dark light.
I put down Michael's skull and held my own.

HER OWN WORDS

W. S. MERWIN

IN THE startling, beautiful, and unsparing title poem of her first collection, *Vesper Sparrows*, Deborah Digges follows, with an eye at once precise and visionary, two images. First, the sparrows themselves. She watches — she loves to watch — how they "sheathe themselves mid-air / shut wings and ride the light's poor spine / to earth…" She is seeing them in a city, New York, "just outside Bellevue's walls" where they touch down "in gutters, in the rainbow / urine of suicides…" The suicides are the other image she traces through the poem: the various fortunes of their remains, and the unnamed and barely imaginable relations between them and the sparrows.

The book was published in 1986, when she was thirty-six. That poem had appeared earlier in *Antaeus*. It seems likely that it was written when she was in her early thirties. By then she had been working at writing poems for ten years or more, with the clear commitment she brought to the things she cared about — the lives she cared about. She was, after all, the daughter of a cancer surgeon and had helped her father in the clinic when she was growing up, getting to see and take in, apparently, a good deal of what was going on there. Her father wanted all ten of his children to follow professional careers in medicine. Her upbringing is behind the assurance of "I have identified so many times that sudden / earnest spasm of the throat in children." *Earnest* spasm.

The aura of violence lingering around the unseen presence of what is left of the suicides, and around the urban landscape itself into which the forest birds have been hatched, takes shape in a few lines of reminiscence — in the first person, as in the lines about identifying "the sudden, earnest spasm in the throats of children." That identification follows: "The first time I saw the inside of anything / alive, a downed bird opened cleanly / under my heel. I knelt / to watch the spectral innards shine and quicken / the heart-whir magnify." A preview of the anonymity of the suicides.

In the poem she is watching the sparrows at evening, at the hour of vespers, but the name is not merely a poetic ascription. They are known to ornithologists as the Eastern Vesper Sparrow (*Pooecetes gramineus*), marked with "the streaked siennas of a forest floor" and conspicuous white outer tail feathers, and she quotes with evident familiarity (by surname alone) one naturalist's attempt to mimic in syllables the long tumbling rapids of the bird's song. These birds are nesting in traffic lights, and "hundreds flock down" at evening to the piles of hospital garbage "for the last feed of the day"—a moment of ephemeral, wild survival.

The other image from "Vesper Sparrows" is of "the ransacked cadavers" transported up the East River to Potter's Field "as if they were an inheritance," after they have been emptied of everything that could be saved, while the other parts have been "jarred and labeled, or incinerated"—their ashes "professing the virus that lives beyond the flesh." And the relation between these remnants and the birds—where is it as she watches? In the leap from the ledge? Beyond identity in the garbage?

I do not mean to suggest that the theme and imagery of this poem are typical of her poetry and of all her writing. That certainly is not so—even though the next poem in this collection is "Laws of Falling Bodies," in which she turns from a wondering, admiring recollection of accompanying her father on his inspections of post-mastectomy scars of his own patients to a close look at the imprisoned Galileo timing the pulse in his groin all night by the pendulum of a swinging lamp, until "Dawn moved in, whole and terrifying" when "He'd hear the death carts begin in the street" and the Holy Office would make him "stand to watch the daily / executions in the sunblind courtyard / hoping he'd go mad with the next / navigation of the rack's wheel." "Instead," she informs us, "he learned to love the body / for its genius of color, / the alizarin crimsons hooding the heart," and she returns to the image of her father and the tenderness of his attention over the microscope and the way he touched the scars of the women on whom he had operated. She says, "to me it was a kind / of love he made, as he leaned over them …"

That turn, that scope and breadth of view, are indications of the range of poetry that was to follow. There and in her two vivid memoirs, her variety and the integrity of her language are continuous. She can be comical, erotic, radiant, even though her prevailing tone is elegiac. She never repeats herself. By her fourth book, *Trapeze*, some of the poems, including the title poem, become haunted and haunting.

But even in her first collection, the lines I have quoted from "Vesper Sparrows" present qualities that will typify her writing. Authority of tone, deliberate precision of language, and what appears to be openness and intimacy—a closeness at once to the subject and to the reader or the imaginary listener. Yet the poem and the life and death at its heart remain elusive, untouched, beyond knowledge. These qualities are clearly her own.

They are also, of course, qualities of poetry itself, its mystery, its radiance, its enigmatic immediacy.

I MET her only once, before I had read anything she wrote. It was in the late seventies, in Seattle, soon after she and Stanley Plumly, her second husband, were together. Beautiful woman, smiling, poised, quiet. I spoke to her later, or wrote to her, I believe, after the publication of each of her books of poems. I loved them from the moment I read them, and have always thought of hers as one of the unique gifts of a richly talented generation. But I have no sense of having known her. When I set down the telephone after a friend had told me, before the news broke, of her death, in that stunned moment I realized that what she had done was suddenly complete. Leaving us the words.

THE LIZARD, THE CATACOMBS, AND THE CLOCK

The Story of Paris's Most Secret Underground Society

SEAN MICHAELS

"It's a war of knowledge. Whoever knows the most is king."
—Crato

ENTRANCES

ON AUGUST 23, 2004, they discovered a cinema sixty feet beneath Paris.

The sun was shining on the Trocadéro, the Eiffel Tower gleamed across the Seine, and deep below ground, police came across a sign. The officers were on a training mission, exploring the 4.3 miles of catacombs that twist beneath the 16th arrondissement. The former quarries are centuries old and the sign at the mouth of the tunnel read, "No public entry." Police are not the public; they entered. Their headlamps flashed against the limestone walls and then suddenly the officers were surrounded. Invisible dogs snarled and barked from all sides. The men's hearts hammered. They froze in their tracks. They cooed canine comforts into the dark.

In time, the officers' lights found the PA system. They found the stereo, with guard-dog yowls burned onto a CD. They found three thousand square feet of subterranean galleries, strung with lights, wired for phones, live with pirated electricity. The officers uncovered a bar, lounge, workshop, dining corner, and small screening area. The cinema's seats had been carved into the stone itself, with room for twenty people to sit in the cool and chomp on popcorn.

On the floor of one cavern, officers discovered an ominous metal container. The object was fat, festooned with wires. The police called in the bomb squad, they evacuated the surface, they asked themselves, *What have we found?*

They had found a couscous maker.

A few days after the *couscoussière* incident, officers returned to the scene. This time they brought agents from Électricité de France. But they were too late. Already someone had undone the galleries' wiring, disappeared with the equipment, vanished with the booze. What had so recently been a private cinema, a secret hideout, was now just an empty quarry. The cinema's makers had left a note. "*Ne cherchez pas,*" they wrote. Don't search.

Don't search? *For what? For whom?* While the Agence France-Presse reported a possible "extreme right-wing" connection, the BBC speculated on a full-fledged "underground movement." All of Paris dreamed of its subterranean screening society.

However, the people responsible for the cinema under the Trocadéro, a place they dubbed the Arènes de Chaillot, are not quite any of these things. "We are the counterpoint to an era where everything is slow and complicated," they explain. This group also balances the aspect of today that is instant and

He and his co-conspirators met at school in the 1980s, when many Latin Quarter colleges still had basement access into the tunnels. Although Parisians have been sneaking into the catacombs (known as *carrières*) for centuries, Kunstmann and his friends had no taste for the usual "cataphile" hijinks. Too young to drink, not interested in drugs, they instead began to explore, map, and expand the underground network.

Eventually, Kunstmann tells me, they entered a "post-post-exploration phase." After "you go, you survey — then it's time to do something."

Five years after the discovery of the cinema, Kunstmann has written a book exposing the full scale of this "something." In *La culture en clandestins: L'UX*, published by the French imprint Hazan, Kunstmann reveals LMDP as just one wing of a larger clandestine organization called UX. Ux (pronounced "oo-eex," like the French letters) has more than one hundred members, split into more than ten teams. While LMDP are dedicated to events, other branches are devoted to maps, restoration, or key-making. "[We] are determined to make these abandoned places a theater for new experiences," Kunstmann explains in his book. This means more than it seems. In French, the word *expériences* connotes both "experiences" and "experiments." Ux itself, an acronym for Urban eXperiences, borrows the double meaning.

The Arènes de Chaillot were built over a period of eighteen months. Starting in 1999 and continuing every summer until the cinema's discovery, the tunnels hosted Urbex Movies. It was a festival combining careful programming and an unusual locale to present discrete visions of urban life. Shorts and features were grouped by unstated "intention," to allow for each twenty- to thirty-person audience "to discover, or merely to feel." A similar philosophy dominated LMDP's other major film festival, the Sessión Cómoda. Whereas Urbex Movies screened films like *Eraserhead* and Dziga Vertov's *Man With a Movie Camera*, the Sessión Cómoda had a narrower focus on the underground — showing *The Third Man* and Jacques Becker's *Le Trou*.

shameless, hysterically tweeting. They are patient, serious, and they keep their secrets.

After the cinema episode, it would be two years until the city would see their work again.

PORTE-PAROLE

I AM late. Paris's decaying public-transit system almost strands me at Gare du Nord and I arrive at Le Pantalon out of breath, panicked, terrified that Lazar Kunstmann has left. I slip past students in this noisy bar, searching for the face I have seen in a handful of photographs. I crossed the ocean to meet him and I may not get another chance.

Lazar Kunstmann is stocky, in his late thirties. He has a shaved head. He is friendly. Too friendly, almost — the eagerness in his eyes seems utterly unclandestine. This is not the mystery man I envisioned: Kunstmann is warm, cheerful, and talkative.

He first appeared in 2004, the mouthpiece for a group called La Mexicaine de Perforation (LMDP). Though it literally translates as "the Mexican of the Drilling," their moniker is best understood as something like "The Mexican Consolidated Drilling Authority." The organization was named for a bar in the 16th arrondissement's Place de Mexico. LMDP, Kunstmann revealed, was responsible for the cinema under the Trocadéro.

"Two-thousand four was the first big discovery," Kunstmann admits. "We were really caught in flagrante delicto."

I was living in Scotland at the time. The French and British press were enraptured with the underground cinema and so was I. The appeal wasn't just in the breadth of the cinema-builders' imagination but in their meticulous follow-through. "We covered our tracks," Kunstmann reassured *The Guardian*. "Short of digging up every cable in the district there's no way of knowing where we took [the electricity] from."

Giddy and well spoken, Kunstmann was at the centre of every article. He had spent decades going where he wasn't supposed to: climbing onto roofs at age seven, sneaking through the subway at twelve, delving into the Paris catacombs at fourteen.

These screenings took place nearby, but above ground — in the famous Cinémathèque of the Palais de Chaillot. Which isn't to say that the Sessión Cómoda was part of the Cinémathèque's official program. No — LMDP snuck in, week after week, year after year, entering (they claim) from a passage beneath the projectionist's chair.

For both festivals, audiences were drawn from among UX's friends, associates, and members of the public who stumbled across scattered fliers. "The LMDP are simply interested in holding events in a free way," Kunstmann explains. "Clandestinity is really a detail."

It's the detail that allows them to continue what they are doing. UX slip past the functionaries, under the cordons, across miles of red tape. Their high-concept installations use secrecy as a cover, but it's not their raison d'être. "We don't seek out the forbidden," Kunstmann murmurs over radio-pop. "We just repudiate any notion of authorization."

At the same time, UX's anonymity is a major source of their allure. We are drawn by their gall, their pluck, but also the burnished gleam of a mystery. The Arènes de Chaillot would not be the same treasure if they were sanctioned, public-funded. Kunstmann is surely aware of this, yet he balks at being part of "something 'plugged in,' elitist, VIP." Ux do not wish to be a "secret society," he insists. "When I say secret society, you imagine, I don't know, like, in *Eyes Wide Shut*. But it's more basic than that. It's the patronage system. It's taking advantage of a hidden alliance."

The group's operational need for clandestinity is offset by this distaste for old boys' clubs. And so UX leave avenues for strangers to stumble across their works, they have published a book revealing certain details, and years ago they resolved to never hide what was in plain sight. This is why LMDP revealed themselves in 2004. Once the Arènes de Chaillot was discovered, with speculation mounting — "In that instant," Kunstmann says, "we had to clearly explain."

They didn't divulge everything.

D'ENFERS

PARISIANS CALL it a *gruyère*. For hundreds of years, the catacombs under the city have been a conduit, sanctuary, and birthplace for its secrets. The Phantom of the Opera and *Les Misérables'* Jean Valjean both haunted these tunnels, striking students descended in 1968, as did patriots during the Second World War. The Nazis visited too, building a bunker in the maze below the 6th arrondissement.

Honeycombed across 1,900 acres of the city, the vast majority of the tunnels are not strictly speaking "catacombs." They house no bones. Limestone (and, to the north of the city, gypsum) quarries, these are the mines that built Paris. The oldest date back two thousand years to Roman settlers, but most were excavated in the construction boom of the late Middle Ages, providing the stone that became Notre Dame Cathedral and the Louvre. Riddling the Left Bank, these tunnels were at first beyond the city's southern limits. But as Paris's population grew, so did the city — and soon whole neighbourhoods were built on this infirm ground.

The first major cave-in happened in 1774, when an entire street collapsed not far from where the Catacombs Museum stands today. After a similar incident three years later, King Louis XVI created the office of the Inspection Générale de Carrières (IGC, or General Inspection of the Quarries), designated with preventing further collapses. Officials went underground: inspecting, charting, filling chambers with concrete, digging a new labyrinth of maintenance tunnels.

Then came the dead. In the late eighteenth century, Paris's overcrowded central cemeteries leaked. Fetid gases would waft into the cellars of Châtelet, marinating wheels of brie and braids of *saucisson*. Beginning in 1785 and for about a century, the government enacted its grisly solution: it transported six million skeletons to the southern quarries. Five percent of the catacombs remain ossuaries today, and Racine, Robespierre, and Marat are among the dry, dusty residents.

Entrances to the tunnels can be found in the basements of hospitals, the cellars of bars, church crypts, subway tunnels,

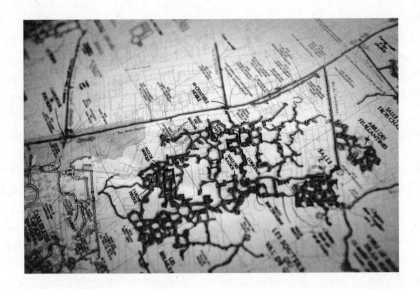

even at the bottom of Paris's tallest skyscraper. Many of these access points have been sealed by the IGC, who both protect the city from the catacombs, and the catacombs from the city. Circulating in the *carrières* was made illegal in 1955.

That didn't stop the catacomb craze. By the time Kunstmann and his friends were in college, almost every Latin Quarter party would end below ground. The IGC fought back, deploying a series of barrier walls that criss-crossed the passages, blocking the flow of visitors. The plan was good, but it only had so much effect: trespassers soon found ways around — and through — the concrete blockades.

By definition, Paris's hundreds of catacomb ramblers, its "cataphiles," decline to follow the rules. They are an odd gang of misfits — "urban explorers," vandals, kids who just want to hang out below ground. They chatter on online message boards, share and hoard maps; they meander, explore, drink, and drill through walls. By night they drop through manholes, or emerge from them, dusty, at dawn.

Members of UX spend time underground, but Kunstmann insists they are not cataphiles. It isn't just a matter of style. "The principle of UX is to provoke experiences using every available part of the city," he says at Le Pantalon. "Not as visitors but as *users*. Users for something other than the simple aesthetic of the places. And for something other than partying."

Their ideas are not new. It is Guy Debord's *détournement* turned loose on geography, Situationism without the politics, a no-nonsense take on Britain's art pranksters, the KLF. Yet these allusions betray UX's modest code — to do interesting things without permission. This credo allows for superficial punkery, sneaking into backyards, but considered seriously, it becomes a formula for being brave, for pursuing dreams. Which is a sappy way of saying, *It grabbed me.*

The first place I looked for UX was on Facebook. I typed "Lazar Kunstmann" into the search box and hit enter. There were no results. So I set my nets wider. I posted a message saying I was looking for contacts in the Paris "underground," figuratively and literally. I did the same on Twitter. I emailed friends in Paris, types who organize concerts in subway cars, asking similar questions. No one knew anything of Kunstmann, or of UX.

Next I scoured cataphile message boards, at least those that are public. Although these forums had discussed the group's works and media coverage, I found no traces of UX's authors. As Kunstmann later scoffed, these boards are full of typical internet posturing—resentful quips and knee-jerk LOLs.

I finally found Kunstmann through private correspondence with another journalist. They gave me an email address; that address told me to telephone a secret number. I asked for "Lazar," Kunstmann answered, and we met at Le Pantalon.

"Ordinary" cataphile contacts are less difficult to make. My online searchlights were glimpsed by a friend of friends, pseudonym Cavannus, who does "urban exploration" in Montreal. Cavannus put me in touch with one of his cataphile pals in Paris—a man with a fake Facebook account named for a celebrated guru. He tells me to meet him at Saint-Pierre de Montrouge church, to look for a guy "on crutches." Two days after meeting Kunstmann, as I ride the subway and climb up to Alésia Square, there seem to be broken-legged people everywhere. I imagine this as cataphile ground zero, a place where everyone has limestone dust in their hair.

The cataphile who meets me looks about thirty, his dark hair pulled into a ponytail. He gestures at his crutches and says he slipped coming out of a manhole, on the rain-soaked street. He is called BHV.

"Underground, everyone has a nickname," BHV explains to me. He didn't choose his own, an acronym that refers to a famous department store. Someone else picked it about a dozen years ago, and it stuck. Other names are more esoteric, like Sork, or Crato, the man who eventually takes me into the tunnels. Some conjure deliberate images. One of the catacombs' most notorious mischief-makers is Lézard Peint, the Painted Lizard, a "devil" with alleged Fascist connections, who has been known to steal fellow cataphiles' lights or to seal up their intended exits.

"What you are on the surface, you are underground," Crato later says, sucking on a cigarette. "When you are a violent person, given to fighting—you're the same below." Scoundrels like Lézard aside, the cataphile community is civil. "In general we look out for each other," BHV agrees. They share knowledge, lighters, cans of beer (never bottles, which are still heavy when empty). "People know that if they get too drunk or if they get hurt, it'll be hard to get out."

BHV's and Crato's first descents were similar—they saw a hole, or heard about a hole, and they entered. Telling me, BHV begins to cough. "Sorry," he wheezes, "I still have dust in my throat." On that first journey, he and his friends ran into some unlikely mentors—off-duty police officers who offered to give them a tour—"and then I spent the whole night underground."

BHV's story is beguilingly simple. *I could go*, I realize. I could find an entrance on the internet, slip inside, wander until I find an off-duty police officer or a shy, kindly filmmaker. "It's a very supernatural setting," BHV murmurs. "You're completely autonomous. There's no light. There's no electricity. Just stones and water."

But I am here to understand UX and this is not the way that UX works. That group does not rely on word of mouth, happenstance, the kindness of strangers. UX sets goals and quietly executes them. They never get lost.

I find Crato online, just as I found BHV. Whereas BHV, becrutched, does not volunteer to play tour guide, Crato—lanky, vaguely grumpy—makes the offer. "There are a lot of reasons to go down," he allows. "There are those who want to find a calm and pleasant spot. There are those who go down to meet a partner. There are those who go to party. There are even those who go to watch movies. Everyone has their own reasons."

We rendezvous on a bridge over train tracks. It's the middle of the afternoon, cars whizzing by, clouds meandering across a dirty blue sky. We're not far from Denfert-Rochereau, site of the official Catacombs Museum. That plain stone building offers historical displays, dioramas, entry onto a sanitized one-mile circuit of "legal" catacombs. This is not, cataphiles emphasize, the "real thing." Besides — you have to pay admission.

We look both ways and, one at a time, jump the bridge wall. It is thick, high as my shoulders. My jump is less deft than Crato's. I struggle for a moment and then I'm over, feet in the weeds, scrambling down the slope to the tracks. This is the Petite Ceinture, one of the city's abandoned railways. It is almost silent. We walk.

Crato has been visiting the catacombs for ten years. He tells me how the original quarries were built just wide enough for a man with a wheelbarrow — six feet by three feet. How they are a permanent 55° Fahrenheit, day and night, winter and summer. "I remember once it was hot in Paris, really hot, really horrible. Instead of dining in an overheated apartment, we went down into the catacombs to eat."

After a time, Crato and I come to a large train tunnel. The sunlight falls away behind us. It is easy to trip on the wooden ties of the tracks or on the irregular stones to either side. We turn on our flashlights yet I can see neither end of the tunnel. I assume the problem is fog, but Crato speaks of *fumis*, cataphile smoke bombs, made by mixing saltpetre with sugar and flour. They are hiding something down here.

Ten minutes into the gloom, Crato swings his flashlight to the right. The darkness slips into focus. Before me, where the tunnel wall meets the earth, is a hole.

In 2009, this is the "grand entrance" to the catacombs. A craggy break in the rock, no more than two feet wide. Cataphile refuse is strewn nearby — empty beer cans, juice cartons, white paste from carbide lanterns. This is just the second "grand entrance" that Crato has known. One day the IGC will close it up, he says, fill it with concrete like the last one. But Crato hopes his fellow cataphiles do not dig a replacement straight away. Better to give the losers, the troublemakers, time to get bored and find something else to do. The committed ones already know different ways to get in. The committed ones are patient. Even Crato seems to think that secrets are best.

DEEPER

FOR KUNSTMANN and his associates, there is little appeal to wandering around underground. Their cinema aside, the catacombs are a means, not an end: a way to access UX work sites or to hide their tracks. But as a first-time visitor plunging into these grey chambers, the experience is thrilling. It is a labyrinth of branching channels and sudden openings, cool and quiet. Most of the catacombs are dry, tall enough to stand in — but from time to time we duck or crawl, or swish into ankle-high water. Still, they are not the dank, sweaty caves I imagined. Even wading into a passage called Banga, whose thigh-high water swirls like miso soup, the tunnel's soft silence recalls a theatre, a wine cellar, an attic.

In Kunstmann's book, cataphiles like Crato are called "*bodzaux*," for their wet and dirty boots, or "Ravioli," for their tendency to dine on boxed dumplings. ("I prefer wine and sausage," my guide retorts.) Ravioli seek to "consecrate" the underground, Kunstmann argues, guarding it from precisely the kind of transformation that UX enjoy. "[They] are protecting an image [of the catacombs] and they want to keep this image intact for the feelings it evokes in them."

Crato speaks of these feelings without actually speaking of them. He talks about how years ago, he and his now-wife would spend all of Saturday night in the tunnels, wandering until four in the morning. They would emerge, dust themselves off, go to sleep — and on Sunday they would walk the same route, retrace the same steps, above ground, hand in hand.

While this is a beautiful image, it is the opposite of what UX hope to accomplish. "It's a typically Parisian phenomenon," Kunstmann sighs. "Nostalgia for a period we didn't know. Areas 'flashed' in time. The work of UX is to de-flash, to thaw, to transform."

As Crato and I weave beneath the 14th arrondissement, the subway murmurs in a passage over our heads. You could walk these caves in jeans and sneakers, I think. I have read how the Painted Lizard has ordered people to do the circuit naked for his own wicked entertainment. I am in knee-high boots and a cardigan. Crato wears the basic cataphile uniform: hip waders, waterproof backpack, strong flashlight, gloves, a cap to keep off the dust. The athletics stores of Paris, he says with a grin, sell a disproportionate number of fishermen's boots and impermeable packs.

Although the catacombs are covered in graffiti tags, there are also sudden instances of art—amateur gargoyles, carved castles, life-sized sculptures of cataphiles. Crato brings me to La Plage, "the beach," a large gallery with a sand-packed floor. Our flashlights sweep across wide murals: Hokusai waves and Max Ernst–like portraits. In the Hall of Anubis we sit at a table chiselled out of stone. We light candles, drink beer, share cookies and chocolate. I am absolutely enchanted. I have no idea of the time.

For the most part, cataphiles don't dispute Kunstmann's characterization of them. BHV says his friends enjoy "taking photos, exploring a particular area, repairing things, going to spots where no one has visited for a long time." The community's holy grail, he suggests, is to clandestinely enter the Catacombs Museum. I balk at this—the same place you can visit for just eight euro, six days a week? "Yes," he agrees, "but that's the goal of tons of cataphiles. And they succeed almost every year—every year there's a hole that's drilled."

When cataphiles do stage large events, they tend to be one-off parties—not permanent "transformational" cinema installations. Crato remembers someone bringing down oysters—stupid, silly, "just as heavy on the way back as on the way down." BHV has organized two Breton-themed shindigs, where more than three hundred people joined dancers, musicians, and amateur chefs cooking subterranean crêpes. Among the largest celebrations was a farewell to Commandant Jean-Claude Saratte in 2000. Head of the catacomb police for twenty-one years, Saratte was respected for his knowledge, instincts, and moderation—pursuing the drug user, vandal, or "tibia collector" instead of the gentle catacomb geek.

Today, officers of BICS (la Brigade d'Intervention de la Compagnie Sportive) patrol the catacomb thoroughfares handing out €65 tickets. The *catacops* are regarded with resentment and disdain. But they force cataphiles to be vigilant: listening, looking out for standard-issue lights, sniffing for aftershave. It is illegal to drink on public streets, Crato proposes, but not beneath them.

"When you're caught, you have the chance to recognize or not recognize an infraction," he explains to me. "If you choose the latter, you're supposed to get an appointment with a judge." Crato has been awaiting his court date for years—and counting down the days until the automatic amnesty triggered by each presidential election.

We emerge from the maze three hours later, flashlights still shining, and again we are wreathed in smoke. It is dark as night. The opening of the railway tunnel is a circle of gold-white light in the far distance. Treading toward the open air, out and past the wild bright green of the weeds, it's as if we're passing through stained glass.

On our way back along the tracks we meet a quartet of cataphiles in black hoodies and running shoes, acquaintances of Crato's. We talk. The conversation is a mixture of bravado, feigned indifference, outbursts of earnest feeling. They talk of girls, parties, police, numbskulls with smoke bombs.

These men seem so gentle. Watching them smile, UX's rejection of this community seems unkind. No, Ravioli are not engaged in the same activities; no, their ambitions are not to the same scale. But if UX want to be something other than a secret club, at least they could be friendly with their neighbours.

Kunstmann sees it differently. Ux are absolutely unrelated to these cataphiles, separate "from the start." "We were *learning* from one experience to another," he says. "We had an intention for these places." Besides, his group is not based in the catacombs. As Paris was to learn, they hide in the above ground as well.

FLYING SAUCER

ON DECEMBER 24, 2006, after fifty years of silence, the clock of the Paris Panthéon began to ring.

Two and a half years later, I arrive at the building for a tour. My group's guide is a man in his fifties, bird-haired, who talks in clipped and concentrated French. He doesn't mention the Panthéon's clock. Nor are there any references in the written program. After the tour ends, as the other tourists disperse, I ask him a question: "Didn't something happen with this clock?" We are standing directly beneath the three-foot minute hand.

The guide looks startled. "There are these people…" he begins to say. He does not make eye contact. "They infiltrated the Panthéon." This group had all the keys; he doesn't know how. The clock had been broken. They fixed it. They have also held plays here, and projected films. He explains everything with a weird, wry solemnity, like he both hates and relishes being asked. "Untergunther," he says finally, though he doesn't know how to spell it. "Look it up on the internet."

What the internet will tell you is that the Untergunther are a branch of UX. Whereas the Mexican Consolidated Drilling Authority are dedicated to events, the Untergunther are the organization's restorers. In September 2005 they came here, to one of Paris's most important monuments—and they went to work.

The Panthéon was commissioned by Louis XV in 1744, as a tribute to Saint Geneviève. By the time it was finished in 1789, the French Revolution had guillotined the church idea. Instead, the domed neo-classical cathedral became a mausoleum for great French citizens. Voltaire, Rousseau, Émile Zola, and Victor Hugo are buried in its crypt; so are Marie Curie, Louis Pasteur, and Louis Braille. In the centre of the Panthéon's floor, where architect Soufflot had imagined a statue of Ste. Geneviève, Foucault's pendulum swings. Tourists like me come and gape at the way this simple experiment, commissioned by Napoleon, offers evidence of the rotation of the planet. It is such an unassuming marvel.

Another modest wonder lies at the end of the main hall, on the left, above a doorway. The Panthéon's clock is not an elaborate timepiece, like the Prague Orloj. The face is about as tall as a person, mounted on frosted glass. The clock hands and roman numerals look like they are made of cast iron. Built by the house of Wagner in 1850, it is plain, even austere. But for one year, this was the Untergunther's project.

"[The Untergunther] have compiled a huge list of slowly degrading places," Kunstmann told a *National Geographic* reporter in 2006. "The list is too big to ever be completed in our lives so each year we choose [just] one." The Untergunther have only three conditions for accepting a restoration project. First, to have the technical ability. Second, to have the means. And third, to have the desire. By 2009, they claim to have completed about twelve projects, including the Panthéon, a hundred-year-old government bunker, a twelfth-century crypt, and a First World War air-raid shelter.

"[We] are only interested in a very precise part of [French] cultural inheritance," Kunstmann writes in his book. "The part that is non-visible." These are not just places that are inaccessible or hidden to the public, like the mechanisms of a clock, but also sites that are invisible to their administrators. Since the city administration scarcely has enough money to maintain what is in plain view, UX suggest, they are doomed to ignore what is not.

This is a beautiful idea, but only compelling if acted upon. The Untergunther could be fakers, blowhards taking credit for conveniently hidden restorations. Yet as with the LMDP and their rock-hewn cinema, the endeavour at the Panthéon dismisses doubt.

The Panthéon's nineteenth-century clock had been broken since the 1960s, left to decay, but it caught the eye of a man called Jean-Baptiste Viot. Viot is a clockmaker, formerly head of restoration for the Swiss house Breguet. He is also a member of UX. Viot observed the rust caked on the Wagner's machinery and ruled that it was a "now or never" moment. If the Panthéon's clock were ever to tick again, it would need the Untergunther's help.

On September 18, 2005, the group formally adopted the project. Soon after, an eight-person "core"—including Viot and Untergunther leader Lanso—went to work. Using a copied

key, they infiltrated the building after dusk, dodged security agents, and made their way up. High above the clock that had lured them there, the Untergunther arrived at a cavity along the base of the building's dome. This dusty, neglected space became their home.

They called it the *Unter und Gunther Winter Kneipe*, the Untergunther's Winter Tavern, taking their inspiration from a door marked UGWK. A similar whimsy had inspired the Untergunther's naming, back when they were just known as "the restoration wing." Unter and Gunther, Kunstmann says, were the names of the imaginary guard dogs in the Arènes de Chaillot's security system.

For the next twelve months, the Panthéon was the Untergunther's playground. They learned every nook and cranny, copied every key, learned the habits of every guard. It was made easier by relatively lax security. When I visited in 2009, there were still no real security badges, and both of my tour guides failed to count the group with their clickers. According to Kunstmann's stories, UX had already used the Panthéon to stage plays and other events; the Untergunther's residency was just a difference of scale, of persistence.

First they had to figure out what was wrong with the clock. The UGWK became a makeshift library, stocked with books on vintage timepieces and easy chairs that transformed into inconspicuous wooden crates. Gradually the team concluded that one of the clock's integral components, the escapement wheel, had been sabotaged—likely by an employee decades ago. The mechanism had eventually been replaced with an electric mechanism, but this, too, had been sabotaged. Finally, they learned that fully restoring the Wagner clock would not just mean fiddling around behind its face—the antique mechanism had machinery located in several different parts of the building.

The "flying-saucer-shaped" atelier of the Untergunther became a not-quite-state-of-the-art clockmaker's workshop. The Untergunther carried up thousands of euros in tools, materials, and chemicals. They installed thick red curtains along its chilly outer wall, because, Viot said, "a clockmaker can't do anything with mittens on." They posed for photos among the Panthéon's statues; they watched fireworks from the roof; they made a new escapement wheel and cleaned the clock machinery piece by piece.

Usually, Kunstmann writes, sites restored by the Untergunther remain "just as inaccessible and unknown as they were before their repair." The Untergunther do not need to trumpet their accomplishments: they seek only the immediate satisfaction of renewing part of their city. Often, the sites' invisibility even shields them from further damage. Alas for the Panthéon's clock, this obscurity was not to be.

STOPPING TIME

UX DOESN'T have a blog. Members share a single email account. Lazar Kunstmann is not on Facebook, and the group's other members do not speak to the press. In this era of full disclosure, of never-ending networking, forwarding, and sharing, it is an organization that refuses friend requests. Members have only as many contacts as they require and they will not invite you to events.

The group's secrecy makes it hard to check their facts. Almost everything one *can* check out *does* check out. For the rest, you have to believe or disbelieve their claims. Kunstmann says the group has between one hundred and one hundred and fifty members ranging from age eleven to fifty-six. They are mostly professionals in their late thirties and early forties. UX's groups formed "by accident" in the early 1990s, gradually formalizing and adopting names. They are the product of "aggregation," the regrouping of kindred spirits within "the same, very reduced, geographic area."

Of the dozen teams that Kunstmann says exist, only three have been revealed—LMDP, the Untergunther, and a group called the Mouse House, recent inductees, allegedly an all-female "infiltration unit." All members benefit "from access to a [Paris-wide, universal, integrated] map, all the possible keys, all the possible knowledge." By sharing resources, pooling expertise, everyone is able to "work less for the same results, or to work the same amount for a better result."

Viewed a certain way, UX offers the same thing as Wikipedia or Google Earth—information for the community to do with as they please. But whereas Wikipedia relies on the wisdom of the masses to perfect its frustratingly imperfect data, while flash-mobs rally as many participants as possible, UX remains private. They reject openness, spurn crowds. The group's discretion allows them to slip below the authorities' radar, to operate with impunity, but there is more to it than that: by closing the network, they accomplish better works. There is no need to screen a film before thousands, to trumpet mysteries from the rooftops, to bring dancers and musicians and chefs making crêpes. Ux quietly create wonders, carefully rescue treasures. Members are expected to be capable, informed, autonomous. "Everything is dedicated to avoiding wasted time," Kunstmann says. The doing, not the discussion, is what matters.

Because of this pragmatism, the Untergunther always knew they would have to reveal their venture to the Panthéon staff. "If you want a monumental clock to work, someone has to mount and maintain it," Kunstmann explains. Two, ten, or fifty years after the gears are set in motion, they must still be regularly tended. "The logic always being to minimize the amount of work for a given project; it's a conversation we had with the whole group. At a certain point, the administrator would need to be clued in."

Standing with my tour guide under the clock's black hands, I ask him whether the mechanism still works.

"No."

"Why not?"

"Management took a piece away."

"Why?"

I glimpse the tiniest sarcastic roll of the eyes. "Pfft. I don't know."

At the end of September 2006, the Untergunther claim they met with Bernard Jeannot, administrator of the Panthéon, and his assistant Pascal Monnet. (In the book, Monnet's name loses an *n*.) Jeannot was thrilled, delighted with the Untergunther's ingenuity, marvelling at their secret workshop and horological handiwork. Monnet was less enthused. Still, everything seemed set for the clock to be mounted, for it to resume functioning—except that it didn't. Weeks passed. The administration, UX allege, did not want to reveal their failure to maintain the clock, or the way it had been restored.

With real sorrow in his voice, Kunstmann confesses they "misjudged the internal tensions that ruled at the CNM [the organization responsible for Paris's monuments] and the administration of the Panthéon. How different interests would exploit this affair to pursue their own agendas." Shortly after the UGWK was revealed, Bernard Jeannot left—or was forced out of—his job. Monnet ascended to the top seat. "That was the defeat," Kunstmann says. "That was the fuck-up. That we underestimated these factors."

It was an oddly naive mistake. Most citizens of Paris—indeed, most citizens of the world—know to never underestimate the hopelessness of their bureaucrats. Blinded by their own panache, UX assumed their work would be embraced by the people they shamed. Instead, two months later, the clock still had not been mounted.

The Untergunther are usually content for their restorations to remain hidden, but they were curious about their Panthéon handiwork. Ux did not know whether their repair job had even been successful. They decided to test it on a day when the Panthéon was closed. The options were few—Christmas Eve, New Year's Day, May 1.

On December 24, the Untergunther once again slipped past security and into the building. They mounted the clock. It began to chime. The mechanism was found to lose less than one minute per day—Viot deemed it "acceptable."

But when Monnet returned from his holiday, he marched up the Panthéon's steps and gazed furiously at the tick-tick-ticking

timepiece. He called a clockmaker to unmake the clock. The man who came, reportedly from the Maison Lepaute, refused to sabotage the mechanism. Instead, he removed the escapement wheel — the same piece damaged those decades before, rebuilt by Viot. At 10:51, the Wagner mechanism stopped.

Kunstmann is still livid. "The notion of conservation, the value of the objects in Monnet's care, don't concern him. He thinks only of his career, to have a good retirement."

I write to Monnet, asking for his version of events. The Panthéon administrator responds in an unmistakable tone: "I absolutely refuse to discuss this file. It is part of an active case and the law prohibits me from commenting."

After the story of the clock repair broke, journalists swarmed — and Kunstmann once again came forward, revealing all. "Underground 'terrorists' with a mission to save city's neglected heritage," shrieked the *Times of London*'s headline. Monnet agreed with this characterization, pursuing the Untergunther in court. But there was one problem: they didn't seem to have committed a crime. Nothing was damaged during the Untergunther's stay at the Panthéon, and at the time there was no such thing as "trespassing" on public property. (This has since been rectified, with a bill passed in December 2008.) Authorities had to wait almost an entire year before finding a reason to bring UX in.

On August 14, 2007, Panthéon security claimed to find four members trying to force the building's locks. The case was heard on November 23, 2007, before the 17th Chambre du Tribunal de Grande Instance. The CNM sought a total of €51,394.76 for damage to public property. The accused: Sophie Langlade (surely Lanso, the Untergunther's leader), thirty-five, unemployed; Dorothée Hachette, thirty-nine, nurse; Christophe Melli, thirty-eight, artistic director; Eric Valleye, thirty-eight, filmmaker. Four members of Untergunther, revealed before the court.

"A real experiment never presumes its results," Kunstmann says. "If someone had asked us, 'What are the chances that one day you will appear in court to talk about the repair of the clock?'

We would have said, 'Zero percent? One percent?' The improbable is still within the realm of the possible."

The charges were ultimately dismissed. Kunstmann says UX took back the removed escapement wheel, stealing it from Monnet's office. LMDP claim to have used the Panthéon for another full year, staging photo exhibits and a festival of police films. And the clock? "[It] is simply waiting for its chance to run again," Kunstmann told *The Architects' Journal*.

The way that Untergunther tell it, this acquittal was inevitable. Ux's members are so clever, after all. They are so sophisticated. They are a world away from hoi polloi like Crato, caught in the catacombs and awaiting presidential amnesty. Ux are not Ravioli. And you would certainly never see Kunstmann in the same room as the Painted Lizard.

LA-ZAR KUNST-MANN

THE PAINTED Lizard, wrote American journalist Christopher Ketcham, is "one of the nastiest pranksters in the underworld." Cavannus, a former Parisian now living in Montreal, says something similar: "Dangerous. To avoid." Another catacomb rat goes further. "The guy's a megalomaniacal jerk and deserves no publicity of any kind," G—— wrote in an email, asking that I not use his name. "He is a lesser human being."

Ketcham recalls seeing a photograph of the Lézard (and a black friend) in Nazi SS uniforms, "singing old German war songs at full throttle, stomping through the tunnels, sieg heiling, the songs echoing down the halls for a half-mile." He's a Fascist, G—— tells me. "In the 1990s him and another guy going by the name of Ktu used to beat people up. They had the network shared, one 'gang' held the south, the other the north.... Idiots are in awe of him because he can break into anywhere [but] an asshole is always an asshole."

I obtain the Untergunther's court records less than a week after my visit to the catacombs. I Google the names — Sophie Langlade, Dorothée Hachette, Christophe Melli, Eric Valleye. Slim pickings, except for Valleye. He is named in Ketcham's

2002 article for *Salon*. Valleye, Ketcham writes, is the real name of the Lézard Peint.

"We dress up as Nazis, sure," the Lizard said, "but we have no politics, none whatsoever. This is all…theater. A game of transformations, masks."

I consider the Lizard, reformed, assisting the patient restorers of the Panthéon's clock. Perhaps he met them below ground. And then suddenly the darkness slips into focus. *Lazar*, after all, sounds an awful lot like *Lézard*. Kunstmann, the German word "art-man." Lazar Kunstmann — *Lézard art-man?*

After that, I'm running. I dig into the Untergunther website, UGWK.org. I discover the site's files reside on a different server, and I note the URL: http://web.mac.com/peint/UGWK.

I scour cataphile forums for photographs of the Lizard, search Flickr. Most photographers lack UX's discretion. I find the Lizard, head bowed, in a series of subterranean snaps. It is the same man with whom I clinked glasses at Le Pantalon.

When I go back to speak to BHV, his ankle has healed. I ask the question whose answer he neglected to volunteer last time. Yes, the cataphile admits, "Lazar and Lézard Peint are the same single person."

I do not know how to feel. Thrilled by my discovery? Proud of my detective skills? Or utterly deflated, imagining UX as an asshole's practical joke? It is as if I am back underground. This time I have no leader.

"Lazar always had a group of friends, but they didn't particularly have a name," BHV says. He suggests they adopted the name LMDP after the discovery of the cinema, Untergunther after the discovery of the clock, UX after the publication of his book. Whereas UX claim to have more than a hundred members, BHV and Cavannus guess that "Kunstmann's group" are no more than twenty. The Untergunther say they have completed a dozen different projects, LMDP to have hosted dozens of events, but there's scant evidence. Perhaps it is because these actions were secret. Or perhaps they didn't happen.

BHV points to another sign of obfuscation in Kunstmann's book. The volume is peppered with comic relief courtesy of Olrik and Peter, UX's goofy, incompetent jester duo. Olrik is real, well known underground. But Peter? "He is maybe Lazar," BHV supposes. "I looked into it. It might be him." *Peter*, I note, is the French word for *farting*.

At that noisy, crowded bar, as I set a pint of Leffe before him, Kunstmann had confessed that he sometimes "gives simple answers to questions that deserve complicated ones." Months later, I contemplate UX as a tall tale, an exaggeration, the invention of an arrogant catacomb trickster. And yet the truth still feels just out of reach, beyond the beam of my flashlight. It is as if I can hear the footfalls.

MISDIRECTION

ALMOST A month after our meeting, I confront Lazar Kunstmann (a.k.a. Lézard Peint, a.k.a. Eric Valleye) over email. Fifteen hours later, I receive a reply. Kunstmann says the Painted Lizard does not exist. He claims that this character's reputation is intentional, invented, part of a concentrated effort to muddle perceptions of UX. Stories of villainous cataphiles quickly take over the discourse, masking any other activities. I am reminded of a comment he made at the bar that night. "A secret launches any information," he said, leaning forward in his chair. "It's a very simple principle. 'I'm going to tell you something. It's a secret — above all don't tell it to anyone.' You will see two other people and say to them, 'I'm going to tell you something. It's a secret — above all don't tell it to anyone.' In four seconds, everybody knows." The greater the tale, the bigger the lizard, the faster word spreads.

Kunstmann admits that one "operation," between 1985 and 1987, "was mildly violent" — but never, he insists, "physically violent." "For a Ravioli," he writes, "anything outside of routine is psychologically violent." He does concede that one of Ktu's friends might have knocked some heads.

And then I receive a message from Lanso. This is unexpected. The head of the Untergunther does not relish the spotlight, hasn't written any books, never talks to journalists. She has not contacted me before. "I know that [catacomb adventures] are very entertaining to foreign readers," she writes, her verbiage precise. "It's the exoticism of 'subterranean Paris.' But it's not what defines [UX]. We are people who realize projects without asking permission. That's all."

From there, Lanso acknowledges that UX's cast of regulars, the nicknames most often cited, may now seem like mischievous cataphiles. But she says these are part of a "media group" led by Kunstmann—a team meant to dazzle and distract the press, mesmerizing us with catacomb talk.

"The small world of the catacombs, which is apparently your place of departure, easily amplifies the importance of Lazar's band of rascals," Lanso writes. "Lazar is a good spokesman...but all of the intox and [media] diversions that he has been able to do, he and his friends, both in the press and [among cataphiles], gets linked to *our* activities, which they have nothing to do with." Kunstmann is an important member, Lanso admits, but the Untergunther and most of the rest of UX "have nothing to do with 'cataphiles,' nor even the catacombs. Nothing to do with Ravioli forums nor the beliefs and myths of these places. Nothing to do with the dozens of confusing articles conceived by Lazar and his cohorts between 1985 and 2004. Nothing to do with the folklore of the Latin Quarter so dear to the previously-mentioned."

Kunstmann's tales, the activities he recounts, the cataphile culture he invokes—it is, Lanso suggests, a *fumis*. It is smoke. It is the smoke that fills our vision, fills newspaper pages, conceals the group's true projects and real work.

Look to the Untergunther website, available in French and English, a kind of souped-up press release, useful documents for journalists. Look to Zone Tour, maintained by Olrik and Kunstmann, ostensibly a website for Paris cataphiles but purely in English. Look to an article in *Zurban* magazine, two years before the "restoration wing" of UX announced themselves. There are the "Untergunther," doing nothing more than run-of-the-mill culture jamming, changing George V subway station signs to George W. Fog, smoke, misdirection.

As for what this "real work" is, Lanso will not say. These projects, she underlines, are secret. "Don't think that I say this against you, or against journalists in general. It's the same for everyone. To be able to do what we do, this is how it has to work."

I have reached a dead end. Lanso's secrets are tantalizing, but I can neither confirm nor deny them. Ux's deepest riddles cannot be Googled. The question I ask is, *Do I believe them?* And then I ask, *Do I want to believe them?* And then I know my answer.

EXITS

DESPITE THEIR unassailable secrecy, UX still have something to offer the rest of us trapped on the far side of the smokescreen. Kunstmann talked about this as we finished our beers that night. "Over time," he said, "I've noticed that the principal reason that UX completes its projects is that we dismiss past inhibitions."

The organization simply *tries* things. If one idea doesn't work, they move on to the next. And whereas doubt inhibits, precedents inspire new experiments. "If someone says tomorrow, 'Ah, I'd love to fly across the Atlantic,' no one would say, 'It's impossible! It will never work!'" Kunstmann said. "If it's already been created, it must be possible to re-create."

We cannot join UX. They will not tell us who they are, or what lies at the heart of the maze. But we can do as they did. We can make our own maps.

THE HERE AND NOW

CHARLES FORAN

MORDECAI RICHLER once confessed his impatience with biographies that opened upon fifty pages of ancestry. Anxious to be off on the experience of a life, the reader instead encounters the subject's grandfather from Poland. The place is Łódź and the year is 1908. Grandpa is a Hasidic rabbi renowned for his translations of the Zohar and mischievous retellings of the Golem and Maharal tales. Bearded and severe, the zeda has fathered eleven children with two women and practises homeopathy and, by the by, draws miniature horsemen. Then there is the grandmother, she of the dark eyes and fragrant poppyseed cake. Married at seventeen by arrangement, the bubbe stoically gives birth to baby after baby, seven of whom survive childhood. Hesil, Aaron, Mair, and Sureh belong to the first wife. From her own womb spring Binyamin, Chana, Israel, Broche, Rivkah, Leah, and Avrum. Life in Łódź may be joyful—the songs and dancing, the cherished company and values—but it is never easy. Not with the state anti-Semitism and, out in the countryside, the pogroms. Not with the poverty that is the lot of the itinerant rabbi. Grandpa steers his sons through studies of Maimonides and the code of Jewish law known as the *Shulchan Aruch*. Grandma reads aloud from the *Tseno-Ureno* to her daughters on the Sabbath. Certain prayers that she recites—"Do not forsake me in my old age," for instance—bring her unfailingly to tears.

Subsequent migrations from Galicia to the New World, Yiddish to English, are no less essential background. Consider those fifty pages a corridor of family photographs. Granted, the photos, many never in focus to start with, are now badly faded, trimmed in sepia as though burned by fire. The corridor itself is dim and dusty, being so rarely visited. But here is the Old Testament patriarch in round fur hat and sidelocks and there is the humble matriarch in babushka and apron, thick glass lenses refracting the camera flash. Individual shots of toddler boys attired in regrettable frills and gaggles of yet-unmarried daughters in patterned dresses, of the scholarly brother who took special heed of his father's teachings of Jewish law in proud rabbinical attire, and of the one who perhaps paid closer attention to *A Guide for the Perplexed* and so wound up a Yiddish theatre actor and playwright, in bow tie and jaunty fedora—all are evidence of a bequeathment, the very richness of that past.

Then there is the magisterial family portrait, taken on the occasion of the rabbi's seventieth birthday. Three generations, including the protagonist's own parents and older brother, gather under one Montreal roof. Resemblances among siblings are striking; one daughter is her mother's mirror image. And in a couple of the uncles, even in the zeda himself—the yet-thick head of hair and high flat brow, the significant nose and sensual lips, a quietly distinguished, and distinctly masculine, countenance—the viewer can't help glimpsing aspects of the face, in focus and free of sepia, likely to grace the biography's dust jacket. Finally, the proto-subject. Finally, the reason for all this fuss.

ONLY TWO more years, and another ten pages, until the blessed birth.

RICHLER'S COMPLAINT was essentially that of a reader. Major biographies, while never actually judged by their heft, disavow pith the way sumo wrestlers reject skinny. Size matters a great deal, and the aesthetic wisdom of being swift and nimble between the covers appears forever outweighed by the need to be gargantuan, regardless if the bulk is either pleasing or pure muscle. Reader patience with buffed, toned details about the subject's life, beginning, say, with the name of the midwife and the manufacturer of the bassinette, frequently runs short when such precision spills over, or spills back, into the jaunty Ford sidecar driven, erratically, by suffragette Aunt Rivkah during the Roaring Twenties or the rumours of Uncle Binyamin's forays, disastrous, into the Soviet Union during the early days of the revolution. Such details may, in fact, be quietly telling—in the brief sketch of Richler's maternal ancestors, the Rosenbergs, keen eyes may have registered the horseman and Golem as motifs from his novels—but at times they seem to be telling too damn much.

A biography of Mordecai Richler has an additional excuse for bypassing that ancestral corridor. Though not averse to relaying his background in print or interview, and even fond, for philosophical reasons, of the family story of how he was originally destined to be American (his father's father had a train ticket to Chicago; on board the ship crossing the Atlantic he swapped with another emigrant and so wound up settling in Montreal), he declined his share of the writer's rightful inheritance: his own very rich past, the zedas and bubbes and Rivkahs and Binyamins, story-made and ready for the dramatic rendering.

The absence of a Richler novel set on that immigrant ship, or in the lively Polish city where Jews thrived against the odds, is one degree of refusal. But the non-dramatizing of scrap dealer Shmarya Richler's hardscrabble early days in the streets of Montreal's Griffintown is quite another. The same holds true for Rabbi Rosenberg, pillar of the city's Hasidic community during the 1920s. For his battles to control the kosher meat-blessing business alone, the rabbi might have merited a short story, sardonic and wry, from his grandson. Shmarya Richler's yard may have been located near the canal, where the equally poor Irish lived, but his community could be found on Colonial and St. Dominique, Clark and St. Lawrence—a.k.a. "The Main." From his apartment on Esplanade facing Fletcher's Field, Yudel Rosenberg would have walked to most butchers whose products he sanctified.

Who laid powerful claim to these streets? "Our world was largely composed of the five streets that ran between Park Avenue and The Main," Richler wrote in an essay about his childhood. "Jeanne Mance, Esplanade, Waverly, St. Urbain, and Clark." St. Urbain, of course, became "the Street," Canadian literature's most ardently mapped and faithfully dramatized urban terrain. Landmarks include particular apartments and laneways, synagogues and schools, pool halls, soda fountains, and barbershops; among the cast of reoccurring characters are almost certainly versions of actual Richler/

Rosenbergs, along with neighbours, schoolmates, and local celebrities from the era. But all this busyness, sharply, obsessively, lovingly, rendered over the course of a half-century-long writing career, is bracketed at the near end by Richler's death on July 3, 2001, and at the far end by, or around, his birth in January 1931. The near bracket requires no comment. That distant punctuation, however, must be explained.

Take the tale of the grandfather's swapping train tickets with another Polish Jew. What likely appealed to the grandson about the story wasn't that he could just as easily have wound up an American, Chicago-born. Almost certainly it was the randomness of the event, a fleeting friendship and hasty decision that ended up redirecting two lives and, by inference, the hundreds of lives of those in their generational orbits. Life, Richler believed, was fundamentally absurd and arbitrary. Better evidence could scarcely be found than in a fable of how fates could be so affected by the mere trading of stubs of paper.

Even then, the anecdote about Shmarya Richler on the boat from Poland never migrated in dramatized form into any of his ten novels. Aside from *Solomon Gursky Was Here*, a work of distinct dimensions and intents, Richler did not arc back into the worlds on either shore of the Atlantic that preceded the historical bracket of his own birth. Leaving the rabbi's kosher meat conflict untransformed by fiction represented neither a show of disrespect for family lore, nor any Walt Whitman–like assertion of singing himself electric, nor of a modernity or literary movement starting fresh and unique with the midwife's slap of the writerly baby bottom. It was, rather, an ongoing dramatization of artistic purpose.

Over and over Mordecai Richler spoke of his ambition to be a witness to his age. His writing was about the search for values, for how "in this time a man can live with honour." As with all things, he was steadfast about what he did and why he did it, be it through fiction, memoir, journalism, or scriptwriting. Witnesses are authoritative only about what

their senses register. Values certainly change. Even the ground beneath the feet of notions of honour tend to shift. For such a writer the time frame has to be, can only be, his own actual lifespan — from 1931 onward, in "his" time and, once he settled the problem of place in his head, "his" Montreal streets, the ones he eventually made it his business to capture on the page.

THE FRAMING of Richler's creative canvas is a natural concern of this biography. For the moment, it is enough to mention the most obvious influences, and to remark that they belong — in chronological sequence, at least — to the first half of the twentieth century and, more precisely still, the 1930s and 1940s. *In Our Time*, Ernest Hemingway's slim 1924 volume of reportage and short fiction, served to announce almost through its title alone an imperative for those writers who wished to take what they did, and how they did it, as seriously as the era demanded. The call, broadly, was to directness of prose and intent, to capturing the here and now, flinching from neither political engagement nor personal alienation; to being more than just alive to the times; to being out in them, witnessing, reporting, then crafting art from realities as vast and apparently defeating as Stalinism or the civil war in Spain. As a sensibility, it was manly and tough-minded, a way to live as much as a way to write. That Hemingway the blowhard and Hemingway the industry later cast a shadow over or, worse, smothered in a blanket of kitsch, an artistic stance of such integrity is a shame. It was certainly irresistible in its day, and its influence over generations of aspiring writers is beyond dispute. Among the aspiring was a restless Montrealer in the late 1940s.

But before the books, by Hemingway or anyone else, there was the Second World War. Picture young Mordecai Richler in the family apartment on St. Urbain. He is eight years old when Churchill declares war on Nazi Germany and fourteen when the Japanese surrender. He and his friends have already re-enacted the Battle of Guadalcanal in the snowbanks, shouting "Die, you crazy Japs!" Putting aside such childish games a couple of years later, the adolescent tacks a map of the world to his bedroom wall. Using newspapers and CBC radio, he follows the march of Canadian troops up the boot of Italy. He cheers each Russian counterattack and bombing of a German city. After D-Day, he inks in the map to chart the Allied advance on Berlin during the winter of 1944–45. To "every German on the face of the earth" the ardent fourteen-year-old wishes no less than "an excruciating death."

All this in advance of the early eyewitness accounts of the mounds of corpses and still-warm crematoriums at Treblinka and Auschwitz. All this before the trials at Nuremberg. For Richler, as for so many others, the Holocaust opens a Grand Canyon in their sense of history, rendering it forever divided, the chasm unbridgeable. Not yet eighteen, not yet really writing, and only just beginning to be a serious reader—Camus, Sartre, and Celine, Waugh, Orwell, and Maugham await him in Europe—he is nonetheless already in the character that he would inhabit for, in effect, the second half of the twentieth century. He is simultaneously absorbing the Nazi attempt to annihilate European Jewry while completing his noisy renunciation of the orthodox Judaism that had birthed and reared him. He is a card-carrying member of the local Zionist youth movement, half-heartedly plotting with Habonim comrades to make *aliyah* to the new Eretz Israel, there to live stout and righteous lives committed to Zion, while likewise readying to apprentice himself as a novelist in that most goyish and, with any luck at all, decadent of finishing schools, Paris: where ex-pats got to wear berets in Montmartre and sip cognac in Pigalle and claim they sat at the next table over from Sartre and de Beauvoir at Les Deux Magots.

To use a favourite Richler word, he is exactly as "charged" with contradictions and complexities as the age that has likewise shaped him. In Paris, in Spain, and eventually in the London he called home for the better part of the next twenty years, his readings and encounters confirm the rightness of a literary engagement that is direct and temporal, with the leisure neither for niceties (what more glaring confirmation of the absurdity of existence than the Holocaust?) nor for glances too far forward or back. In Europe Mordecai Richler finds an urgent philosophy to match his own urgent impulses, as well as social and political times begging for such a rough, hands-on approach.

Born is a serious-minded young writer hard on the search for values, for how a man/author can live with honour in such existential times. It is that author who opens a 1965 essay titled "The Holocaust and After" with a line of bracing frankness and minimal tact: "The Germans are still an abomination to me." It is likewise that author who, explaining his decision to repatriate permanently to Canada a few years later, confesses that he is afraid that if he stays in London, further and further cut off from those Montreal streets, he might wind up writing historical novels or books set on other planets. A woeful fate, apparently.

By 1972, Richler is returning to a Canada in the thrall of a cultural self-awakening so striking in its intensity and earnestness it is akin to a teenager being raised in a house without mirrors who suddenly discovers his own image in a glass. All at once there are reflections everywhere. All at once everyone is busy self-regarding. Twenty years earlier the nation, or English Canada to be exact, had been muddling along with few quality literary depictions of its own outline to contemplate. The past wasn't a foreign country: it was mostly foreign books on local shelves or local books of colonized technique and voice. If a national literature is a road lit by the brilliant lights of individual achievements, and if writers are continually encouraged by those lights, in particular those that illuminate their own locality, then Mordecai Richler in 1950 was glancing back at a highway cast in shade or even darkness, the only flickers courtesy of the softly falling snow. While this wasn't entirely true, it might well have seemed so to a Jewish kid from The Main as anxious as the next neophyte to find a tradition he could appear to spring from. He was also possibly more needful.

NOW, A biography is under no obligation to respect its subject's convictions, let alone abide his aesthetics. With literary biographies, a certain disrespect may even be wise, given the intersection of forms. Sharing a medium can be tricky. It can also be compromising. Mordecai Richler's own stated views on the value of personal details in helping understand an author's work, views formed early and held fiercely, could also be taken as spurs to book-about-book independence, if not outright rebellion. What he told one interviewer in 1991—"The only interesting thing about a novelist is the work that goes out. The rest is gossip"—was merely the condensed version of a 1971 vivisection of the conventional biographical premise. "Anything you could say about me or feel about me is gossip," he asserted then. "Whether a writer is a marvellously charming, agreeable, generous man or whether he beats his wife and tortures his children is beside the point. That's private. The books are what matter one way or another, and the two should not be confused." At this stage in the encounter he had already driven a stake through the heart of the biographical vampire. "You know," Richler said, "sometimes it may be a mistake to meet the writer. I'm quite serious."

Well.

Meet Mordecai Richler.

Or maybe not.

IF THIS biography opens, as indeed it does, with a description of the Jewish neighbourhood in Montreal, and the goings-on in an apartment at 5300 Esplanade in the days after the birth of Lily and Moses Richler's second son on January 27, 1931, it won't be for fear of annoying the author from beyond the grave with fifty pages of Eastern European shtetl-lore and steerage encounters. Instead, it will be a modest assertion about how a portrait of a writer can succeed in providing a felt experience of a life that is otherwise impossibly subjective and interior; unknowable, more or less, like any life, regardless of the diaries in the archive or the family and friends with vivid memories or even of the published memoir by the subject's own mother, bursting with details and incident. Experiencing his life and times, in contrast, however fleetingly, isn't out of the question. A version of what it felt like to be a male Jewish Montrealer within those chronological brackets can be reconstructed. Thus, to better experience how Mordecai Richler experienced the world, it seems wise to accept his conditions of engagement, to start with his own start. To glimpse, even, what he saw as the boy called Muttle, Mutty, or sometimes Mordy. Not every writer believes his sensibility is formed in childhood and thus is forever informed by what he absorbed, soft as a sponge, during those years. But since Mordecai Richler did believe this, it seems wise to also try experiencing that boy, that childhood, and certainly that Montreal, as vividly as possible.

ipsum

ipse ipsa ipsum pronoun and adjective

[IS+PSE, of disputed origin] himself (herself, itself, oneself, etc.) as opposed to others; for his (her, etc.) own part; in person (as opposed to through intermediaries, letters, etc.); the actual himself (herself, etc.) as opposed to persons more remotely connected; the real state of affairs, the fact, reality; acting or considered alone by himself; himself and no other; this or that very; just, the very; the master 'himself'; *ipse tristis* the sad one.

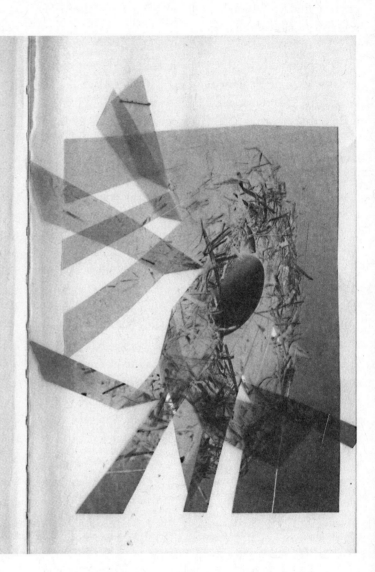

IN CONVERSATION
WITH ANNE CARSON

ELEANOR WACHTEL

I'VE ADMIRED *Canadian poet, essayist, Greek and Latin scholar, and librettist Anne Carson for a long time now. I think I first heard about her as a professor of classics at McGill University who was writing amazing stuff, starting with her quirky academic treatise,* Eros the Bittersweet, *where she mixes classical philosophy with witty, ironic brilliance.*

Next she produced two remarkable books of poetry combined with essays. She was hailed as an original by Harold Bloom, Susan Sontag, and Annie Dillard. She won both a Guggenheim and a Lannan Foundation Fellowship, and the MacArthur "genius" award. With her 2001 book, The Beauty of the Husband: A Fictional Essay in 29 Tangos, *she became the first woman to receive England's T. S. Eliot Prize for Poetry. It also took Canada's Griffin Prize. Along the way, she had a crossover success with another unusual book,* Autobiography of Red, *subtitled "A Novel in Verse." It blends a modern homosexual romance with Greek myth, set in small-town Ontario and Peru. See what I mean?*

Anne Carson's latest work is yet another surprising, and haunting, book called Nox, *or "Night." An elegy to her brother — "an epitaph," as she calls it, a notebook of memories and fragments of photographs, let-ters, and paintings — it's a moving reflection on absence. As she writes in her first entry: "I wanted to fill my elegy with light of all kinds. But death makes us stingy. There is nothing more to be expended on that, we think. He's dead. Love cannot alter it. Words cannot add to it. No matter how I try to evoke the starry lad he was, it remains a plain, odd history."*

I had the opportunity to speak to her in June 2011 at the Banff Centre, where she was part of their International Literary Translators residency.

EW   Much of your work invokes the ancient Classical period, references to Greek myths, translations from Greek or Latin, essays on ancient thought. What first drew you to that world?

AC   I think it was in a shopping mall in Hamilton, Ontario, in about 1965; I was trolling around the bookstore and for some reason they had a bilingual edition of *Sappho* by Willis Barnstone, the translator and editor, with the Greek on the left, the English on the right, and it just looked so fascinating I thought I should learn this. The next year we moved to Port Hope and I went to a high school where the Latin teacher knew Greek. When she found I was interested she offered to teach me on my lunch hour. So I owe my career and happiness to Alice Cowan in Port Hope High School.

EW   And what was it? Was it that the language looked so alien, or enticing?

AC   It was partly the look and just the aesthetic but also at that time I was fancying myself a reborn Oscar Wilde, and the whole world of intellectual life in Oscar Wilde's time, which included a lot of Latin and Greek, was sort of a myth to me and I thought, If I learn Greek I could be all the more like Oscar Wilde. It seemed the natural next step.

EW   A reborn Oscar Wilde.

AC   I had an Oscar Wilde costume that I wore now and again for special occasions. I thought he was the most interesting fellow.

EW   Did you drop bon mots and witticisms?

AC   As we will discover in the course of the interview, no, I'm not quick-witted but I appreciate wit.

EW   Once you started to study Latin and Greek, especially Greek, do you remember what the first myths you heard were?

AC   I think probably the ones that Sappho refers to, which are not in general the standard ones. Niobe, for example, who was turned into a rock because she wept so much; and most pointedly I remember from that book the myth of Tithonus. Tithonus was the young man who fell in love with the goddess of the dawn and they were having a pleasant affair, then one day he asked her to make him immortal. He wanted to be a god and live with her forever. So she went to Zeus and said, "Can you make Tithonus immortal?" And Zeus said, "Sure" and made him immortal but he didn't make him ageless. So poor Tithonus withered away into a little cricket of himself and that wasn't much fun for the goddess of the dawn any more.

EW   Pay attention to the fine print.

AC   The wording, yes. The wording is key.

EW   Tell me a bit more about studying Greek. I mean, obviously you stuck with it and it became your subject, but can you say more about what attracted you to it, about the culture, the language, the complexity?

AC   I think it's partly the content of the works. They're some of the most thoughtful pieces of literature anyone's ever come up with. But also the mental activity of being inside a translation is something I simply love. It's like doing an endless crossword puzzle but with a valuable product. And that *puzzle mode* of mind is simply the best thing.

EW   You've said that the ancients don't necessarily have much relevance to our world today, and I have to say that surprised me because we always seem to be able to extract relevance from everything in the past.

AC   I didn't mean it that way, I meant it upside down — that it's more our task to be relevant to them, to go back and see what they were really doing, doing from their side. John Cage says, "No one can have an idea once he really starts listening," and I think that's what's important about studying the past, to listen to the ancients rather than replacing them with your own ideas of how they are relevant to you.

EW   And is it partly that they saw the world so differently, or they're just so far away from us in time and language that we have to apprehend?

AC   They're at the root of things that then grew up and formed the trees where we now live — they're fresh, the ideas still have dew on them. And thousands of years later our ideas have some of that left in them but they're all kind of crusted over and centuries in between. The newness of the world keeps dawning on the Greeks.

EW   Do you know at what point you determined that this would be your life subject?

AC   Immediately when I studied it with Mrs. Cowan.

EW   Oh yes?

AC   Yes, it was unquestionable.

EW   A *coup de foudre*.

AC   Yes. And she was a very unusual person. She smelled of celery all the time. And after that year she disappeared. Quit, I guess, and somebody told me she ended up in Africa. Some decades later when I did a reading somewhere—I think Montreal—and mentioned her because I read some Greek stuff, a woman came up to me afterwards and said, "Alice Cowan's my mother and she now lives on a farm in northern Ontario. She's kind of a hermit. She'd probably like to hear from you but she won't answer." So I wrote her a letter and indeed she didn't answer. So that's all I know about Alice Cowan.

EW   That was near the end of high school.

AC   That was grade thirteen.

EW   Your latest book, *Nox*, is a kind of grief project, an epitaph for your brother who died in 2000. You structure the work by translating word by word a poem by Catullus, a Roman poet who lived in the first century B.C.E. Each Latin word of the poem gets its own page, and then you set your own poetry, thoughts, images, all kinds of things, on the opposite page. Where did that idea come from?

AC   Probably from the structure of the bilingual translation, because I spend a lot of my life looking at books with left-hand-page Greek or Latin, and right-hand-page English, and you get used to it, you get used to thinking in the little channel in between the two languages where the perfect language exists.

EW   I can see that it would also appeal because it forces one to slow down when you have each word with its expanded lexicographical definition—

AC   Oh, well, I'm glad to hear that. I wondered when I did it if people would bother to read the left-hand page or just look at it and think, I don't want to plough through that, and go on to the next. So I hope it slows them down. The lexical entries are drawn from the lexicon but a bit fiddled with, and I did want people to gradually notice that and follow the clues of it; it's a bit of a puzzle.

EW   Because you manipulate the Oxford Latin lexicon entries a bit.

AC   Yes, I manipulate them to put in more *nox*.

EW   I read somewhere you quote Jacques Lacan, the French psychoanalyst and philosopher, who said we don't go to poetry for wisdom but for the dismantling of wisdom. How does poetry do that?

AC   I feel it's a kind of fervour of mine to get away from whatever body of information I rest on when I give opinions. And I think poetic activity is a method for doing that—you leap off the building when you think poetically; you don't amass your data and then move from point to point, you have to just know what you know in that moment. Something freeing about that.

EW   Maybe I'm being too literal-minded when I think of dismantling because when I think of taking the poem apart word by word—

AC   Yes, it is a mantle, the confidence that you can ever know what words mean because really we don't. They're just these signs that we pretend to nail down in dictionaries, tokens of usage, but frankly they're all wild integers. Disassembling it is a way of exposing that myth at the bottom of language.

EW   Is that the myth you're referring to?

AC   The myth that you can know it ever definitively. Use it, yes. Make sense, yes. But know it, I'm not sure.

EW   Now, this isn't your first attempt to translate Catullus's poem "101." When did you first try?

AC   I think probably in that same year with Mrs. Cowan. And it's probably Catullus's most well-known poem, so everybody tries it. It's deceptively simple on the surface, impossible to capture underneath. The ideal poem.

EW   And why is it so difficult to translate?

AC   Well, that's complicated. Partly because of the nature of Catullus's diction, which is a reinvention, in a way, of Latin poetic language, through an infusion of common talk. He wrote a lot of poetry in street language, much of it scatological or obscene, and he keeps the energy of street language even in his more formal works. But also he just has a way of, it feels to me, economizing a situation and telling you exactly the bones of it and no more, which is hard to capture in another language.

EW   Although I think both aspects would appeal to you, both the conjunction of idiomatic language and the more dignified or elegiac verse.

AC   It's true I do mix registers of discourse, maybe inadvertently. I believe Catullus did it as a program, sort of a renovation of his language because he was tired of the way people were doing poetry. I'm not sure I'm that committed. But there is this same energy.

EW   And is that difficulty of translation the very thing, or among the things, you admire about Catullus?

AC   I don't admire it as give-me-a-problem-I-can't-solve but as having something to flail away at daily.

EW   And this time, you felt you could finally translate? I know you've said you tried hundreds of times to translate this poem, but this time, in the case of *Nox*, you could, or you just resigned yourself to a certain way of translating?

AC   It was more a resignation. I think a translation always has a context and this one needed to fit into that book and it needed, therefore, to be somewhat plain. I didn't want to decorate anything.

EW   And tell me a bit about the poem, the context for it, like how Catullus came to…

AC   He wrote it in honour of his brother, whom we don't know much about except he died in the Troad, in Asia Minor. Catullus travelled from Italy to Asia Minor to bury him and stand at the grave. He wrote the elegy sometime around then.

EW   And the Troad, that's near Troy?

AC   Yes, there was a Roman settlement on the site of what they thought was the ancient city of Troy.

EW   A sense of mystery infuses *Nox*. I mean, there is the difficulty of elegizing a brother who had disappeared from your life long before his death. What did you know about his life around the time he left?

AC   I didn't know very much. We both went to university — different ones — more or less at the same time. I was immersed in my Greek and Latin, a world he had no interest in or patience with. And he diverged from me in taste and moral standards and everything else that makes you a person, so I didn't really know him any more. Then he began to deal drugs and that seemed stupid to me so we argued about it. And then he got arrested and decided to jump bail and leave the country.

EW   And that was 1978, which was the last time that you saw him.

AC   Right.

EW   In your book, there's a photo of your brother when he was around ten years old, and he's standing on the ground with some other boys above him in a tree house. What do you see when you look at that?

AC   It just breaks my heart, frankly, because he always wanted to hang out with boys too old for him; I guess because it, I don't know, enhanced his view of himself. They always picked on him and exploited him. So there he is at the bottom of the tree. They've taken up the ladder so he can't come up. And he looks just so stalwart about it. He looks like it's just another one of those setbacks, he's going to get through it and come out to a brighter day. He always was like that. He had a certain absolutely unfounded optimism that things would get better. They didn't.

EW   Because in the text you say that, years later when your brother began to deal drugs, you'd get a sinking feeling because of a sideways invisible look that he wore in that photo. Why is that look so troubling to you?

AC   I'm not sure. Photographs are stunning that way. They give you so much information that you can't paraphrase. But when I looked at that photograph after he died, it seemed to me his whole life is in that look. He'll never win and he'll never believe that the next throw of the dice isn't going to be a win.

EW   It's interesting you say optimism because in so many of the photos he's bashed up. He's wearing a sling or a bandage or something.

AC   Isn't that odd? I didn't notice that until I got the photographs out to make the book, I was struck by the fact that he always has a broken arm or a bandage on his leg. I don't remember all those injuries but there it is. Yet he was not deterred. He'd break his arm and go right on, join the hockey team.

EW   Partly, I think, hanging around with the older boys would do it. Did he have trouble making friends?

AC   No, he was very charming. He could make friends with anyone, so I don't know why they beat him up so much. There are these mysteries with one's siblings.

EW   Your brother was four years older than you, and when you were in your teens and both in high school, he liked you to do his homework, but also he called you "Professor" or "Pinhead." How would you describe your relationship?

AC   Rueful. I think he put up with me once I started doing his homework for him—he kept failing French and got put back in school a few times. I had an ambivalent attitude toward him, I guess. When we were younger he was my total hero and I followed him around everywhere, got told to go home. But later I didn't understand his decisions and couldn't reason with him, it all got to be kind of fractious. I think I still saw him as a kind of mythic person because of that strange optimism. And he had a sort of glow. He would come into a room and everybody would look at him. He was very handsome—tall and blond—and as I say he had this charmingness. I was never charming. Certainly not glowing.

EW   You mention twice in the book about this "pinhead" thing. Could you read this short passage?

AC   "His voice was like his voice with something else crusted on it, black, dense—it lighted up for a moment when he said pinhead (so, pinhead, d'you attain wisdom yet?), then went dark again. All the years and time that had passed over him came streaming into me, all that history. What is a voice?"

EW   And on the following page you write, "I love all the old questions." Does that refer back to this?

AC   What is a voice? Yes. I've been so long fascinated by all the information conveyed in a voice.

EW   And do you think that "pinhead–professor" was an affectionate play?

AC   I think it was, yes. He also gave me, I think when I turned sixteen—no, it was Christmas when I was sixteen—*Roget's Thesaurus* because he wanted me to be a writer and I wanted to be a writer. I still have this book. But it was in two volumes and he only gave me volume one. Never got around to volume two. It's a clue to certain things about my writing.

EW   You favour the first half of the alphabet?

AC   Yes, I'm much more versatile with that half, for some reason.

EW   *Nox* itself is presented as an artefact. It's a fold-out, accordion-style book with pieces of paper stapled or glued on, sometimes with text, or photos, or painted images, or fragments of a handwritten letter. It's very tactile. In fact, I kept touching it thinking there would be a staple there. But of course each page is a reproduction of all those things. Why this presentation, why did you physically want to build a book?

AC   Because I made the book myself at first. I bought an empty book and filled it with stuff, painted it, glued it, stapled it, and so on. It was a grand day when I discovered you could staple instead of gluing, that was really an advance in method. Anyway, Currie, my husband, said that the thing about this book is, because it's handmade, when you read it, you're pulled into these people and these thoughts and the thing that it is. If you want to reproduce it, it has to have that quality still. So he fooled around with ways of Xeroxing to make the pages look, as you say, three-dimensional. If you Xerox or scan something perfectly, it looks glossy like a cookbook but if you let a little light into the Xerox machine and make it a bad Xerox, you get all those edges and life, you get what Currie calls the "decay" put back in. So it was really important to me to have that in the experience of the reader.

EW   You even soaked some of the typescript in tea to make it look like parchment.

AC   I did.

EW   Why? You made the book in the year 2000. Why did you want it to look ancient?

AC   It was a fancy of mine to make the left-hand pages, the Catullus pages, look like an old dictionary because when I was learning these languages I always had very old, faded dictionaries with yellowed pages. The experience of reading Latin, to me, is an old dusty page you could hardly make out. So I thought, Well, I'll just stain them with tea and it'll look magical. And they did look magical for about twenty-four hours, and then the tea dried and it all turned white again.

EW   And the original process for you of making the book, what was that like? I mean, was it a way of working through grief? How did it engage you?

AC   It was not so much grief…I mean, yes, grief partly, but more the puzzle of understanding him. Because actually, just before he died, he had telephoned me for the first time since 1978. This was in the year 2000, we had a very strange, awkward conversation and I arranged to go to Copenhagen where he turned out to be living, to meet with him. But a week before I was to go I got a phone call from a woman who said, "You don't know me, but your brother has just died in my bathroom." And that was his wife in Copenhagen, whom he'd been married to for seventeen years.

EW   He didn't mention that on the phone.

AC   He did mention it but on the phone, his wife didn't iden-tify herself, she just said, "You don't know me." So I went to Copenhagen and met her and the dog and found out some things about his life but the more I found out the more I didn't understand about who he had been those twenty-two years he was gone. So I started the book as an effort of understanding, just trying to put strands of things I could say about him into one place and see what it added up to. As it went on, it became what I called an epitaph, a way of praising him.

EW   When he called, did you know what prompted that call? Was it a premonition of his own death?

AC   No idea, he never said. He was laconic. Just felt like getting in touch.

EW   After all those years.

AC   After all those years. You see it's puzzling.

EW   How did he die?

AC   Aneurysm. I think he'd lived a hard life, drugs and so on, his system gave out. He was only in his fifties.

EW   Some of the photos that you use are fragments, and many don't have people in them. One features a shadow of a person more than the humans in the distance. A chair, a shed, an empty swing, some stairs, a wall. There is a sense of absence. What do you see when you look at them?

AC   The puzzle of him. Breaking it down, two things. When I was young and idolized him he was always gone—he didn't want to spend time with me, he managed to vanish. Later on when I was puzzling over who he had been in his later years, I just couldn't get it. It was like Aeneas in the Underworld, you know, when he meets his dead mother and tries to embrace her. Three times he holds out his arms and tries to hold her, three times she vanishes from his grip. So I wanted to put the vanishing into the pictures, and if you cut out the people, there's a lot of vanishing there. And some of them were empty anyway, oddly—another thing you discover when you look at your old family photographs, a lot of them are pictures of nothing. Very evocative pictures of nothing.

EW   And did you tear some of them for the book?

AC   I did. I tore them, cut them.

EW   Was that hard, to tear?

AC   Surprisingly no. I'd go into work mode and rip on through it.

EW   The information about your brother the last time you saw him — when he ran away in 1978 travelling on a false passport, only one letter home in all those years — is repeated several times in a row, sometimes with slightly different punctuation or minute differences in the marks on the paper. On the fourth repetition, it becomes almost a fragment itself. Why that repetition?

AC   The repetition is only in the printed book. In the original, the letter is glued in as a folded thing, so to make the fold visible in the printed book we had to repeat the information. It's a mechanical solution to the problem of not having the original book.

EW   I thought the repetition might have something to do with trying to understand the revealed in repetition. Sometimes we say what we know over and over in a way to make sense of it.

AC   Sometimes it helps to hear what you think by saying it more than once. That came to me as we were doing it. Incidental benefit of my imperfect method. But I can't say I thought of it before.

EW   And you say that you didn't understand your brother's decisions in those days of self-exile. Did you try to imagine what his life was like?

AC   I got anecdotes from his widow and other people in Copenhagen who were his friends. But it was like reading bits of a synopsis of a movie that you never see; it just didn't add up. Somebody would say, "Oh yeah, I knew your brother in his gold-smuggling days." Well that was news to me! So things like that. Little chips of data. They didn't make any pattern.

EW   About halfway through the book there's a line that says, "Always comforting to assume there is a secret behind what torments you."

AC   A secret — meaning something that would make sense — the answer rather than just all these bits. I mean, most of us, to be honest, are just a collection of bits that don't make sense. It's a nice idea that there's a coherent self in each of us with a story that another person could tell, but it's a fiction. And with somebody like my brother, you really come up against that fiction. Because he did not want to be known.

EW   I think that must be the difference because even though all of us might be these fragments that are a fiction, we try to present — we give narratives that make it seem to have coherence.

AC   We do. At some point he gave up on that, I think.

EW   Your mother described your brother as the light of her life, and he wrote occasional postcards and one letter to her. She didn't see him for the last twenty years of her life. Can you talk about their relationship, how his absence affected her?

AC   It ruined her life. She died not knowing if he was still alive. And she was simply sad for all those years. On the other hand she never gave up hoping he'd reappear. I did. But she never quite abandoned that notion and it made her life be sort of the wrong life, you know. The right life would have been the one where he came in the door. He was her golden child. She had a little lock of his hair from when he was a baby. I don't know how to measure that sort of sorrow. And when he called me that time I mentioned this. He just said, "Yes, I guess that's true."

EW   She had already died by then.

AC   She had died three years before. And I said, "She had a lot of pain because of you." And he said, "Yes, I guess that's true." So, cut off from himself at some level.

EW   And you describe how eventually you and your mother stopped talking about your brother, which you say was a relief. Why, what had it been like when you did talk about him?

AC   I think I said in the book it was like a smell of burning hair dropping through every conversation. There was nowhere for it to go. It blackened the day, and I didn't think it was a problem with any solution.

EW   Although you still describe, every time a car would pull up, she'd look up out the window—

AC   Gravel on the road. She thought it might be him. Sad.

EW   At one point you ask, "Why do we blush before death?" I found that a surprising word. Have you found an answer to that?

AC   No. It surprised me too. I found that in another poem of Catullus. I don't remember the exact passage, but he's talking about death, it's an elegy for a friend, and he uses the blush, it's a puzzling passage. It often happens to me trying to translate something in Latin or Greek that I come to a piece that doesn't make sense, but it still seems true, it seems like a nub of something I should get to, so I just secrete it into writing and hope it'll work its truth by itself without me knowing how to control it. I'm still thinking about the blush.

EW   And there's an interesting image nearby, it's not on the same page, I don't think, but there's some quite lurid red that's…

AC   Well, I thought *blush*, good! I'll use my red paint. Nothing subtle about me. You know I loved making that book, despite the context. I gave myself the task of trying to do something different on each page than I had done on any page previous, mechanically, physically, it was just a joy.

EW   Without being too literal, was that enabling you to turn the page in a way?

AC   In a way, yes.

EW   You quote the seventh-century B.C.E. historian Herodotus, who said that history is by far the strangest things humans do, all this asking and searching, because it doesn't give a clear or helpful account. Do you agree with that?

AC   They call Herodotus the first historian when what he invented was a picture of history as all these chips of data that don't make sense. He collects them and hands them over.

EW   And this reflected on what you felt you were doing.

AC   Yes, that sort of assembling without any final control of the sense.

EW   But Herodotus also suggests that he as a historian didn't have to believe everything everyone reported. He says, "So much for what is said by the Egyptians. Let anyone who finds such things credible make use of them." Or "I have to say what is said, I don't have to believe it myself."

AC   He has a good sense of humour, Herodotus. But I think he's not kidding. He does hand over opinions, as well as facts, and he doesn't try to distinguish too much among opinions as to the good ones and the bad ones. Trusts the reader to do that. An admirable tolerance.

EW   And did this reflect on your own search in some way?

AC   I think in that book, or in everything I write, there is an attempt at tolerance, to put down as much as I can figure out and let the reader make what sense they make.

EW   And sometimes the sense is, as you alluded to earlier, in the crack between the pages, because on the very next page of "I have to say what is said, I don't have to believe it myself" is, in your brother's handwriting, "love you, love you, Michael," a fragment from a letter.

AC   Isn't that haunting, when people write things twice. Why would he write it twice? I don't know.

EW   You also say history and elegy are kin. How are they connected?

AC   They're both a way of telling a story, giving the shape of a person or an event by—as Herodotus says—this searching, asking, without arriving. It's the non-arrival that makes them akin, the struggle and then the non-arriving.

EW   Did anything change for you after finishing *Nox*, either in how you saw your brother or the whole idea of elegy and investigation?

AC   I don't think anything changed in my view of him. It was more storied but not more complete. Elegy, I don't know. It's a difficult form, I would say. It's hard to keep the dignity of the subject without getting your own fingerprints all over it.

EW   That's an interesting way to put it because it seems to me a very apt description of elegy, that whoever — and maybe I'm conflating it with eulogizing — but whoever is doing the eulogy has their fingerprints all over it. It seems like it's about them, it's not even about the deceased.

AC   It's very hard to get the right place to stand, to elegize or eulogize somebody. But I thought by making these pages instead of just writing them, it helped me do that, because making is somehow…I don't know…seems less egotistical, I don't know why.

EW   At one point you say, "A brother never ends. I prowl him."

AC   I had this sense of him as a room where I was groping around, finding in the dark, here a chair, there a book, there a switch, and not getting a sense of the floor plan ever but just being in that room every day, working with it. And the poem was like that too, disassembling the poem, also a dark process.

EW   Do you see Catullus's poem differently now? I mean, of course, as an elegy for a brother, your own brother's death would lend a certain resonance.

AC   Yes, it has a resonance. But I always thought it one of the best things in the world and I still do. There it lies, untranslatable.

EW   Well, there's not that much that's explicit in *Nox*. It's still a very personal, intimate work. What made you decide to make it public?

AC   The fact that it got lost. For a number of years, seven or eight years, I used to show the book to people one by one and then I met by chance a German publisher who does art books and fashion books who said, "I think I can do that in a respectful way, why don't we try?" So I said okay and he took it to Germany then lost it for three years. He didn't answer emails and he had no phone so there was a certain interval of anguish about this object I thought I'd never see again. Then one day it showed up in a FedEx package. So I thought, Time to make this permanent. Then Currie figured out how to make it work as a replicated book.

EW   We alluded to it earlier, but it's interesting, on the left-hand pages with the definitions of the Latin word, you almost always add idiomatic expressions with the word *nox*, meaning night. But when it comes to defining *frater*, brother, the subject of the book, there's no idiomatic expression with *nox*. That was deliberate, obviously.

AC   I couldn't add to that one. It didn't seem respectable, or fair. And a way of putting the boundaries around him that he wanted put there. He wasn't noble, didn't want to be noble, and *frater* is an impersonal word for that.

EW   Your book *Autobiography of Red* is your first novel in verse. It also takes a story from the ancients as its starting point, the myth of Herakles and the monster Geryon. Can you tell me a bit about that story?

AC   Herakles is that person you probably know from Saturday-morning cartoons who did the famous labours. Hercules they call him in American. One of his labours was to travel to the island of a supposed monster named Geryon and capture his magic red cattle. So he did that, killed Geryon, took the cattle. I just changed that story a bit.

EW   A bit.

AC   A moderate bit.

EW   Well, the mythical Geryon has wings, and so does your incarnation. They're another marker of his difference. What did attract you to this story?

AC   His monstrosity. We all feel we're monsters most of the time. But also there is a very tantalizing set of fragments about this myth from the Greek poet Stesichorus, who isn't very much read or known. He doesn't write attractive love poetry like Sappho but these fragments are quite beautiful. I got involved in translating them for my own pleasure, then got frustrated because I couldn't work into the translations most of what I thought was interesting in the original language. For some reason.

EW   What do you mean?

AC   The differences between Greek and English set up some barriers to what you can say and how you say it. Plus the myth being somewhat unknown to most readers meant that the context was missing. I couldn't talk about Geryon and have the audience say, "Oh yes, the red guy with wings." So a lot of explanatory blah-blah-blah would have been necessary to make the fragments intelligible as such and I didn't want to do that, so I thought maybe I could do it in another form. What's another form? I've never written a novel, let's try that.

EW   Did you actually first try it as a straight prose novel?

AC   Yes, I tried it a lot of ways. Prose, various kinds of prose and then one day messing around with the lines I worked out those couplets that are long and short alternations, which seemed to work so I went ahead with it. And then it proved to be quite nice to do. Before that was a bit hellish, whole paragraphs of prose. I really wanted to write a novel, you know, an Arthur Hailey novel that people would read in airports.

EW   Arthur Hailey novel?

AC   I mean something huge and substantial with lots of manly activity, and of course I couldn't do it. But anyhow, the verse form eventually extracted itself from my efforts and that was obviously right.

EW   In *Autobiography of Red*, Geryon and Herakles are modern-day lovers. What did you see in the ancient myth that inspired this interpretation?

AC   Absolutely nothing. In the ancient myth Herakles goes there, confronts Geryon and kills him and the story is over. But in other ancient sources, for example the *Iliad*, there's a certain amount of reference to homoerotic tenderness and it's interesting to me how that works in a story and I wanted to give Geryon a fun part to his life.

EW   There's a great line: "They were two superior eels at the bottom of the tank and they recognized each other like italics." What is the nature of the attraction that you imagined between them?

AC   Probably mutual strangeness. I think that's why I used italics. Everyone else is roman font then these two people show up slanted and they see that. Automatic lightning.

EW   You give another view of love in your book *The Beauty of the Husband*. It's described as a fictional essay in twenty-nine tangos. At one point the wife in the story describes their interaction as characteristic or ideal. In what way ideal?

AC   Based on beauty. Beauty being a romantic ideal that works itself out in various ways. You desire the one you've invented rather than the one who exists.

EW   Because the one who exists knows more about the Battle of Borodino than he does about his wife's body. It's such a great line!

AC   And his beauty partly consists in that.

EW   This is a complex relationship that's described here. The husband lies and cheats, but he's not ashamed of this. He says he loves her, he even says he wants to be worthy of her. What kind of love is this for him?

AC   It may be ideal from his point of view in the sense that he idealizes himself as the agent of perfect or beautiful actions, but I'm not sure that either the wife or the novel knows what his view of it is.

EW   Or what he's looking for.

AC   Or what he's looking for, no. There are a few places in there where the narrative structure tries to put things from a husband's point of view but it becomes external; it's mostly what he says and what he does, not what he thinks.

EW   And for some years the wife continues to sustain the relationship. What kind of love is it for her?

AC   I think desperate. I think the kind of love — as with Herakles and Geryon — based on that original moment of recognizing the other person in italics, without whom you can't be your own italic self, so you have to keep that going as long as possible.

EW   Although it's giving power to the other over oneself.

AC   That's the paradox of it, isn't it? But I think, again, because there's a desperation in it, there's nothing else to do.

EW   It's refreshing to hear the wife admit that she wasn't ashamed to say she loved her husband for his beauty. For some reason we very often are reluctant to admit beauty's power over us.

AC   Isn't that odd? And it's so much a part of all of Western culture, that beauty's what makes love happen. Even if the person isn't beautiful you convince yourself they are.

EW   And you quote a passage from Keats before each tango or section, and it was Keats of course who wrote famously, "Beauty is truth, truth beauty." How does beauty speak of truth?

AC   I don't think it does. I think that's all a big mistake, but there's so much power in believing it, and so many of the decisions of life, especially early life — with the adolescent emotions — identify those two, and think that the person who's beautiful is also true and the feelings that come from beauty lead you to truth. I don't believe it works out usually.

EW   Certainly not in the beauty of this husband.

AC   No.

EW   I don't want to presume autobiography here, but did you bring some of your experience to *The Beauty of the Husband*?

AC   Some of it. But it's very manipulated and beautified, not to put too fine a point on it.

EW   Did your first husband take your notebooks? Did he return your notebooks? That's what I want to know.

AC   He did. And eventually he did.

EW   The poet, or the wife, sometimes tells her story to a listener whom she addresses as *You*. Is that a particular *You*? Who was the *You*?

AC   Not a particular *You*. It's the generalized *You* of lyric poetry. Catullus invented this, I think, for the Romans, and the *You* is sometimes unnamed, a persona who forms as the poem forms, a sort of ideal listener.

EW   And that started with Catullus? Because you're right, it's certainly a convention in lyric poetry.

AC   He used it extensively. Probably took it from Sappho.

EW   Near the end of *The Beauty of the Husband*, the wife contrasts her earlier view of beauty, her pure early thought, with a later experience of it. Before she wanted to recognize it without desiring it. Now her advice is "Hold, hold beauty." What has changed for her?

AC   I guess her sense of where she stands in the whole question. She can hold it if she doesn't need it.

EW   Which has to do with not wanting to desire.

AC   Yes, it has to do with getting the desperation out of it.

EW   Although at one point the wife wonders what not wanting to desire means, and one could associate that with a kind of freedom, but on the other hand it feels like giving up.

AC   A kind of deadness.

EW   Utter resignation or something.

AC   Or turning entirely inward. I think that's not where she wants to end up. But I believe it's left open whether she does end up there or not.

AN ODE TO CURLING

R. CHANDRAN MADHU AND COLUM MCCANN

I WAS TEACHING an Ovid course at The New School in New York City last spring. To try to give the students a feel for how difficult it is to write in dactylic hexameter, I assigned each of them the task of composing two lines that scanned perfectly. A line in dactylic hexameter has six dactyls (LONG-short-short, like "murmuring"). The trick is that any of the six dactyls might be replaced by a spondee (LONG-long, like "hemlock"). For instance, the first line of the *Aeneid* is D-D-S-S-D-S: *Arma viRUMque caNO troIAE qui PRImus ab Oris*. The subject was imposed on them — there is something about Ovid's subject matter that's forced and artificial, in contrast with the ease and naturalness of his language and versification. At the time, I was consumed by the Olympic curling competition, particularly by Kevin Martin, who has the athletic charisma and intensity of Michael Jordan in the body of Wallace Shawn. He deserved epic. It was a good bet that none of the students would be interested in curling, so for me it seemed the perfect training ground for future poet laureates. But when the students turned in their work, only one of the eighteen lines scanned. They kept at it until a respectable (for the U.S.) accuracy rate of sixty percent, or ten lines, was achieved. I tried to pull them together, but the thematically discontinuous couplets would not mix. (I'd say this argues for the Homeric unitarians — you can't really do this stuff by committee.)

The original goal was an epic opener: that seven-line majestic statement of purpose you find in the *Iliad* and *Aeneid* (the *Odyssey* uses ten, Dante three, and Milton can't seem to get the job done in twenty-six), that grand opening chord from which the next ten thousand lines flow naturally and inevitably. So I shredded their lines and stitched together seven that I felt had some epic potential. Then Colum came along to put an English or rather Irish accent on the translation.

— *R. Chandran Madhu*

THIS STORY, like all stories, is so many stories. Recently I was asked by sportswriter George Kimball to write an essay for the Library of America about boxing. Truth is, I know little or nothing about boxing, but I've always had a fascination with the literature of the sport. I like the idea that boxers get told to imagine punching a spot behind their opponent's head, to reach in so far that they can extend the destruction to the back of your mind. It's the same thing with writers. We want to disturb your imaginative ecstasy with the deepest punch, though the truth is we generally hit air.

During the course of the boxing essay, I wrote a throwaway line, saying that I hadn't yet read a good poem about curling — and didn't really anticipate finding one. (All Joyce scholars will recognize what "throwaway" means in this context and how inevitably it leads to the Homeric horse race of poetry.) In any case I met my friend, Chandran Madhu, on New Year's Eve. He had read my boxing essay and told me that he had a poem about curling. I thought he was kidding me at first, but

Curling –
Toronto. 16.1.43
"Soop it up – Soop it up!
Jist break an egg on that
stane – oh play gently &
lay it on the pat lid "!

he unfolded a Latin poem from his pocket. He read it to me and I was rocked back on my toes. I loved the sound and the fury of it. However, the English translation was a little tame: it didn't have the rhythmic swerve and daring of the original.

Like boxing, I don't know a thing about Latin either, but I wanted to try to "re-music" the translation, so we sat together over a few bottles and worked and reworked the lines until 2010 ticked over into 2011. What we wanted to do was to marry the meaning with the "inscape" of the poem. Really, it's Chandran's work with a little help from his students, and I'm an accidental interloper. I've always wanted to be a poet of some sort, though the idea that I would be working from the Latin dactylic hexameter is bizarre. Life continues to deal its surprises. It's the most fun I've had writing in quite a while.

— *Colum McCann*

THE GOLDEN AGE OF CURLING
DAWNS BRIGHT

A paean for
Kevin Martin
on the occasion of the victory of the
Canadian Men's curling team, Calgary 2010.

By M. Alexander, K. Grant, B. Horton, D. Lenard,
    E. Light, R. C. Madhu, C. McCann, J. Melo,
    H. Northington, I. Omar, and E. Sherman

Saxa virumque cano, strepitumque gravem glacierum.
Saxa virumque cano, strepitumque gravem glacierum.
Stones and the man I sing, the deep roar of ice.

Ecce, senex (sic terra in acerni alcisque vocatur)
Ecce, senex (sic terr- in acern- alcisque vocatur)
Behold him — called in land of maple, moose —

ursus, cui manus atque animusque oculusque cohaeret,
ursus, cui manus atqu- animusqu- oculusque cohaeret,
Bear, for whom hand, heart, and eye, are one,

et sua prodiga verrendo turma, optima et audax,
et sua prodiga verrendo turm-, optim- et audax,
with crew peerless, vigorous, sweeping, brave,

immodicis insignes bracis mox superabit.
immodicis insignes bracis mox superabit.
vanquishes the fancy-trousered slave.

Aurea crispandi aetas lucescet manifesta
Aurea crispand- aetas lucescet manifesta
The golden age of curling dawns bright

cum petrarchus malleum acerbum iecerit auro.
cum petrarchus malle- acerbum iecerit auro.
as stone-skipped anvils hammer unto light.

AFTERWORD

I FIRST HEARD of it at a Toronto party for another magazine in an east-end condo. The music was terrible. "*Brick*?" I shouted. "I don't think I know it!"

The soft-spoken assistant editor replied oh-so-casually: "That's because we're the best magazine you've never heard of." I strained to catch his words; I almost missed them.

When I finally traced *Brick* to its lair, hidden away in the top corner of an old red-brick manse in Toronto, it looked just as I'd imagined it would, down to the crowded bookshelves and waning houseplants. The magazine itself brimmed with character: there were candid conversations between writers; lush, startling images; and tributes to writers who'd gone before, who'd changed the way successive generations thought and wrote. It was a privilege to join its ranks, but the first reaction I recall was *relief*. It was just as I hoped it would be.

In my years at *Brick*, we struggled to find ways to talk about the magazine: a literary dinner party, perhaps, with all your favourite authors around the table? How, then, to extend the invitation? Most of our readers seemed to find us when a friend, companion, loved one, or complete stranger passed them a copy, and they latched on tight. They wrote us kind, witty letters and regularly sent cheques, like distant relatives. They appeared loyal, chatty, eager, and funny — and they were too few in number to sustain us.

A venture like *Brick* relies on a lot of help, financial and otherwise, and side projects like this anthology offer us a new opportunity to introduce the magazine around, as well as celebrate "the writing life and the arts in general." I left the magazine in 2010 for Scotland, and though I'd been working on *The New Brick Reader* for some months, it was far from finished. I would never have been able to take it any further without the guidance and support of everyone at *Brick*, particularly Nadia, Linda and Michael, Michael and Michael, and Liz, Laurie, Allison, and Mark. I am also grateful to House of Anansi Press for agreeing to publish it, and of course to all the contributors who so generously let us reproduce their work. It has been a labour of love for so many, for so long (the list of people I'm in debt to stretches even longer). It's no wonder a contributor once suggested we subtitle the magazine, *A Love Journal*.

This anthology is a sampling of the very best of *Brick*, and the magazine itself has, over forty-five years, proved to be tougher, smarter, and more gorgeous than anything I can compare it to in the Canadian literary landscape — the most charming and raucous dinner party of them all. So, how best to extend the invitation? Surely not online, for as Jim Harrison once wrote to us, "I am so proud I have never seen a website — the home doubtless of poisonous spiders." Perhaps not by post, as one invitee kindly returned our last direct mail brochure shredded into tiny pieces and stuffed into our own postage-paid envelope. Once we spoke of travelling cross-country with a van full of *Brick*s, physically putting them in people's hands. But, the *environment*...

Maybe best of all is to whisper its name at parties like all secrets worth knowing. The real readers will find it anyway, and the others would be too busy to bother looking. Ascend that staircase in the old brick house and watch the light filter through the stained glass window. Water the plants and buy half a dozen back issues; we'll cut you a great deal. It smells like furniture wax up there, mixed with coffee brewing and the sweat of more than a few literary titans. *Another Brick being born.*

—*Tara Quinn*

CONTRIBUTORS

PAULE ANGLIM is the owner of Gallery Paule Anglim in San Francisco.

MARGARET ATWOOD is the author of more than fifty books of fiction, poetry, and critical essays. Her new novel is *MaddAddam*.

RUSSELL BANKS lives in Miami and upstate New York. His most recent novel is *Lost Memory of Skin*. A collection of stories, *A Permanent Member of the Family*, will be published in November 2013.

REZA BARAHENI (born in 1935 in Iran, now living in Canada) is an Iranian-Canadian poet, novelist, and literary critic who has written more than two dozen books of fiction, poetry, and literary criticism in Persian. Many of his major works have been translated into English, French, and other languages, and his poetry and fiction have been anthologized alongside some of the major poets and writers of the world. A founder of the Writers Association of Iran, Baraheni has also been a member of PEN International, a president of PEN Canada, and the winner of several human rights and literary awards.

JOHN BERGER is an art critic, novelist, painter, and poet. His novel *G.* won the Booker Prize in 1972, and his essay "Ways of Seeing" has become a set text on art criticism in universities around the world. He lives in France.

CLARK BLAISE, OC, lives in New York and San Francisco. His most recent book is *The Meagre Tarmac* (Biblioasis), linked stories of Indian-immigrant life in the U.S. and Canada.

ALASTAIR BLAND is a freelance writer based in San Francisco. He writes about science, the environment, food, and travel, and his work has appeared in such publication as *Smithsonian*, *Slate*, and NPR.

ROBERTO BOLAÑO (1953–2003) was a celebrated Chilean writer whose Rimbaudian life in Mexico among a ragged tertulia of poet-misfits is mythologized in *The Savage Detectives*. Bolaño founded the infamous Infrarealism Movement. An English translation of his poems, *The Unknown University*, was published by New Directions this year.

ROO BORSON'S latest book is *Rain; Road; An Open Boat*, published in 2012 by McClelland & Stewart. She also writes, with Kim Maltman, under the pen name Baziju.

DIONNE BRAND is a poet, novelist, and essayist. She teaches in the School of English and Theatre Studies at the University of Guelph.

STÉPHAN BUREAU is a journalist with twenty-five years of experience in broadcasting and the creator and host of the documentary series *Contact*.

SEMI CHELLAS is a writer, screenwriter, and co-creator of the television series *The Eleventh Hour*. Most recently, she adapted Linda Spalding's *Who Named the Knife* into a television movie, *Murder on Her Mind*.

ROBERT CREELEY (1926–2005) was the author of more than sixty books of poetry.

DON DELILLO is the author of fifteen novels including *White Noise*, *Libra*, and *Underworld*. His most recent book is *The Angel Esmeralda: Nine Stories* (2011). He has won the

National Book Award, the Pen/Faulkner Award for Fiction, the Jerusalem Prize for his complete body of his work, and the PEN/Saul Bellow Award.

LEON EDEL (1907–1997) was the Pulitzer Prize–winning biographer of Henry James, and the author of *Bloomsbury: A House of Lions*. He wrote about his time in Paris in the 1920s and 1930s in his last book, *The Visitable Past: A Wartime Memoir*.

JEFFREY EUGENIDES is the author of the novels *The Virgin Suicides*, *Middlesex* (which was awarded the Pulitzer Prize in 2003), and *The Marriage Plot*.

CHARLES FORAN is the author of ten books, including *Mordecai: The Life and Times*, and a regular contributor to *Brick*. He lives in Toronto.

ROBERT FYFE became a high school teacher and is now a principal at a Chinese international school in Beijing.

FORREST GANDER is a writer and translator with a degree in geology. His *Core Samples from the World* was a finalist for the Pulitzer Prize and National Book Critics Circle Award.

HELEN GARNER, born in Australia in 1942, writes fiction, essays, journalism, and long-form non-fiction. Her most recent book is a novel, *The Spare Room*.

GRAEME GIBSON is the acclaimed author *Five Legs*, *Perpetual Motion*, and *Gentleman Death*.

PETER HARCOURT, C.M., is the author of *Six European Directors* (Penguin, 1974) and *Movies & Mythologies* (CBC, 1977). He has written regularly for *Cinema Canada*, *The Canadian Forum*, *Descant*, *POV*, and for *cineAction!*.

JIM HARRISON'S most recent book is a collection of novellas, *The River Swimmer*, published by Grove Press.

ROBERT HASS is the author, recently, of *What Light Can Do*, a book of essays, and *The Apple Trees at Olema: Selected Poems*, both from Ecco Press. He teaches literature at the University of California at Berkeley.

ELIZABETH HAY'S eight books include short fiction, creative non-fiction, and novels. Among them, *Small Change*, *A Student of Weather*, *Garbo Laughs*, *Late Nights on Air*, and most recently *Alone in the Classroom*. A former radio broadcaster, she has lived in Ottawa for many years.

MICHAEL HELM is the author of *The Projectionist* (short-listed for the Giller Prize), *In the Place of Last Things*, and *Cities of Refuge* (both shortlisted for the Rogers Writers' Trust Fiction Prize). He is an editor of *Brick*.

FANNY HOWE has written numerous books of fiction and poetry and two collections of essays, *The Wedding Dress* and *The Winter Sun*.

CRAIG HOWES is the Director of the Center for Biographical Research at the University of Hawai'i at Mānoa. In 1996/97, he conducted a series of life history interviews with Leon Edel.

A. L. KENNEDY is a Scottish comedian and writer of novels, short stories, and non-fiction. Her second novel, *So I Am Glad*, won the Encore Award, and her novel *Day* won Costa Book of the Year in 2007.

JONATHAN LETHEM is the author of nine novels, including the forthcoming *Dissident Gardens*. He lives in Los Angeles and Maine.

TIM LILBURN'S most recent book is *Assiniboia*. He teaches at the University of Victoria.

R. CHANDRAN MADHU teaches Latin at The New School in New York City. He recently published a translation of Gomez Pereira's argument that animals lack sensation.

COLUM MCCANN'S latest novel is *TransAtlantic*.

ALISTAIR MACLEOD is from Cape Breton Island, Nova Scotia. He is the author of many books of short stories and the novel *No Great Mischief*, for which he won the International IMPAC Dublin Literary Award.

W. S. MERWIN was born in New York City and educated at Princeton University. *A Mask for Janus*, his first book, in 1952, was selected for the Yale Series of Younger Poets. His book *Migration: Selected Poems 1951–2001* won the National Book Award for poetry in 2005. He has twice won the Pulitzer Prize for Poetry, in 1971 for *The Carrier of Ladders*, and in 2009 for *The Shadow of Sirius*. In addition to his own collections of poetry, Merwin has published more than twenty books of translation and numerous plays and books of prose. In 2010, he was named Poet Laureate of the United States.

SEAN MICHAELS has written for publications including the *Walrus*, the *Guardian*, *McSweeney's*, and the music blog *Said the Gramophone*. The piece appearing in this anthology won a National Magazine Award in 2011. His first novel, *Us Conductors*, will be published by Knopf Canada/Tin House Books in 2014. He lives in Montreal.

ALBERT NUSSBAUM (1934–1996), a notorious bank robber in the 1960s, was once on the FBI's Ten Most Wanted list. Known as the "brains" of a bank robbery operation in upstate New York, he spent his time behind bars competing in high-level chess tournaments by correspondence and developing his skills as an expert photographer, mechanic, and draftsman.

MICHAEL ONDAATJE'S prose works include *Coming through Slaughter*, *In the Skin of a Lion*, *The English Patient*, *Running in the Family*, *Anil's Ghost*, *Divisadero*, and *The Cat's Table*. His poetry books include *The Collected Works of Billy the Kid*, *The Cinnamon Peeler*, *Secular Love*, and *Handwriting*. He was an editor at *Brick* from 1983–2013.

MICHELLE ORANGE is the author of *This Is Running for Your Life*. She lives in New York City.

DON PATERSON is a Scottish poet, writer, and musician. His most recent collection of poetry is *Rain*, which won the Forward Poetry Prize. He teaches at the University of St Andrews and is poetry editor of Picador.

ANNIE PROULX lives in back-country Wyoming where she is working on a novel about forests, from Quebec to Indonesia.

CLAYTON C. RUBY is one of Canada's leading lawyers specializing in criminal, constitutional, administrative, and civil rights law. He received his LL.B. from the University of Toronto and his LL.M. from the University of California (Berkeley) and currently practices law with the firm of Ruby Shiller Chan Hasan in Toronto. In 2006, Mr. Ruby was awarded membership in the Order of Canada. In 2012 the Lieutenant Governor of Ontario presented him with the Queen Elizabeth II Diamond Jubilee Medal.

JANE RULE (1931–2007) was born in New Jersey, but moved to British Columbia in 1956 and spent the last thirty years of her life on Galiano Island. Her first novel, *Desert of the Heart*, was published in 1964 to great acclaim and controversy, and the movie version (called *Desert Hearts*) quickly became a lesbian classic. She went on to publish many more works of fiction and non-fiction, including *Contract with the World*, *Memory Board*, and *Taking My Life*. She was awarded the Order of British Columbia and Order of Canada in 1998 and 2007 respectively.

SALMAN RUSHDIE is the author of seventeen books, including *Midnight's Children*, which won the Booker Prize in 1981. *The Moor's Last Sigh* won the Whitbread Prize in 1995 and the European Union's Aristeion Prize for Literature in 1996. In

2007, Salman Rushdie was awarded a Knighthood for services to literature. He is a Fellow of the Royal Society of Literature and a Commandeur de l'Ordre des Arts et des Lettres.

ESTA SPALDING is a poet and screenwriter. Her most recent book of poetry is *The Wife's Account*. Her most recent screenwriting work is as a writer/producer for FX's *The Bridge*. She lives in L.A. and is an editor of *Brick*.

SARMISHTA SUBRAMANIAN is a managing editor of *Maclean's* magazine. She lives in Toronto.

COLM TÓIBÍN'S novels include *The Master*, *Brookyn*, and *The Testament of Mary*. His two volumes of short stories are *Mothers and Sons* and *The Empty Family*. He is Mellon Professor of English and Comparative Literature at Columbia University in New York.

GEORGE TOLES is Distinguished Professor of English and Film at the University of Manitoba. For twenty-five years, he has been a screenwriting collaborator of director Guy Maddin, most recently co-authoring the original screenplay for Maddin's feature film *Keyhole*. George is currently working on a monograph on the films of Paul Thomas Anderson.

ELEANOR WACHTEL is the host and co-founder of CBC Radio's *Writers & Company* and *Wachtel on the Arts*. Her latest books are *Original Minds* and *Random Illuminations: Conversations With Carol Shields*.

MELORA WOLFF has published work in *Best American Fantasy*, *The Normal School*, *Gettysburg Review*, and the *New York Times*. She is a Notable Essayist of 2011 in *Best American Essays*.

JAMES WOOD is a staff writer at *The New Yorker*. He is the author of a novel, *The Book Against God* (2003), and four books of criticism, most recently *The Fun Stuff and Other Essays* (2012). His work has appeared in *Best American Essays* and won the National Magazine Award for 2010.

C. D. WRIGHT'S most recent book is One With Others: a little book of her days. She is currently researching beech trees. She is on the faculty at Brown University and lives outside of Providence.

CREDITS

Image credits

Page xiv: Photograph of John Hawkes by Rob Kinmonth. Every effort has been made to obtain permission for this use.

Page 5: Image courtesy of Valance Archives.

Page 17: Drawing of Jorge Luis Borges and translation by Steven Heighton, reprinted with his kind permission.

Page 22: Image courtesy of the Art Gallery of Ontario. Reprinted here by kind permission of Paul Schaefer.

Page 26: Photograph by David Hlynsky.

Page 38: Garry and Melissa Winogrand by Lee Friedlander, courtesy of Fraenkel Gallery, San Francisco.

Pages 44–46, 76, & 107: Line drawings by Michael Winter.

Page 49: Still from *À bout de souffle* is courtesy of the TIFF Film Reference Library.

Page 60: Photograph of Jim Harrison by Jean-Luc Bertini.

Page 62: Illustration from http://upload.wikimedia.org/wikipedia/commons/5/53/1855_Colton_Map_or_Chart_of_the_World's_Mountains_and_Rivers_-_Geographicus_-_Mts-Rvrs2-colton-1855.jpg

Page 82–90: Drawings with this piece by Mark Byk.

Page 96: Image of Donald Westlake courtesy of Abigail and Paul Westlake.

Page 101: Courtesy of Valance Archives.

Pages 115 & 197: Image from the International Dada Archive at the University of Iowa.

Page 122: Photograph of Gabrielle Buffet-Picabia and Paule Anglim at the home of Mme Picabia in 1976, courtesy of Paule Anglim.

Page 125: Drawing by stef lenk.

Page 126: Drawing by Mark Byk

Page 131: Photograph of Francis Picabia.

Pages 141–143: Jack Spicer's questionnaire is from *My Vocabulary Did This to Me: The Collected Poetry of Jack Spicer,* edited by Peter Gizzi and Kevin Killian, and published by Wesleyan University Press in November 2008. Reprinted by kind permission of the publisher.

Page 148: "Fish Guitar" by Mark Byk.

Page 150: "Spin Art" by Rick/Simon.

Pages 156 & 161: Photographs by Baroness Pannonica de Koenigswarter and published by Abrams Images in *Three Wishes: An intimate look at Jazz Greats.* Reprinted here by kind permission of Shaun de Koenigswarter.

Pages 168 & 171: Boxer photographs reprinted with kind permission of Jennifer Kawaja. Copyright © Jennifer Kawaja, producer of Sienna Films.

Page 178: Image of Pier Paolo Pasolini provided by the TIFF Film Reference Library.

Page 183: Photograph by Col. Manuel Romero, ca. 1870. Reproduced from *Retratos de Mexicanos 1939–1986* (Fondo de Cultura Economica, 1991).

Pages 186–187: Courtesy of the estate of William Faulkner and Jill Faulkner Summers. Copyright © 2006 Jill Faulkner Summers. All rights reserved. Obtained through the Department of Archives & Special Collections at the University of Mississippi.

Page 199: Page of James Salter's manuscript, reprinted with his kind permission.

Page 200: Stills from the rushes of *Brand Upon the Brain!* reprinted with kind permission of Guy Maddin.

Pages 212–223: Photographs of Mavis Gallant, with her notes, reproduced with her kind permission.

Page 225: Portrait of Roberto Bolaño by David Bolduc, reprinted with kind permission of Blaise DeLong.

Page 228: Passport photos of Leon Edel courtesy of Craig Howes.

Page 244: Photograph of Deborah Digges by Stephen Digges, reprinted with kind permission of Charles Digges.

Pages 250 & 258: Photographs by Zoriah. © zoriah/www.zoriah.com.

Page 255: Photograph of the Panthéon clock by Sean Michaels.

Page 262: Picture of Mordecai Richler and his brother Avrum courtesy of Charles Foran.

Page 268: Pages from Anne Carson's *Nox* have been reprinted by permission of the author.

Page 281: Drawing of people curling on the Bay of Toronto, 1843, by Sir J. E. Alexander—collection of the Library and Archives Canada.

Pages 282–283: Photograph of Kevin Martin courtesy of the Canadian Curling Association.

Text Credits

The following reprinted works are used by permission of the authors, except where other permissions are noted. All rights are held by the authors.

"The Lover of the Hummingbird: Remembering John Hawkes," by Jeffrey Eugenides, appeared in *Brick* 65/66, Fall 2000.

"The Writer's Life," by Elizabeth Hay, appeared in *Brick* 63, Fall 1999.

"An Interview with W. G. Sebald," by James Wood, first appeared in Brick 59, Spring 1998, and then with a new introduction in *Brick* 69, Fall 2001.

"Bargains With the Land," by Robert Fyfe, first appeared in *Brick* 41, Summer 1991.

"I Want to Speak Ill of the Dead," by Jane Rule, first appeared in *Brick* 58, Winter 1998. It appears by permission of Hedgerow Press where it appeared in *Loving the Difficult* (2008).

"The Writings of Hugh MacLennan," by Alistair MacLeod, appeared in *Brick* 44, Summer 1992.

"Garry Winogrand's Moment of Exposure," by Michael Helm, appeared in *Brick* 64, Spring 2000.

"What I'd be if I were not a Writer," by E. Annie Proulx, Dionne Brand, Robert Creeley, Salman Rushdie, C. D. Wright, Margaret Atwood, Graeme Gibson, and Russell Banks, appeared in *Brick* 50, Fall 1994. Work by Salman Rushdie used by permission of the Wylie Agency LLC, copyright © 1994.

"Sites of Citation," by Peter Harcourt, appeared in *Brick* 53, Winter 1996.

"Don't Go Out Over Your Head," by Jim Harrison, appeared in *Brick* 80, Fall 2007/Winter 2008.

"Antarctic Voyage," by Helen Garner, appeared in *Brick* 60, Fall 1998.

"A Conversation with David Malouf," by Michael Ondaatje, appeared in *Brick* 47, Summer 1993.

"Fall of the Winter Palace," by Melora Wolff, appeared in *Brick* 88, Winter 2012.

"Persimmons," by Roo Borson, appeared in *Brick* 67, Spring 2001, and is excerpted from *Short Journey Upriver toward Oishida* by Roo Borson. Copyright © 2004 Roo Borson. Reprinted by permission of McClelland and Stewart.

"An Inside Look at Donald Westlake," by Albert Nussbaum, appeared in *Brick* 83, Summer 2009, and was first published in *Take One* magazine by Joe Medjuck.

"Yoked in Gowanus," by Jonathan Lethem, appeared in *Brick* 67, Spring 2001.

"Getting Into the Cabri Lake Area," by Tim Lilburn, appeared in *Brick* 68, Fall 2001.

"A Minor Mistake in the Evin Prison," by Reza Baraheni, appeared in *Brick* 68, Fall 2001.

"Fielding Dawson Remembered: Fee-Fi-Fo-Fum," by Robert Creeley, appeared in *Brick* 70, Winter 2002.

"An Interview with John Orange, on Completing the Ceiling of the Sistine Chapel, a Jigsaw Puzzle," by Michelle Orange, appeared in *Brick* 70, Winter 2002.

"An Interview with Gabrielle Buffet-Picabia," by Paule Anglim, appeared in *Brick* 83, Summer 2009, and has been edited for this book.

"Au Hasard Suicide," by Fanny Howe, appeared in *Brick* 71, Summer 2003.

"Swimming Pools," by A. L. Kennedy, appeared in *Brick* 71, Summer 2003.

"Counterpoint: Three Movies, a Book, and an Old Photograph," by Don DeLillo, was first published in *Grand Street*, and appeared in *Brick* 74, Winter 2004. Copyright © 1984 by Don DeLillo.

"How Scientists Party," by Alastair Bland, appeared in *Brick* 75, Summer 2005.

"Manos de Piedra," by Dionne Brand, appeared in *Brick* 76, Winter 2005.

"An Interview with David Sedaris," by Esta Spalding, appeared in *Brick* 76, Winter 2005.

"The Chorus is in Our Heads," by John Berger, appeared in *Brick* 78, Winter 2006.

"Why I Ride a Bicycle," by Sarmishta Subramanian, appeared in *Brick* 78, Winter 2006.

"A Delayed Disclosure," by Clark Blaise, appeared in *Brick* 78, Winter 2006. It also appeared in his *Selected Essays* (Biblioasis, 2008) and is used by permission of Biblioasis and the author.

"A Visit from Jean Genet," by Clayton Ruby, appeared in *Brick* 79, Summer 2007.

"Tomas Transtromer: A Tribute," by Robert Hass, appeared in *Brick* 80, Fall 2007/Winter 2008.

"Silent Cinema: An Aesthetic Call to Arms," by George Toles, appeared in *Brick* 80, Fall 2007/Winter 2008.

"An Interview with Mavis Gallant," by Stéphan Bureau, appeared in *Brick* 80, Fall 2007/Winter 2008 and has been edited for this book.

"Two Encounters with Nicanor Parra," by Roberto Bolaño and Forrest Gander, appeared in *Brick* 81, Summer 2008. Roberta Bolaño's essay is copyright © 2004 by the heirs of Roberto Bolaño. Copyright © 2004 by Editorial Anagrama, S.A. Used by permission of New Directions Publishing Corporation, New York.

"A Visit with G. Bernard Shaw," by Leon Edel, appeared in *Brick* 82, Winter 2009.

"Music," by Colm Tóibín, appeared in *Brick* 83, Summer 2009.

"Phantom," by Don Paterson, appeared in *Brick* 83, Summer 2009, and is included in his collection *Rain*, published by Faber, 2009.

"Her Own Words: Thinking of Deborah Digges," by W. S. Merwin, appeared in *Brick* 84, Winter 2010. Copyright © 2010 by W. S. Merwin, used by permission of the Wylie Agency LLC.

"The Lizard, the Catacombs, and the Clock: The Story of Paris's Most Secret Underground Society," by Sean Michaels, appeared in *Brick* 85, Summer 2010.

"The Here and Now," by Charles Foran, appeared in *Brick* 86, Winter 2011. It is an unused introduction from his book, *Mordecai: The Life and Times* (Toronto: Alfred A. Knopf Canada, 2010).

"In Conversation with Anne Carson," by Eleanor Wachtel, appeared in *Brick* 89, Summer 2012, and has been edited for this book. A version of this conversation was broadcast on CBC Radio's Writers and Company and produced by Mary Stinson.

"The Golden Age of Curling Dawns Bright," by Colum McCann and R. Chandran Medhu, appeared in *Brick* 87, Summer 2011.

PUBLISHER & MANAGING EDITOR: Nadia Szilvassy
EDITORS: Michael Helm, Michael Ondaatje,
Michael Redhill, Rebecca Silver Slayter, Esta Spalding,
Linda Spalding
CONTRIBUTING EDITORS: Robert Hass, Anne McLean, Tara
Quinn, Colm Tóibín
ASSISTANT EDITOR/CIRCULATION MANAGER:
Laurie Graham
PUBLIC RELATIONS SPECIALIST: Liz Johnston
DESIGN: Mark Byk
EDITORIAL ASSISTANT: Allison LaSorda
ORIGINAL DESIGN: Gordon Robertson, Rick/Simon
LOGOS: David Bolduc
COPY EDITOR: Heather Sangster
WEBSITE DESIGN: Mark Byk with Mike Stringer
FOUNDERS: Stan Dragland & Jean McKay

"Works of art are of an infinite loneliness and with nothing to be so little appreciated as with criticism. Only love can grasp and hold and fairly judge them."

—Rainer Maria Rilke